GRAMMAR MASTER 1

WorldCom Edu

Grammar Master
구성과 활용법

01 복습과 예습을 한 번에!

어려운 문법 용어를 알기 쉽게 풀이 했어요.

학습할 Lesson들의 주요 내용만을 간추려 미리 예습 할 수 있으며, 또는 배운 내용들을 마지막에 한 번 더 확인할 수 있어요.

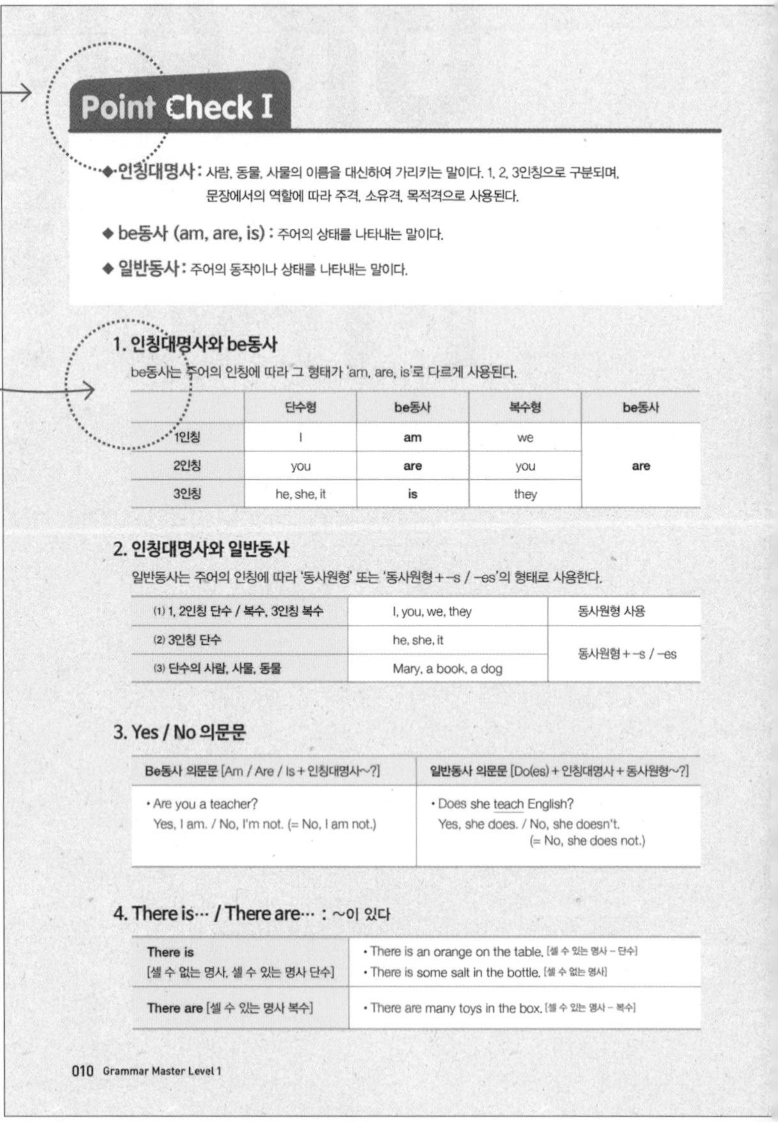

Point Check I

◆ 인칭대명사 : 사람, 동물, 사물의 이름을 대신하여 가리키는 말이다. 1, 2, 3인칭으로 구분되며, 문장에서의 역할에 따라 주격, 소유격, 목적격으로 사용된다.

◆ be동사 (am, are, is) : 주어의 상태를 나타내는 말이다.

◆ 일반동사 : 주어의 동작이나 상태를 나타내는 말이다.

1. 인칭대명사와 be동사

be동사는 주어의 인칭에 따라 그 형태가 'am, are, is'로 다르게 사용된다.

	단수형	be동사	복수형	be동사
1인칭	I	am	we	are
2인칭	you	are	you	
3인칭	he, she, it	is	they	

2. 인칭대명사와 일반동사

일반동사는 주어의 인칭에 따라 '동사원형' 또는 '동사원형+-s / -es'의 형태로 사용한다.

(1) 1, 2인칭 단수 / 복수, 3인칭 복수	I, you, we, they	동사원형 사용
(2) 3인칭 단수	he, she, it	동사원형+-s / -es
(3) 단수의 사람, 사물, 동물	Mary, a book, a dog	

3. Yes / No 의문문

Be동사 의문문 [Am / Are / Is + 인칭대명사~?]	일반동사 의문문 [Do(es) + 인칭대명사 + 동사원형~?]
• Are you a teacher? Yes, I am. / No, I'm not. (= No, I am not.)	• Does she teach English? Yes, she does. / No, she doesn't. (= No, she does not.)

4. There is··· / There are··· : ~이 있다

There is [셀 수 없는 명사, 셀 수 있는 명사 단수]	• There is an orange on the table. [셀 수 있는 명사 - 단수] • There is some salt in the bottle. [셀 수 없는 명사]
There are [셀 수 있는 명사 복수]	• There are many toys in the box. [셀 수 있는 명사 - 복수]

010 Grammar Master Level 1

02 Note

지문의 단어를 정리한 부분이에요.

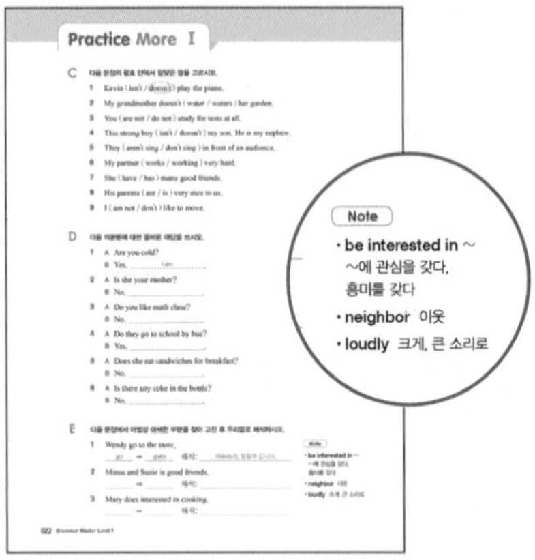

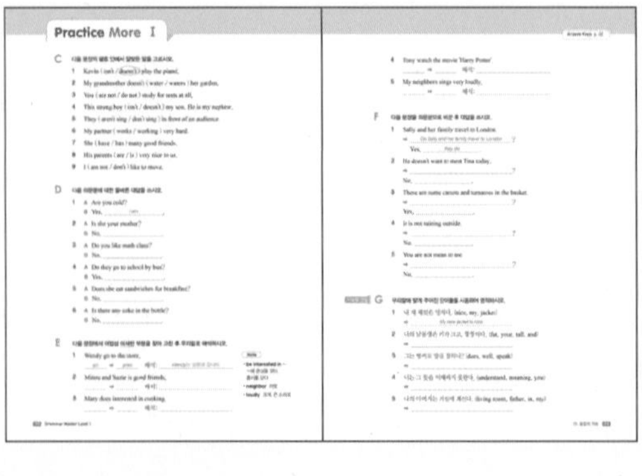

다양한 유형의 문제풀이!

앞서 학습한 내용들의 확실한 이해를 돕기 위한 다양한 유형과 난이도를 가진 문제 풀기 연습을 통해 문법에 대한 자신감을 높여 줄 수 있어요.

Lesson 1-1

문장의 종류
인칭대명사와 be동사

- **명사**: 이름이 있는 사람, 동물, 사물을 말한다.
  ex) Susie, Tom, a cat, a book, Seoul, Korea
- **인칭대명사**: 명사를 대신하여 나타내는 말을 가리킨다.

1. 인칭대명사와 be동사

	인칭대명사	be동사	줄임말		인칭대명사	be동사	줄임말
단수	I	am	I'm (= I am)	복수	we	are	we're (= we are)
	you	are	you're (= you are)		you		you're (= you are)
	he she it	is	he's (= he is) she's (= she is) it's (= it is)		they		they're (= they are)

2. be동사의 쓰임

(1) [be동사 + 명사] ~이다
- I **am Woody** from *Toy Story*.

(2) [be동사 + 형용사] ~이다
- She **is kind**.

(3) [be동사 + 형용사 + 명사] ~이다
- We **are good friends**.

(4) [be동사 + 전치사 + 장소] ~에 있다
- He **is in Seoul, Korea**.

Grammar Plus +

be동사 뒤에 오는 형용사, 명사 단어를 '보어'라고 한다. be동사 뒤에 오는 이 단어들이 주어를 보충 설명하고 있기 때문이다.
I am an engineer. (*I = an engineer*)
➡ "내"가 "기술자"라는 것을 보충 설명해 준다.

Check up!

Answer Keys p. 01

A 다음을 인칭대명사(I, you, we, they, he, she, it)로 바꾸어 쓰시오.

1 my cat ➡ *it*　　2 Jack and me ➡ ______
3 her brother ➡ ______　　4 our sisters ➡ ______
5 Mary and you ➡ ______　　6 the oranges ➡ ______
7 a short boy ➡ ______　　8 you and I ➡ ______
9 this long ruler ➡ ______　　10 their cousins ➡ ______

01. 문장의 기초 011

03 단계별 설명과 문제풀이!

많은 분량의 문법을 단계적으로 나누어 학습하는데 부담을 덜어 주었어요.

04 Grammar Plus +

본문에서 다루어진 핵심 문법사항보다 좀 더 심화된 내용을 살펴볼 수 있어요.

05 Check up

학습한 내용에 맞는 반복적인 문제풀이 연습을 통해 문법을 확실히 이해할 수 있도록 했어요.

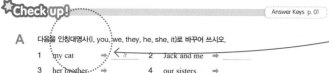

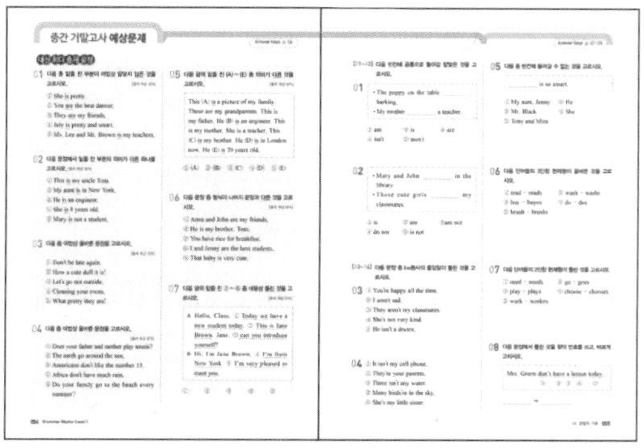

내신대비를 위한 마지막 단계!

내신 최다 출제 유형

전국 중학교의 중간/기말고사 기출 문제들을 분석하여 가장 많이, 자주 출제되는 문제들의 유형을 파악하고 학습해요.

내신 대비 문제

해당 Chapter의 문법을 이용한 다양한 유형의 문제풀이로 내신에 완벽 대비할 수 있어요.

Grammar Master

Grammar Master Level 1

CHAPTER 01 문장의 기초

문장의 종류

문장의 구성요소와 5형식

CHAPTER 02 동사의 시제

현재시제

과거시제

미래시제

CHAPTER 03 조동사

CHAPTER 04 명사와 관사

CHAPTER 05 대명사

CHAPTER 06 형용사

CHAPTER 07 부사

CHAPTER 08 비교구문

CHAPTER 09 부정사

CHAPTER 10 동명사

CHAPTER 11 수동태

CHAPTER 12 분사

CHAPTER 13 접속사

CHAPTER 14 전치사

01 Chapter 문장의 기초

Point Check I

◆ **인칭대명사 :** 사람, 동물, 사물의 이름을 대신하여 가리키는 말이다. 1, 2, 3인칭으로 구분되며, 문장에서의 역할에 따라 주격, 소유격, 목적격으로 사용된다.

◆ **be동사 (am, are, is) :** 주어의 상태를 나타내는 말이다.

◆ **일반동사 :** 주어의 동작이나 상태를 나타내는 말이다.

1. 인칭대명사와 be동사

be동사는 주어의 인칭에 따라 그 형태가 'am, are, is'로 다르게 사용된다.

	단수형	be동사	복수형	be동사
1인칭	I	**am**	we	**are**
2인칭	you	**are**	you	
3인칭	he, she, it	**is**	they	

2. 인칭대명사와 일반동사

일반동사는 주어의 인칭에 따라 '동사원형' 또는 '동사원형 + -s / -es'의 형태로 사용한다.

(1) 1, 2인칭 단수 / 복수, 3인칭 복수	I, you, we, they	동사원형 사용
(2) 3인칭 단수	he, she, it	동사원형 + -s / -es
(3) 단수의 사람, 사물, 동물	Mary, a book, a dog	

3. Yes / No 의문문

Be동사 의문문 [Am / Are / Is + 인칭대명사~?]	**일반동사 의문문** [Do(es) + 인칭대명사 + 동사원형~?]
• Are you a teacher? Yes, I am. / No, I'm not. (= No, I am not.)	• Does she teach English? Yes, she does. / No, she doesn't. (= No, she does not.)

4. There is… / There are… : ~이 있다

There is [셀 수 없는 명사, 셀 수 있는 명사 단수]	• There is an orange on the table. [셀 수 있는 명사 - 단수] • There is some salt in the bottle. [셀 수 없는 명사]
There are [셀 수 있는 명사 복수]	• There are many toys in the box. [셀 수 있는 명사 - 복수]

Lesson 1-1

문장의 종류

인칭대명사와 be동사

• **명사**: 이름이 있는 사람, 동물, 사물을 말한다.
ex) Susie, Tom, a cat, a book, Seoul, Korea

• **인칭대명사**: 명사를 대신하여 나타내는 말을 가리킨다.

1. 인칭대명사와 be동사

	인칭대명사	be동사	줄임말		인칭대명사	be동사	줄임말
단수	I	am	I'm (= I am)	복수	we	are	we're (= we are)
	you	are	you're (= you are)		you		you're (= you are)
	he she it	is	he's (= he is) she's (= she is) it's (= it is)		they		they're (= they are)

2. be동사의 쓰임

(1) [be동사 + 명사] ~이다
• I **am Woody** from *Toy Story*.

(2) [be동사 + 형용사] ~이다
• She **is kind**.

(3) [be동사 + 형용사 + 명사] ~이다
• We **are good friends**.

(4) [be동사 + 전치사 + 장소] ~에 있다
• He **is in Seoul, Korea**.

Grammar Plus +

be동사 뒤에 오는 형용사, 명사 단어를 '보어'라고 한다. be동사 뒤에 오는 이 단어들이 주어를 보충 설명하고 있기 때문이다.
I am an engineer. (*I = an engineer*)
➡ "내"가 "기술자"라는 것을 보충 설명해 준다.

Check up!

Answer Keys p. 01

A 다음을 인칭대명사(I, you, we, they, he, she, it)로 바꾸어 쓰시오.

1 my cat ➡ *it*
2 Jack and me ➡ ________
3 her brother ➡ ________
4 our sisters ➡ ________
5 Mary and you ➡ ________
6 the oranges ➡ ________
7 a short boy ➡ ________
8 you and I ➡ ________
9 this long ruler ➡ ________
10 their cousins ➡ ________

Check up!

Answer Keys p. 01

B 다음 문장의 빈칸에 알맞은 be동사(am, are, is)를 쓰시오.

1 My mother ___is___ a teacher.

2 He and she ________ lovers.

3 That boy ________ a soccer player.

4 You and I ________ twins.

5 Mr. Smith ________ very kind.

6 Her parents ________ doctors.

7 You and I ________ not working.

8 The girls ________ singing loudly.

9 Tom ________ my brother's friend.

10 She ________ a famous writer.

C 다음 문장에서 밑줄 친 단어들의 줄임말을 쓰시오. (없으면 X표 하시오.)

1 They are very nice to their students. ➡ ___They're___

2 Her friends are tall and beautiful. ➡ ____________

3 He is a singer. ➡ ____________

4 My uniform is very dirty. ➡ ____________

5 We are interested in music. ➡ ____________

6 She is very angry. ➡ ____________

7 Those apples are very fresh. ➡ ____________

8 I am a police officer. ➡ ____________

9 You are a little tired. ➡ ____________

10 His eyes are green. ➡ ____________

Lesson 1-2

be동사의 부정문

주어	be동사+not	줄임말		
I	am not	I am not	➡	I'm not
he she it	is not	he is not she is not it is not	➡ ➡ ➡	he isn't (= he's not) she isn't (= she's not) it isn't (= it's not)
you we they	are not	you are not we are not they are not	➡ ➡ ➡	you aren't (= you're not) we aren't (= we're not) they aren't (= they're not)

- She **is not (isn't)** beautiful.
- We **are not (aren't)** teachers at this school.
- The books **are not (aren't)** boring.

Check up!

Answer Keys p. 01

A 다음 밑줄 친 부분을 줄임말로 다시 쓰시오.

1 I am not a student. ➡ *I'm not*

2 Your daddy is not a singer. ➡ ______________

3 Her brothers are not kind. ➡ ______________

4 You are not fat. ➡ ______________

5 It is not my bag. ➡ ______________

6 They are not oranges. ➡ ______________

B 다음 문장의 괄호 안에서 알맞은 말을 고르시오.

1 I (am not / are not) a student.

2 Her sister (is not / are not) young.

3 My parents (isn't / aren't) here.

4 Our brother (are not / is not) an athlete.

5 My cat's legs (aren't / isn't) broken.

Lesson 1-3 일반동사

• **일반동사의 현재형:** 주어의 인칭에 따라 동사원형을 쓰거나, 동사 뒤에 '-s / -es'를 붙여서 사용한다.

1. 일반동사의 현재형 변화

	주어	일반 동사		주어	일반 동사
1, 2인칭 단수 / 복수 및 3인칭 복수	I you we you they	동사원형 (read, like, walk, watch)	3인칭 단수	he she it	동사+-s / -es (read**s**, like**s**, walk**s**, watch**es**)

• We **read** a book about wild animals.

• He **goes** for a walk in the park.

• They **watch** the horror movie.

2. 일반동사의 현재형 동사 형태 바꾸기

(1) 대부분의 일반동사: 동사원형 뒤에 '-**s**'를 붙인다.

• eat - eat**s** • see - see**s** • choose - choose**s**

(2) '**-o, -s, -x, -ch, -sh**'로 끝나는 동사는 '-**es**'를 붙인다.

• wash - wash**es** • do - do**es** • catch - catch**es**

※ 예외: have - has

(3) '**자음+y**'로 끝나는 동사는 y를 'i' 로 고치고, '-**es**'를 붙인다.

• study - stud**ies** • cry - cr**ies** • fly - fl**ies**

Check up!

Answer Keys p. 01

A 다음 동사들의 3인칭 단수형을 쓰시오.

1 read ➡ *reads* 2 watch ➡ ____________

3 try ➡ ____________ 4 love ➡ ____________

5 work ➡ ____________ 6 go ➡ ____________

7 study ➡ ____________ 8 look ➡ ____________

9 play ➡ ____________ 10 brush ➡ ____________

Check up!

Answer Keys p. 01

B 다음 문장에서 밑줄 친 동사를 알맞게 바꾸시오.

1 She make a mistake all the time. ➡ makes

2 Mary and I watches TV. ➡ ______

3 They goes to the hospital. ➡ ______

4 His dog run very fast. ➡ ______

5 John always agree with me. ➡ ______

6 Everyone love Mr. Smith, our math teacher. ➡ ______

7 He take a nap in the afternoon. ➡ ______

8 They does their homework. ➡ ______

9 My daddy usually wash the dishes. ➡ ______

10 She try to clean her room. ➡ ______

C 다음 문장에서 어법상 어색한 부분을 찾아 바르게 고치시오.

1 We goes to school. goes ➡ go

2 Mike have some money. ______ ➡ ______

3 Tom and Mary likes each other. ______ ➡ ______

4 They watches movie 'Jurassic Park'. ______ ➡ ______

5 My sister cry loudly. ______ ➡ ______

6 Peter and John plays tennis. ______ ➡ ______

7 I listens to music in the evening. ______ ➡ ______

8 My father read the newspaper every morning. ______ ➡ ______

9 Justin always wash his hands. ______ ➡ ______

10 My friends likes to play football. ______ ➡ ______

Lesson 1-4

일반동사의 부정문

- 일반동사의 부정문: 동사 뒤에 'not'을 붙이지 않고, 조동사 'do / does'를 사용한다.
  1, 2인칭과 복수형태의 주어는 'do'를, 3인칭 단수는 'do'를 변형한 'does'를 'not'과 함께 사용한다.
- **'do / does + not' 뒤에는 동사원형이 온다.**

◈ 일반동사의 부정형

	주어	do동사	줄임말	일반동사의 원형
단수	I you	do not	don't	read like walk watch
	he **she** **it**	**does not**	**doesn't**	
복수	we you they	do not	don't	

1. 1, 2인칭 단수 / 복수 및 3인칭 복수: [do not + 동사원형]
   - I **do not (don't)** like him.
   - You **do not (don't)** have to play outside.

2. 3인칭 단수: [does not + 동사원형]
   - He **does not (doesn't)** eat at all.
   - She **does not (doesn't)** like to play baseball.

Check up!

Answer Keys p. 01

A 다음 문장의 괄호 안에서 알맞은 말을 고르시오.

1 They don't (play / plays) musical instruments.
2 You (don't / doesn't) have to clean the house.
3 I don't (go / goes) to my grandma's house.
4 They (do not / does not) enjoy any sports.
5 The bus (do / does) not have any passengers.
6 We (do / does) not (have / has) breakfast.

Check up!

Answer Keys p. 01

B 다음 문장에서 괄호 안의 동사를 부정문으로 바꾸시오.

1 That old man ___*doesn't play*___ the violin well. (play)

2 Sam ______________ his homework. (do)

3 My friend, Mia ______________ New York. (visit)

4 Lucy ______________ an electric guitar. (have)

5 We ______________ in this pool. (swim)

6 My brother ______________ a calculator. (use)

7 Mary and Tom ______________ to read books. (like)

8 You ______________ me science. (teach)

9 I ______________ new clothes. (buy)

10 Sally ______________ any vegetables. (eat)

C 다음 주어진 문장을 부정문으로 바꿔 쓰시오.

1 My daddy cooks well.

➡ ___*My daddy doesn't cook well.*___

2 Anna and her sister go fishing.

➡ ______________________________

3 Emma speaks English well.

➡ ______________________________

4 Sammy likes to sing songs.

➡ ______________________________

5 She plays the drum well.

➡ ______________________________

6 Tony loves that TV show.

➡ ______________________________

Lesson

1-5 Yes / No 의문문

- **Yes / No의문문:** 질문에 대한 답을 'Yes / No'로 하는 문장을 말한다.
- **be동사의 의문문:** 주어와 동사의 위치를 바꾸고 문장 끝에 '물음표(?)'를 붙인다.
- **일반동사의 의문문:** 'Do / Does + 주어 + 동사원형'의 형태를 만들고 문장 끝에 '물음표(?)'를 붙인다.

◈ be동사와 일반동사의 의문문

be동사의 의문문		일반동사의 의문문	
동사 + 주어~?	대답	Do(es) + 주어 + 동사원형~?	대답
Am I ~?	Yes, you are. No, you aren't.	Do I + 동사원형~?	Yes, you do. No, you don't.
Are you ~?	Yes, I am. No, I'm not.	Do you + 동사원형~?	Yes, I do. No, I don't.
Are we ~?	Yes, you are. No, you aren't.	Do we + 동사원형~?	Yes, you do. No, you don't.
Are they ~?	Yes, they are. No, they aren't.	Do they + 동사원형~?	Yes, they do. No, they don't.
Is he (she / it) ~?	Yes, he (she / it) is. No, he (she / it) isn't.	Does he (she / it) + 동사원형~?	Yes, he (she / it) does. No, he (she / it) doesn't.

1. be동사의 의문문: [Be (Am, Are, Is) + 주어~?]

A **Am I** your father?
B **No, you are not (aren't).**

A **Is she** a kind dentist?
B **Yes, she is.**

Grammar Plus +

be동사 뒤에 올 수 있는 것: 형용사, 명사, '전치사 + 장소', '형용사 + 명사'

2. 일반동사의 의문문

(1) **1, 2인칭 단수 / 복수 및 3인칭 복수:** [Do + 주어 + 동사원형~?]

A **Do you** like your school?
B **Yes, I do.**

(2) **3인칭 단수:** [Does + 주어 + 동사원형~?]

A **Does he** wash the dishes?
B **No, he does not (doesn't).**

Check up!

Answer Keys p. 02

A 다음 문장의 괄호 안에서 알맞은 말을 고르시오.

1 (Do / Does) you like puppies?

2 (Is / Am) she a basketball player?

3 (Am / Are) I a polite person?

4 (Are / Is) Anna and Mary good friends?

5 (Do / Does) you water the garden every day?

B 다음 의문문의 올바른 대답을 고르시오.

1 Does Jenny help people often?
➡ Yes, (she does / Jenny does).

2 Do they study together in the library?
➡ No, (they don't / they do).

3 Are you going to the shopping mall?
➡ Yes, (you are / I am).

4 Is she your mother?
➡ Yes, (she is / she does).

5 Do they drink coffee?
➡ No, (they aren't / they don't).

C 다음 문장을 의문문으로 바꿔 쓰시오.

1 My family is going to the zoo.
➡ *Is my family going to the zoo?*

2 Sam wants to go to the party.
➡ ______________________________

3 John and his father go to the same health center.
➡ ______________________________

4 I write in my diary every day.
➡ ______________________________

5 You are kind to people.
➡ ______________________________

Lesson 1-6 There is / There are

• **There is / are**: '~이 있다'라는 뜻으로 문장 맨 앞에 온다.
'There is / are'에서 there는 따로 해석하지 않으며, 바로 뒤에 문장의 주어가 온다.

1. There is / There are

There is	셀 수 있는 명사의 단수 셀 수 없는 명사	• **There is** a long rope. • **There is** much homework today.
There are	셀 수 있는 명사의 복수	• **There are** many pages in this book.

2. There is / are 부정문: ~이 없다

(1) There is not + 명사

• **There is not (There isn't)** water in the glass.

• **There is not (There isn't)** an eraser in the pencil case.

※ 'there is not'은 'there isn't'로 줄여 쓸 수 있다.

(2) There are not + 명사

• **There are not (There aren't)** any notebooks in my bag.

※ 'there are not'은 'there aren't'로 줄여 쓸 수 있다.

3. There is / are 의문문: ~이 있는가?

(1) Is there~?

A **Is there** any cinnamon powder?

B **Yes, there is. / No, there isn't (there is not).**

(2) Are there~?

A **Are there** any pink ribbons?

B **Yes, there are. / No, there aren't (there are not).**

Grammar Plus +

'There is / are'와 함께 사용하는 'some / any'

① 'some, any'는 셀 수 있는 명사, 없는 명사에 모두 사용할 수 있다.

② 'some'은 긍정문에, 'any'는 부정문, 의문문에 주로 쓰인다.

Check up!

Answer Keys p. 02

A 다음 문장의 괄호 안에서 알맞은 말을 고르시오.

1 There (is / are) some milk.

2 (There is / There are) some honey in the cup.

3 There is not (any / some) ice in the refrigerator.

4 (Is / Are) there any vegetables in the refrigerator?

5 (Is there / Are there) much money in the bag?

6 (There isn't / There aren't) (some / any) water in the stream.

Practice More I

Answer Keys p. 02

A 다음 문장의 빈칸에 보기 에서 알맞은 단어를 찾아 쓰시오.

보기

am　　are　　is　　are not　　is not

[긍정문]

1 Aunt Mary ___is___ a math teacher.

2 You ________ my best friends.

3 There ________ some boys in the reading club.

4 The weather ________ wonderful today.

5 I ________ a kind person.

[부정문]

6 You and I ___are not___ twins.

7 My sister ________ ugly.

8 The dogs and cats ________ good each other.

9 There ________ a handsome man in our company.

10 Mr. and Mrs. Smith ________ husband and wife.

B 다음 괄호 안의 동사를 알맞은 형태로 바꿔 빈 칸에 쓰시오.

1 My teacher ___teaches___ music well. (teach)

2 Ann and her mother ________ shopping together. (go)

3 We ________ comic books a lot. (read)

4 Sam and I ________ the dishes for our mother. (wash)

5 He ________ some chocolate. (buy)

6 My brother ___doesn't use___ a calculator. (use, not)

7 Mary ________ to play tennis. (like, not)

8 You ________ to exercise. (need, not)

9 Ian and his wife ________ breakfast every morning. (cook, not)

10 Sally ________ the bugs well. (catch, not)

Practice More I

C 다음 문장의 괄호 안에서 알맞은 말을 고르시오.

1 Kevin (isn't / doesn't) play the piano.

2 My grandmother doesn't (water / waters) her garden.

3 You (are not / do not) study for tests at all.

4 This strong boy (isn't / doesn't) my son. He is my nephew.

5 They (aren't sing / don't sing) in front of the audience.

6 My partner (works / working) very hard.

7 She (have / has) many good friends.

8 His parents (are / is) very nice to us.

9 I (am not / don't) like to move.

D 다음 의문문에 대한 올바른 대답을 쓰시오.

1 A Are you cold?
B Yes, ___*I am*___.

2 A Is she your mother?
B No, ______________.

3 A Do you like math class?
B No, ______________.

4 A Do they go to school by bus?
B Yes, ______________.

5 A Does she eat sandwiches for breakfast?
B No, ______________.

6 A Is there any coke in the bottle?
B No, ______________.

E 다음 문장에서 어법상 어색한 부분을 찾아 고친 후 우리말로 해석하시오.

1 Wendy go to the store.
___*go*___ ➡ ___*goes*___ 해석: ___*Wendy는 상점에 갑니다.*___

2 Minsu and Suzie is good friends.
________ ➡ ________ 해석: ______________

3 Mary does interested in cooking.
________ ➡ ________ 해석: ______________

Note
- **be interested in ~** ~에 관심을 갖다, 흥미를 갖다
- **neighbor** 이웃
- **loudly** 크게, 큰 소리로

Answer Keys p. 02

4 Tony watch the movie 'Harry Potter'.
________ ➡ ________ 해석: ________________________

5 My neighbors sings very loudly.
________ ➡ ________ 해석: ________________________

F 다음 문장을 의문문으로 바꾼 후 대답을 쓰시오.

1 Sally and her family travel to London.
➡ *Do Sally and her family travel to London*?
Yes, *they do*.

2 He doesn't want to meet Tina today.
➡ ________________________________?
No, ____________________.

3 There are some carrots and tomatoes in the basket.
➡ ________________________________?
Yes, ____________________.

4 It is not raining outside.
➡ ________________________________?
No, ____________________.

5 You are not mean to me.
➡ ________________________________?
No, ____________________.

서술형 연습 G 우리말에 맞게 주어진 단어들을 사용하여 영작하시오.

1 내 새 재킷은 멋지다. (nice, my, jacket)
➡ *My new jacket is nice.*

2 너의 남동생은 키가 크고, 뚱뚱하다. (fat, your, tall, and)
➡ ________________________________

3 그는 영어로 말을 잘하니? (does, well, speak)
➡ ________________________________

4 너는 그 뜻을 이해하지 못한다. (understand, meaning, you)
➡ ________________________________

5 나의 아버지는 거실에 계신다. (living room, father, in, my)
➡ ________________________________

Point Check Ⅱ

◆ **'Wh-' 의문문 :** 'Wh-'로 시작하는 의문사로 된 의문문을 말하며, 'Yes / No'로 답할 수 없다.

◆ **선택의문문 :** A와 B 중에서 어떤 것을 고를지 묻는 의문문을 말하며, 'or'를 사용한다.

◆ **부가의문문 :** 상대방에게 동의를 구하기 위해 문장의 끝에 짧게 덧붙이는 의문문을 말한다.

1. 'Wh-' 의문문

Who	When	Where	What	Why	How

• [Wh-의문사 + be동사 + 주어~?]

A **When is** your birthday?

B It's on April 14th.

• [Wh-의문사 + do / does + 주어 + 동사원형~?]

A **What do you have**?

B I have a new basketball.

2. 선택의문문

(1) **Which + or**

A **Which** do you like better, English **or** math?

B I like English better.

(2) **Be동사 + or**

A **Is** she a teacher **or** a student?

B She is a teacher.

(3) **일반동사 + or**

A **Do** you go shopping **or** go fishing?

B I go shopping.

3. 부가의문문

• They are beautiful, **aren't they**? (O) • They are beautiful, **are not they**? (X)

※부가의문문은 항상 줄임말로 표현한다

• The boys are so brave, **aren't they**?

※주어가 명사일 때도 부가의문문의 주어는 항상 대명사를 사용한다.

Lesson 1-7

Wh- 의문문

- **'Wh–' 의문문:** 'who, when, where, what, why, how'로 시작하는 의문문을 말한다.
- 'Wh–' 의문문에는 'Yes / No'로 대답하지 않고, 질문에 알맞은 내용으로 답한다.

Who	When	Where	What	Why	How

- **be동사와 함께 사용할 때:** [의문사 + be동사 + 주어~?]
- **일반동사와 함께 사용할 때:** [의문사 + do(does) + 주어 + 동사원형~?]

1. **Who :** 사람에 대해 물을 때 사용

(1) who : 누가 _ 문장에서 주어나 목적어로 쓰인다.

A **Who** is she? **B** She is my English teacher.

(2) whom : 누구를 _ 'who'가 목적어로 쓰일 때 'whom'을 대신 사용하기도 한다.

A **Who(m)** does he meet? **B** He meets Jane.

(3) whose : 누구의(것) _ 소유관계에 대해 물을 때 사용한다.

A **Whose** is this book? [누구의 것] **B** It's Harry's.

(= Whose book is this? [누구의])

2. **What :** 무엇이, 무엇을 _ 사물이나 사람의 직업, 이름을 물을 때 사용

A **What** do they want to do? **B** They want to play basketball.

3. **When :** 언제 _ 시간이나 날짜 등을 물을 때 사용

A **When** do you go to school?

B I go to school from Monday to Friday.

Grammar Plus +

'when'이 시간을 물어보는 표현으로 사용될 경우 'what time'으로 바꿔 쓸 수 있다.

When do you eat dinner?
= **What time** do you eat dinner?

4. **Where :** 어디에, 어디에서 _ 장소나 위치 등을 물을 때 사용

A **Where** does he live? **B** He lives in Seoul.

5. **Why:** 왜 _ 원인이나 이유를 물을 때 사용

A **Why** are you so sad? **B** Because I lost my favorite pen.

6. **How:** 어떤, 어떻게, 얼마나 – 안부, 상황, 방법, 나이, 키, 빈도 등을 물을 때 사용

A **How** do I go to the concert hall? **B** You should take a subway line No. 2.

A **How** is the weather today? **B** It's cloudy and windy.

※ 'how' 는 '어떻게'라는 의미로 방법을 물을 때와, '어떠한'이란 의미로 날씨를 물을 때도 사용한다.

Check up!

Answer Keys p. 03

A 다음 우리말에 맞게 빈칸에 알맞은 의문사를 쓰시오

1 너는 언제 점심을 먹니?
➡ ___When___ do you eat lunch?

2 너의 취미는 무엇이니?
➡ ________ is your hobby?

3 저 여자는 어디 출신입니까?
➡ ________ is that woman from?

4 그는 피자와 햄버거 중 어떤 음식을 좋아할까?
➡ ________ food does he like, hamburgers or pizza?

B 주어진 문장의 대답에 알맞게 보기 에서 알맞은 의문사를 골라 쓰시오.

보기

who when where what why

1 A ___Why___ are you so happy?
B Because I got the first prize.

2 A ________ do you arrive here?
B It's in 20 minutes.

3 A ________ do you want to be?
B I want to be a scientist.

4 A ________ is your birthday?
B It's July 26th.

C 다음 보기 에서 알맞은 대답을 골라 쓰시오.

보기

① Because she was very sick. ② She usually gets up at 7.
③ I don't know. ④ I want to go Gangwondo.

1 A Where do you want to go this weekend?
B ___④ I want to go Gangwondo.___

2 A Why was she absent yesterday?
B ________________

3 A How old is your new teacher?
B ________________

4 A What time does she get up usually?
B ________________

Lesson **1-8**

선택의문문

- **선택의문문:** A와 B 중에서 어떤 것을 고를지 묻는 의문문을 말한다. 대답할 때는 'Yes / No'로 하지 않고, 자신이 선택한 것으로 말한다.
- **'or' 가 있는 선택의문문**에는 'what' 대신에 **'which'**를 사용한다.

A **Which** do you like better, oranges **or** tomatoes?
B I like oranges better. (= Oranges.)

A **Is** he a doctor **or** a nurse?
B He is a doctor. (= A doctor.)

A **Do** you want to listen to the pop music **or** the classical music?
B I want to listen to the classical music. (= The classical music.)

Check up!

Answer Keys p. 03

A 다음 그림을 보고 빈칸에 알맞은 말을 쓰시오.

1 **A** ___*Which*___ do you want to drink, water ___*or*___ juice?
B ___*Water*___ please.

2 **A** __________ is your favorite subject, English __________ science?
B I like __________.

3 **A** __________ is your teacher, Mrs. Kim __________ Mrs. Brown?
B She is __________.

4 **A** __________ she eat a sandwich __________ a hamburger?
B She eats __________.

5 **A** __________ they musicians __________ magicians?
B They are __________.

Lesson 1-9

부가의문문

- **부가의문문**: 상대방에게 사실을 확인하거나 동의를 구하기 위해 문장의 맨 마지막에 짧게 덧붙이는 의문문을 말한다.
- 부가의문문을 만들 때 긍정문의 뒤에는 부정 의문문이, 부정문의 뒤에는 긍정 의문문이 온다.

◈ 부가의문문 만들기

	긍정문의 부가의문문	부정문의 부가의문문
be동사 부가의문문	He **is** a kind teacher, **isn't he**? 그는 친절한 선생님이야, 그렇지 않니?	She **isn't** a nurse, **is she**? 그녀는 간호사가 아니야, 그렇지?
조동사 부가의문문	Mary **will** go abroad, **won't she**? Mary는 해외에 갈 거야, 그렇지 않니?	They **won't** go picnic, **will they**? 그들은 소풍 가지 않을 거야, 그렇지?
일반 동사 부가의문문	They **study** English together, **don't they**? 그들은 함께 영어공부를 해, 그렇지 않니?	You **don't like** him, **do you**? 너는 그를 좋아하지 않아, 그렇지?

※ 부가의문문의 동사는 주절의 동사와 같은 것을 사용한다.

1. 부정의 부가의문문: 반드시 줄임말을 사용한다.

➡ They are nice, **aren't they**? (O) They are nice, are not they? (X)

2. 부가의문문은 대명사만을 사용한다.

➡ The girls are pretty, aren't **they**?

Grammar Plus +1

- **부가의문문에 대한 대답 :** 부가의문문의 긍정/부정과는 상관 없이 의문문과 같은 방식으로 한다.
  A You studied hard, didn't you? **B** Yes, I did. →(= Did you study hard? Yes, I did.)
- **'I' 의 부가의문문 :** 'I' 의 be동사인 'am' 은 부정형으로 할 때 줄임말을 쓸 수 없다. (**amn't** →X)
  'I' 의 부정형태가 부가의문문으로 올 때는 'aren't I' 를 사용한다.
  A I am a good student, **aren't I**? **B** Yes, you are.

Grammar Plus +2

- **명령문과 청유문의 부가의문문**
  ⓐ **명령문 :** [명령문, will you?] - Listen carefully, **will you**?
  ⓑ **청유문 :** [Let's~, shall we?] - Let's study together, **shall we**?
  → 명령문과 청유문의 부가의문문은 주절이 긍정이든, 부정이든 상관없이 'will you?' 와 'shall we?' 를 사용

Check up!

Answer Keys p. 03

A 다음 괄호 안에서 알맞은 말을 고르시오.

1 That is Jenny's pencil case, (isn't this / isn't it)?

2 She likes dancing, (dose she / doesn't she)?

3 You can't swim well, (can't you / can you)?

4 It is a sunny day, (is not it / isn't it)?

5 My brother doesn't know her, (does he / doesn't he)?

B 다음 문장의 빈칸에 알맞은 부가의문문을 쓰시오.

1 Sammy doesn't like watching TV, ___*does he*___?

2 You didn't sleep well last night, ______________?

3 They are so wonderful, ______________?

4 Her new car is awsome, ______________?

5 Jane and I are the same class, ______________?

6 Kate and Alice aren't doctors, ______________?

7 This statue was made by metal, ______________?

8 Tony has enough money to buy this bike, ______________?

9 Maria and Jenny don't like Richard, ______________?

10 I am good at science, ______________?

Practice More Ⅱ

A 다음 우리말에 알맞은 의문사를 쓰시오.

1 누가 ➡ who
2 언제 ➡ ________
3 어디서 ➡ ________
4 무엇을 ➡ ________
5 왜 ➡ ________
6 어떻게 ➡ ________
7 어느 것 ➡ ________

B 다음 문장의 괄호 안에서 알맞은 말을 고르시오.

1 (Who / Which) is that girl?
2 (When / What) is Harry's favorite food?
3 Mary drives a car very well, (doesn't she / doesn't Mary)?
4 (When / What time) will your father come back? – He'll come back tomorrow.
5 (Which / Do) do you choose, blue one or green one?
6 Jimmy wants to marry with Anna, (does he / doesn't he)?
7 (What / Which) day is it today?
8 We don't have to study hard, (are we / do we)?
9 The horrible movie makes us scared, (isn't it / doesn't it)?
10 He never goes out for a walk, (does he / doesn't he)?

C 다음 주어진 대답에 맞게 빈칸에 알맞은 의문사를 쓰시오.

1 A What does he like to do?
B He likes to do dishes.

2 A ________ wants to eat this pie?
B It's me!

3 A ________ are you so surprised?
B Because I think you are my mother.

4 A ________ do you go to school?
B At 7:50.

Answer Keys p. 03

5 A __________ do you study English?
B I always listen and repeat.

6 A __________ is my pencil case?
B It's under your desk.

7 A __________ do you like, comic books __________ novels?
B I like comic books.

8 A __________ you go fishing __________ go shopping?
B I go shopping.

9 A __________ she a doctor __________ a nurse?
B : She's a nurse.

10 A __________ makes you happy, John or Sam?
B John makes me happy.

D 다음 빈칸에 알맞은 부가의문문을 써 넣으시오

1 Harry is not ugly, ___*is he*___?

2 Mary and Gina are teachers, __________?

3 They always help other people, __________?

4 You don't like to eat meat, __________?

5 Mr. Lee is never late for work, __________?

6 Mrs. Green doesn't teach Chinese, __________?

7 Harry and his friends don't play baseball, __________?

8 You and I are in the same class, __________?

9 It's not windy and cloudy, __________?

10 You and Mary like to take pictures, __________?

E 다음 질문에 알맞은 대답을 찾아 연결하시오

1 ___*What*___ time do you go to bed? • • ⓐ He lives in New York.

2 __________ made this model airplane? • • ⓑ I go to bed at 10:30.

3 __________ is the weather today? • • ⓒ Jinsu made it.

4 __________ does Sam live? • • ⓓ It's windy.

Practice More Ⅱ

Answer Keys p. 03

F 다음 문장에서 어법상 어색한 부분을 찾아 바르게 고치시오

1 The girls are go to middle school.
  are (go) ➡ X (going)

2 She doesn't watches TV. ______ ➡ ______

3 Who time does he meet you? ______ ➡ ______

4 Which is your favorite idol group, EXO or Big Bang?
  ______ ➡ ______

5 He goes to the book store, does he?
  ______ ➡ ______

6 When do you go after school? ______ ➡ ______

7 Anna and Tony are playing the piano together, aren't Anna and Tony? ______ ➡ ______

8 It's such a wonderful weather, is not it?
  ______ ➡ ______

9 A When do we go to the gallery?
  B We go there by subway. ______ ➡ ______

10 A Did you eat kimbap and bread?
  B I ate kimbap. ______ ➡ ______

서술형 연습 **G** 우리말에 맞게 주어진 단어들을 사용하여 문장을 완성하시오.

1 그들은 언제 칠면조를 요리하나요? (turkey, cook)
  ➡ When do they cook turkey?

2 그는 왜 그렇게 운동을 열심히 해? (why, exercise)
  ➡ ______________ so hard?

3 너는 항상 지하철을 타고 다녀, 그렇지 않니? (subway, take)
  ➡ You always __________, __________?

4 그녀는 농장에 있지 않아, 그렇지? (farm, she)
  ➡ She isn't __________, __________?

5 Jim은 농부이니, 어부이니? (farmer, fisherman)
  ➡ Is Jim ______________?

Point Check Ⅲ

◆ **명령문 :** '~ 해라', '~ 하지 마라'의 뜻으로 상대방에게 무언가를 시킬 때 사용하는 문장을 말한다.

◆ **감탄문 :** 'How'나 'What'으로 시작하는 문장으로서, 어떠한 광경, 물건 등을 보고 감탄하는 것을 표현한 문장을 말한다.

1. 명령문

- **Be** kind to everyone.
- **Don't** be shy.
- **Clean** your room.

※ be동사의 부정 명령문에도 **'Don't'**을 사용한다.

2. 명령문의 부가의문문

- Be careful, **will you**?
- Don't be silly, **will you**?
- Don't make a mess, **will you**?

※ 명령문의 부가의문문은 긍정, 부정 모두 **'will you?'**를 사용한다.

3. Let's의 부가의문문

- Let's go picnic, **shall we**?
- Let's not swim, **shall we**?
- Let's pick up the garbage, **shall we**?

※ Let's의 부가의문문은 긍정, 부정 모두 **'shall we?'**를 사용한다

4. 감탄문

(1) [How + 형용사 + 주어 + 동사!]

It is so beautiful.

➡ **How beautiful (it is)!**

(2) [What + a/an + 형용사 + 명사 + 주어 + 동사!]

He is a very honest man.

➡ **What an honest man (he is)!**

Lesson 1-10 명령문

• **명령문:** '~ 해라', '~ 하지마라' 라고 상대방에게 무엇을 시킬 때 사용하는 문장을 말한다.

• 명령문은 주어를 빼고 동사원형으로 문장을 시작한다

1. 명령문

상대방에게 '~해라', '~하지 마라' 라고 무엇을 시킬 때 사용하는 문장으로 긍정명령문과 부정명령문이 있다.

- You are quiet in the class. ➡ **Be** quiet in the class.
- You do your best. ➡ **Do** your best.
- You don't have to be afraid of it. ➡ **Don't** (Do not) be afraid of it.
- You don't have to touch anything. ➡ **Don't** (Do not) touch anything.

※ 부정을 강조할 때 'Don't' 대신에 'Do not'을 사용하기도 한다.

2. [명령문, + and~] (~해라, 그러면~)와 [명령문, + or~] (~해라, 그렇지 않으면~)

- Study hard, **and** you will get a good grade.
  ➡ If you study hard, you will get a good grade.
- Hurry up, **or** you will miss the train.
  ➡ If you don't hurry up, you will miss the train.

3. [Let's + 동사원형] (~하자) 와 [Let's + not + 동사원형] (~하지 말자)

- **Let's** go shopping together.
- **Let's not go** outside.

※ 'Let's'는 'Let us'의 줄임말이다.

Grammar Plus +

'Why don't we + 동사원형~?' 은 '~하지 않을래?' 라는 뜻의 제안하는 표현으로 'Let's + 동사원형' 으로 바꿔 쓸 수 있다.

Check up!

Answer Keys p. 04

A 다음 괄호 안에서 알맞은 말을 고르시오.

1 (Are / Be) quiet everyone.

2 (Wash / Washes) your hands first.

3 (Let's not / Let not us) go inside.

4 Don't (be / is) late again.

5 (Don't tell / Don't tells) anybody about your secret.

Check up!

Answer Keys p. 04

B 다음 문장을 부정명령문으로 바꿔 쓰시오

1 Run in the hall.

➡ ___Don't run in the hall.___

2 Let's make a noise.

➡ ______________________

3 Be unkind to the others.

➡ ______________________

4 Eat only meat.

➡ ______________________

5 Let's throw the garbage.

➡ ______________________

C 다음 문장을 괄호 안의 지시에 따라 바꿔 쓰시오.

1 You prepare the umbrella.

➡ ___Prepare the umbrella___. (명령문)

2 Shall we meet at five?

➡ ______________________. (Let's)

3 You clean your room.

➡ ______________________. (명령문)

4 You don't make a mess.

➡ ______________________. (Let's)

5 Why don't we go to the movies?

➡ ______________________. (Let's)

D 다음 문장을 명령문으로 바꿀 때 알맞은 말을 빈칸에 쓰시오

1 If you get up early, you won't miss the first lesson.

➡ Get up early, ___and___ you won't miss the first lesson.

2 If you don't wash your hands, you can't have dinner.

➡ Wash your hands, _______ you can't have dinner.

3 If you study hard, you will get a good grade.

➡ _______ hard, _______ you will get a good grade.

4 If you are scared of it, you never go forward.

➡ _______ _______ scared of it, _______ you never go forward.

Lesson 1-11

명령문의 부가의문문

- 명령문으로 부가의문문을 만들 경우 긍정, 부정에 상관없이 문장의 끝에 항상 'will you'를 붙이며, '~알겠니?'라고 확인을 하는 의미로 사용된다.
- 'Let's'의 부가의문문은 'shall we'를 붙여서 '어때?'하고 동의를 구할 때 사용된다.

1. 명령문의 부가의문문

- Be honest, **will you**?
- Don't forget your promise, **will you**?
- Don't be a liar, **will you**?
- Throw the ball here, **will you**?

2. Let's의 부가의문문

- Let's have lunch together, **shall we**?
- Let's not go inside, **shall we**?
- Let's take a trip to Jeonju, **shall we**?
- Let's not run away, **shall we**?

Check up!

Answer Keys p. 04

A 다음 명령문의 문장에 대한 부가의문문을 쓰시오.

1 Wait for me for a second, ___*will you*___?

2 Please be quiet in the library, _______________?

3 Don't be silly like that, _______________?

4 Let's stay here, _______________?

5 Don't worry, _______________?

6 Let's not go out for a walk, _______________?

7 Be diligent more, _______________?

8 Leave me alone, _______________?

9 Let's not drink cold water too much, _______________?

10 Drive slowly, _______________?

Lesson 1-12 # 감탄문

- **감탄문**: How나 What으로 시작하는 문장을 말한다.
  '정말~하구나'라는 뜻을 가지며, 문장의 끝에는 항상 '감탄사(!)'를 붙인다.
- 주어와 동사의 생략이 가능하다.

1. How + 형용사 + 주어 + 동사!

- She is very beautiful.
  ➡ **How beautiful (she is)!**
- The Great Wall is very awesome.
  ➡ **How awesome The Great Wall is!**

2. What + a/an + 형용사 + 명사 + 주어 + 동사!

- He is a very handsome actor.
  ➡ **What a handsome actor (he is)!**
- That is a really wonderful view.
  ➡ **What a wonderful view (that is)!**

Grammar Plus +

- 감탄문에 형용사나 부사만 있을 경우 'what'은 쓸 수 없다.
- 감탄문에 주어를 제외한 또 다른 명사가 있는 경우 대부분 'what'을 써서 감탄문을 만든다.
- 감탄문을 만들 때 누구나 알고 있는 일반적인 사실을 말할 때는 '주어 + 동사'의 생략이 가능하다.

Check up!

Answer Keys p. 04

A 다음 문장을 감탄문으로 바꿀 때 빈칸에 알맞은 말을 쓰시오.

1 She is very kind to them.
➡ ___How___ kind to them ___she___ is!

2 It has a very long neck.
➡ ________ a long neck it ________!

3 Martin is very handsome.
➡ ________ handsome ________ is!

4 They are great athletes.
➡ ________ great athletes they ________!

5 He is a very nice man.
➡ ________ a nice man ________ is!

Practice More Ⅲ

A 다음 괄호 안에서 알맞은 말을 고르시오.

1 (Is / Be) nice to the others.

2 (Brushing / Brush) your teeth every three times a day.

3 (Let's / Let not us) follow the rules.

4 (Don't let / Let's not) enter the dangerous place.

5 Don't (you throw / throw) garbage on the street.

6 Don't be late, (will you / shall you)?

7 Let's not go to the zoo, (will we / shall we)?

8 Read a lot of books, (do you / will you)?

9 Let's take a picture, (shall we / will you)?

10 You won't go anywhere, (shall you / will you)?

B 다음 문장들을 명령문으로 고쳐 쓰시오.
(긍정문은 긍정명령문, 부정문은 부정명령문으로 고치시오.)

1 You turn on the light.
➡ ___Turn on___ the light.

2 You are kind to your friends.
➡ ____________ your friends.

3 You help people all the time.
➡ ____________ all the time.

4 Shall we drink some soda pop?
➡ ____________ some soda pop.

5 Why don't we watch the parade?
➡ ____________ the parade.

6 You shouldn't make noise in the library.
➡ ____________ in the library.

7 You don't throw food to the animals.
➡ ____________ food to the animals.

8 You don't waste water.
➡ ____________.

Answer Keys p. 04

9 You shouldn't touch dry ice for a long time.
➡ __________________ for a long time.

10 You shouldn't hit little puppies.
➡ __________________ little puppies.

C 다음 명령문의 부가의문문을 쓰시오.

1 Keep your secret please, ___will you___?
2 Don't forget your homework, _________?
3 Let's not ride a bike here, _________?
4 Stay here, _________?
5 Let's have lunch, _________?
6 Don't be upset easily, _________?
7 Let's take a taxi, _________?
8 Don't laugh at your friends, _________?
9 Let's take a dance class, _________?
10 Clean the house for your mom, _________?

D 다음 문장을 명령문으로 바꿀 때 알맞은 말을 빈칸에 쓰시오.

1 If you go out now, you will get wet.
➡ ___Don't___ go out now, ___or___ you will get wet.

2 If you sleep well, you will be able to study well.
➡ _______ well, _______ you will be able to study well.

3 If you don't brush your teeth, you will get a cavity.
➡ _______ your teeth, _______ you will get a cavity.

4 If you spend too much money, you will go bankrupt.
➡ _______ spend too much money, _______ you will go bankrupt.

5 If you do your best, you can get the gold medal.
➡ _______ your best, _______ you can get the gold medal.

Note
- set wet 젖다
- sleep well 잘 자다
- a good condition 좋은상태
- cavity 충치
- go bankrupt 파산하다

Practice More Ⅲ

Answer Keys p. 04

E 다음 괄호 안의 주어진 단어를 사용하여 우리말에 맞게 빈칸을 채워 감탄문을 완성하시오.

1 Sam은 정말 느리구나!
➡ ___How___ ___slow___ Sam is! (slow)

2 저 여자 배우는 정말 아름다운 사람이다!
➡ ________ ________ ________ actress she is! (beautiful)

3 이 물은 정말 차갑다!
➡ ________ ________ this water is! (cold)

4 그것은 정말 굉장한 무덤이다!
➡ ________ ________ ________ tomb it is! (awesome)

F 다음 문장을 감탄문으로 고쳐 쓰시오.

1 She has a wonderful camera.
➡ ___What a wonderful camera she has___!

2 They are really horrible.
➡ ________________________!

3 Jenny is very smart.
➡ ________________________!

4 It is a really mysterious scene
➡ ________________________!

서술형 연습

G 다음 괄호 안에 있는 단어들을 배열하여 문장을 완성하시오.

1 (person, Be, positive, a)
➡ ___Be a positive person___.

2 (will, won't, fall down, cry, if, you, you, you)
➡ ________________________?

3 (Let's, homework, do, in the library)
➡ ________________________.

4 (How, room, clean, your, is)
➡ ________________________!

Point Check IV

◆ **문장의 구성 :** '**주어, 동사, 목적어, 보어**'로 이루어져 있다.

◆ **문장의 5형식 :** 문장을 구성하는 요소를 크게 5가지로 구분하여 나눠 놓은 것을 말한다.

◆ **1형식 :** 주어＋동사

◆ **2형식 :** 주어＋동사＋보어

◆ **3형식 :** 주어＋동사＋목적어

◆ **4형식 :** 주어＋동사＋간접목적어＋직접목적어

◆ **5형식 :** 주어＋동사＋목적어＋목적격보어

1. 문장의 기본 구성 요소

(1) 주어: **Sarah** sings very well.

(2) 동사: He **practices** soccer every day.

(3) 목적어: She teaches **math**.

(4) 보어: We are **middle school students**.

2. 문장의 5형식

(1) 1형식 문장: [주어＋동사]

The baby / cries.
주어 / 동사

(2) 2형식 문장: [주어＋동사＋보어]

Mrs. Brown / is / a teacher.
주어 / 동사 / 보어 ⇨ Mrs. Brown = a teacher

(3) 3형식 문장: [주어＋동사＋목적어]

They / sing / a song.
주어 / 동사 / 목적어 ⇨ They ≠ a song

(4) 4형식 문장: [주어＋동사＋간접목적어＋직접목적어]

Our teacher / makes / us / some cookies.
주어 / 동사 / 간접목적어 / 직접목적어

(5) 5형식 문장: [주어＋동사＋목적어＋목적격보어]

He / makes / her / smile.
주어 / 동사 / 목적어 / 목적격보어

3. 4형식 문장에서 3형식으로 전환하기

4형식 We / **ask** / him / some questions.
주어 / 동사 / 간접목적어 / 직접목적어

3형식 We / **ask** / some questions / **of** him.
주어 / 동사 / 직접목적어 / of＋간접목적어

to를 쓰는 동사	give, send, show, teach, tell, write
for를 쓰는 동사	buy, cook, find, get, make
of를 쓰는 동사	ask

Lesson 1-13

문장의 구성 요소와 5형식

문장의 기본 구성 요소

• 문장을 구성하는 기본 요소: 주어 / 동사 / 목적어 / 보어

1. **주어**: 동작을 행하는 주체이며, 우리말 '~은 / 는 / 이 / 가'에 연결된다.
   - **She** dances well.
   - **His family** likes to watch TV.

2. **동사**: 주어의 동작이나 상태를 나타내며, 우리말 '~이(있)다, ~하다'에 해당한다.
   - Tom **writes** a letter to her every day.
   - They **have** a Christmas party.

3. **목적어**: 동사가 의미하는 동작의 대상이 되며, 우리말 '~을 / 를'에 연결된다.
   - I can speak **English**.
   - You can touch **this animal**.

4. **보어**: 주어를 설명하면 주격보어, 목적어를 설명하면 목적격보어라고 한다.
   - Mary is **a kind nurse**.
   - We see the man **drawing pictures**.

Grammar Plus +

목적어와 보어 구분하기: 동사 다음에 오는 단어가 '~을' 이라고 해석이 되면 목적어, 그렇지 않으면 보어이다.

Check up!

Answer Keys p. 05

A 다음 문장의 주어에 밑줄을 그으시오.

1 <u>My family</u> plants some trees every year.

2 We water the flowers.

3 They are good people.

4 Mary and Jane like me.

Check up!

Answer Keys p. 05

B 다음 문장의 동사에 밑줄을 그으시오.

1 The birds fly in the sky.

2 She has lunch at school.

3 The hat looks nice.

4 I arrived here on time

C 다음 문장의 목적어에 밑줄을 그으시오

1 You don't like him.

2 Sam tells the truth.

3 Michael sings a serenade for her.

4 She makes a mistake.

D 다음 문장의 보어에 밑줄을 그으시오.

1 My new teacher is Mr. Black.

2 Everyone thinks him to be honest.

3 I became a cook.

4 We feel cold.

E 다음 문장의 밑줄 친 부분의 문장의 구성 요소를 보기 에서 골라 쓰시오.

보기
주어 동사 목적어 주격보어 목적격보어

1 Mary is so happy. ➡ 주어

2 Tom and Jerry are nurses. ➡ ______

3 She always makes me sad. ➡ ______

4 I like my job. ➡ ______

5 They don't hate me. ➡ ______

6 Mr. Smith loves us so much. ➡ ______

Lesson 1-14

문장의 1, 2형식

• 영어의 문장은 주어, 동사, 목적어, 보어가 있고, 없느냐에 따라 5가지 문장 형식으로 나뉘는데, 이를 문장의 5형식이라고 한다.

1. 1형식 문장 : [주어 + 동사]

• The birds(주어) sing(동사).

• The sun(주어) shines(동사) *in the sky*.

※ 1형식의 동사를 **완전자동사**라고 한다.

Grammar Plus +

• **1형식에 많이 쓰이는 동사**: rise, leave, come, run, shine, sing, consist
1형식은 문장에 부가적인 내용을 더하기 위하여 시간/장소 등의 부사(구)를 함께 사용하기도 하는데, 부사구는 문장의 형식을 결정하는데 아무런 역할도 하지 않는다.

• **Some oranges are** in the bag. (in the bag-부사구)

• **He comes** late. (late-부사)

• 부사 외에도 전치사구, 명사구 등이 부사구가 될 수 있다.

2. 2형식 문장 : [주어 + 동사 + 보어]

2형식의 보어는 주어를 설명하는 말로 '주격 = 주격보어'의 관계가 성립된다.

• Mr. Brown(주어) is(동사) a dentist(보어). ⇨ *Mr. Brown = a dentist*

• The woman(주어) is(동사) polite(보어) *to us*. ⇨ *The woman = polite*

※ 2형식의 동사를 **불완전자동사**라고 한다.

※ 전치사구는 생략이 가능하므로 문장의 요소에 넣지 않는다.

Grammar Plus +

• 2형식의 동사는 be동사를 사용하지만 감각동사도 사용할 수 있다. 형태는 일반동사에 속하지만 형용사와 함께 쓰여서 2형식의 동사로 사용된다.

• **감각동사**: look(~하게 보인다), feel(~하게 느껴지다), sound(~하게 들리다), smell(~한 냄새가 나다), taste(~한 맛이 나다)

※ 특히 'like'와 함께 쓰이며, 이때의 'like'는 전치사로서 '~같은'이라는 뜻으로 쓰인다.

Check up!

Answer Keys p. 05

A 다음 보기 에서 같은 형태의 문장을 찾아 기호를 쓰시오.

보기

ⓐ She cries. ⓑ It tastes good.
ⓒ Mary is a kind girl. ⓓ We run fast.
ⓔ They are at the beach.

1 Tom is a bad boy. ➡ ⓒ
2 He worked all day long ➡ ______
3 She looks so young. ➡ ______
4 My uncle Jim comes. ➡ ______
5 Anna and I are in the library. ➡ ______

B 다음 문장이 어떤 형식인지 쓰고, 동사를 찾아 밑줄을 그으시오.

1 Her father is angry. ➡ 2형식
2 The birds live in a nest. ➡ ______
3 The cat runs. ➡ ______
4 I felt happy. ➡ ______
5 The flower smells good. ➡ ______

C 우리말에 맞게 괄호 안의 단어를 배열하여 문장을 완성하시오.

1 Tom은 잘생겨 보인다. (looks, handsome)
➡ Tome *looks handsome*.

2 Mr. and Mrs. Brown은 부부이다. (husband and wife, are)
➡ Mr. and Mrs. Brown ______.

3 밤하늘에 많은 별들이 있다. (stars, a lot of, are)
➡ ______ in the night sky.

4 Amy는 친절한 간호사이다. (a, nurse, kind)
➡ Amy is ______.

5 Tim과 Jerry는 같은 회사에서 일한다. (Tim, Jerry, and, work)
➡ ______ in the same company.

Lesson 1-15 문장의 3, 4형식

• **3형식 문장**: '주어+동사+목적어'의 형태로 나타내며, 목적어는 주어가 행하는 동작을 설명한다.
• **4형식 문장**: '주어+동사+간접목적어+직접목적어'의 형태로 나타내며, 2개의 목적어를 갖는다. 간접목적어에는 주로 사람이, 직접목적어에는 주로 사물이 나온다.

1. 3형식 문장: [주어+동사+목적어]

• I draw a picture.
주어 동사 목적어 ⇨ *I ≠ picture*

• Tom drinks some coffee *with Mary*.
주어 동사 목적어 ⇨ *Tom ≠ some coffee*

※ 3형식의 동사를 **완전타동사**라고 한다.

Grammar Plus +

3형식으로만 사용되는 동사:
explain, say, introduce, announce, report 등

2. 4형식 문장: [주어+동사+간접목적어+직접목적어]

'~에게'로 해당하는 간접목적어와, '~을 / 를'에 해당하는 직접목적어가 있다.

• My mom gives us some cookies.
주어 동사 간접목적어 직접목적어

• Santa gives us some gifts *for Christmas.*
주어 동사 간접목적어 직접목적어

※ 4형식의 동사를 **수여동사**라고 한다.

Grammar Plus +

• **간접목적어**: 동작을 받는 대상으로 주로 사람이다.
• **직접목적어**: 동작의 대상으로 주로 사물이다.

Check up!

Answer Keys p. 05

A 다음 문장의 목적어를 찾아 밑줄을 그으시오.

1 Mr. Brown drinks <u>coffee</u> everyday.

2 I bought some flowers.

3 She finds her cat.

4 Mrs. Smith asked a question.

5 An old woman points me.

Answer Keys p. 05

B 다음 문장에서 목적어를 찾아 밑줄을 긋고, 간접목적어는 '간목', 직접목적어는 '직목'이라고 쓰시오.

1 He told us a fairy tale.
간목 직목

2 They gave me a present.

3 We make our son a big kite.

4 I bring her a glass of water.

5 You'll send her an email.

6 She tells us good news.

C 다음 문장의 밑줄 친 부분을 바르게 고치시오.

1 The baker baked a big cake us.
➡ The baker baked ___us a big cake___.

2 Mary buy me an ice-cream cake.
➡ Mary __________ me an ice-cream cake.

3 She showed a picture us.
➡ She showed __________.

4 Mrs. Green like her cat.
➡ Mrs. Green __________ her cat.

5 A handsome boy looks at I.
➡ A handsome boy looks at __________.

6 She explain the symbolism of that color.
➡ She __________ the symbolism of that color.

7 Harry made some pecan pies for she.
➡ Harry made some pecan pies for __________.

Lesson

1-16 4형식 문장의 3형식 전환

- 두 개의 목적어를 가진 4형식의 문장을 3형식으로 전환할 때는 간접목적어와 직접목적어의 위치를 바꾸면서 간접목적어 앞에 전치사를 넣어준다.
- **간접목적어와 함께 쓰는 전치사**: to, for, of

1. 4형식 문장에서 3형식으로 전환하기

4형식 My daddy **bought** me a new smart phone.
(주어 / 동사 / 간접목적어 / 직접목적어)

3형식 My daddy **bought** a new smart phone **for** me.
(주어 / 동사 / 직접목적어 / for + 간접목적어)

2. to를 쓰는 동사: give, send, show, teach, tell, bring, write

Maria **writes** me a love letter.

➡ Maria **writes** a love letter **to** me.

3. for를 쓰는 동사: buy, cook, find, get, make

She **makes** him a wonderful kite.

➡ She **makes** a wonderful kite **for** him.

4. of를 쓰는 동사: ask, inquire, require

You can **ask** me a question.

➡ You can **ask** a question **of** me.

Check up!

Answer Keys p. 05

A 다음 괄호 안에서 알맞은 것을 고르시오.

1 My boss introduced a new project (us / to us) in the morning.

2 We required a charity donation (of him / him).

3 Lucy teaches (I / me) a song.

4 He reads (we / us) a storybook every night.

5 The waiter brings (she / her) a menu.

Answer Keys p. 05

B 다음 빈칸에 알맞은 전치사를 쓰시오.

1 I will buy my mother a gift.
➡ I will buy a gift ___for___ my mother.

2 She likes to tell us scary stories.
➡ She likes to tell scary stories ________ us.

3 The manager sent me an email yesterday afternoon.
➡ The manager sent an email ________ me yesterday afternoon.

4 Tommy made his wife a beautiful ring.
➡ Tommy made a beautiful ring ________ his wife.

5 I asked him some questions.
➡ I asked some questions ________ him.

6 I found him a watch.
➡ I found a watch ________ him.

C 다음 4형식 문장을 3형식으로 고치시오.

1 Maria asked me a difficult question.
➡ ___Maria asked a difficult question of me___.

2 He cooked her spaghetti.
➡ ________________.

3 We bought you some apples.
➡ ________________.

4 Mrs. Green gives me some chocolate.
➡ ________________.

5 Sam showed me a pearl necklace.
➡ ________________.

6 Anna requires me some advice.
➡ ________________.

Lesson

1-17 문장의 5형식

• 5형식 문장: '주어+동사+목적어+목적격보어'의 형태로 나타내며, 목적어를 보충 설명하는 목적격보어에는 명사, 형용사, to부정사, 원형부정사가 온다.

1. 5형식 문장: [주어+동사+목적어+목적격보어]

5형식의 문장에는 목적어를 설명해 주는 목적격보어가 목적어 뒤에 온다.
(목적어 = 목적격보어)

• We(주어) will elect(동사) her(목적어) the president(목적격보어) *of our country.*

• He(주어) calls(동사) me(목적어) 'angel'(목적격보어) *all the time.*

※ 5형식의 동사를 **불완전타동사**라고 한다.

2. 5형식 문장의 동사

(1) 사역동사: have, let, make, get

(2) 지각동사: feel, hear, watch, see, taste, notice

※ 사역동사, 지각동사는 원형부정사를 목적어로 한다.

Grammar Plus +

• **4형식의 make: ~에게 …을 만들어주다**
She usually makes me steak. (me≠steak)
그녀는 자주 나에게 스테이크를 만들어준다.

• **5형식의 make: ~을 …하게 만들다**
He makes me happy. (me=happy)
그는 나를 행복하게 해준다.

Check up!

Answer Keys p. 05

A 다음 문장에서 목적어와 목적격보어를 찾아 쓰시오.

1 She made her son a great architect.
목적어: *her son* 목적격보어: *a great architect*

2 Our teacher let us not go out during class.
목적어: ________ 목적격보어: ________

3 This umbrella will keep you dry from the rain.
목적어: ________ 목적격보어: ________

4 He had his car washed.
목적어: ________ 목적격보어: ________

5 This movie made them happy.
목적어: ________ 목적격보어: ________

Practice More IV

Answer Keys p. 06

A 다음 문장에서 주어와 동사를 찾아 쓰시오.

1 My grandparents live near my house.
➡ 주어 : *My grandparents* 동사 : *live*

2 Jenny and I are in the haunted house.
➡ 주어 : ________ 동사 : ________

3 That monster is very naive.
➡ 주어 : ________ 동사 : ________

4 At last, Michael came to us.
➡ 주어 : ________ 동사 : ________

5 That pretty girl is my sister.
➡ 주어 : ________ 동사 : ________

Note

- **naive** 순진한
- **at last** 결국엔, 마침내
- **loyal** 충성스러운
- **a household account book** 가계기록부
- **artist** 화가
- **shine** 빛나다
- **environment** 환경
- **old fashioned** 오래된, 유행이 지난

B 다음 문장에서 목적어와 보어를 찾아 쓰시오. (없는 경우에는 X로 표시하시오.)

1 The cat eats fish.
➡ 목적어 : *fish* 보어 : *X*

2 People think dogs are "loyal animals".
➡ 목적어 : ________ 보어 : ________

3 Jack makes me happy.
➡ 목적어 : ________ 보어 : ________

4 My mom keeps a household account book.
➡ 목적어 : ________ 보어 : ________

5 My dad is an artist.
➡ 목적어 : ________ 보어 : ________

C 다음 문장이 몇 형식인지 쓰시오.

1 The moon shines in the night sky. 1형식

2 She is a scientist. ________

3 They write an essay about the environment. ________

4 Aunt Annie comes to my house. ________

5 Mr. Black teaches us music. ________

6 Mrs. Han gives some candies to them. ________

7 Dad cooks us dinner every weekend. ________

8 I think him a smart boy. ________

Practice More IV

D 다음 괄호 안에서 알맞은 것을 고르시오.

1 My sister writes (me / to me) a letter.

2 They make (her / for her) a model boat.

3 You bought a rose (for / to) her.

4 John sometimes calls (me "Puppy" / "puppy" me).

5 Tony found (me / for me) my lost cat.

6 I will get my daughter to (participate / participates) in the Miss Korea Beauty Contest.

7 The music is (impress / impressive).

8 Suzie asked (I / me) a riddle .

9 I know that old (man / men)

10 Sam and you are very (kind / kindly).

E 다음 4형식의 문장을 3형식으로, 3형식의 문장을 4형식으로 바꾸시오.

<4형식 ➡ 3형식>

1 Sammy sends his boss an email.
➡ Sammy ___*sends*___ an email ___*to*___ his boss.

2 They showed him the magic tricks.
➡ They showed ______________.

3 The waitress brought me some cold water.
➡ The waitress __________ some cold water __________ me.

4 Maria tells me a scary tale.
➡ Maria tells __________ me.

5 Mr. Han teaches us math.
➡ Mr. Han __________ math __________.

<3형식 ➡ 4형식>

6 My brother cooks pizza for me.
➡ My brother ___*cooks me pizza*___.

7 Wendy found his favorite pen for Jack.
➡ Wendy found __________.

8 Minsu inquired some information of her.
➡ Minsu inquired ____________________.

9 We gave a new oven to him.
➡ We gave ____________________.

10 Jane writes Christmas cards to her friends.
➡ Jane writes ____________________.

F 다음 밑줄 친 우리말과 뜻이 같도록 빈칸에 알맞은 말을 쓰시오.

1 그 소식은 그를 기쁘게 만들었다.
➡ The news makes *him happy*.

2 그녀는 내게 그 신문을 읽기를 조언했다.
➡ _______________ me to read the newspaper.

3 Jenny는 우리에게 그 파티에 가자고 말했다.
➡ Jenny told us to _______________.

4 나는 그가 정직한 사람이라고 생각한다.
➡ I think _______________.

5 나는 그들이 에세이를 빨리 끝내도록 했다.
➡ I had _______________ the essay quickly.

서술형 연습 G 우리말에 맞게 주어진 단어들을 사용하여 문장을 완성하시오.

1 Lucy는 노래를 아주 잘 부른다. (Lucy, well, sings, very)
➡ *Lucy sings very well*.

2 Jenny와 Sammy는 매일 책을 읽는다.
(Jenny, Sammy, books, read, every day, and)
➡ ____.

3 돌은 딱딱한 느낌이 난다. (feels, a, hard, stone)
➡ ____.

4 그는 나에게 장미꽃 한 다발을 주었다.
(a bunch of, me, roses, he, gave)
➡ ____.

5 나는 그들을 영웅들이라고 부른다. (heroes, them, I, call)
➡ ____.

중간 기말고사 예상문제

Answer Keys p. 06

내신 최다 출제 유형

01 다음 중 밑줄 친 부분이 어법상 알맞지 않은 것을 고르시오. [출제 예상 90%]

① She is pretty.
② You are the best dancer.
③ They are my friends.
④ July is pretty and smart.
⑤ Ms. Lee and Mr. Brown is my teachers.

02 다음 문장에서 밑줄 친 부분의 의미가 다른 하나를 고르시오. [출제 예상 90%]

① This is my uncle Tom.
② My aunt is in New York.
③ He is an engineer.
④ She is 8 years old.
⑤ Mary is not a student.

03 다음 중 어법상 올바른 문장을 고르시오. [출제 예상 90%]

① Don't be late again.
② How a cute doll it is!
③ Let's go not outside.
④ Cleaning your room.
⑤ What pretty they are!

04 다음 중 어법상 올바른 문장을 고르시오. [출제 예상 90%]

① Does your father and mother play tennis?
② The earth go around the sun.
③ Americans don't like the number 13.
④ Africa don't have much rain.
⑤ Do your family go to the beach every summer?

05 다음 글의 밑줄 친 (A)~(E) 중 의미가 다른 것을 고르시오. [출제 예상 90%]

> This (A) is a picture of my family. These are my grandparents. This is my father. He (B) is an engineer. This is my mother. She is a teacher. This (C) is my brother. He (D) is in London now. He (E) is 20 years old.

① (A) ② (B) ③ (C) ④ (D) ⑤ (E)

06 다음 문장 중 형식이 나머지 문장과 다른 것을 고르시오. [출제 예상 90%]

① Anna and John are my friends.
② He is my brother, Tom.
③ You have rice for breakfast.
④ I and Jenny are the best students.
⑤ That baby is very cute.

07 다음 글의 밑줄 친 ①~⑤ 중 내용상 틀린 것을 고르시오. [출제 예상 90%]

> **A** Hello, Class. ① Today we have a new student today. ② This is Jane Brown. Jane, ③ can you introduce yourself?
> **B** Hi, I'm Jane Brown. ④ I'm from New York. ⑤ I'm very pleased to meet you.

① ② ③ ④ ⑤

Answer Keys p. 07~08

[01~02] 다음 빈칸에 공통으로 들어갈 알맞은 것을 고르시오.

01

- The puppy on the table ________ barking.
- My mother ________ a teacher.

① am ② is ③ are
④ am not ⑤ aren't

02

- Mary and John ________ in the library.
- Those cute girls ________ my classmates.

① is ② are ③ am not
④ do not ⑤ is not

[03~04] 다음 문장 중 be동사의 줄임말이 틀린 것을 고르시오.

03
① You're happy all the time.
② I amn't sad.
③ They aren't my classmates.
④ She's not very kind.
⑤ He isn't a doctor.

04
① It isn't my cell phone.
② They're your parents.
③ There isn't any water.
④ Many birds're in the sky.
⑤ She's my little sister.

05 다음 중 빈칸에 들어갈 수 없는 것을 고르시오.

________ is so smart.

① My aunt, Jenny ② He
③ Mr. Black ④ She
⑤ Tony and Mira

06 다음 단어들의 3인칭 현재형이 올바른 것을 고르시오.

① read – reads ② wash – washs
③ buy – buyes ④ do – dos
⑤ brush – brushs

07 다음 단어들의 3인칭 현재형이 틀린 것을 고르시오.

① need – needs ② go – goes
③ play – plays ④ choose – chooses
⑤ work – workes

08 다음 문장에서 틀린 곳을 찾아 번호를 쓰고, 바르게 고치시오.

Mrs. Green don't(①) have(②) a(③) lesson(④) today(⑤).

________ ➡ ________

[09~10] 다음 주어진 문장을 부정문으로 고쳤을 때 알맞은 것을 고르시오.

09

Anna visits her grandparents every weekend.

① Anna don't visits her grandparents every weekend.
② Anna doesn't visits her grandparents every weekend.
③ Anna isn't visit her grandparents every weekend.
④ Anna aren't visit her grandparents every weekend.
⑤ Anna doesn't visit her grandparents every weekend.

10

Sam and Tony are the best friends.

① Sam and Tony aren't the best friends.
② Sam and Tony isn't the best friends.
③ Sam and Tony am not the best friends.
④ Sam and Tony doesn't the best friends.
⑤ Sam and Tony don't the best friend.

[11~12] 다음 주어진 문장을 의문문으로 고쳤을 때 알맞은 것을 고르시오.

11

You eat vegetables.

① Are you eat vegetables?
② Am I eat vegetables?
③ Do you eat vegetables?
④ Does you eat vegetables?
⑤ Is you eat vegetables?

12

Her new dress is very pretty.

① Is her new dress is very pretty?
② Are new dress very pretty?
③ Does her new dress very pretty?
④ Is her new dress very pretty?
⑤ Do her new dress is very pretty?

[13~14] 다음 의문문에 대한 대답으로 알맞은 것을 고르시오.

13

Are Mr. and Mrs. Smith teachers?

① Yes, she is. ② No, he isn't.
③ Yes, they do. ④ No, they aren't.
⑤ Yes, he is.

14

Does Jack watch TV every night?

① Yes, she does. ② No, he don't.
③ Yes, he does. ④ No, Jack does.
⑤ Yes, he is.

15 다음 문장을 명령문으로 바꿨을 때 올바른 것을 고르시오.

You are polite to old people.

① Polite to old people.
② Let's polite to old people.
③ Be polite to old people.
④ Let's not be polite to old people.
⑤ Shall we be polite to old people?

16 다음 문장에서 'not'이 들어갈 알맞은 곳을 고르시오.

> I and ① my sister ② are ③ going ④ to the ⑤ zoo.

[17~18] 다음 주어진 문장과 같은 뜻이 되도록 빈칸에 알맞은 단어를 쓰시오.

17

> Shall we go out for a walk?
> ➡ ________ go out for a walk.

18

> You don't make a mess in your room.
> ➡ ________ a mess in your room.

19 다음 문장 중 올바른 것을 고르시오.

① Sam and I doesn't go to school.
② Mian and Minsu is students.
③ We are go shopping today.
④ John catches a ball.
⑤ I has a break time.

20 다음 문장 중 틀린 것을 고르시오.

① She takes a shower.
② They don't have to hurry.
③ I doesn't know the answer.
④ We take the subway.
⑤ You always study hard.

★★★
21 다음 중 대화가 잘못된 것을 고르시오.

① **A** Who is the girl in this picture?
B She's my cousin, Ellen.
② **A** Where are you going?
B I'm going to the shopping mall.
③ **A** What do you like?
B I don't buy it.
④ **A** Why are you sad?
B Because my mom got mad me.
⑤ **A** How's the weather?
B It's sunny.

★★★
22 다음 중 대화가 올바른 것을 고르시오.

① **A** What do you want to buy?
B I don't think so.
② **A** When do you go back home?
B At the bus stop.
③ **A** Where do you go this weekend?
B I'm at the hospital.
④ **A** How are you today?
B It's very hot.
⑤ **A** What's your favorite subject?
B I like English very much.

23 다음 문장의 빈칸에 알맞은 말을 보기에서 찾아 쓰시오.

> 보기
> When What Who Where How

(1) ________ do you go to bed?
(2) ________ does Mr. Green live?
(3) ________ is your favorite teacher?
(4) ________ is the matter? You look sad.
(5) ________ do you go to work?

[24~25] 다음 주어진 대답을 보고 빈칸에 알맞은 단어를 써 대화를 완성하시오.

24 A ________ do you want, milk ______ water?
B I want milk, please.

25 A ______ she a doctor ______ a nurse?
B She is a nurse.

[26~27] 다음 문장 중 부가의문문이 틀린 것을 고르시오.

26 ① Mary goes to the hospital, doesn't she?
② He sings songs well, doesn't he?
③ 'Cats' doesn't play in this hall,does it?
④ I like to draw pictures, do I?
⑤ You don't have much money, do you?

27 ① Susie is a kind nurse, isn't she?
② We are very diligent, aren't we?
③ Sam is a tall boy, is he?
④ John isn't a teacher, is he?
⑤ They aren't good engineers, are they?

28 다음 괄호 안의 단어를 바르게 배열한 것을 고르시오.

> My father (a chocolate cake, me, bakes)

① bakes a chocolate cake
② bakes me a chocolate cake
③ a chocolate cake bakes me
④ me a chocolate cake
⑤ bakes a chocolate cake me

29 다음 문장의 빈칸에 올 수 없는 단어를 고르시오.

> Jenny's mother gives ________ some candies.

① us ② me ③ I
④ you ⑤ them

30 다음 문장의 빈칸에 올 수 있는 단어를 고르시오.

> John requires some information ________ us.

① for ② to ③ of
④ from ⑤ in

[31~32] 다음 문장을 감탄문으로 알맞게 바꾼 것을 고르시오.

31

> The ice structure is really amazing.

① How amazing the ice structure is!
② What amazing the ice structure is!
③ What an amazing the ice structure is!
④ How an amazing the ice structure is!
⑤ How amazing the ice structure!

32

It is a very tall statue.

① How tall that it is!
② What a tall statue it is!
③ How a tall statue it is!
④ What tall statue it is!
⑤ What a tall statue is!

[33~34] 다음 두 문장에 들어갈 알맞은 단어들끼리 짝 지어진 것을 고르시오.

★★★
33

• He will teach English ________ us.
• I cook some spaghetti ________ you.

① to – for ② to – of ③ for – to
④ in – for ⑤ for – of

★★★
34

• She asked some information ________ me.
• They tell a story of an honest man ________ us.

① of – for ② to – of ③ of – to
④ for – to ⑤ to – for

[35~36] 다음 문장에 대한 대답으로 알맞은 것을 고르시오.

35

How do I get to the Green gallery?

① You can take a taxi.
② You are in the gallery.
③ You don't have a car.
④ It's eight o'clock.
⑤ It goes to the gallery.

36

What time do you meet Anna?

① I meet her at the bookstore.
② Anna meets me here.
③ I and Anna are meeting now.
④ I will meet her at 5.
⑤ I don't know.

★★★
37 다음 중 밑줄 친 like의 쓰임이 다른 하나를 고르시오.

① Susie likes to read books.
② They like pizza and coke.
③ He is like his father.
④ We like to study English.
⑤ I like that movie star.

38 다음 문장에 들어갈 be동사가 다른 하나를 고르시오.

① The animals at the zoo ______ sleeping.
② The dress and the shoes ______ new.
③ My kittens ______ all white.
④ This ______ your favorite pen.
⑤ They ______ my cousins.

39 다음 빈칸에 알맞은 것끼리 짝지어진 것을 고르시오.

• He always does his best, ________?
• They don't play football at lunch time, ________?

① does he – do they
② doesn't he – don't they
③ isn't he – are they
④ doesn't he – do they
⑤ don't he – don't they

40 다음 중 문장의 형식이 다른 하나를 고르시오.

① It looks like a butterfly.
② The baby cries in the bed.
③ He is a gentleman.
④ They are nice and sweet.
⑤ She feels cold.

[41~42] 다음 글을 읽고 물음에 답하시오.

> Gijun lives in Korea. He usually has six classes every day. He usually has classes in the same classroom. ⓐ He has ten-minutes breaks between classes. His favorite subject is history.
> ⓑ On Tuesdays he studies *samullori* in a club. He plays the *drum*.
> Does he enjoy it? Yes, he does.
> Wendy lives in Canada. ⓒ She goes to school by school bus. She has classes from Monday to Friday. ⓓ Each classes are about 35 minutes. All her classes are in different rooms. She eats lunch during her second or third break. After school, ⓔ she plays soccer with the soccer club members. 그녀는 좋은 선수이다.

41 ⓐ~ⓔ 중에서 어법상 옳지 않은 것으로 짝지어진 것을 고르시오.

① ⓐ, ⓑ ② ⓒ, ⓓ ③ ⓓ, ⓔ
④ ⓐ, ⓓ ⑤ ⓑ, ⓔ

42 윗글의 밑줄 친 우리말을 영작하시오.

➡ ______________________

★★★
43 다음 중 문장의 전환이 잘못된 것을 고르시오.

① She made me some cookies.
→ She made some cookies for me.
② He bought her a pen.
→ He bought a pen for her.
③ Sam brought me a puppy.
→ Sam brought a puppy to me.
④ You sent her an email.
→ You sent an email for her.
⑤ I gave her a book.
→ I gave a book to her.

★★★
44 다음 중 문장의 전환이 바르게 된 것을 고르시오.

① John makes her some muffins.
→ John makes some muffins to her.
② We write them letters.
→ We write letters to them.
③ Jenny bought me a pencil case.
→ Jenny bought a pencil case to me.
④ He showed us the magic trick.
→ He showed the magic trick for us.
⑤ She gave me a glass of juice.
→ She gave a glass of juice for me.

[45~46] 다음 주어진 문장과 형식이 같은 것을 고르시오.

45

> He drives me crazy all the time.

① I made a kite.
② She teaches us science.
③ Mary makes me happy.
④ She stayed four days.
⑤ I got the mail.

46

They are very famous singers in the world.

① He likes melons.
② She looks like her grandmother.
③ They go to the doctor.
④ I really hate snakes.
⑤ He showed me the pictures.

◇◇◇◇◇◇◇◇◇◇ 서술형 평가 ◇◇◇◇◇◇◇◇◇◇

47 다음 빈칸에 알맞은 부가의문문을 쓰시오.

- They are beautiful, __________?
- Mary is not tall and thin, ________?

[48~49] 다음 두 문장의 뜻을 같게 할 때, 빈칸에 알맞은 단어를 쓰시오.

48

- If you help the poor people, they thank to you.
  = Help the poor people, __________ they thank to you.

49

- If you eat only junk food, you'll be fat and weak.
  = Don't eat junk food, __________ you'll be fat and weak.

50 다음 주어진 문장을 부정문으로 바꿔 쓰시오.

The patient suffers from a toothache.

➡ ________________________________

51 다음 주어진 문장을 의문문으로 바꿔 쓰시오.

Tom Sawyer is a brave boy.

➡ ________________________________

52 다음 명령문의 부정문을 쓰시오.

Let's go into the haunted house.

➡ ________________________________

★★★
53 다음 문장을 감탄문으로 고쳐 쓰시오.

Michael Jackson was a very great singer.

➡ ______________________

54 다음 문장에서 틀린 것을 찾아 바르게 고쳐 쓰시오.

The roses smells very sweet.

__________ ➡ __________

55 다음 글의 괄호 안에서 알맞은 동사를 고르시오.

I (am / like) cheetahs a lot. They (are / do) the fastest animals.
They (have / has) strong legs.
Most of cheetahs (is / live) in Africa.

★★★
56 다음 3형식 문장을 4형식으로 고쳐 쓰시오.

The man tells the truth to us.

➡ ______________________

★★★
57 다음 4형식 문장을 3형식으로 고쳐 쓰시오.

Jenny brings them some cake.

➡ ______________________

58 다음 괄호 안에 있는 단어들을 우리말에 맞게 배열하여 쓰시오.

Mr. Brown은 우리를 웃게 만든다.
(Mr. Brown, laugh, us, makes)

➡ ______________________

[59~60] 다음 명령문의 부가의문문을 쓰시오.

59

Let's share our food.

➡ Let's share our food, __________?

60

Don't be afraid anymore.

➡ Don't be afraid anymore, __________?

02

Chapter 동사의 시제

Point Check I

◆ **현재시제 :** 현재에 일어나는 일이나 반복적이고 습관적인 일을 나타낼 때 쓰인다.
현재시제는 (단순)현재형과 현재진행형 두 가지로 구분하여 사용한다.

1. 현재형 : 현재의 상태, 습관, 반복, 사실, 불변의 진리, 속담 등을 표현할 때 쓰인다.

- She is a pianist. [현재 상태]
- He brushes his teeth three times a day. [반복]
- Seoul is the capital of Korea. [사실]
- The sun sets in the west. [진리]
- Time is money. [속담]

대부분의 동사	-s	like – likes sing – sings	spend – spends draw – draws
-o, -s, -x, -ch, -sh	-es	go – goes mix – mixes	wash – washes pass – passes
'자음+y'로 끝나는 경우	'y'를 'i'로 바꾸고 -es	carry – carries	study – studies
'모음+y'로 끝나는 경우	-s	buy – buys	enjoy – enjoys

2. 현재진행형 : [be동사(am, are, is) + 동사-ing] ~하고 있는 중이다, ~하고 있다

- We **are taking** some pictures now.

현재진행형의 일반동사 변화

대부분의 동사	-ing	read – reading	park – parking
'자음+-e'로 끝나는 경우	-e를 빼고 -ing	come – coming	make – making
'-ie'로 끝나는 경우	'-ie'를 'y'로 바꾼 후 -ing	lie – lying	die – dying
'단모음+단자음'으로 끝나는 경우	자음을 한 번 더 쓰고 -ing	put – putting	run – running

3. 진행형이 불가능한 동사

소유	have belong to
상태	like hate want know understand remember resemble

※ have: '먹다', '시간을 보내다'의 뜻을 가질 경우 '-ing'가 가능하다.

She **is having** some ice cream. [먹다]
They **are having** a nice weekend at the beach. [시간을 보내다]

Lesson 2-1

현재시제

일반동사 3인칭 단수 (1)

• **현재형:** 현재의 습관, 반복적인 일상, 속담 등을 표현할 때 사용한다. 일반동사의 경우 주어에 따라 동사의 형태가 달라진다.

1. be동사 현재형: 주어에 따라 'am, are, is'를 사용한다.

• Mrs. Green **is** my history teacher.

• We **are** on the same team.

2. 일반동사 현재형:

(1) 주어가 1, 2 인칭 단/복수, 3인칭 복수일 경우 동사원형을 쓴다.

(2) 주어가 3인칭 단수(he, she, it)일 경우 동사 뒤에 '-s' 또는 '-es'를 붙인다.

◈ 3인칭 단수 동사 변화

대부분의 동사	-s	like – likes sing – sings	spend – spends draw – draws	walk – walks take – takes
-o, -s, -x, -ch, -sh	-es	go – goes mix – mixes	pass – passes wash – washes	cross – crosses touch – touches

• He **sings** songs very well.

• Sam and Anna **cross** the street.
→ 주어에 이름이 두 개일 때는 단수가 아니라 복수이다.

Check up!

Answer Keys p. 09

A 다음 빈칸에 알맞은 be동사를 쓰시오.

1 I ___am___ a good painter.

2 She ________ happy when she plays tennis.

3 Sue and Tom ________ hungry when they finish playing.

4 You and I ________ in the same class.

5 Tony ________ my best friend.

Check up!

Answer Keys p. 09

B 다음 동사들의 3인칭 현재 단수형을 쓰시오.

1	ask	*asks*	2	stand	________
3	clean	________	4	read	________
5	agree	________	6	meet	________
7	find	________	8	wear	________
9	sit	________	10	know	________
11	reach	________	12	wish	________
13	teach	________	14	arrive	________
15	miss	________	16	dress	________
17	pass	________	18	go	________
19	brush	________	20	have	________

C 다음 괄호 안에 주어진 동사를 활용하여 빈칸을 채우시오.

1 Jane *wants* to drink a glass of ice water. (want)

2 My father ________ his old jacket. (wear)

3 Sue and Jenny ________ some eggs and vegetables. (mix)

4 Jack ________ his mother by himself. (draw)

5 Some doctors ________ the poor in Africa. (help)

6 Ian ________ his shoulder. (touch)

7 My sister ________ the dishes after meals. (do)

8 My kitten ________ a nap in the afternoon. (take)

9 The red sports car ________ through the gate. (pass)

10 The cat ________ a mouse. (catch)

Lesson **2-2**

일반동사 3인칭 단수 (2)

• **현재형:** 현재에 일어나는 일이나 반복적이고 습관적인 일을 나타낼 때 쓰는 표현이다.

◈ 3인칭 단수 동사 변화 2

'자음+y'로 끝나는 경우	'y'를 'i'로 바꾸고 -es	carry – carries	study – studies	try – tries
'모음+y'로 끝나는 경우	-s	buy– buys	enjoy – enjoys	play – plays

• A bird **flies** in the sky.

• Joe **enjoys** tap dancing.

Check up!

Answer Keys p. 09

A 다음 동사들의 3인칭 현재 단수형을 쓰시오.

1 envy *envies*　　2 lay ________

3 hurry ________　　4 fly ________

5 say ________　　6 copy ________

7 cry ________　　8 marry ________

9 stay ________　　10 obey ________

11 pay ________　　12 dry ________

13 worry ________　　14 supply ________

B 다음 괄호 안의 동사를 문장에 맞게 현재형으로 바르게 고쳐 쓰시오. (긍정문)

1 Jerry *brings* some coffee. (bring)

2 Anna and Mary ________ about their test results. (worry)

3 Tom ________ some pancakes for his mom. (make)

4 I like to ________ kites in winter. (fly)

5 His brother ________ one credit card. (carry)

6 She ________ up early in the morning. (wake)

7 Tony usually ________ in the library. (study)

8 He ________ to be a kind person. (try)

Lesson

2-3 일반동사 현재형

• **일반동사 현재형:** 주어의 인칭에 따라 동사에 변화가 있지만 뜻은 변하지 않는다.
현재에 일어나는 일이나 반복적이고 습관적인 일을 나타낼 때 쓰기도 하며,
미래를 나타내는 단어(부사)와 함께 쓰여 가까운 미래를 표현하기도 한다.

1. 일반동사의 현재형: [주어 + 동사원형 (–s / –es)]

• She **practices** the violin every day.

• They **play** tennis on Sundays.

2. 현재형을 사용하는 경우

(1) 현재의 사실이나 상태
• I **live** with my family.
• Fiona **goes** to Seoul National University.

(2) 습관적, 반복적으로 일어나는 일
• We **go** to school from Monday to Friday.
• She **writes** in her diary every night.

(3) 일반적인 사실이나 변하지 않는 진리
• Bears **sleep** during the winter.
• The earth **goes** around the sun.

(4) 속담이나 격언
• All roads **lead** to Rome.
• Knowledge **is** power.

Check up!

Answer Keys p. 09

A 다음 괄호 안의 단어를 현재형에 알맞게 바꾸어 빈칸에 쓰시오. (긍정문)

1 Kevin *watches* TV after lunch. (watch)

2 I always ________ up early. (get)

3 The woman ________ her daughter. (miss)

4 My grandmother ________ the newspaper in the morning. (read)

5 My friends ________ happy because they don't have homework today. (look)

6 The mind ________ heaven of hell and hell of heaven. (make)

Answer Keys p. 09

7 Mina ________ to a girls' high school. (go)

8 One good turn ________ another. (deserve)

9 Min ________ a good chance. (have)

10 Captain Jack ________ his team. (call)

B 다음 문장의 괄호 안에서 알맞은 말을 고르시오.

1 The oranges in the basket (taste / tastes) great.

2 Lisa (walk / walks) in the park every morning.

3 Babies (cry / cries) when they are sleepy.

4 My son (go / goes) to bed at 9p.m.

5 She (writes / write) in her diary every day.

6 The sun (rise / rises) in the east and (sets / set) in the west.

7 A friend in need (is / are) a friend indeed.

8 The weather (change / changes) from day to day.

9 Reading (make / makes) a full man.

10 The leaves (fall / falls) down in winter.

11 They always (says / say), "Be honest."

12 He (tries / try) to find a hero.

13 I (make / makes) them happy.

14 Mr. Jackson (have / has) three children.

15 She (sends / send) an email to her teacher.

Lesson 2-4 현재진행형

• **현재진행형:** '지금 ~하는 중이다'라는 뜻을 가지고 있으며, 지금 당장 일어나고 있는 상황에 대하여 말할 때 쓴다.

1. 현재진행형 만들기: [동사(am, are, is)+동사-ing] ~하고 있는 중이다, ~하고 있다

2. 일반동사의 진행형

대부분의 경우	-ing	read – reading	park – parking
'자음+-e'로 끝나는 경우	-e를 빼고 -ing	come – coming	make – making
'-ie'로 끝나는 경우	'-ie'를 'y'로 바꾼 후 -ing	lie – lying	die – dying
'단모음+단자음'으로 끝나는 경우	자음을 한 번 더 쓰고 -ing	put – putting	run – running

• Dorothy **is watching** TV now.

• Robert and I **are doing** homework right now.
→ 현재진행형은 보통 'now, right now, at the moment'와 함께 쓰인다.

3. 진행형이 불가능한 동사

소유	have	belong to		
상태	like	hate	want	know
	understand	remember	resemble	

※ have는 (먹다(eat)', '시간을 보내다(spend)'의 뜻을 가질 경우 진행형이 가능하다.

• I **am having** my dinner.

• I **am having** a great time with my friends.

4. 현재진행형의 부정문: [주어+am/are/is not+동사 -ing] ~하고 있지 않는 중이다

• We **are not singing** now.

5. 현재진행형의 의문문: [Am/Are/Is+주어+동사 -ing~?] ~하고 있는 중인가?

• **A** **Is** he **taking** a test?
B **Yes, he is. / No, he isn't.**

Check up!

Answer Keys p. 09

A 다음 동사들의 -ing형을 쓰시오.

1 call – calling
2 draw – ___________
3 wait – ___________
4 fly – ___________
5 enter – ___________
6 write – ___________
7 bring – ___________
8 save – ___________
9 cut – ___________
10 begin – ___________

B 다음 문장을 현재진행형으로 바꿀 때 빈칸에 알맞은 말을 쓰시오.

1 Mary reads a newspaper.
➡ Mary is reading a newspaper.

2 The rain pours down outside.
➡ The rain ___________ down outside.

3 A man stands in front of our classroom.
➡ A man ___________ in front of our classroom.

4 I send a message to you.
➡ I ___________ a message to you.

5 Helen makes a card for her grandfather's birthday.
➡ Helen ___________ a card for her grandfather's birthday.

C 다음 문장을 괄호 안의 지시어에 맞게 올바른 형태로 바꾸어 쓰시오.

1 Birds are flying over the bridge. (의문문)
➡ Are birds flying over the bridge?

2 She is making a cake for her mother. (부정문)
➡ ___________ a cake for her mother.

3 He is using the computer now. (의문문)
➡ ___________ the computer now?

4 We are drawing some flowers. (부정문)
➡ ___________ some flowers.

5 They are building a tower now. (부정문)
➡ ___________ a tower now.

6 The flowers are blooming right now. (부정문)
➡ ___________ right now.

Lesson

2-5 현재형과 현재진행형

• **현재형과 현재진행형의 차이**
현재형은 늘 반복되는 일이나 항상 일어나는 일들을 말할 때 쓰고, 현재진행형은 지금 바로 일어나고 있는 일에 대하여 말할 때 쓴다.

1. 현재형

(1) 반복적이거나 습관적인 일을 나타내는 말에 쓰인다.

• It **snows** a lot in winter.

(2) 현재형은 문장 끝에 'every day, all the time' 등과 함께 쓰인다.

• Students **go** to school every day.

2. 현재진행형

(1) 말하는 시점에 일어나고 있는 일을 나타낼 때 쓰인다.

• Peter **is doing** a puzzle.

(2) 현재진행형은 문장 끝에 'now, right now, at the moment'와 함께 쓰인다.

• Sumi **is eating** lunch now.

• Minsu and Mary **are studying** in class right now.

Grammar Plus +

• **현재형과 함께 쓰이는 부사** every (day, month, time), all the time, 빈도부사 (always, usually, sometimes)등

• **현재진행형과 함께 쓰이는 부사:** now, right now, at the moment

• **현재형, 현재진행형이 미래를 나타내는 부사구와 함께 쓰이면 가까운 미래를 표현하기도 한다.**
tomorrow, next week (day, month) after

Check up!

Answer Keys p. 10

A 다음 괄호 안의 단어를 문맥에 맞게 현재형 또는 현재진행형으로 바르게 고쳐 쓰시오.

1 He always ___drinks___ coffee before he goes to sleep. (drink)

2 Tiffany __________ to church on Sundays. (go)

3 Sara and I __________ in class right now. (sing)

4 Please wait a minute, I __________ a letter right now. (write)

5 Children __________ to play computer games. (like)

6 Lucas and I __________ in front of the big gate now. (dance)

7 She sometimes __________ comic books. (read)

8 We __________ the piano together all the time. (practice)

Practice More Ⅰ

Answer Keys p. 10

A 다음 중 동사의 원형과 -ing형이 올바르게 짝지어진 것을 고르시오

1 ① stay – staing
② turn – turnning
③ bike – biking
④ arrive – arriveing
⑤ fly – fling

2 ① put – puting
② feed – feding
③ visit – visitting
④ study – studing
⑤ drink – drinking

3 ① sleep – sleepping
② drive – driveing
③ break – breaking
④ burn – burnning
⑤ come – comming

4 ① build – building
② eat – eatting
③ cheer – cheerring
④ get – geting
⑤ tie – tieing

5 ① cut – cuting
② fall – falling
③ camp – campping
④ have – haveing
⑤ write – writeing

6 ① bring – bringing
② collect – collectting
③ lie – lieing
④ sing – singging
⑤ save – saveing

B 다음 문장의 괄호 안에서 알맞은 말을 고르시오.

1 My book (look / looks) more interesting than hers.
2 I (keeps / keep) quiet when my sister sleeps.
3 Daniel (is knowing / knows) a lot about making kimchi.
4 It (is raining / rains) a lot this week.
5 The bus (is coming / comes) into the station now.
6 Jungmin (has / is having) an interesting book.
7 They (are not drawing / not are drawing) a car.
8 He (is liking / likes) her very much.
9 He (is going / goes) to the park every morning.
10 Children (are not practicing / not are practicing) the piano right now.

Practice More I

C 다음 괄호 안의 동사를 문맥에 맞게 현재형 또는 현재진행형으로 고쳐 쓰시오. (긍정문)

1 She ___goes___ to the library to study science. (go)

2 John __________ the piano with his brother. (play)

3 My sister __________ a bike at the park in the evening. (ride)

4 Lisa __________ at seven every morning. (get up)

5 Jim __________ to study hard to get an A on the English test. (try)

6 I ____________ Japan the day after tomorrow. (leave)

7 She __________ some flowers for her mother at the moment. (buy)

8 I am going to __________ my grandmother next week. (visit)

9 Today, she _____________ to meet her old friend. (plan)

10 Mrs. Lee __________ English to us now. (teach)

D 다음 문장에서 어법상 어색한 곳을 바르게 고치시오.

1 Kate and I going to school by bus.

___going___ ➡ ___are going___

2 My parents take a trip to Canada right now.

_______________ ➡ _______________

3 I know that the Earth is going around the sun.

_______________ ➡ _______________

4 She looks for her ring now.

_______________ ➡ _______________

5 Sue and Tim is writing a letter to their teacher.

_______________ ➡ _______________

6 The house is belonging to Jim.

_______________ ➡ _______________

7 He is walking his dog every day.

_______________ ➡ _______________

8 I am remembering what happened yesterday.

_______________ ➡ _______________

Answer Keys p. 10

9 The Koreans are speaking Korean.

_______________ ➡ _______________

10 Tom and Lilly is having dinner together now.

_______________ ➡ _______________

E 다음 우리말과 뜻이 같도록 빈칸에 알맞은 말을 쓰시오.

1 Emma는 아버지를 돕고 있는 중이니?

➡ ___Is___ Emma ___helping___ her father?

2 Steve는 사진을 찍고 있는 중이니?

➡ _______ Steve _______ pictures?

3 우리는 매일 아침마다 우유를 마신다.

➡ We _______ milk every morning.

4 우리는 즐거운 시간을 보내고 있다.

➡ We _______ _______ a good time now.

5 태양은 서쪽으로 진다.

➡ The Sun _______ in the west.

서술형 연습 F 우리말에 맞게 주어진 단어들을 사용하여 영작하시오.

1 Isabella는 나를 비웃고 있다. (Isabella, laughing at, is, me)

➡ ___Isabella is laughing at me.___

2 Kim은 Robert 옆에 앉아 있다. (sitting, next to, Kim, Robert, is)

➡ ______________________________

3 나는 지금 안경을 찾고 있는 중이다. (looking for, glasses, am, I, now, my)

➡ ______________________________

4 그는 아침 8시 30분에 학교를 간다.(in the morning, goes, he, at 8:30, school, to)

➡ ______________________________

5 그녀는 지금 통화하고 있는 중이 아니다. (she, talking, on, phone, the, now, is, not)

➡ ______________________________

Point Check Ⅱ

◆ **과거시제 :** 과거에 일어났던 일이나 상태를 표현할 때 쓰는 말이다.
과거의 일을 전체적으로 말하는 단순 과거형과 과거의 어느 시점에 일어나고 있었던 일을 말하는 과거진행형이 있다.

1. be동사 과거형

(1) **be동사 과거** : [주어 + was / were ~] ~였다, ~에 있었다
- She **was** a comedy writer.

(2) **be동사 과거 부정문** : [주어 + was / were not ~] ~가 아니었다, ~에 없었다
- He **was not(wasn't)** at the park.

(3) **be동사 과거 의문문** : [Was / Were + 주어 ~?] ~였습니까?, ~에 있었습니까?
- A **Were they** in the theater together?
  B **Yes, they were. / No, they weren't.**

2. 일반동사 과거형

(1) **일반동사 과거** : [주어 + 동사-d/-ed ~] ~했다
- We **played** basketball together yesterday.

(2) **일반동사 과거 부정문** : [주어 + did not + 동사원형 ~] ~하지 않았다
- You **did not (didn't)** need this pencil at that time.

(3) **일반동사 과거 의문문** : [Did + 주어 + 동사원형 ~?] ~했었습니까?
- A **Did** John **get** a good score?
  B **Yes, he did. / No, he didn't.**

3. 과거진행형

(1) **과거진행형** : [주어 + was / were + 동사-ing] ~하고 있던 중이었다
- It **was playing** with the yarn.

(2) **과거진행형 부정문** : [주어 + was / were not + 동사-ing] ~하지 않던 중이었다
- John and Mary **were not going** to the theater.

(3) **과거진행형 의문문** : [Was / Were + 주어 + 동사-ing ~?] ~하고 있던 중이었습니까?
- A **Were** you **watching** TV then?
  B **Yes, I was. / No, I wasn't.**

Lesson 2-6

과거시제

be동사 과거형

과거형: 과거에 이미 일어났던 일이나 과거의 반복적 습관에 대해 말할 때 사용한다.

1. be동사 과거형

(1) 'was'와 'were'가 있으며 주어의 인칭에 따라 다르게 쓰인다.

(2) 과거를 나타내는 부사어 'yesterday, last week, ago, then, at that time' 등과 함께 쓰인다.

주어	be동사 현재형	be동사 과거형
I	am	was
you, we, they	are	were
he, she, it	is	was

- I **was** at school at that time.
- They **were** very tired and sleepy.
- She **was** busy last week.

2. be동사 과거형_부정문: [주어 + was / were not]

주어	be동사 과거형 + not	줄임말
I	was not	wasn't
you, we, they	were not	weren't
he, she, it	was not	wasn't

- We **were not (weren't)** happy then.
- He **was not (wasn't)** angry yesterday.

3. be동사 과거형_의문문: [Was / Were + 주어~?]

(1) 주어와 동사의 위치를 바꾼다.

- **It was** funny.
- **Was it** funny?

(2) 대답할 때 긍정은 [Yes, 주어 + was / were.], 부정은 [No, 주어 + was / were not.]이다.

A **Were you** in America last month?

B **Yes, I was. / No, I wasn't.**

Check up!

Answer Keys p. 10

A 다음 빈칸에서 알맞은 말을 고르시오.

1 I (was / were) happy when the test was finished.

2 We (are / were) sad because we lost the game.

3 (Were / Are) they in Busan three days ago?
– Yes, they (are / were).

4 Park and I (were not / was not) sad and lonely.

5 (Was / were) this towel wet?
– No, it (was not / were not).

B 다음 대화의 빈칸에 알맞은 be동사를 써 넣으시오.

1 A Was Jenny absent yesterday?
B No, she __wasn't (was not)__.

2 A __________ Max and Sam in the class?
B Yes, they __________.

3 A __________ your parents taking a nap then?
B No, they __________________.

4 A Was she cooking Korean food?
B Yes, she __________.

5 A __________ Tommy sad?
B No, he __________________.

6 A __________ you surprised?
B Yes, I was.

7 A Was I your best friend?
B Yes, you __________.

8 A __________ your teachers kind to students?
B Yes, they __________.

Lesson **2-7**

일반동사의 과거형 _ 규칙동사 변화

• **일반동사의 과거형:** 동사원형에 '–d / –ed'가 붙어 규칙적으로 변하는 동사들이 쓰인다.

1. 일반동사의 과거형 _ 규칙변화

대부분의 경우	-ed	visit – visited	walk – walked
-e로 끝나는 경우	-d	save – saved	dance – danced
'모음+y'로 끝나는 경우	-ed	play – played	stay – stayed
'자음+y'로 끝나는 경우	'y'를 'i'로 바꾸고 -ed	cry – cried	try – tried
'단모음+단자음'으로 끝나는 경우	자음을 한 번 더 쓰고 -ed	plan – planned	stop – stopped

• He **played** soccer last weekend.

• Tom and Jerry **planned** to travel to Europe last month.

2. 일반동사의 과거형_부정문: [주어 + did not + 동사원형 ~]

• We **did not (didn't)** save the money.

• She **did not (didn't)** study for the test at all.

3. 일반동사의 과거형_의문문: [Did + 주어 + 동사원형~?]

(1) 문장의 맨 앞에 'Did'를 붙이고, '주어+동사원형'을 사용한다.

• **She visited** New York last year.
➡ **Did she visit** New York last year?

(2) 대답할 때 긍정은 [Yes, 주어 + did.], 부정은 [No, 주어 + did not.] 이다.

A **Did** they **try** to study hard?
B **Yes, they did. / No, they didn't.**

Check up!

Answer Keys p. 10

A 다음 동사의 과거형을 쓰시오.

1 stop *stopped*　　2 raise ________

3 discuss ________　　4 happen ________

5 talk ________　　6 live ________

Check up!

Answer Keys p. 10

7	shop	________	8	answer	________
9	worry	________	10	clean	________
11	hug	________	12	plan	________
13	hop	________	14	work	________
15	play	________	16	escape	________
17	cook	________	18	study	________
19	invent	________	20	serve	________

B 다음 문장을 괄호 안의 지시대로 바꿔 쓸 때 빈칸에 알맞은 말을 쓰시오.

1 Jack worked a lot last week. (의문문)
➡ __*Did*__ Jack __*work*__ a lot last week?

2 I lived in Seoul last year. (부정문)
➡ I ______________ in Seoul last year.

3 They played basketball after school. (부정문)
➡ They ______________ basketball after school.

4 She bought some cakes. (의문문)
➡ ________ she ________ some cakes?

5 John studied for the final test. (의문문)
➡ ________ John ________ for the final test?

6 My brother and I thought about the future. (부정문)
➡ My brother and I ______________ about the future.

7 Everyone had lunch at the cafeteria. (의문문)
➡ ________ everyone ________ lunch at the cafeteria?

8 The leaves fell off all in the fall. (부정문)
➡ The leaves ______________ off all in the fall.

9 He drew a picture of me. (부정문)
➡ He ______________ a picture of me.

10 She showed him fantastic magic tricks. (의문문)
➡ ________ she ________ him fantastic magic tricks?

Lesson 2-8

일반동사의 과거형 _ 불규칙동사 변화

• 일반동사의 과거형을 쓸 때 동사가 불규칙하게 변하는 것들이 있다.

1. **AAA형** (원형, 과거형, 과거분사형이 같은 것)

원형	과거형	과거분사형	뜻
cost	cost	cost	비용이 들다
hit	hit	hit	치다
hurt	hurt	hurt	다치다
let	let	let	~하게 하다
put	put	put	놓다
read	read	read	읽다
set	set	set	놓다
spread	spread	spread	퍼지다

2. **ABB형** (과거형과 과거분사형이 같은 것)

원형	과거형	과거분사형	뜻
bring	brought	brought	가져오다
build	built	built	짓다
burn	burned / burnt	burned / burnt	타다
buy	bought	bought	사다
catch	caught	caught	잡다
dream	dreamed / dreamt	dreamed / dreamt	꿈꾸다
feed	fed	fed	먹이다
feel	felt	felt	느끼다
fight	fought	fought	싸우다
find	found	found	발견하다
get	got	got	얻다
have	had	had	가지다
hear	heard	heard	듣다
hold	held	held	잡다, 지니다
keep	kept	kept	유지하다
lay	laid	laid	놓다, 낳다

lead	led	led	인도하다
leave	left	left	떠나다
lend	lent	lent	빌려주다
lose	lost	lost	잃어버리다
make	made	made	만들다
mean	meant	meant	의미하다
meet	met	met	만나다
pay	paid	paid	지불하다
say	said	said	말하다
sell	sold	sold	팔다
send	sent	sent	보내다
sit	sat	sat	앉다
sleep	slept	slept	자다
slide	slid	slid	미끄러지다
smell	smelled / smelt	smelled / smelt	냄새맡다
spend	spent	spent	소비하다
stand	stood	stood	서다
teach	taught	taught	가르치다
tell	told	told	말하다
think	thought	thought	생각하다
understand	understood	understood	이해하다
win	won	won	이기다

3. **ABC형** (원형, 과거형, 과거분사형이 다른 것)

원형	과거형	과거분사형	뜻
be	was/were	been	~이다, 있다
bear	bore	born	낳다
begin	began	begun	시작하다
bite	bit	bitten	물다
blow	blew	blown	불다
break	broke	broken	깨뜨리다
choose	chose	chosen	선택하다
do	did	done	하다

draw	drew	drawn	그리다
drink	drank	drunk	마시다
drive	drove	driven	운전하다
eat	ate	eaten	먹다
fall	fell	fallen	떨어지다
forget	forgot	forgotten	잊다
fly	flew	flown	날다
give	gave	given	주다
go	went	gone	가다
grow	grew	grown	자라다
know	knew	known	알다
ride	rode	ridden	타다
ring	rang	rung	울리다
rise	rose	risen	오르다
see	saw	seen	보다
sing	sang	sung	노래하다
show	showed	showed / shown	보여주다
speak	spoke	spoken	말하다
swim	swam	swum	수영하다
take	took	taken	가지고 가다
throw	threw	thrown	던지다
wake	woke	woken	깨다
wear	wore	worn	입다
write	wrote	written	쓰다

4. **ABA형** (원형과 과거분사형이 같은 것)

원형	과거형	과거분사형	뜻
become	became	become	되다
come	came	come	오다
run	ran	run	달리다

Check up!

Answer Keys p. 11

1 spread – *spread* – *spread*
2 cost – ______ – ______
3 read – ______ – ______
4 catch – ______ – ______
5 burn – ______ – ______
6 find – ______ – ______
7 hold – ______ – ______
8 feed – ______ – ______
9 keep – ______ – ______
10 make – ______ – ______
11 mean – ______ – ______
12 slide – ______ – ______
13 stand – ______ – ______
14 think – ______ – ______
15 put – ______ – ______
16 dream – ______ – ______
17 sit – ______ – ______
18 tell – ______ – ______
19 win – ______ – ______
20 be – ______ – ______
21 wear – ______ – ______
22 sleep – ______ – ______
23 lay – ______ – ______
24 bear – ______ – ______
25 begin – ______ – ______
26 bite – ______ – ______
27 wake – ______ – ______
28 ride – ______ – ______
29 run – ______ – ______
30 grow – ______ – ______

Lesson 2-9 과거진행형

• 과거형은 단순히 과거에 있었던 일을 전체적으로 말하는 것이고, 과거진행형은 과거의 어떤 시점을 짚어서 그 시간에 하고 있었던 일을 나타낸다.

1. **과거진행형:** [주어 + was / were + 동사 -ing] ~하고 있던 중이었다
   • Maria **was playing** a computer game.
   • They **were singing** a song at that time.

2. **과거진행형의 부정문:** [주어 + was / were not + 동사 -ing] ~하지 않던 중이었다
   • I **was not dancing** then.

3. **과거진행형의 의문문:** [Was / Were + 주어 + 동사 -ing ~?] ~하고 있던 중이었습니까?
   A **Were** you **walking** in the park?
   B **Yes, I was. / No, I wasn't.**

Check up!

Answer Keys p. 11

A 다음 밑줄 친 부분을 과거진행형의 형태로 바꾸어 쓰시오.

1 Balloons flew up into the sky.
➡ *were flying*

2 They enjoyed the party at that time.
➡ ______________

3 I made some cookies for Sue's birthday.
➡ ______________

4 My puppy White dug the ground.
➡ ______________

5 A hen laid some eggs.
➡ ______________

6 Some birds sang in the tree.
➡ ______________

7 Jamie wrote a letter to me.
➡ ______________

 Answer Keys p. 11

B 다음 문장을 괄호 안의 지시어에 따라 '진행형'의 형태로 고쳐서 빈칸에 알맞은 말을 쓰시오.

1 She ran at the park last night. (의문문)
➡ ___Was___ she ___running___ at the park last night?

2 He cared for his dog because his dog was sick. (의문문)
➡ ________ he ________ for his dog because his dog was sick?

3 The man looked for some nice shoes. (의문문)
➡ ________ the man ________ for some nice shoes?

4 She didn't have lunch then. (부정문)
➡ She __________________ lunch then.

5 I listened to music yesterday. (부정문)
➡ I __________________ to music yesterday.

6 Wandong spoke English very well. (부정문)
➡ Wandong __________________ English very well.

7 Sally didn't ask some questions. (의문문)
➡ ________ Sally ________ some questions?

8 Donna and Jack crossed the street at the red light. (부정문)
➡ Donna and Jack __________________ the street at the red light.

9 My grandfather watered the garden. (의문문)
➡ ________ my grandfather ________ the garden?

10 She lied to everyone. (부정문)
➡ She __________________ to everyone.

C 다음 주어진 단어를 이용하여 우리말을 영어로 바르게 영작하시오.

1 우리는 TV를 보고 있던 중이 아니었다. (watch TV)
➡ ___We weren't watching TV.___

2 그들은 그때 시험 공부를 하고 있던 중이었다. (study, for the test, at that time)
➡ ______________________________

3 그녀는 수영장에서 수영을 하던 중이었습니까? (swim, in the pool)
➡ ______________________________

Practice More Ⅱ

Answer Keys p. 11

A 다음 동사의 과거형을 쓰시오.

1 do ➡ did 2 spread ➡ ______

3 sing ➡ ______ 4 study ➡ ______

5 eat ➡ ______ 6 mean ➡ ______

7 keep ➡ ______ 8 burn ➡ ______

9 speak ➡ ______ 10 wear ➡ ______

B 다음 괄호 안에서 알맞은 것을 고르시오.

1 I (am / were / was) happy because I ate delicious pizza.

2 We (are / were / is) quite busy last week.

3 Sam (is / are / was) interested in playing chess when he was eight.

4 My father (was / is / are) handsome 30 years ago.

5 The leaves (is / was / were) yellow and red last month.

6 They (go / went / goes) to the swimming pool last week.

7 My grandmother (left / leave / leaving) the hospital yesterday.

8 Jerry and his sister (cooks / cooking / cooked) some food for Mother's Day.

9 Margaret (think / thought / was thinking) that Jack was silly.

10 We (brings / are / brought) some cake for her.

C 다음 문장을 괄호 안의 지시에 따라 과거형으로 바꾸어 쓰시오.

1 She washed her hands. (부정문)
➡ She did not (didn't) wash her hands.

2 Helen liked her new coat. (의문문)
➡ ______________ her new coat?

3 Jack finished homework early. (부정문)
➡ ______________ homework early.

4 I was ready for the trip. (부정문)
➡ ______________ ready for the trip.

5 Jane ran to the amusement park. (의문문)
➡ ______________ to the amusement park?

6 She left China last year. (의문문)
➡ ________________ last year?

7 The concert was really exciting. (부정문)
➡ ________________ really exciting.

8 He came to the party yesterday. (의문문)
➡ ________________ to the party yesterday?

9 They slept well last night. (의문문)
➡ ________________ well last night?

10 Joe and Helen were good friends. (부정문)
➡ ________________ good friends.

D 다음 대화의 빈칸에 알맞은 말을 쓰시오.

1 A __*Did*__ __*they*__ go hiking yesterday?
B No, they __*didn't*__.

2 A ________ Mina playing tennis yesterday?
B Yes, ________ ________.

3 A ________ Ann give you a birthday present?
B No, she ________. Maybe she forgot my birthday.

4 A ________ he in the library with Jane?
B Yes, ________ ________.

5 A ________ Sara send an email to you?
B No, ________ ________.

6 A ________ Jack and you having lunch together at that time?
B No, ________ ________.

E 다음 주어진 단어를 이용하여 문장을 완성하시오.

1 What were you doing yesterday? (play computer games)
➡ I __*was playing computer games*__.

2 What were they doing at that time? (read the newspaper)
➡ They ________________.

3 What was Harry doing then? (wash his car)
➡ Harry ________________.

Answer Keys p. 11~12

4 What did Mother do last week? (watch a movie)

➡ Mother ____________________.

5 What did you do? (my homework)

➡ I ____________________.

6 What did Wendy and Jack bring? (a loaf of bread)

➡ They ____________________.

F 다음 중 밑줄 친 부분을 어법상 바르게 고치시오.

1 Does he studying English last night? ___Was___

2 Hana was moving to Seoul in 2014. ____________

3 Mr. Ahn were having an interview at that time. ____________

4 I not was taking a picture then. ____________

5 They going for a walk yesterday morning. ____________

6 Wendy stays up late last night. ____________

7 He practices the piano a lot before the last concert. ____________

8 They enjoys Helen's birthday party last month. ____________

서술형 연습

G 다음 우리말에 맞게 괄호 안에 있는 단어들을 배열하여 문장을 완성하시오.

1 그녀는 어제 낮잠을 자고 있었습니까? (was, taking, a nap)

➡ ___Was___ she ___taking a nap___ yesterday?

2 Diana는 3시에 테니스를 치고 있었습니까? (playing, tennis, was)

➡ ________ Diana ____________ at three o'clock?

3 그들은 어젯밤에 과학 공부를 하지 않았다. (not, did, study)

➡ They ____________________ science last night.

4 나는 그때 잠을 자고 있지 않았다. (sleeping, was, not)

➡ I ____________________ then.

5 Daniel은 기타를 치지 않았다. (play, not, did)

➡ Daniel ____________________ the guitar.

Point Check Ⅲ

◆ **미래시제 :** 미래에 일어날 일에 대하여 표현한 것을 말한다.

◆ 미래를 뜻하는 조동사 'will / be going to'를 사용하여 표현한다.

◆ 현재진행형과 미래를 나타내는 부사를 함께 써서 가까운 미래를 표현하기도 한다.

1. will과 be going to

will	be going to
[주어 + will + 동사원형] Mary will play the piano at the concert.	[주어 + be(am / are / is) going to + 동사원형] They are going to swim in the river.

2. 현재형 / 현재진행형으로 미래를 표현하는 경우

현재형의 미래 표현	현재진행형의 미래 표현
(1) **왕래발착 동사:** go, come, leave, start, arrive ➡ They come back here in 30 minutes. (2) **시간, 조건의 부사절:** when(~할 때), after(~후에), before(~전에), until(~할 때까지), if(~한다면), unless(~하지 않는다면) ➡ We will go on a picnic unless it rains next week.	• 미래를 나타내는 부사구: tomorrow, next week, later → She is making a diet video next month.

3. will과 be going to의 부정문과 의문문

(1) **will의 부정문:** [주어 + will not + 동사원형] ~하지 않을 것이다

• Phillip **will not** go abroad this summer.

(2) **will의 의문문:** [Will + 주어 + 동사원형~?] ~할 것인가?, ~할 계획인가?

• **A** **Will** Lucy and Eddie go to Japan this winter?
  B **Yes, they will. / No, they will not (won't).**

(3) **be going to의 부정문:** [주어 + be동사 + not going to + 동사원형] ~하지 않을 것이다

• We **are not going to** make the same mistakes again.

(4) **be going to의 의문문:** [be동사 + 주어 + going to + 동사원형 ~?] ~할 예정인가?, ~할 것인가?

• **A** **Is** Jerry **going to** sing a main song with the band?
  B **Yes, he is. / No, he is not (isn't).**

Lesson 2-10

미래시제

will / be going to

미래형은 가까운 미래부터 계획되거나 계획되지 않은 미래에 일어날 일을 표현한다.
'will'과 'be going to'를 써서 나타낸다.

1. will: [주어 + will + 동사원형] ~할 것이다, ~할 예정이다

미래를 나타내는 조동사 will의 뒤에는 주어의 인칭에 상관없이 항상 동사원형이 온다.

- It **will** be sunny and warm this Saturday.
- Nisha **will** go to the airport.

2. be going to: [주어 + be(am / are / is) going to + 동사원형] ~할 것이다, ~할 예정이다

(1) be going to의 뒤에도 주어의 인칭에 상관없이 항상 동사원형이 온다.

(2) be는 주어에 따라 'am / are / is'로 바꾸어 쓴다.

- Tom **is going to** arrive at the station.
- They **are going to** go to the library.

3. will과 be going to의 부정문과 의문문

(1) will 부정문: [주어 + will not + 동사원형] ~하지 않을 것이다

- You **will not** do the work with him.

(2) will 의문문: [Will + 주어 + 동사원형~?] ~할 것인가?, ~할 계획인가?

- **A** **Will** Jessica study hard this semester?
  B **Yes, she will. / No, she will not(= won't).**

(3) be going to 부정문: [주어 + be not going to + 동사원형] ~하지 않을 것이다

- He **is not going to** take the final exam.

(4) be going to 의문문: [Be + 주어 + going to + 동사원형 ~?] ~할 예정인가?, ~할 것인가?

- **A** **Are** you **going to** eat out tonight?
  B **Yes, we are. / No, we are not (aren't).**

Check up!

Answer Keys p. 12

A 다음 괄호 안에서 알맞은 말을 고르시오.

1 They will (be / are) here in thirty minutes.

2 You (will play / will plays) the violin at the next concert.

3 Jack (will not / not will) send an email to his professor.

4 She (will not / is not) going to eat fast food.

5 Are you (will / going to) go to your uncle's farm to help him?

6 They (aren't going to / won't going to) go on a picnic this Saturday.

7 I am (going to / will) have an audition next month.

B 다음 문장의 밑줄 친 부분을 바르게 고쳐 쓰시오.

1 I am going to running when Susan comes back home.
➡ *am going to run*

2 Tim will goes to the concert tomorrow.
➡ ________________

3 She is going to met her grandfather next week.
➡ ________________

4 We will taking part in the contest next month.
➡ ________________

5 They is going to wake up early next morning.
➡ ________________

6 She will not going to have some ice cream.
➡ ________________

7 You will taking a shower after playing sports.
➡ ________________

8 Jennifer and I isn't going to be late for school.
➡ ________________

9 Are they go shopping this weekend?
➡ ________________

C 다음 대화나 문장의 빈칸에 알맞은 말을 쓰시오.

Note
• recital 독주회

1 A Are you *going* *to* play a game after school?
B Yes, *we* *are*. We are going to play bingo.

2 A ________ he teach us Spanish?
B No, he won't. He ________ teach us English.

3 A ________ Mary ________ ________ visit her grandparents next month?
B Yes, ________ ________. She's going to go there by train.

4 He ________ ________ ________ ________ give a violin recital. (be going to 부정)

5 You ________ ________ get a chance like this again. (will 부정)

Lesson 2-11

현재형의 미래 표현

미래를 표현할 때 'will / be going to' 외에 '현재형 + 미래형 부사구'로 나타낼 수 있다.

1. 현재형으로 미래를 표현하는 경우

(1) 'go, come, start, leave, arrive' 등의 왕래발착(가다, 오다, 출발하다, 도착하다) 동사는 '현재형' 형태로 미래를 나타내는 부사(구)와 함께 쓰여 가까운 미래를 표현한다.

- The train **departs** in ten minutes.
- I **leave** for England tomorrow morning.

(2) 'when (~할 때), after (~후에), before (~전에), until (~할 때까지), if (~한다면), unless (~하지 않는다면)'가 있는 시간, 조건의 부사절에는 미래형 대신 현재형을 쓴다.

- He will not start **if** it **snows** tomorrow.

2. 현재진행형으로 미래를 표현하는 경우

(1) 현재진행형으로 미래를 표현할 때는 계획된 일과 계획되지 않은 일에 모두 사용할 수 있다.

(2) 미래를 나타내는 부사구: tomorrow, next week, later 등

- I'**m coming** to pick you up.
- **Is** she **going** to Seoul tomorrow?

Check up!

Answer Keys p. 12

A 다음 괄호 안에서 알맞은 말을 고르시오.

1 If it (will / (is)) sunny, we will go to the beach.

2 When you (will play / play) the violin, all of your friends will be surprised.

3 I will send a message to him when he (arrives / will arrive) home.

4 She will cry if you (will leave / leave) without a message.

5 She (does / is doing) homework tomorrow.

6 We (are visiting / visit) our grandmother on our next vacation.

7 Sam and Sunny (are going to / is going to) Gyeongju next week.

8 They (will / are) going to ride bicycles at the park.

9 She is going to (reads / read) a new novel.

10 The vending machine (will / is) be fixed tomorrow.

Practice More Ⅲ

Answer Keys p. 12

A 짝지어진 두 문장의 의미가 같도록 빈칸을 채우시오.

1 I will go to a job interview next week.
= I ___am going to go___ to a job interview next week.

2 He will visit his parents this weekend.
= He ________________ his parents this weekend.

3 It will snow tomorrow. I am going to make a snowman.
= It ________________ tomorrow. I ______________ a snowman.

4 We will pass the entrance exam.
= We ________________ pass the entrance exam.

5 They will tell you a secret.
= They ________________ you a secret.

6 He will have a date with Kate.
= He ________________ with Kate.

7 She is going to join the club.
= She ________________ join the club.

8 My grandparents will be back tomorrow.
= My grandparents ________________ tomorrow.

9 John will be a great actor some day.
= John ________________ a great actor some day.

10 Emma and I will play tennis next month.
= Emma and I ________________ tennis next month.

B 다음 괄호 안에서 알맞은 것을 고르시오.

1 I'm going to (help / helps) my mother with cooking.

2 She will (is / be) a dancer in the future.

3 Tim will (carry / carries) the bag for you.

4 We are going to (go / going) to Jejudo Island next month.

5 The train (arrive / will arrive) at eight.

Answer Keys p. 12

C 다음 문장에서 어색한 부분을 찾아 고쳐 쓰시오.

1 What is he do this weekend? ___is___ ➡ ___will___

2 Jin and Alex will drinks orange juice. ________ ➡ ________

3 The woman will makes my new coat. ________ ➡ ________

4 He is go fishing with his brother. ________ ➡ ________

5 I am going to doing my homework tomorrow.
________ ➡ ________

6 Harry will starts to teach English. ________ ➡ ________

7 They will stayed there for five days. ________ ➡ ________

8 I'm going to painting my room tonight. ________ ➡ ________

9 Jerry will going to the store to buy cookies. ________ ➡ ________

10 He will starts to work in Korea next week. ________ ➡ ________

D 다음 주어진 동사를 빈칸에 알맞게 바꾸어 쓰시오.

1 When she ___leaves___ here, I will really miss her. (leave)

2 We are ________ there soon. (come)

3 If you ________ her, she will be happy. (love)

4 The party will be delayed until Jack ________. (arrive)

5 It will be difficult to solve unless you ________ me tonight. (help)

6 She will be angry when I ________ the truth. (tell)

서술형 연습

E 다음 문장을 괄호 안에 주어진 표현에 맞게 고쳐 쓰시오.

1 Sam leads the soccer team this year. (will)
➡ Sam will lead the soccer team this year.

2 Minsu and Jihye quit the band. (be going to)
➡ ________________________________

3 The news makes him happy. (will not)
➡ ________________________________

4 The bad rumor spreads all over the world. (be not going to)
➡ ________________________________

Practice More Ⅲ

Answer Keys p. 12

서술형 연습 **F** **우리말 해석에 맞게 문장을 완성하시오.**

1 날씨가 좋으면 소풍을 갈 것이다. (will / be)
➡ I ___*will go*___ on a picnic if it ___*is*___ fine.

2 그 비행기는 9시에 서울을 떠날 예정이다. (be going to / leave)
➡ The plane ________________ Seoul at nine.

3 내일 밤에 무엇을 볼 예정이니? (will / watch)
➡ What ________ you ________ tomorrow night?

4 나는 오늘 밤에 책을 읽을 거야. (be going to / read)
➡ I ________________ a book tonight.

5 Susan이 5분 안에 오면 우리는 기차를 놓치지 않을 거야. (arrive / miss)
➡ If Susan ________ in five minutes, we ________ the train.

6 내일 비가 오면 계획을 취소할 것이다. (will cancel / rain)
➡ We ________ our plans if it ________ tomorrow.

7 영화는 3시 30분에 시작될 예정이다. (be going to / start)
➡ The movie ________________ at 3:30.

8 그들은 Sam을 찾으면 그에게 전화할 거야. (will call / find)
➡ They ________ him when they ________ Sam.

9 엄마는 내 숙제를 도와 주실 거야. (help)
➡ Mom ________________ me do my homework.

10 내일 Julian을 몇 시에 만날 예정이니? (be going to / meet)
➡ What time ________________ Julian tomorrow?

중간 기말고사 예상문제

Answer Keys p. 13

내신 최다 출제 유형

01 다음 중 어법상 올바르지 않은 것을 고르시오.

[출제 예상 90%]

① My dad makes dinner for me.
② Jenny is playing tennis.
③ Does your history teacher nice?
④ They are playing a computer game.
⑤ His old brother is kind.

02 다음 문장 중 그 쓰임이 어색한 것을 고르시오.

[출제 예상 85%]

① It's a long walk to school.
② Does Minsu play the flute well?
③ Do Jacky live in London, England?
④ When do Jenny and her friends get up?
⑤ What is your favorite color?

03 다음 중 어법상 틀린 곳이 있는 문장을 모두 고르시오.

[출제 예상 85%]

① Everything in the classroom are so clean and nice.
② I'm going to show you a picture of my sister and brother.
③ Do they get ready for their first day of school?
④ Are your teacher in the classroom now?
⑤ She's going to go shopping tomorrow.

04 다음의 일기를 읽고 ⓐ~ⓔ의 빈칸에 들어갈 동사의 형태가 맞는 것을 고르시오.

[출제 예상 90%]

> Saturday, July 5th, Rainy
> I got up late so I didn't ___ⓐ___ breakfast. I ___ⓑ___ to the school and ___ⓒ___ twelve subjects. After lunch, I played soccer and ___ⓓ___ in the swimming pool.
> When I came back home, I ___ⓔ___ a book.

① ⓐ had ② ⓑ go ③ ⓒ studyed
④ ⓓ swam ⑤ ⓔ readed

05 다음 중 올바로 쓰인 동사를 모두 고르시오.

[출제 예상 90%]

> Gijun is a middle school student. Yesterday he ① playing baseball with his friends.
> And he ② enjoys it so much. After that, he ③ met his uncle and went shopping. Yesterday was his dad's birthday. He ④ buys a tie for his dad. He ⑤ felt happy.

06 다음 밑줄 친 곳에 알맞은 단어를 고르시오.

[출제 예상 85%]

> This is my sister, Sara.
> She is ________ her room.

① makes ② cleaning ③ played
④ do ⑤ finish

중간 기말고사 예상문제

[01~03] 다음 중 동사의 기본형과 3인칭 단수 현재형이 잘못 짝지어진 것을 고르시오.

01 ① talk – talks ② go – goes ③ build – builds ④ watch – watchs ⑤ bake – bakes

02 ① come – comes ② play – playes ③ cry – cries ④ wash – washes ⑤ have – has

03 ① sit – sits ② raise – raises ③ marry – marries ④ wash – washs ⑤ work – works

[04~06] 다음 중 동사와 과거형의 연결이 어색한 것을 고르시오.

04 ① discuss – discussed ② stay – stayed ③ write – wrote ④ lay – lain ⑤ meet – met

05 ① take – took ② burn – burnt ③ feed – feeded ④ lose – lost ⑤ draw – drew

06 ① lead – led ② drink – drank ③ build – built ④ bear – bore ⑤ ride – ridded

[07~08] 다음 빈칸에 공통으로 들어갈 알맞은 것을 고르시오.

07

- I played the piano __________.
- We went to the museum __________.

① tomorrow ② someday ③ last week ④ later ⑤ next month

08

- She __________ travel to Korea next week.
- I __________ visit my grandmother after I finish homework.

① will ② is ③ are ④ am ⑤ were

★★★

09 다음 대화의 괄호 ⓐ ~ ⓒ에 알맞은 말이 순서대로 짝지어진 것은?

A Did you ⓐ (hear / heard) the news? Sarah and Tim won the race last week. They ⓑ (got / get) the first prize in the race. It was awesome!

B Really? I didn't ⓒ (expect / expected) that! Let's have a party for them!

① heard – got – expected
② heard – got – expect
③ hear – got – expected
④ hear – got – expect
⑤ hear – get – expected

10 다음 중 밑줄 친 '동사원형＋-ing'형이 바르지 못한 것을 고르시오.

① Willy is listening to music on his phone.
② A bulldog is lying on the sofa.
③ He was wining the marathon.
④ My mother is reading a book for us.
⑤ I'm making a flower vase.

[11~12] 다음 문장의 빈칸에 들어갈 말로 알맞은 것을 고르시오.

11

• She ________ to Incheon last week.

① goes ② will go ③ went
④ is going to ⑤ was go

12

• I ________ at 11 p.m. every day.

① go to slept ② go to is sleeping
③ go to was sleeping ④ go to sleep
⑤ go to is sleep

[13~15] 다음 대화의 빈칸에 들어갈 알맞은 말을 고르시오.

13

A Did Eric help you work?
B ________________________.

① Yes, he does. ② Yes, he didn't.
③ No, he did. ④ No, he doesn't.
⑤ Yes, he did.

14

A What are you going to do?
B ________________________.

① Yes, I go.
② I like to go.
③ I'm going to go on a picnic with father.
④ No, I went to school.
⑤ She is going to meet her boyfriend.

15

A Are you fifteen now?
B Yes, I am. I ________ fourteen last year.

① did ② were ③ is
④ am ⑤ was

★★★
16 다음 문장 중 do의 성격이 다른 하나를 고르시오.

① Do you have some money?
② Do they go to school every day?
③ I do not know the answer.
④ We always do our homework.
⑤ They don't play sports.

[17~18] 다음 빈칸에 공통으로 쓸 수 있는 것을 고르시오.

17

• Jack didn't ________ dinner.
• Do you ________ the time?

① has ② eat ③ have
④ know ⑤ play

18

• Lucy __________ the guitar at the concert.
• Jack __________ tennis with Harry.

① had ② played ③ do
④ are played ⑤ have

[19~20] 다음 중 어법상 잘못된 문장을 모두 고르시오.

★★★
19 ① He pushes the kids onto the ground.
② Taylor skips breakfast all the time.
③ The soccer players uses only hands.
④ Do you going to church on Sundays?
⑤ We listen to music at the break time.

★★★
20 ① Do you and your brother fight sometimes?
② Jack and Amy is a students.
③ They live in an apartment.
④ I don't do my homework sometimes.
⑤ Helen is comes back tomorrow.

[21~23] 다음 문장을 괄호 안의 지시대로 바르게 고친 것을 고르시오.

21

Amy likes to climb mountains.
(과거형 부정문)

① Amy liked not to climb mountains.
② Amy doesn't like to climb mountains.
③ Amy didn't like to climb mountains.
④ Amy wasn't like to climb mountains.
⑤ Amy didn't likes to climb mountains.

22

Jerry likes to dance on the street.
(과거형 의문문)

① Liked Jerry to dance on the street?
② Does Jerry like to dance on the street?
③ Do Jerry likes to dance on the street?
④ Was Jerry like to dance on the street?
⑤ Did Jerry like to dance on the street?

23

I watched a movie with my cousin, John. (현재진행형)

① I watching movie with my cousin, John.
② I watch movie with my cousin, John.
③ I is watch movie with my cousin, John.
④ I am watch movie with my cousin, John.
⑤ I am watching a movie with my cousin, John.

[24~25] 다음 대화의 빈칸 (A)와 (B)에 들어갈 말이 바르게 짝지어진 것을 고르시오.

24

A Will you ___(A)___ with me in the library?
B Yes, I ___(B)___.

	(A)	(B)
①	study	would
②	studied	will
③	studies	won't
④	studying	will not
⑤	study	will

25

A Were you and Jack ___(A)___ tennis at that time?
B No, we ___(B)___.

	(A)	(B)
①	playing	weren't
②	played	were
③	play	are
④	plays	were not
⑤	playing	were

[26~27] 다음 밑줄 친 부분의 쓰임이 나머지와 다른 것을 고르시오.

★★★
26 ① I am going to see my grandparents next week.
② They are going to go fishing tomorrow.
③ We are going to go to a department store next Saturday.
④ Suran is going to the bookstore.
⑤ You are going to go to the zoo.

★★★
27 ① Jack cleans up his house this Sunday.
② Mary takes a trip to take pictures next week.
③ I go to school from Monday to Friday.
④ They sell some handmade cards tomorrow.
⑤ We move to a small town next month.

[28~29] 다음 빈칸에 들어갈 수 있는 말을 모두 고르시오.

28

They bought a lot of meat for the barbecue party ________.

① next week
② yesterday
③ the day after tomorrow
④ last week
⑤ three hours later

29

Sam is taking a trip to Kenya ________.

① last month
② next month
③ last week
④ tomorrow
⑤ yesterday

[30~31] 다음 대화의 빈칸에 들어갈 수 있는 의문문을 고르시오.

30

A ____________________?
B Yes, we were.

① Were they baking cookies?
② Was your baby sister crying a lot?
③ Were you and Jack making sandwiches?
④ Were Jane and I going to the hospital?
⑤ Were she and he having dinner?

31

A ______________________?
B No, they didn't.

① Did you go back to school?
② Did Tom and you study together?
③ Did he get the first prize?
④ Did Sophia and Harry sing a song together?
⑤ Did I swim in the swimming pool?

[32~33] 다음 문장의 형식이 나머지와 다른 것을 고르시오.

32
① The old man is walking along the river.
② I am throwing a large ball.
③ She is going to have lunch.
④ They are doing their homework together.
⑤ We are watering the garden right now.

33
① Mr. Lee was teaching at that time.
② My friends and I were dancing.
③ Paul was playing the drums in the band.
④ Lucy sang a famous song at the concert.
⑤ They were watching movies.

[34~35] 다음 주어진 우리말을 바르게 영작한 것을 고르시오.

34

그는 어제 라디오를 고치지 않았다.

① He didn't fixed the radio yesterday.
② He didn't fix the radio yesterday.
③ He wasn't fix the radio yesterday.
④ He didn't fixing the radio yesterday.
⑤ He doesn't fix the radio yesterday.

★★★
35

내가 집에 왔을 때 그들은 과학 공부를 하고 있던 중이었다.

① They were studying science when I came home.
② They weren't studying science when I came home.
③ They were studying science when I was coming home.
④ They studied science when I was coming home.
⑤ They were studying science when I come home.

36 다음 밑줄 친 것 중 어법상 틀린 것을 모두 고르시오.

Phillip ① was meeting Gina yesterday. They ② ate some sandwiches and ③ drink some coke. They ④ went to the theater and watched the movie 'Star Wars.' ⑤ Phillip bought a rose to Gina and Gina was very happy.

[37~38] 다음 주어진 문장과 같은 뜻이 될 수 있는 문장을 고르시오.

37

Jane will have a pajama party tonight.

① Jane is going to a pajama party tonight.
② Jane will having a pajama party tonight.
③ Jane is going to have a pajama party tonight.
④ Jane having a pajama party tonight.
⑤ Jane is going have a pajama party tonight.

38

Harry is going to go to the dentist next Monday.

① Harry is going the dentist next Monday.
② Harry will is going to the dentist next Monday.
③ Harry is going to the dentist next Monday.
④ Harry will going to go to the dentist next Monday.
⑤ Harry will to the dentist next Monday.

39 다음 중 어법상 올바른 것을 고르시오.

① Jack washed the dishes for his mom tomorrow.
② Jinsu watched a magic show on TV.
③ Jake liked to playing baseball.
④ We are going shopping mall yesterday.
⑤ Does you and Jane buy some apples?

40 다음 중 어법상 바르지 않은 것을 고르시오.

① Mirae and Changsu are best friends.
② They're going to the same university next year.
③ Seoul National University is the best in Korea.
④ We were bringing some cookies at tomorrow's party.
⑤ Jane's grandmother cooks very well.

◇◇◇◇◇◇◇◇◇◇ 서술형 평가 ◇◇◇◇◇◇◇◇◇◇

[41~42] 다음 두 문장의 같은 뜻이 되도록 빈칸에 알맞은 말을 쓰시오.

41

• Tom and I will go to the concert next week.
= Tom and I ________ ________ ________ go to the concert next week.

42

• Wendy is not going to school tomorrow. It's Sunday.
= Wendy ________ ________ go to school tomorrow. It's Sunday.

43 주어진 두 문장의 의미가 같도록 만들 때 빈칸에 들어갈 알맞은 단어를 쓰시오.

• They ① ______________ climb the mountain next Sunday.
= They ② ______________ the mountain next Sunday.

➡ ① ______________
② ______________

Answer Keys p. 13~14

[44~46] 다음 글을 읽고 물음에 답하시오.

> Gina has a special pet at home.
> When (A) <u>she walked along the river</u>, she see it.
> It was a little bird.
> The bird hurt its wings.
> Gina takes it home and looked after it.
> Gina named the bird Titi. Now Titi can fly and it wakes Gina up every morning.

44 글의 흐름상 문법적으로 <u>어색한</u> 단어 <u>2개</u>를 골라 올바르게 고쳐 쓰시오.

➡ ①____________, ②____________

45 윗글의 (A) she walked along the river를 과거진행형으로 바꿔 쓰시오.

➡ ________________________

46 윗글의 내용과 일치하도록 질문에 답하시오.

(1) Does Gina have a pet cat?

➡ ________________________

(2) What is Gina's pet?

➡ ________________________

[47~49] 다음 주어진 문장을 괄호 안의 지시대로 바꿔 쓰시오.

47 Dan goes on a picnic next Tuesday.
(현재진행형)

➡ ________________________

48 She doesn't bring any money at all.
(과거형의 부정)

➡ ________________________

49 We studied English for the final exam.
(과거진행형)

➡ ________________________

[50~52] 우리말에 맞게 주어진 단어를 이용하여 영작하시오.

50

> 그녀는 내일 싱가폴로 떠날 것이다.
> (Singapore / leave / will)

➡ ________________________

51

> 나와 Tom은 매일 학교에 걸어서 간다.
> (on foot / go to school)

➡ ________________________

03

Chapter
조동사

Point Check I

◆ **조동사:** 다른 동사를 도와주는 역할을 하는 보조 동사이며, 홀로 쓰일 수 없다.

◆ 조동사의 뒤에는 반드시 동사원형이 오며, 부정문은 조동사 뒤에 'not'을 붙여 만든다.

1. 조동사의 종류

미래	will	Anita will play the violin at the concert.
	be going to	We're going to be on time.
가능/허가	can	They can recycle their cans.
	be able to	She is able to speak Chinese.
	could	Could you lend me a pen?
추측/허가	may	You may go through the gate.
의무	have to	We have to listen carefully in class.
	must	You must adopt the class rules.
조언	should	She should put on a warm coat.
	had better	I had better go now.
소망	would like (to)	He would like to move to Seoul.

2. 미래형 will / be going to

	will	be going to
긍정문	[will + 동사원형] Anna will play the cello at the concert.	[be(am, are, is) going to + 동사원형] I am going to watch the movie tonight.
부정문	[will not + 동사원형] Jerry will not(won't) go there.	[be(am, are, is) not going to + 동사원형] You are not(aren't) going to take a test.
의문문	[will + 주어 + 동사원형~?] A: Will they meet tomorrow? B: Yes, they will. / No, they won't(will not).	[Be(Am, Are, Is) + 주어 + going to + 동사원형~?] A: Is she going to go on a picnic? B: Yes, she is. / No, she isn't(is not).

Lesson 3-1

조동사의 종류와 역할

- 조동사는 be동사나 일반동사와 함께 쓰여 능력, 허가, 요청, 추측, 제안, 의무, 충고의 의미를 더해준다.
- 조동사는 주어의 인칭에 상관없이 항상 형태가 같으며 반드시 뒤에는 동사원형이 와야 한다.

1. 조동사의 종류

조동사	will [= be going to]	can [= be able to]	may	must [= have to]	should [= had better]
의미	미래 ~할 것이다	가능 · 능력 ~할 수 있다 허가 ~해도 된다	추측 ~일지도 모른다 허가 ~해도 된다	추측 ~인 것이 틀림없다 의무 반드시 ~해야 한다	의무 · 당연 ~해야 한다 조언 ~하는 것이 낫겠다
부정형	will not (won't) be not going to	cannot (can't) be not able to	may not	must not (mustn't) do(es) not have to	should not (shouldn't) had better not

2. 조동사의 규칙

(1) 주어의 인칭에 따른 형태의 변화가 없다.

- Jerry **will** go to church. **(O)**
- Jerry wills go to church. **(X)**

(2) 조동사 뒤에는 동사원형이 온다.

- Jenny will **listen** to the music. **(O)**
- Jenny will listens to the music. **(X)**

(3) 조동사 부정문: [조동사 + not + 동사원형]

- Jerry **will not (= won't) stay** with us. (O)
- Jerry will doesn't stay with us. **(X)**

(4) 조동사 의문문: [조동사 + 주어 + 동사원형~?]

- Will Jenny collect comic books? **(O)**
- Will collect Jenny comic books? **(X)**

(5) 조동사끼리는 함께 쓰이지 않는다.

- Amy will be going to play badminton with us. **(X)**
- Amy will play badminton with us. **(O)**
  (= Amy is going to play badminton with us.)

Check up!

Answer Keys p. 15

A 다음 괄호 안에 주어진 단어 중 알맞은 것을 고르시오.

1 I can (swim / to swim) in that lake.

2 Mary will (go / goes) to the zoo this weekend.

3 You don't have to (eat / eating) spicy food.

4 Chris thinks that he can (does / do) anything.

5 You should (stop / stopping) taking the medicine.

6 Kim may (comes / come) to class.

7 You have to (pays / pay) attention to his opinion.

8 I'm not able to (accept / accepting) your proposal.

9 We must (get / got) ready for the hot summer.

10 He should (suggesting / suggest) a great idea tomorrow.

B 다음 중 밑줄 친 부분을 어법상 바르게 고치시오.

1 It may <u>snows</u> tomorrow. ___snow___

2 You <u>will can</u> go now. ________

3 He can <u>makes</u> a delicious cake. ________

4 Will <u>study Alex</u> English tonight? ________

5 She <u>not may</u> like this song. ________

6 Kate will <u>didn't</u> bring her hat. ________

7 We should <u>going</u> to the doctor. ________

8 They <u>going to</u> go to the jungle gym. ________

9 Can I <u>drawing</u> a picture now? ________

10 Rachel <u>has</u> better practice more. ________

Lesson 3-2

미래형 will

• 조동사 will : 미래를 예측하는 단순 미래와 의지를 표현하는 미래로 구분할 수 있다.

1. 단순 미래

(누군가 / 무언가) ~일 것이다 : 단순히 미래에 일어날 일을 이야기하거나 예측

• It **will** be sunny tomorrow afternoon.

• She **will** leave here in a few hours.

2. 의지의 미래

(1) ~할 것이다 : 말하는 사람의 의지

I **will** practice the piano.

(2) ~할 것인가? : 말 듣는 사람의 의지

Will you study hard from now on?

Check up!

Answer Keys p. 15

A 조동사 will을 사용하여 미래시제 문장으로 바꾸어 쓰시오.

1 She goes to a concert to see Big Bang.

➡ She ___*will go*___ to a concert to see Big Bang.

2 My mom makes a beautiful dress.

➡ My mom ________ a beautiful dress.

3 I send a postcard to a pen pal.

➡ I ________ a postcard to a pen pal.

4 She does her homework with her father.

➡ She ________ her homework with her father.

5 Jane has dinner with her parents.

➡ Jane ________ dinner with her parents.

6 Anna finishes her project by tomorrow.

➡ Anna ________ her project by tomorrow.

7 David has a date with Jessy.

➡ David ________ a date with Jessy.

8 Paul participates in music contests.

➡ Paul ____________ in music contests.

Lesson 3-3

will의 부정문과 의문문

1. **will의 부정문:** [주어 + will not + 동사원형] ~하지 않을 것이다

- I **will not (won't)** go there again.
- This machine **will not (won't)** work tomorrow.
  ➡ 'will not'은 'won't'로 줄여 쓸 수 있다.

2. **will의 의문문:** [Will + 주어 + 동사원형 ~?] ~할 것인가?
   대답: 긍정 [Yes, 주어 will.]
   부정 [No, 주어 + will not (won't).]

- **A** **Will** Jerry **watch** the movie this Saturday?
  B **Yes, he will. / No, he will not (won't).**

Check up!

Answer Keys p. 15

A 다음 문장을 괄호 안의 지시대로 바꿔 쓰시오.

1 Mr. Han will go to school. (부정문)
➡ *Mr. Han will not (won't) go to school.*

2 She will bring some delicious cookies for Jane. (의문문)
➡ ______________________

3 My teacher will be upset because of Tom. (부정문)
➡ ______________________

4 This robot will clean the floors. (의문문)
➡ ______________________

5 Helen will buy a cup of coffee. (부정문)
➡ ______________________

6 Will Jenny take a test next week? (긍정문)
➡ ______________________

7 Steven will practice soccer harder. (의문문)
➡ ______________________

8 Will they go to Africa to help sick people? (긍정문)
➡ ______________________

Lesson

3-4 미래형 be going to

• 조동사 be going to : 미래를 나타내는 표현으로, 가까운 미래에 계획된 일이나 예정된 일을 말하려고 할 때 사용한다.

1. be going to의 긍정문: [주어 + be going to + 동사원형] ~할 것이다

• You **are going to** visit your grandparents.

2. be going to의 부정문: [주어 + be not going to + 동사원형] ~하지 않을 것이다

• I **am not going to** go fishing.

3. be going to의 의문문: [Be + 주어 + going to + 동사원형 ~?] ~할 것인가?
대답 : 긍정 [Yes, 주어 + be(am, are, is)] 응, 그럴 것이다.
부정 [No, 주어 + be(am, are, is) not] 아니, 그러지 않을 것이다.

• **A** **Is** she **going to** go to the shopping mall?
B **Yes, she is. / No, she is not (isn't).**

Grammar Plus +

• **미래형 be going to vs. 현재진행형 be going to**
• 미래형: 'be going to' 뒤에 동사원형이 온다. ➡ She **is going to** go to school.
• 현재진행형: 'be going to' 뒤에 명사가 온다. ➡ She **is going to** school.

Check up!

Answer Keys p. 15

A 다음 괄호 안에서 알맞은 것을 고르시오.

1 I (will not / not am going to) tell anyone his secret.

2 I (will / going to) make some chocolate.

3 Emma (will / be going to) be a great singer some day.

4 Jack and I (am going to / are going to) go to a movie this weekend.

5 She (will be not / is not going to) take a math test today. It was canceled.

Answer Keys p. 15

B 다음 문장을 주어진 단어를 이용하여 미래 시제(be going to)로 바꾸어 쓰시오.

1 I draw some flowers. (be going to, next week)
➡ I ___am going to draw___ some flowers ________.

2 She writes a letter to Mr. Lee. (be not going to, tomorrow)
➡ She ________________ a letter to Mr. Lee ________.

3 They take some pictures for their parents. (be going to, today)
➡ They ________________ some pictures for their parents ________.

4 Mark brings his cat to the hosital. (be not going to, tonight)
➡ Mark ________________ his cat to the hosital________.

5 Jena and Elly join a club. (be going to, next semester)
➡ Jena and Elly ________________ a club ________.

C 다음 대화의 빈칸에 알맞은 말을 써 넣으시오.

1 A Is she going to buy a present for him?
B No, ___she isn't (is not)___.

2 A ________ Thomas and Max __________ go fishing tonight?
B Yes, they ________.

3 A Where are they going to go tomorrow?
B They __________ go camping tomorrow.

4 A Are you __________ have dinner with him?
B No, I ________________.

5 A What is he going to do this summer vacation?
B He __________ take a trip.

Practice More I

Answer Keys p. 15~16

A 다음 괄호 안에서 알맞은 것을 고르시오.

1 Tim should (watches / watch) his step.

2 He will (goes / go) to school tomorrow.

3 Minji can (swim / swimming) in the sea.

4 I could (wash / washing) my dirty car in there.

5 Mr. Seo will (have / has) a cup of tea.

6 This large dog might (bark / barked).

7 Our teacher may (coming / come) to English class.

8 Tiffany often (write / writes) letters to her mom.

9 I will (studies / study) English for the next exam.

10 I could (remember / remembered) everything about you.

B 다음 주어진 문장들을 미래시제 문장으로 바꿔 쓰시오.

〈will 긍정문〉

1 I make pizza for my family.

➡ *I will make pizza for my family.*

2 Sam goes hiking with his brother.

➡ ____________________

3 He finishes his project.

➡ ____________________

4 Jinju travels all around the world this year.

➡ ____________________

5 My grandmother goes there.

➡ ____________________

〈be going to 긍정문〉

6 Daniel and you visit Japan on a tour.

➡ ____________________

7 The library is closed during the summer vacation.

➡ ____________________

8 I go to John's birthday party.

➡ ____________________

9 Mom buys a new coffee machine.

➡ ____________________

10 Phillip sings a song from *The Phantom of the Opera*.

➡ ____________________

C 다음 주어진 문장을 괄호 안의 지시어대로 알맞게 바꿔 쓰시오.

1 Mary will tell her brother an interesting story. (의문문)

➡ *Will Mary tell her brother an interesting story?*

2 I am going to practice tennis every weekend. (부정문)

➡ ____________________

3 He will watch the baseball game tonight. (부정문)

➡ ____________________

4 They are going to leave Busan tomorrow. (의문문)

➡ ____________________

5 She will stay here for a few days. (부정문)

➡ ____________________

D 다음 주어진 문장에서 어법상 어색한 부분을 찾아 바르게 고치시오.

1 She not is going to go to school next week.

not is going to ➡ *is not going to*

2 Mom will wants to do something special.

__________ ➡ __________

3 Harry will moving to another place.

__________ ➡ __________

4 Sam wills play baseball after school.

__________ ➡ __________

5 It is going to be rain.

__________ ➡ __________

6 Will Jack goes to the museum tomorrow?

__________ ➡ __________

7 I will to give you something to drink.

__________ ➡ __________

Answer Keys p. 15~16

8 She isn't going writing a letter to him.

_______________ ➡ _______________

9 Does she going to take the bus?

_______________ ➡ _______________

10 The hip-hop festival will is held here.

_______________ ➡ _______________

Note

• be held
열리다, 개최되다

서술형 연습 **E** 우리말에 맞게 주어진 단어를 바르게 배열하여 영작하시오.

1 나는 내일 초콜릿 케이크를 만들 거야.
(I / tomorrow / a chocolate cake / make / will)
= *I will make a chocolate cake tomorrow.*

2 그들은 이번 주 일요일에 축구를 할 거야.
(will / this Sunday / they / play / soccer)
= _______________________________

3 Linda는 우리를 위해 점심을 준비하지 않을 거야.
(Linda / for / lunch / isn't going to / us / make)
= _______________________________

4 너희들은 오늘 밤에 거기 있을 거니?
(will / tonight / you / there / be)
= _______________________________

5 Sam은 미래에 훌륭한 과학자가 될 것이다.
(in the future / will / a great scientist / become / Sam)
= _______________________________

F 다음 주어진 영어 문장을 우리말로 해석하시오.

1 Denny will join our reading club next semester.
➡ *Denny는 다음 학기에 우리 독서 동아리에 가입할 것이다.*

2 I have an audition for the role of Harry Potter next week.
➡ _______________________________

3 Mr. Moon is not going to come today.
➡ _______________________________

4 Will your family move to Seoul next month?
➡ _______________________________

Note

• reading club
독서 동아리
• have an audition
오디션을 보다
• role of ~의 역할
• move to ~로 이사 가다

Point Check Ⅱ

◆ **can / could :** '~할 수 있다'의 뜻으로 '가능, 능력'을 나타낼 때 사용하기도 하고, '~해도 된다'의 뜻으로 '허가'를 나타낼 때도 사용한다.

◆ **be able to :** '~할 수 있다'의 뜻을 가지며, '가능, 능력'에 관하여 미래를 표현할 때 주로 사용된다.

◆ **may :** '허가' 또는 '추측'의 의미를 가지고 있다.

1. can

(1) **가능 / 능력**

- We **can** understand this rule. [가능]
- He **cannot** play soccer well. [능력]

(2) **허가**

- You **can** drink some water.

(3) **요청**

- **Can** I wash my hands first?

2. be able to

(1) **현재형** : [be(am, are, is) + 동사원형]

Jerry **is able to** jump high.

(2) **과거형** : [be(was/were) able to + 동사원형]

We **were not able to** talk when we were one year old.

(3) **미래형** : [will be able to + 동사원형]

They **will be able to** travel next week.

3. could

(1) **can의 과거형**

She **could not (couldn't)** sing very well. [능력]

(2) **요청 및 허가**

- **Could (Can)** you lend me some money? [요청]
- **Could (Can)** he take a rest? [허가]

4. may

- It **may** be a real snake. [추측]
- **May** I get some rest? [허가]

Lesson 3-5

can

• can: '~할 수 있다', '~해도 된다'라는 뜻을 가지는 조동사로서 주어의 인칭에 따라 형태는 변하지 않으며, 뒤에 항상 동사원형이 온다.

1. '가능/능력'의 can: ~할 수 있다

• We **can** understand this situation. [가능]

• He **can** play basketball well. [능력]

2. '허가'의 can: ~해도 된다

• You **can** leave now.

• She **can** stay here.

Grammar Plus +

'can'이 가능/능력의 의미로 '~할 수 있다'의 뜻을 가지면 'be able to'와 바꿔 쓸 수 있다.
Jenny can dance very well.
= Jenny is able to dance very well.

Check up!

Answer Keys p. 16

A 다음 문장에서 어색한 부분을 찾아 바르게 고치시오.

1 I can making melon juice. ___making___ ➡ ___make___

2 She cans speak Japanese well. ________ ➡ ________

3 Mr. Park can to play the violin. ________ ➡ ________

4 We can discussed how to enjoy reading.
________ ➡ ________

5 She says that Thomas can plays soccer now.
________ ➡ ________

B 다음 문장을 우리말로 고쳐 쓰시오.

1 Can you help me?
➡ ___나를 도와 주시겠습니까?___

2 Jack can make friends easily.
➡ ________________

3 They can hand in their test paper now.
➡ ________________

4 Can we go there on foot?
➡ ________________

5 Can I watch TV tonight?
➡ ________________

Note
• **hand in** 제출하다

Lesson

3-6 can의 부정문

• cannot은 '~할 수 없다'는 뜻을 가지며, not을 붙일 때는 띄어 쓰지 않고 붙여 쓴다. cannot 뒤에는 동사원형이 오며, can't로 줄여 쓸 수 있다.

1. '불가능'의 cannot: ~할 수 없다

• They **cannot (can't)** sing well.
• Toddlers **cannot (can't)** go to school.

2. '금지'의 cannot: ~하면 안된다

• We **cannot (can't)** go to that dangerous place.
➡ 'cannot'을 'can not'으로 띄어 쓰지 않는다.

Check up!

Answer Keys p. 16

A 다음 문장의 괄호 안에서 알맞은 것을 고르시오.

1 I (can't / can) solve the problem because it is so difficult.

2 You (can / cann't) watch TV after you finish your homework.

3 I'm full. I (can / can't) eat anymore.

4 You look hot. You (can / can't) open the window.

5 It is too cold today. We (can / can't) go hiking.

6 I have a math test tomorrow. So, I (can / can't) play a game tonight.

B 다음 주어진 문장을 부정문으로 고쳐 쓰시오.

1 Monkeys can swing the branches.
➡ *Monkeys cannot (can't) swing the branches.*

2 They can go up the mountain.
➡ ______________________

3 Children can run here and there all day.
➡ ______________________

4 An ant can hold up heavy things.
➡ ______________________

Note
• **here and there** 여기저기로
• **go up** ~에 오르다
• **branch** 나뭇가지
• **all day** 하루종일
• **hold up** ~을 들다, 붙잡다

Lesson

3-7 can의 의문문

- '~할 수 있는가?'라는 뜻의 의문문을 만들 때 [Can + 주어 + 동사원형 ~?]의 형태를 가진다. 대답이 긍정일 경우 [Yes, 주어 can.], 부정일 경우 [No, 주어 can't.]로 말한다.

◈ 의문문의 can

(1) **가능:** ~할 수 있니?

A **Can** you **drive** a car?

B **Yes, I can. / No, I can't.**

(2) **요청:** ~해 줄 수 있니?

Can I borrow your English notebook?

(3) **허가:** ~해도 될까?

A **Can** I open the window?

B **Yes, you can. / No, you can't.**

Check up!

Answer Keys p. 16

A 다음 괄호 안에서 알맞은 것을 고르시오.

1 My sister can (speak / speaks) Chinese well.

2 I don't know what Hansu (can / cans) do well.

3 Can I use your eraser? – Yes, you (can / cannot).

4 They (can't / can not) find the answers.

5 (Can / Are) you play football? – No, I (can / can't).

B 다음 대화의 빈칸을 알맞게 완성하시오.

1 **A** ___Can___ I ___park___ here?

B No, ___you can't___. Parking is banned here.

2 **A** ________ I ________ your black coat?

B Yes, ________.

3 **A** ________ you ________ to a concert today?

B Sorry, ________. I'm busy today.

4 **A** ________ he ________ the violin?

B Yes, ________. He ________ also play the piano.

5 **A** ________ you ________ off the radio, please?

B Yes, ________.

Note

- **be banned** 금지되다

Lesson 3-8

be able to

• be able to: 능력을 나타내는 can과 같은 표현으로 '~할 수 있다'의 뜻을 가진다.

1. **긍정문**: [주어+be(am, are, is) able to+동사원형] ~할 수 있다
   - Barbara **is able to** dance well.

2. **부정문**: [주어+be(am, are, is) not able to+동사원형] ~할 수 없다
   - Jerry and Anna **are not (aren't) able to** work together.

3. **의문문**: [Be(Am, Are, Is)+주어+able to+동사원형~?] ~할 수 있니?
   - **A** **Are** you **able to** go to the concert tonight?
     B **Yes, I am. / No, I'm not.**

➡ 주어의 인칭에 따라 'be' 대신에 'am, are, is'를 사용한다.
➡ 대답할 때는 be동사에 맞춰서 답한다.

Check up!

Answer Keys p. 16

A 주어진 문장과 같은 뜻이 되도록 빈칸을 완성하시오.

1 I can't drive a car.
➡ I ___am not able to___ drive a car.

2 Mark can speak English.
➡ Mark ____________ speak English.

3 You can stay here.
➡ You ____________ stay here.

4 Lilly can't fly a kite.
➡ Lilly ____________ fly a kite.

5 We can't find the answer.
➡ We ____________ find the answer.

6 Mom can cook all kinds of food.
➡ Mom ____________ cook all kinds of food.

7 Can you dance with her?
➡ ________ you ________ dance with her?

8 Lucas can't remember her.
➡ Lucas ____________ remember her.

9 Can rabbits run fast?
➡ __________ rabbits __________ run fast?

10 You can't say anything now.
➡ You ____________________ say anything now.

B 다음 중 어법상 어색한 부분을 찾아 바르게 고치시오.

1 He is able to playing the piano.
playing ➡ *play*

2 Susan are able to take a picture.
__________ ➡ __________

3 I am able not to read this book.
__________ ➡ __________

4 Is he able to using fax machine?
__________ ➡ __________

5 She ables to sing a song.
__________ ➡ __________

6 We is able to go fishing today.
__________ ➡ __________

7 Richard is able to runs fast.
__________ ➡ __________

8 You not are able to use a dictionary.
__________ ➡ __________

9 Are you able to helped me, Dad?
__________ ➡ __________

10 Tina does able to fix the chair.
__________ ➡ __________

Lesson 3-9

be able to의 과거와 미래

1. be able to의 과거형

- [주어 + be(was/were) able to + 동사원형] ~할 수 있었다
  과거형을 만들 때 be동사는 과거 형태인 'was / were'로 바꾸어 사용한다.

- I **was able to** solve the question. [긍정문]
- Ian **was not (wasn't) able to** climb a tree. [부정문]
- **A** **Were** you **able to** read English books well? [의문문]
  B **Yes, I was. / No, I was not (wasn't).**

2. be able to의 미래형

- [주어 + will be able to + 동사원형] ~할 수 있을 것이다
  'will' 뒤에는 반드시 동사원형이 와야 하므로 주어의 인칭에 상관 없이 'will be able to'를 사용한다.

- Mr. Brown **will be able to** teach science next year. [긍정문]
- Hansu **will not (won't) be able to** fly a kite. [부정문]
- **A** **Will** Jack and Mary **be able to** present at the meeting? [의문문]
  B **Yes, they will. / No, they will not (won't).**

Check up!

Answer Keys p. 17

A 다음 우리말 해석에 맞게 be able to를 이용하여 문장을 완성하시오.

1 그는 치즈케이크를 만들 수 있었다.
= He ___was able to___ make cheese cake.

2 Nick은 그 문제를 풀 수 없었다.
= Nick ______________ solve the problem.

3 나는 내일 새 자전거를 탈 수 있을 것이다.
= I ______________ ride a new bike tomorrow.

4 너는 답이 무엇인지 알 수 없을 것이다.
= You ______________ know what the answer is.

5 그녀는 사진을 찍는 법을 알 수 있었다.
= She ______________ know how to take a picture.

6 우리는 컴퓨터 게임을 할 수 있었나요?
= __________ we __________ play computer games?

Lesson

3-10 could

• **could**: can의 과거형으로 '~할 수 있었다'의 뜻으로 사용된다.

• 'could'는 '~하겠습니까?'라는 뜻으로 상대방에게 정중히 요청하는 표현으로도 사용된다.

1. **긍정문**: [주어 + could + 동사원형] ~할 수 있었다

He **could** hurry a little more before.

2. **부정문**: [주어 + could not + 동사원형] ~할 수 없었다

I **could not** walk and talk when I was a baby.

3. **의문문**: [Could + 주어 + 동사원형 ~?]

(1) 가능/능력: ~할 수 있었니?

• **A** **Could** you go to the market on foot?

B **Yes, I could. / No, I could not (couldn't).**

(2) 요청: ~해 줄 수 있니?

• **Could** you do me a favor?

➡ 요청을 의미할 때의 'could'는 'can'보다 조금 더 정중한 표현이다.

Check up!

Answer Keys p. 17

A 다음 표를 보고 Jenny와 Sam이 할 수 있었던 것과 없었던 것을 구분하여 문장을 완성하시오.

	could	could not
Jenny	ride a bike	ride in-line skate
Sam	ski	play badminton

1 Jenny could __________. She ________________ ride in-line skate.

2 Sam __________ ski. He couldn't ______________.

Check up!

Answer Keys p. 17

B 다음 밑줄 친 부분을 어법상 알맞은 형태로 고쳐 쓰시오.

1 He <u>can</u> study more last year. *could*

2 We could <u>played</u> basketball. ____________

3 <u>Can</u> I send a message to him yesterday? ____________

4 I could <u>eat not</u> garlic when I was 13. ____________

5 Sam <u>could</u> go to the concert tonight. ____________

6 He and I <u>not could</u> move the heavy box. ____________

7 She could <u>has</u> an early dinner. ____________

8 I <u>didn't could</u> take pictures here. ____________

9 The repairman could <u>fixing</u> anything. ____________

10 We couldn't <u>to go</u> camping last week. ____________

Lesson 3-11

may

• may : '~일지도 모른다'의 추측의 의미와 '~해도 좋다'는 허가의 의미를 갖는다.
주어의 인칭에 따라 형태가 변하지 않으며, 반드시 뒤에 동사원형이 온다.

1. 추측의 may: ~일지도 모른다

• She **may** visit her grandparents next week.

• We **may** join the reading club.

2. 허가의 may: ~해도 좋다

• You **may** go to the bathroom now.

• You **may** drink milk after washing your hands.

Grammar Plus +

• **might**: '추측'의 의미로 쓰일 때는 may보다 실현 가능성이 희박한 불확실한 추측을 나타낸다.
They might be in the classroom. 그들은 교실에 있을지도 모른다.

Check up!

Answer Keys p. 17

A 다음 밑줄 친 may의 의미를 괄호 안에서 고르시오.

1 Daniel may be tired now. (추측 / 허가)

2 May I come in? (추측 / 허가)

3 He may take pictures here. (추측 / 허가)

4 She may love him. (추측 / 허가)

5 We may pass the exam. (추측 / 허가)

6 You may go out alone at night. (추측 / 허가)

7 It may be true. (추측 / 허가)

8 He may be sick. (추측 / 허가)

9 You may watch this movie. (추측 / 허가)

10 Helen may come back tomorrow. (추측 / 허가)

Check up!

Answer Keys p. 17

B **다음 우리말과 뜻이 갈도록 빈칸에 알맞은 말을 쓰시오.**

1 그녀는 배우일지도 모른다.
= She *may be* an actress.

2 다음 주에 비가 올지도 모른다.
= It ______________ next week.

3 너는 가서 야구를 해도 좋다.
= You ______________ and __________ baseball.

4 Harry는 Mr. Choi의 컴퓨터를 써도 좋다.
= Harry ______________ Mr. Choi's computer.

5 Charles는 화가 났을지도 모른다.
= Charles ______________ angry.

6 우리 집에 와도 좋다.
= You ______________ to my house.

7 나는 곧 런던으로 떠날지 모른다.
= I ______________ for London soon.

8 그녀는 천재일지도 몰라.
= She ______________ a genius.

9 그는 축구를 아주 잘할지도 몰라.
= He ______________ soccer very well.

10 너희들은 음식을 좀 먹어도 좋다.
= You ______________ some food.

11 그와 그녀는 부부일지도 몰라.
= He and she ______________ husband and wife.

12 우리들은 낮잠을 자도 된다.
= We ______________ a nap.

13 그와 그녀는 칭찬을 받아도 된다.
= He and she ______________ praise.

14 너는 나가서 놀아도 된다.
= You ______________ outside to play.

15 너는 아침에 조깅을 해도 된다.
= You ______________ in the morning.

Lesson 3-12

may의 부정문과 의문문

• May의 부정문 : 추측의 의미일 때는 '~하지 않을지도 모른다'라는 뜻으로 사용하며, 허가의 의미일 때는 '~해서는 안 된다'라는 뜻으로 비교적 약한 금지를 표현할 때 사용된다.

• May의 의문문 : 허락을 묻는 표현으로 '~해도 될까요?'라는 뜻으로 사용한다.

1. may의 부정문: [주어 + may not + 동사원형]

(1) 추측: ~하지 않을지도 모른다

I **may not** pass the exam.

(2) 허가: ~해서는 안 된다

We **may not** throw trash on the street.

2. may의 의문문: [May + 주어 + 동사원형 ~?] ~해도 될까요?

'Can I~?' 보다는 공손한 표현으로 윗사람에게 사용한다.

(1) 주문 받을 때

May I take your order?

(2) 전화할 때

May I speak to Mr. Jones, please?

(3) 허락을 구할 때

- **May** I use this pencil?
- **May** I drink some water, *please*?

➡ 상대방의 허락을 구할 때 뒤에 'please'를 붙이면 더욱 공손한 표현이 된다.

Grammar Plus +

'May'의 의문문에 대한 대답

• 긍정: 'Yes, you may.'(정중한 대답)
  - 'Of course you can. / Sure. / Certainly.'로 대답할 수 있다.
• 부정: 'No, you may not.'
  - 'I'm afraid you can't. / I'm sorry you can't.'를 사용하기도한다.

Check up!

Answer Keys p. 17

A 다음 괄호 안에서 알맞은 것을 고르시오.

1 (I may / May I) bring some cookies?

2 May I (went / go) out with him?

3 Justin (not may / may not) keep his promise.

4 You may not (tell / to tell) his secret.

5 May I (using / use) this video?

6 (May / May be) I go to the meeting, please?

7 They (not may / may not) be here on time.

8 We may not (throw / throwing) the ball toward the people.

B 다음 우리말과 뜻이 같도록 빈칸에 알맞은 말을 쓰시오.

1 이곳에서 사진을 찍어도 될까요?
= ___May___ I ___take___ a picture here?

2 너는 오늘 밤에 영화를 보러 가도 좋다.
= You ______________ to the theater tonight.

3 우리는 그 문제를 풀 수 없을지도 모른다.
= We ______________ the problem.

4 숙제를 다하기 전까지 Harry는 TV를 봐서는 안 된다.
= Harry ______________ TV before he finishes his homework.

5 질문을 해도 될까요?
= __________ I __________ a question?

6 사람들은 이곳에 들어와서는 안 된다.
= People ______________ in here.

7 모두에게 Linda를 소개해도 될까요?
= __________ I __________ Linda to everyone?

8 이 검은 가방을 사도 될까요?
= __________ I __________ this black bag?

9 너는 이곳에 앉으면 안 된다.
= You ______________ here.

10 John과 통화할 수 있나요?
= __________ I __________ to John?

Practice More Ⅱ

Answer Keys p. 17~18

A 다음 주어진 문장의 의미가 같도록 빈칸을 알맞게 채우시오.

1 I can give you an answer.
= I ___am able to___ give you an answer.

2 She isn't able to remember the boy.
= She ______________ remember the boy.

3 We could make a large pizza for our family.
= We ______________ make a large pizza for our family.

4 Sam couldn't pass the math exam.
= Sam ______________ pass the math exam.

5 He can play the piano and violin.
= He ______________ play the piano and violin.

6 He and I can bake bread.
= He and I ______________ bake bread.

7 Sue could learn how to write Korean.
= Sue ______________ learn how to write Korean.

8 Can you speak French?
= __________ you __________ speak French?

9 He could buy some clothes for his mother.
= He ______________ buy some clothes for his mother.

10 She can't ride a bike.
= She ______________ ride a bike.

B 다음 문장에서 어법상 어색한 것을 찾아 바르게 고치시오.

1 He cans speak English fluently.
___cans___ ➡ ___can___

2 May I has some juice?
______________ ➡ ______________

3 You may to go fishing with her.
______________ ➡ ______________

4 He will can move that box.
______________ ➡ ______________

5 Sam could ate some cakes.
______________ ➡ ______________

6 Can he plays chess?

_______________ ➡ _______________

7 May I speaking to Linda?

_______________ ➡ _______________

8 She may can go there.

_______________ ➡ _______________

9 Rabbits is able to run fast.

_______________ ➡ _______________

10 Can you reading a newspaper for me?

_______________ ➡ _______________

C 다음 문장을 괄호 안의 지시어에 맞게 고치시오.

1 I can borrow some books. (의문문)

➡ *Can I borrow some books?*

2 He may go there because of his sister. (부정문)

➡ _______________

3 Sean is able to go hiking with his father. (부정문)

➡ _______________

4 Mary is able to drive a car. (의문문)

➡ _______________

5 My sister could make kimchi. (부정문)

➡ _______________

6 They can bring some cookies. (의문문)

➡ _______________

7 He may go to the airport tonight. (부정문)

➡ _______________

8 They could borrow some pens. (의문문)

➡ _______________

9 She is able to go home early. (부정문)

➡ _______________

10 I can cook well. (부정문)

➡ _______________

Answer Keys p. 17~18

D 다음 문장 중 나머지 넷과 뜻이 다른 것을 고르시오.

1 ① Sarah can play the flute very well.
② We can go there by taxi.
③ Can he draw pictures?
④ Can we take a break?
⑤ You can do your best.

2 ① You may leave now.
② He may be a kind person.
③ We may not have dinner tonight.
④ They may not be on a diet.
⑤ You may have a hard time there.

3 ① Can you bring me some chocolate?
② Can you do me a favor?
③ Can I have some chicken?
④ Can you tell me the story?
⑤ Can you stop talking please?

4 ① Could she do that instead of me?
② Could he come together?
③ Could I have some drink?
④ Could you read a book in Chinese when you were in college?
⑤ Could I give you some advice?

서술형 연습

E 우리말과 같은 뜻이 되도록 주어진 단어를 배열하여 문장을 완성하시오.

1 나는 그 자동차를 살 수 없었다.
(was, the car, not, able to, I, buy)
➡ *I was not able to buy the car.*

2 그들은 어제 콘서트에 갈 수 있었다.
(They, yesterday, to, could, the concert, go)
➡ ____________________

3 문을 닫아도 될까요? (the door, may, close, I)
➡ ____________________

4 그녀는 그 가구를 혼자서 옮길 수 없었다.
(she, alone, not, was, able to, move the furniture)
➡ ____________________

Point Check Ⅲ

◆ **must :** 강한 의무를 표현하며 주로 법, 규칙 등을 이야기할 때 사용한다.
'must'가 추측의 의미로 사용될 때는 'must be'로 표현한다.

◆ **have to :** 'must'와 함께 강한 의무를 표현하며, 강제적으로 하지 않아도 될 때에 쓰인다.

◆ **should :** 약한 의무를 표현하기도 하지만, 주로 충고나 조언의 의미로 더 많이 쓰인다.

1. must

(1) **강한 의무 :** [must + 동사원형]
You **must** know exactly what you want.

(2) **강한 추측 :** [must be + 명사 / 형용사]
She **must be** a great actress.

(3) **부정문 :** [주어 + must not + 동사원형]
They **must not (mustn't)** play baseball near the window.

(4) **의문문 :** [Must + 주어 + 동사원형 ~?]
Must I respect my teachers?

2. have to

	I, you, we, they	he, she, it	
긍정문	have to	has to	+ 동사원형
부정문	don't(do not) have to	doesn't(does not) have to	
의문문	Do 주어 have to ~?	Does 주어 have to ~?	

- She **has to** wake up early in the morning.
- They **don't have to** learn how to dive.
- **Do** you **have to** get there by tomorrow?

3. should

(1) **의무 / 충고 / 조언:** [should + 동사원형]
- He **should** listen to her advice. [의무]
- You **should** go on a diet. [충고 · 조언]

(2) **부정문:** [should not + 동사원형]
They **should not (shouldn't)** tell the story.

(3) **의문문:** [Should + 주어 + 동사원형~?]
Should I use some colored pencils?

Lesson 3-13 must

• must: '~해야만 한다'의 뜻으로 강한 의무를 나타낼 때 사용한다. 또 be동사와 함께 사용해서 '~인 것이 틀림없다'라는 강한 추측의 의미를 갖기도 한다.

1. 강한 의무의 must: [주어 + must + 동사원형] 반드시 ~해야만 한다

주로 규칙이나 꼭 지켜야 하는 법에 관련하여 사용하며, 그 외의 강한 의무의 표현에는 'have(has) to'와 바꿔 쓸 수 있다.

- We **must** obey the rules of this school.
- They **must** finish the job by tomorrow.

2. 강한 추측의 must: [주어 + must be + 명사 / 형용사] ~인 것이 틀림없다, ~이 분명하다

- He **must be** a liar.
- She **must be** saying the truth.

➡ 강한 추측을 나타낼 때 must 뒤에 주로 'be'를 사용한다.

Check up!

Answer Keys p. 18

A 다음 우리말과 같도록 빈칸을 알맞게 채우시오.

1 그가 배가 고픈 것이 틀림없다.
= He ___must be___ hungry.

2 너는 그 상자를 옮겨야만 한다.
= You ______________ this box.

3 Hana는 새로운 집을 찾아야만 한다.
= Hana ______________ a new house.

4 우리는 약속을 잘 지켜야 한다.
= We ______________ our promises.

5 Sue와 Emma는 자매인 것이 틀림없다.
= Sue and Emma ______________ sisters.

6 그는 집에 일찍 돌아와야 한다.
= He ______________ home early.

7 Henry는 유명한 가수인 것이 틀림없다.
= Henry ______________ a famous singer.

Check up!

Answer Keys p. 18

B 다음 문장에서 어법상 어색한 부분을 찾아 바르게 고치시오.

1 Players must obeys the rule of the game.
   obeys ➡ obey

2 Robin must turning the volume down.
   ______ ➡ ______

3 Student must studying hard.
   ______ ➡ ______

4 She have to come home before the sun sets.
   ______ ➡ ______

5 It must being wrong.
   ______ ➡ ______

6 He must is a teenager.
   ______ ➡ ______

7 Sally and Tom must be hide something.
   ______ ➡ ______

C 다음 주어진 우리말을 영어로 바르게 영작하시오.

1 그들은 정직함이 틀림없다.
   ➡ They must be honest.

2 너희들은 지금 놀면 안 된다.
   ➡ ______________.

3 그녀는 간호사임이 틀림없다.
   ➡ ______________.

4 우리는 빨간불에 길을 건너면 안 된다.
   ➡ ______________ at the red light.

5 나는 내일까지 숙제를 끝내야만 한다.
   ➡ ______________ by tomorrow.

Lesson

3-14 must의 부정문과 의문문

• **must의 부정문**: '~해서는 안 된다'의 의미로 강한 금지의 뜻을 가지고 있다.
must의 부정문은 'have to의 부정문'과 바꿔 쓸 수 없다.

• **must의 의문문**: '~해야만 하나요?'의 뜻을 가지기도 하고, 허락을 묻는 표현으로 '~해도 될까요?'라는 뜻으로도 사용한다.

1. **must의 부정문**: [주어 + must not + 동사원형] ~해서는 안 된다

- You **must not** park here.
- We **mustn't** laugh at other people.

➡ 'must not'은 'mustn't'으로 줄여 쓸 수 있다.

2. **must의 의문문**: [Must + 주어 + 동사원형 ~?] ~해야만 하나요?

- **Must** they write in their diary every night?
- **Must** she leave here tonight?

Check up!

Answer Keys p. 18

A 다음 문장을 보고 맞으면 O, 틀리면 X를 쓰시오.

1 I mustn't play a computer game. (○)

2 Must Jane stays here? (   )

3 You must not keep your room dirty. (   )

4 Must quit he smoking? (   )

5 Sally must not eats chocolate. (   )

B 다음 우리말에 맞게 빈칸에 알맞은 말을 보기에서 찾아 써 넣으시오.

보기

must   must not

1 너는 거짓말을 해서는 안 된다.
= You ___must not___ tell a lie.

2 Sam이 매일 운동을 해야 하나요?
= ________ Sam exercise every day?

3 학생들은 지각을 하면 안 된다.
= Students ____________ be late.

4 그가 꼭 병원에 가야 하나요?
= ____________ he go to the hospital?

5 도서관에서는 크게 얘기하면 안 된다.
= You ____________ speak loudly in the library.

C 주어진 단어들을 이용하여 우리말 해석에 맞는 문장을 쓰시오.

1 그녀는 동물을 때려서는 안 된다.
(must not / she / animals / hit)
= *She must not hit animals.*

2 남자들은 오늘 밤 검은 모자를 꼭 써야 하나요?
(a black hat / men / must / tonight / wear)
= ______________________________

3 너는 너무 많이 먹으면 안 된다.
(you / too / much / eat / must not)
= ______________________________

4 너는 친구들에게 친절해야만 한다.
(you / kind / must / to / your / be / friends)
= ______________________________

5 그는 우리를 비웃으면 안 된다.
(at / us / not / must / he / laugh)
= ______________________________

6 우리는 에너지를 아껴야만 한다.
(must / we / energy / save)
= ______________________________

7 그들은 코미디언들인 것이 틀림없다.
(comedians / they / be / must)
= ______________________________

Lesson 3-15

have to

• **have to**: '~해야 한다'의 뜻으로 의무를 나타낼 때 사용한다. 주어가 3인칭 단수일 경우 'has to'로 사용한다. must보다는 조금 약한 의무를 나타내며, 강제적으로 하지 않아도 될 경우에 사용한다.

◈ 주어의 인칭에 따른 'have to'

I, you, we, they	he, she, it
have to	has to

have(has) to: ~해야 한다

• Jerry **has to** finish his homework before dinner.

• Jerry and Anna **have to** start studying for the English test right now.

Check up!

Answer Keys p. 18

A 다음 빈칸에 have(has) to를 이용하여 문장을 완성하시오.

1 It is so cold. We ___*have to*___ wear a coat.

2 We ____________ be quiet in the museum.

3 She ____________ walk home because she missed the train.

4 I ____________ sleep now. I will go on a the picnic tomorrow.

5 She ____________ fix her bike. It is broken.

6 Monday is Tim's birthday. We ____________ plan his birthday party.

7 He ____________ return the book today.

8 Minsu ____________ take medicine. He must be sick.

9 We ____________ love ourselves.

10 Sumi ____________ study English hard because he wants to be an English teacher.

Check up!

Answer Keys p. 18

B 다음 문장에서 어법상 어색한 것을 찾아 바르게 고치시오.

1 I has to go to church now.

has ➡ have

2 Mike has to practicing playing tennis.

______ ➡ ______

3 John and I has to study hard.

______ ➡ ______

4 She has to helped her mother.

______ ➡ ______

5 I have to studied 10 hours every day.

______ ➡ ______

6 We has to wear uniforms.

______ ➡ ______

7 Jina have to take care of her baby.

______ ➡ ______

8 He has stopped watching TV.

______ ➡ ______

9 You has to keep your room clean.

______ ➡ ______

10 The news have to be true.

______ ➡ ______

Lesson 3-16

have to의 부정문과 의문문

- **have to의 부정문**: '~하지 않아도 된다', '~할 필요가 없다'의 의미로 불필요한 것에 대해 나타낼 때 사용한다.
- **have to의 의문문**: 허락을 묻는 표현으로 '~해도 될까요?', '~해야 하나요?'라는 뜻으로 사용한다.

◈ 부정문과 의문문에서의 'have to'

	I, you, we, they	he, she, it
부정문	don't(do not) have to	doesn't(does not) have to
의문문	Do 주어 have to ~?	Does 주어 have to ~?

1. have to의 부정문: ~하지 않아도 된다, ~할 필요가 없다

- You **don't have to** worry about that.
- She **doesn't have to** wait for him.

2. have to의 의문문: ~해도 될까요?, ~해야 하나요?

- **A** **Do** they **have to** stand in line?
  B **Yes, they do. / No, they don't.**

Grammar Plus +

'Do(es) not have to'는 'do(es) not need to' 또는 'need not'으로 바꿔 쓸 수 있다.
둘 모두 '~할 필요가 없다'의 뜻으로 불필요함을 나타낸다.
You **don't have to** wake up early today.
= You **don't need to** wake up early today. / You **need not** wake up early today.

Check up!

Answer Keys p. 18

A 다음 괄호 안에 알맞은 것을 고르시오.

1 We (doesn't / don't) have to finish this work early.
2 (Does / Do) you have to help your mom?
3 You (don't / doesn't) have to do something.
4 I don't (have taking / have to take) a bus.
5 Thomas (don't have / doesn't have) to eat more.
6 Does she (has / have) to take off her shoes?
7 Lisa (don't / doesn't) have to take history class.
8 Do you have to (go / went) surfing?

Lesson 3-17

should

• should : 'must'나 'have to'처럼 '~해야 한다'는 뜻으로도 사용하지만 아주 약한 의미를 가지고 있다. '~하는 것이 좋겠다'라는 뜻으로 부드럽게 조언이나 충고를 할 때 많이 사용한다.

◈ should : [주어 + should + 동사원형]

(1) 약한 의무 : ~해야 한다

• You **should** wear your school uniform when you go to school.
• You **should** take a shower after exercising.

(2) 충고 · 조언 : ~하는 것이 좋겠다

• You **should** get some rest.
• You **should** say sorry to your friend.

Check up!

Answer Keys p. 19

A 다음 우리말과 같도록 알맞은 것을 고르시오.

1 우리는 반드시 교통 규칙을 지켜야 한다.
= You (must / should) follow the traffic rules.

2 Tom는 영어 공부를 열심히 하는 게 좋겠다.
= Tom (should / could) study English hard.

3 그녀는 피곤해 보여. 쉬는 게 좋겠다.
= She looks tired. She (should / must) take a rest.

4 우리는 매일 2리터의 물을 마시는 게 좋다.
= We (should / could) drink two liters of water.

5 너는 9시까지 이 책들을 꼭 다 읽어야 한다.
= You (should / have to) read these books until 9 o'clock.

6 그들은 식사 후에 물을 마셔야 한다.
= They (should / may) drink water after meal.

7 Sujin은 기름 진 음식을 멀리하는 게 좋겠다.
= Sujin (should / have to) keep off greasy food.

8 사람들은 적어도 하루에 8시간은 자야 한다.
= People (should / could) sleep at least eight hours a day.

Lesson 3-18

should의 부정문과 의문문

- **should의 부정문**: '~하지 않는 것이 좋겠다'라는 의미로 사용되며, 'should not'의 줄임말은 'shouldn't'이다.
- **should의 의문문**: 허락을 묻는 표현으로 '~해야 하나요?'라는 뜻으로 사용한다.

1. **should의 부정문**: [주어 + should not + 동사원형] ~해서는 안 된다

   • You **should not (shouldn't)** take my pen.

2. **should의 의문문**: [Should + 주어 + 동사원형 ~?] ~해야 하나요?

   • **Should** I wear a long skirt here?

Check up!

Answer Keys p. 19

A 다음 괄호 안에서 알맞은 것을 고르시오.

1 (Should / Have to) students study hard?

2 I (not should / should not) buy this computer.

3 (Do / Should) she send an email to him?

4 Neil should not (is / be) late.

5 Should everyone (goes / go) to the museum?

6 He should (not to join / not join) the club.

7 Nick (should / don't) not be rude to his parents.

8 Should I (to cut / cut) the paper into pieces?

9 You should not (throwing / throw) bottles here.

10 All of you (should not / may not) forget to do your homework.

Check up!

Answer Keys p. 19

B 다음 우리말 해석에 맞게 보기 에서 알맞은 문장을 찾아 기호를 쓰시오.

보기

ⓐ I should go to sleep early.

ⓑ Charlie should not miss the bus.

ⓒ You should not walk alone late at night.

ⓓ Should I buy a new book tomorrow?

1 늦은 밤에는 혼자 걸어서는 안 된다. (ⓒ)

2 나는 일찍 잠을 자야 한다. (   )

3 내일 새로운 책을 사와야 하나요? (   )

4 Charlie는 그 버스를 놓치면 안 된다. (   )

C 다음 우리말 해석에 맞게 주어진 말을 배열하여 문장을 완성하시오.

1 여기서는 모자를 벗어야 하나요?
(should, my hat, take off, I, here)
= *Should I take off my hat here?*

2 너의 실수에 변명을 하면 안 된다.
(not, mistake, you, make excuses for, should, your)
= ______________________

3 이 마우스를 이곳에 옮겨야 하나요?
(I, the mouse, should, here, move)
= ______________________

4 Tyler는 돈을 너무 많이 쓰면 안 돼.
(money, too, spend, not, should, Tyler, much)
= ______________________

Practice More Ⅲ

Answer Keys p. 19

A 다음 중 밑줄 친 단어가 의미하는 것이 무엇인지 보기 에서 골라 쓰시오.

보기

의무 추측 조언 금지 불필요

1 Students must be careful when they run across the street. [의무]

2 I think she must be a doctor. [ ]

3 Tom should go to the doctor. [ ]

4 I have to finish my homework. [ ]

5 Helen doesn't have to eat dinner again. [ ]

6 You must not be late for school. [ ]

7 She looks so tired. She must be tired. [ ]

8 You must not be outside all day long. Just take a rest. [ ]

9 They don't have to leave here anymore. [ ]

10 I must send an email to my teacher right now. [ ]

B 다음 중 어법상 어색한 곳을 찾아 바르게 고치시오.

1 I has to finish the work.

has to ➡ have to

2 He don't have to buy the book.

________ ➡ ________

3 Do I should wear a raincoat?

________ ➡ ________

4 They doesn't have to go with me.

________ ➡ ________

5 Do you must return to your hometown?

________ ➡ ________

6 He must be stop this bad habit.

________ ➡ ________

Practice More Ⅲ

7 I not should eat chocolate.

_______________ ➡ _______________

8 You must tell not a lie.

_______________ ➡ _______________

9 You should following the rule of the game.

_______________ ➡ _______________

10 Does she has to cancel our plans?

_______________ ➡ _______________

C 다음 우리말 해석에 맞게 빈칸에 알맞은 말을 쓰시오.

1 너는 숙제를 5시까지 끝낼 필요가 없다.
= You ___*don't have to finish*___ your homework begore 5.

2 우리는 내일 아침 일찍 일어나야 하나요?
= __________ we _______________ early tomorrow morning?

3 넌 또 다른 직업을 찾아볼 필요가 없다.
= You ____________________ another job.

4 Joseph은 내일 병원에 가보는 게 좋겠다.
= Joseph ____________________ to the hospital tomorrow.

5 길거리에 쓰레기를 버려서는 안된다.
= You ____________________ the garbage on the street.

6 비 오는 날에는 축구를 하지 않는 게 좋다.
= You ____________________ when it rains.

7 Sam과 Nick은 형제인 것이 틀림없다.
= Sam and Nick ____________________ brothers.

D 다음 주어진 문장을 우리말로 알맞게 해석하시오.

1 They have to get up early tomorrow morning.
➡ ___*그들은 내일 아침 일찍 일어나야 한다.*___

2 I must write in a diary for homework.
➡ ____

3 She doesn't have to finish the work until Friday.
➡ ____

Answer Keys p. 19

4 We have to participate in the English speaking contest.

➡ ______________________________

5 I think students should study hard for their future.

➡ ______________________________

서술형 연습 **E** **우리말에 맞게 주어진 문장의 빈칸에 들어갈 수 있는 단어를 모두 쓰시오.**

1
> 너는 식사 전에 반드시 손을 씻어야만 한다.
> = You __________ wash your hands before meal.

➡ ______________________________

2
> 그는 그 회의에 참석할 필요가 없다.
> = He __________ participate in the meeting.

➡ ______________________________

3
> 너는 그녀의 충고를 받아들이는 것이 낫겠다.
> = You __________ accept her advice.

➡ ______________________________

F **다음 문장을 주어진 지시에 맞게 바꾸어 쓰시오.**

1 She has to buy the doll for her daughter. (의문문)

= *Does she have to buy the doll for her daughter?*

2 Jane and Kate have to go to the hospital. (부정문)

= ______________________________

3 I should take care of them. (의문문)

= ______________________________

4 They should buy the green chair. (부정문)

= ______________________________

5 John must exercise regularly. (부정문)

= ______________________________

Point Check IV

◆ **must not :** 강한 금지를 표현하며 '~해선 안 된다'라는 뜻을 가지고 있다.

◆ **do(es) not have to :** 불필요한 것을 나타내는 표현이며 '~할 필요가 없다'의 뜻으로 사용한다.
must not과 do(es) not have to는 바꿔 쓸 수 없다.

◆ **had better :** 주로 충고나 조언을 할 때 쓰이며 '~하는 것이 낫다'의 뜻을 가진다.

◆ **would like (to) :** 'would like'와 'would like to' 는 '~(하기를) 원한다'의 뜻으로 'to'가 있을 때는 뒤에 동사원형이 오고, 없을 때는 명사가 온다.

1. 'must not'과 'don't (doesn't) have to'

(1) **must not (=mustn't)** : ~해서는 안 된다 (강한 금지의 뜻)
He **mustn't** sleep outside.

(2) **don't (doesn't) have to** : ~할 필요가 없다 (불필요한 것을 나타낼 때 사용)
We **don't have to** do our homework again.

2. should : 가장 약한 의무/조언

You **should** be kind to your friends.

3. have to : 강한/의무

They **have to** arrive there by next Monday.

4. must : 가장 강한 의무/추측

We **must** be late for school.

5. had better : ~하는 것이 낫다

(1) **긍정문** : had better + 동사원형
We **had better** stay at home.

(2) **부정문** : had better not + 동사원형
You **had better not** come here.

6. would like (to) : ~(하기를) 원한다

(1) **would like + 명사**
She **would like** some cookies.

(2) **would like to + 동사원형**
He **would like to** have that toy.

Lesson 3-19

must not과 don't have to의 차이

• must not: '~해서는 안 된다'라는 강한 금지의 뜻을 나타낸다.

• don't(doesn't) have to: '~할 필요가 없다'라는 뜻으로 필요하지 않은 것을 나타낸다.

• You **must not** take off your raincoat here. [강한 금지]
• We **don't have to** hurry. [불필요]

Grammar Plus +

must와 have to(긍정문) 비교하기
'must'는 '개인의 의무'를 표현하고, 'have to'는 규칙이나 의사의 지시 같은 '외부로부터의 의무'를 나타낸다.
I want to be thin. I **must** do exercise. [개인의 의무_내가 원함]
The doctor says he **has to** do exercise regularly. [외부로부터의 의무_의사의 지시]

Check up!

Answer Keys p. 19~20

A 다음 우리말 해석에 맞게 don't(doesn't) have to나 must not을 이용하여 문장을 완성하시오.

1 우리는 일찍 일어날 필요가 없다. 오늘은 일요일이야!
= We ___don't have to___ get up early. Today is Sunday!

2 위험하기 때문에 무단 횡단을 하면 안 된다.
= People ______________ jaywalk because it is dangerous.

3 그녀는 우산을 가져갈 필요가 없다.
= She ______________ bring an umbrella.

4 Alex는 창 밖으로 쓰레기를 버려서는 안 된다.
= Alex ______________ throw the garbage out of the window.

5 나는 비싼 옷을 살 필요가 없다.
= I ______________ buy expensive clothes.

6 할아버지는 멀리 산책 가실 필요가 없다.
= Grandfather ______________ take a long walk.

7 학생들은 결석해서는 안 된다.
= Students ______________ miss the class.

8 너는 그녀를 기다릴 필요가 없다.
= You ______________ wait for her.

9 시험에서 부정 행위를 하면 안 된다.
= We ______________ cheat on an exam.

10 병원에서 뛰어 다니면 안 된다.
= You ______________ run in the hospital.

B **다음 문장 에서 어법상 어색한 것을 찾아 바르게 고치시오.**

1 He don't have to find a new job.
don't ➡ *doesn't*

2 Samantha doesn't have getting up early.
__________ ➡ __________

3 Joe and Yuna doesn't have to go home now.
__________ ➡ __________

4 I don't have to studying all night.
__________ ➡ __________

5 You must not going home alone.
__________ ➡ __________

6 They don't have to cleaned their room.
__________ ➡ __________

7 She doesn't has to go to school.
__________ ➡ __________

8 Eric doesn't must be bad.
__________ ➡ __________

9 We don't must to clean our room now.
__________ ➡ __________

10 She have not to jog every morning.
__________ ➡ __________

Lesson

3-20 should / have to / must

• should / have to / must: 강약의 차이가 있을 뿐 모두 의무의 뜻을 가진다.

1. **should**: 가장 약한 의무/조언
   • You **should** be quiet.

2. **have to**: 강한 의무
   • They **have to** write a diary every night.

3. **must**: 가장 강한 의무/추측
   • She **must** leave here right now.

Grammar Plus +

• **should**
약한 의미의 조언이나 충고를 나타낸다.

• **must**
강한 의무를 나타낸다.

• **have to**
'must'와 비슷하게 강한 의무를 나타내지만, 꼭 해야만 하는 것은 아니다.

Check up!

Answer Keys p. 20

A 다음 괄호 안에서 알맞은 것을 고르시오.

1 People (should / must) help the handicapped.

2 You (have to / should) be careful next time.

3 He (must / should) not fight with his friend.

4 I (don't have to / should not) take a shower. I already did that.

5 We (must / should) stop talking. English class will start.

6 Britney (has to / must) be tired. She looks so sleepy.

7 Mom (must / should not) wear a coat. It is so hot outside.

8 I have a math test tomorrow. I (have to / should) study tonight.

9 You (don't have to / must not) bring your dog here. It is prohibited.

10 You (should not/ have to) wear a helmet while you ride a bike.

Lesson 3-21

had better

• **had better**: '~하는 것이 낫다'의 의미를 가지고 있으며, should보다 더 강한 충고나 권유를 나타낸다.

1. had better: [주어 + had better + 동사원형] ~하는 것이 낫겠다

• He looks tired. He **had better** go to bed early.

➡ had better는 'd better로 줄여 쓸 수 있다.

2. had better의 부정문: [주어 + had better not + 동사원형] ~하지 않는 것이 낫겠다

• They have to hurry. They **had better not** take a bus.

Grammar Plus +

충고나 조언을 할 때 사용하는 'had better'는 'should'보다 강한 충고로 이행하지 않을 경우 안 좋은 결과가 생길 수 있는 것을 의미한다.
상황에 따라 '강요'의 의미로 쓰일 수 있으므로 가까운 사이에서만 사용한다.
You **had better** hurry now, or you will be late.

Check up!

Answer Keys p. 20

A 다음 문장에서 어법상 어색한 것을 찾아 바르게 고치시오.

1 You have better study more.
  have ➡ *had*

2 He had better wearing a coat. It's cold today.
  ________ ➡ ________

3 They had better to take a taxi. They're late.
  ________ ➡ ________

4 Lisa has better take medicine.
  ________ ➡ ________

5 She had not better to go there.
  ________ ➡ ________

6 You had better not listened to music.
  ________ ➡ ________

7 We are had better go to the park to exercise.
  ________ ➡ ________

Lesson **3-22**

would like (to)

- would like: '~을 원하다'의 뜻으로 'want'와 같은 의미이다.
- would like to: '~하기를 원하다'의 뜻으로 'want to'와 같은 의미이다.

1. **would like**: [주어+would like+명사] ~을 원하다
   - **Would** you **like** some coffee?
     = **Do you want** some coffee?

2. **would like to**: [주어+would like to+동사원형] ~하기를 원하다
   - Anna **would like to** travel all over the world.
     = Anna **wants to** travel all over the world.

Check up!

Answer Keys p. 20

A 다음 문장과 같은 뜻이 되도록 빈칸을 채우시오.

1 Do you want a black dress?
= ___Would___ you ___like___ a black dress?

2 Emily wants to eat some spicy food.
= Emily ______________ eat some spicy food.

3 He would like something special to do.
= He __________ something special to do.

4 I want beautiful flowers.
= I ______________ beautiful flowers.

5 She would like to eat pizza and galbi.
= She ______________ eat pizza and galbi.

6 I want to meet Dan.
= I ______________ meet Dan.

7 Would Sara like to get a good grade on a writing test?
= __________ Sara __________ get a good grade on a writing test?

Practice More IV

A 다음 괄호 안에서 올바른 것을 고르시오.

1 A We should get up early tomorrow.
B Oh, I heard that our plan changed.
We (must / don't have to) get up early.

2 A Do you want to go fishing?
B Well, no. I (would like to / could) go hiking.

3 A What is Nick doing?
B He is doing his homework. He (must / had better) finish it by noon.

4 A What do you want for your birthday?
B I (must / would like) to get a beautiful dress.

5 You (must / don't have to) buy the food because we already bought it yesterday.

6 We (had better / would like to) stop eating junk food for our health.

7 We (had better not / must not) go camping because it will snow tomorrow.

8 You (should / must not) stop eating too much for your health.

9 I (should / had not better) study hard to pass the final exam.

B 다음 우리말 해석에 맞게 빈칸을 채우시오.

1 너는 오늘 저녁을 먹을 필요가 없다.
= You *don't have to eat* dinner today.

2 학생들은 이 방에 들어가면 안 된다.
= Students __________ the room.

3 Sally는 이번 주에 할머니를 뵙고 오는 것이 좋겠다.
= Sally __________ her grandmother this week.

4 Tim은 내일 학교에 갈 필요가 없다.
= Tim __________ to school tomorrow.

5 우리들은 약한 사람들을 때리면 안 된다.
= We __________ weak people.

Answer Keys p. 20

6 도서관에서는 조용히 해야 한다.
= In the library, you ________________ quiet.

7 우리는 올해 꽃 축제를 준비할 필요가 없다.
= We ________________ for the flower festival this year.

8 너는 고장 난 의자를 새 것으로 교체하는 것이 낫겠다.
= You ________________ your broken chair for a new one.

9 너는 영어 공부를 하고 있는 동안에 음악을 들으면 안 된다.
= You ________________ to music while you are studying English.

10 Jane은 이 책들을 다 읽을 필요가 없다.
= Jane ________________ all these books.

C 다음 문장과 같은 뜻이 되도록 빈칸을 채우시오.

1 Do you want to go on a picnic with John?
= *Would you like to go* on a picnic with John?

2 I should not plant the trees in the garden.
= I ________________ the trees in the garden.

3 You need not repair the coffee machine because I will buy a new one.
= You ________________ the coffee machine because I will buy a new one.

4 They must follow the safety rules.
= They ________________ the safety rules.

5 What a lovely day! We should go to the Han River to ride a boat.
= What a lovely day! We ________________ to the Han River to ride a boat.

6 You don't have to send an email to him because I already did.
= You ________________ send an email to him because I already did.

Practice More IV

D 다음 문장에서 어법상 어색한 것을 찾아 바르게 고치시오.

1 I would like to going to the beach.

going ➡ *go*

2 She has better leave there early.

________ ➡ ________

3 Mr. Moon should changes his computer.

________ ➡ ________

4 John had better to buy the shirt.

________ ➡ ________

5 They are would like to play soccer.

________ ➡ ________

6 I could like to eat something sweet.

________ ➡ ________

7 Would you like change your hair color?

________ ➡ ________

서술형 연습 **F** 다음 보기에서 알맞은 표현을 골라 문장을 완성하시오.

보기

had better take a rest / don't have to buy / has to go shopping / should exchange it for / had better hurry up / would like to start / have to finish / don't have to eat

1 I don't like this bike. I *should exchange it for* another one.

2 You look so tired. You ________.

3 Mom already made a cake. You ________ it.

4 We ________ the work before meal.

5 We should arrive on time. We ________.

6 Sam ________ with his mom.

7 I ________ something. I'm full.

8 She ________ exercising for her health.

중간 기말고사 예상문제

Answer Keys p. 21

내신 최다 출제 유형

01 다음 중 어법상 올바른 것을 고르시오. [출제 예상 85%]

① Jane will not has lunch.
② They will play soccer tomorrow.
③ Ian won't does his homework.
④ Will Mary goes to the mall?
⑤ We will play and swimming all day.

02 다음 중 어법상 올바른 것을 고르시오. [출제 예상 90%]

① I will can fix the CD player.
② Jenny will be able to solve the math questions.
③ My sister can wrote her name.
④ What was you and your brother doing yesterday?
⑤ When we went into the house, it starts raining.

03 다음 중 can의 쓰임이 나머지와 다른 하나를 고르시오. [출제 예상 95%]

① Can I help you?
② Can I open the door?
③ Can I eat some cookies?
④ Can you drink some juice?
⑤ You can speak English very well.

04 다음 중 어법상 올바른 문장을 모두 고르시오. [출제 예상 80%]

① You could read and write when you were seven.
② We didn't often understood her language.
③ It can means 'a cute person.'
④ My nephew can is a great singer.
⑤ She is able to jump high.

05 다음 빈칸에 들어갈 말이 바르게 짝지어진 것을 고르시오. [출제 예상 95%]

- It is too cold in this room. ________ I close the window?
- You ________ park your car in front of this building. This is not a parking lot.

① Can – will
② May – has to
③ Can – must not
④ May – are going to
⑤ Will – can

06 Which is not grammatically correct? [출제 예상 95%]

① We should walk up the stairs up to the third floor.
② Sam will to have his own Internet site.
③ Are there any books on the desk?
④ They should laugh all at once.
⑤ It's for making the air clean.

중간 기말고사 예상문제

[01~03] 다음 빈칸에 들어갈 단어로 알맞은 것을 고르시오.

01

I'm sorry, but I ________ come to your birthday party.

① should ② may ③ must not
④ have to ⑤ cannot

02

It's getting dark outside. It ________ rain today.

① may ② won't ③ must not
④ cannot ⑤ does not

03

Jason ________ play the flute very well. He will play at the concert.

① should ② cannot ③ must
④ has to ⑤ can

[04~06] 다음 대화의 빈칸 (A)와 (B)에 들어갈 말이 바르게 짝지어진 것을 고르시오.

04

A ________ I help you?
B Yes, please. I ________ find size seven, green color.

	(A)	(B)
①	Can	can
②	May	can't
③	Should	must not
④	Must	should not
⑤	Can	am not

05

A ________ you borrow me a pen, please?
B Of course, I ________. Here you are.

	(A)	(B)
①	Can	could
②	May	can't
③	Should	shouldn't
④	May	can
⑤	Can	can

06

A ________ you like to drink some coffee?
B Yes, ________. Thank you.

	(A)	(B)
①	Should	could
②	May	can't
③	Would	please
④	Would	wouldn't
⑤	Can	can't

[07~09] 우리말과 같은 뜻이 되도록 빈칸에 알맞은 말을 보기 에서 찾아 써 넣으시오.

보기

can must may will should

07

Mia는 아마 겨울 방학에 캐나다에 있는 삼촌을 방문할지도 몰라.

➡ Mia ________ visit her uncle in Canada during winter vacation.

08

나는 올해 중국어 연습을 더 열심히 할 것이다.

➡ I ________ practice Chinese harder this year.

09

내 어린 남동생은 이제 걸을 수 있다.

➡ My little brother ________ walk now.

[10~11] 다음 문장 중 어법상 올바른 것을 고르시오.

10
① She won't go to the theater tomorrow.
② They won't be play the violin.
③ I can't plays badminton very well.
④ She can able to ride a bike.
⑤ We will goes to the department store.

★★★
11
① My sister can played the violin.
② She wasn't able to run fast when she was four.
③ They could played the piano well.
④ She can't be able to buy a new bag.
⑤ We weren't able to carry this heavy box tomorrow.

12 다음 문장 중 밑줄 친 can의 쓰임이 다른 하나를 고르시오.

① Jane can draw a picture well.
② We can speak Japanese.
③ My little sister can dance well.
④ I can ride a bike.
⑤ You can eat some cookies.

★★★
13 다음 문장 중 밑줄 친 may의 쓰임이 다른 하나를 고르시오.

① You may leave now.
② You may listen to the music.
③ You may come with me.
④ It may be false.
⑤ You may go to the bathroom.

★★★
14 다음 문장 중 밑줄 친 must의 쓰임이 다른 하나를 고르시오.

① We must read books all the time.
② They must be sad now.
③ You must hurry up.
④ He must take the first train.
⑤ She must follow the rules.

[15~16] 우리말과 같은 뜻이 되도록 빈칸에 들어갈 가장 알맞은 말을 고르시오.

15

너는 무대에서 노래를 부를 예정이니? ________________________ sing songs on the stage?

① Are you going to
② You are going to
③ Will you going to
④ Going you to
⑤ Will be you going to

16

너는 오늘 밤 놀이공원에 갈 거야?
______________________ tonight?

① Will you going to the amusement park?
② Will you go to the amusement park?
③ Are you going the amusement park?
④ Can you going to the amusement park?
⑤ Are you able to go to the amusement park?

[17~18] 다음 밑줄 친 부분과 바꾸어 쓸 수 있는 것을 모두 고르시오.

17

A May I drink something cold?
B Sure.

① Must ② Do ③ Can
④ Could ⑤ Will

18

A We must pay attention in class.
B You're right.

① should ② don't have to
③ must not ④ have to
⑤ cannot

[19~20] 다음 주어진 우리말을 영어로 가장 잘 옮긴 것을 고르시오.

19

홍차 좀 마실래요?

① Would you drink some black tea?
② Would you like drink some black tea?
③ Would you like to drink some black tea?
④ Would you like to some black tea?
⑤ Would you like to drinking some black tea?

★★★
20

너는 이곳에서 휴식을 취하는 것이 낫겠어.

① You have better take a rest here.
② You has better take a rest here.
③ You had better taking a rest here.
④ You had better take a rest here.
⑤ You had better takes a rest here.

[21~23] 다음 대화에서 질문에 맞는 알맞은 답을 고르시오.

21

A What would you like to buy?
B ______________________.

① I would like to drink some milk.
② She would like some cookies.
③ I would like to buy some cheese.
④ I can bring some cake.
⑤ I should go there.

22

A Can you do a magic trick?
B ______________________.

① Sure, I can't. ② No, I can.
③ Yes, I can. ④ Yes, I could.
⑤ No, I couldn't.

23

A Will you pick up the flowers for me?
B ______________________.

① No, I will. ② Yes, I would.
③ No, I won't to go. ④ Yes, I will.
⑤ No, I would.

Answer Keys p. 21~22

24 다음 문장 중 밑줄 친 부분이 금지의 뜻으로 사용된 문장을 모두 고르시오.

① She can't wear these small jeans.
② They can't buy anything.
③ You can't make noise in a public place.
④ They can't find my glasses.
⑤ We can't run in the restaurant.

25 다음 문장 중 may가 들어갈 수 없는 것을 고르시오.

① ________ I help you?
② She ________ be at home.
③ The rumor ________ be true.
④ ________ I sing here?
⑤ ________ you buy me a flower?

[26~27] 다음 짝지어진 대화 중 어색한 것을 고르시오.

26 ① **A** Will he visit his parents?
B Yes, he will.
② **A** May I make a phone call?
B Yes, you may.
③ **A** She wants to lose weight.
B She should not eat sweets.
④ **A** Can you help me with my homework?
B You mustn't help me.
⑤ **A** Do you have to finish this work by tonight?
B Yes, I have to do it.

27 ① **A** Will you come to my party?
B Yes, I will.
② **A** May I wash my hands first?
B No, I can't.
③ **A** Do your parents want you to study hard?
B Yes, they do.
④ **A** Can you go to the library with me?
B I'm sorry but I can't.
⑤ **A** Is she able to learn quickly?
B Yes, she is.

[28~29] 다음 우리말 영작이 바르지 못한 문장을 고르시오.

28 ① 나는 세수를 할 것이다.
→ I'm going to wash my face.
② 너는 버스를 타서는 안 된다.
→ You must not take a bus.
③ 그녀는 일을 열심히 해야 한다.
→ She has to work hard.
④ Mr. Wang은 한국어를 이해할 수 없다.
→ Mr. Wang can understand Korean well.
⑤ Jenny는 2등인 것이 틀림없다.
→ Jenny must be the second place.

29 ① 그들은 이 호텔에 머물러야 한다.
→ They must stay at this hotel.
② 우리는 비옷을 입어야 한다.
→ We should not wear a raincoat.
③ 너는 의사에게 가 보는 것이 낫겠다.
→ You had better go to the doctor.
④ Tom은 일찍 자야 한다.
→ Tom should go to bed early.
⑤ Jason과 Mary는 일찍 떠나야 한다.
→ Jason and Mary must leave early.

[30~31] 다음 괄호 안의 알맞은 말이 바르게 짝지어진 것을 고르시오.

30

(a) You (must not / not must) cross the street on a yellow light.
(b) We'll (be careful / careful) all the time.
(c) (Can / Are) you able to go there alone?

① must not – be careful – Can
② not must – careful – Are
③ must not – careful – Are
④ must not – be careful – Are
⑤ not must – be careful – Are

31

(a) They (have to / have) wash their hands every time.
(b) We (will / will be) take some pictures.
(c) Would you (like / like to) eat some peaches?

① have to – will be – like to
② have – will – like to
③ have to – will – like to
④ have to – will – like
⑤ have – will be – like

[32~33] 다음 문장 중 어법상 옳은 것을 모두 고르시오.

32
① He is able to edits really well.
② She could compose music when she was 17.
③ I could not attending the concert.
④ Edward will not buy a new car.
⑤ The kids cannot to add numbers quickly.

33
① They were not able to stop running.
② Mina couldn't getting her textbooks.
③ It is a sunny day. I may go on a picnic with him.
④ The big dog may not is afraid.
⑤ She will comes back soon.

[34~35] 다음 문장 중 어법상 틀린 것을 모두 고르시오.

★★★
34
① I will drinking orange juice.
② It will not be a big thing.
③ I should go to the doctor.
④ He is not able speak French.
⑤ She had better hurry up.

35
① You may sit down here.
② Do we have to study hard?
③ She would like some coke.
④ They must been models.
⑤ Hans could write well when he is eight.

Answer Keys p. 21~22

[36~38] 다음 주어진 우리말을 바르게 영작한 것을 고르시오.

36 이 편지는 그녀의 것일 리가 없다.

① This letter cannot be hers.
② This is a letter cannot be hers.
③ This is not her letter.
④ This cannot her letters.
⑤ This letter can be hers.

37 우리는 사람들에게 친절해야 한다.

① They must be kind to people.
② I should be kind to people.
③ We should be kind to people.
④ They should be kind to people.
⑤ You must be kind to people.

38 그녀는 한 나라의 공주인 것이 틀림없다.

① She must be a prince of a country.
② She must be a princess of a country.
③ She may be a princess of a country.
④ She should be a prince of a country.
⑤ She must be a country of a princess.

[39~40] 다음 글을 읽고 물음에 답하시오.

Jenny and Tom are best friends. They ⓐ <u>went to</u> the same high school and the university. But their jobs ⓑ <u>were</u> different now.
Jenny ⓒ <u>can</u> repair computer, radio, TV and so on very well.
Also, she is able to ⓓ <u>make</u> some electronics by herself.
Tom is a positive person. He ⓔ <u>likes</u> give some advice to his friends. So his friends said that (A) <u>그는 상담원이 되는 것이 낫겠다</u>. But he would like to write novels and he's writing now.

★★★
39 윗글의 ⓐ~ⓔ에서 어법상 <u>틀린</u> 것을 <u>모두</u> 고르시오.

① ⓐ ② ⓑ ③ ⓒ ④ ⓓ ⑤ ⓔ

40 Can you guess what Jenny's job is in the story?

① teacher ② engineer ③ scientist
④ doctor ⑤ dentist

41 밑줄 친 (A)의 우리말을 영어로 바르게 옮긴 것을 고르시오.

① He should better a counselor.
② He is a counselor.
③ He had better be a counselor.
④ He must be a counselor.
⑤ He may be a counselor.

◇◇◇◇◇◇◇◇◇◇◇ 서술형 평가 ◇◇◇◇◇◇◇◇◇◇◇

[42~44] 다음 글을 읽고 물음에 답하시오.

There are many kinds of animals around the world. (A) Some animals can jump very well. Kangaroos may be the best jumpers in the world.
They ⓐ (can / can't) jump up to five meters.
How about monkeys?
Monkeys ⓑ (can / can't) jump like them, but they ⓒ (can / can't) swing the branches very well.
Cheetahs have four legs and run very fast in the world. But (B) 그들은 캥거루처럼 높이 뛸 수는 없다.

42 윗글의 밑줄 친 (A)와 같은 뜻이 되도록 빈칸에 알맞은 말을 쓰시오.

(A) Some animals can jump very well.
➡ Some animals ________________ jump very well.

43 윗글의 'ⓐ, ⓑ, ⓒ'에서 알맞은 단어를 골라 쓰시오.

ⓐ ________ ⓑ ________ ⓒ ________

44 (B)의 우리말을 주어진 단어를 사용하여 바르게 영작하시오.

(jump high, can't, They)
➡ ____________________ like kangaroos, either.

[45~46] 다음 주어진 그림에 맞추어 괄호 안의 단어를 바른 순서로 배열하여 문장을 완성하시오.

45

(Kelly / orange juice / drink / would / like / to / some)
➡ ________________________________

★★★
46

(Mr. Brown / at all / so / fast / can't / and / understand / I / speaks)
➡ ________________________________

[47~49] 우리말에 맞게 주어진 단어를 이용하여 영작하시오.

47

Paul은 그녀에게 도움을 줄 것이다.
(give a hand / her)

➡ ________________________________

Note give a hand 도와주다

48

그녀는 유명한 배우인 것이 틀림없다.
(a famous / must / actress)

➡ ________________________________

Answer Keys p. 21~22

49

그는 아마도 나를 기억하지 않을지도 몰라.
(remember / me / may)

➡ ______________________

[50~53] 다음 괄호 안의 단어들을 바르게 배열하여 문장을 완성하시오.

50

(Sumi / go / there / didn't / want / to)

➡ ______________________

51

(We / stayed / weren't / late / last night / we / up / tired)

➡ ______________________ but ______________

52

(he / prize / got / first)

➡ ______________________

[53~55] 다음 주어진 문법을 사용하여 원하는 문장을 만들어 보세요.

53 'be able to + 동사'

➡ ______________________

54 'may', 'may not'
(2개 모두 사용, 다른 문장 만들기)

➡ ______________________
____

55 'must', 'must not'
(2개 모두 사용, 다른 문장 만들기)

➡ ______________________
____

Note

04

Chapter

명사와 관사

Point Check I

◆ **명사 :** 셀 수 있는 명사(보통명사, 집합명사)와 셀 수 없는 명사(물질명사, 추상명사, 고유명사)로 나뉠 수 있다.

1. 명사의 종류

분류	종류		부정관사 a/an
셀 수 있는 명사 (가산 명사)	보통명사	company, gate, lion, flower	단수에 사용
	집합명사	family, team	
셀 수 없는 명사 (불가산 명사)	물질명사	water, money, pepper	사용 불가능
	추상명사	love, friendship, dream	
	고유명사	Jane, Mina, Chinese, French	

- **A flower** smells sweet.
- **Water** is a very necessary resource.
- **Jane** is from **America**.

2. 명사의 복수형

(1) 명사의 규칙변화

명사의 종류	변화	단어
대부분의 명사	-s	computers, pencils, bottles
-s, -x, -ch, -sh로 끝나는 경우	-es	glasses, boxes, benches, bushes
'자음+o'	-es	potatoes
'자음+y'	y를 i로 고치고 -es	baby – babies, country – countries
-f / -fe 로 끝나는 경우	f/fe를 v로 고치고 -es	thief – thieves, life - lives

- There are **two computers** on the desk.
- **Three thieves** are running away.

(2) 명사의 불규칙변화

foot – feet **man – men** **mouse – mice** **child – children**

- **Those women** are the models.
- I believe the **children** are our future.

Lesson 4-1

명사

명사의 종류

- **명사**: 이름이 있는 사람, 사물, 동물 등을 말한다.
  ex) Susie, Tom, a cat, a book, Seoul, Korea
- **명사의 종류**: 셀 수 있는 명사에는 '보통명사'와 '집합명사'가 있고, 셀 수 없는 명사에는 '물질명사, 추상명사, 고유명사'가 있다.

◈ 명사의 종류

분류	종류		부정관사 a/an
셀 수 있는 명사 (가산 명사)	보통명사: 사람이나 사물, 동물을 일반적으로 나타내는 말	school, door, dog, cat	단수에 사용
	집합명사: 사람이나 사물, 동물의 집합을 나타내는 말	family, group, team	
셀 수 없는 명사 (불가산 명사)	물질명사: 정해진 일정한 형태가 없는 것을 나타내는 말	water, money, sugar, sand	사용 불가능
	추상명사: 사람의 생각으로 표현하는 개념이나 감정을 나타내는 말	health, happiness, hope	
	고유명사: • 사람, 사물, 동물, 나라 등이 가지는 각각의 이름을 나타내는 말 • 고유명사의 첫 글자는 대문자로 시작	Jane, Minsu, Korea, America	

Check up!

Answer Keys p. 23

A 다음 보기 의 명사들을 종류 별로 구분하시오.

보기

Mary, family, cow, Russia, Tim, coffee, salt, love, box, hate, pencil, nurse, cattle, cup, computer, John, movie, bread, actor, window.

Note
• cattle 소 떼

1 셀 수 있는 명사

(1) 보통명사: *cow, box, pencil, nurse, cup, computer, movie, actor, window*

(2) 집합명사: ______________________

2 셀 수 없는 명사

(1) 추상명사: __________ (2) 고유명사: __________

(3) 물질명사: __________

Lesson 4-2 명사의 복수형

- **명사의 단수**: 하나를 의미하는 '단수명사' 앞에는 'a'나 'an'이 붙는다.
- **명사의 복수**: 두 개 이상일 경우 '복수명사'라고 하며, 대부분은 뒤에 '–s'를 붙인다.

1. 명사의 규칙변화

명사의 종류	변화	단어
대부분의 명사	-s	ants, balls, books, sons, doors, cups
-s, -o, -x, -ch, -sh, 로 끝나는 경우	-es	-s : buses, glasses　-ch : watches, matches -o : tomatoes, potatoes -sh : bushes, dishes　-x : foxes, axes
'자음+y'	y를 i로 고치고 -es	baby – babies　candy – candies country – countries　lady – ladies story – stories　city – cities
-f / -fe 로 끝나는 경우	f/fe를 v로 고치고 -es	half – halves　leaf – leaves knife – knives　life – lives

예외: '모음 + o'와 '모음 + y'의 경우는 그냥 -s만 붙인다. – kilos, memos, pianos, photos, bamboos, radios, boys, keys, toys

2. 명사의 불규칙변화

woman - women	mouse – mice	child – children	ox – oxen
man - men	goose – geese	foot – feet	tooth – teeth

3. 단수/복수 명사의 형태가 같은 것

deer - deer　**fish - fish**　**sheep - sheep**

4. 쌍으로 이루어져 있는 명사: 복수 취급

glasses　**shoes**　**scissors**　**gloves**　**jeans**　**pants**

5. 숫자 + 단수명사: 숫자와 명사가 하이픈(-)으로 연결되어서 형용사처럼 명사 수식

- I got a **three-week** vacation.
- Mrs. Green is a **fifty-year-old** woman.

Grammar Plus +

쌍으로 이루어진 명사는 항상 복수 취급을 하며, 'a pair of'와 함께 사용하여 한 벌, 두 벌 등으로 표현할 수 있다.

a pair of socks 양말 한 켤레　　**two** pair**s** of socks 양말 두 켤레

Check up!

Answer Keys p. 23

A 다음 명사의 복수형을 쓰시오.

1 kite – *kites*	2 egg – ______
3 hat – ______	4 pen – ______
5 nail – ______	6 dish – ______
7 beach – ______	8 knife – ______
9 ox – ______	10 hero – ______
11 orange – ______	12 umbrella – ______
13 subject – ______	14 apple – ______
15 daughter – ______	16 lady – ______
17 roof – ______	18 window – ______
19 party – ______	20 friend – ______
21 tooth – ______	22 sandwich – ______
23 ring – ______	24 mouse – ______
25 man – ______	26 bath – ______
27 child – ______	28 diary – ______
29 cookie – ______	30 question – ______
31 flower – ______	32 shirt – ______
33 idea – ______	34 bottle – ______
35 belief – ______	36 monkey – ______
37 toy – ______	38 eraser – ______
39 boat – ______	40 mistake – ______

Check up!

Answer Keys p. 23

B 다음 명사의 복수형을 쓰시오.

1	sheep	– *sheep*	2	goose	– ______
3	number	– ______	4	leg	– ______
5	woman	– ______	6	foot	– ______
7	factory	– ______	8	leaf	– ______
9	sport	– ______	10	hour	– ______
11	cliff	– ______	12	fish	– ______
13	deer	– ______	14	problem	– ______
15	church	– ______	16	day	– ______
17	pants	– ______	18	duck	– ______
19	inch	– ______	20	branch	– ______
21	cake	– ______	22	scarf	– ______
23	season	– ______	24	girl	– ______
25	radio	– ______	26	dictionary	– ______
27	car	– ______	28	baby	– ______
29	wife	– ______	30	blouse	– ______
31	key	– ______	32	life	– ______
33	camera	– ______	34	Japanese	– ______
35	story	– ______	36	butterfly	– ______
37	elephant	– ______	38	actress	– ______
39	seed	– ______	40	report	– ______

Practice More I

Answer Keys p. 23~24

A

다음 명사 앞에 알맞은 부정관사(a, an)를 쓰시오. (쓸 수 없는 것은 'X' 하시오.)

1	___X___	water	2	_____	company
3	_____	gate	4	_____	dream
5	_____	information	6	_____	umbrella
7	_____	unicorn	8	_____	potato
9	_____	honest man	10	_____	lives
11	_____	sugar	12	_____	hour
13	_____	countries	14	_____	friendship

B

다음 명사의 복수형을 쓰시오.

1	company –	*companies*	2	hero –	__________
3	candy –	__________	4	dish –	__________
5	echo –	__________	6	key –	__________
7	class –	__________	8	mistake –	__________
9	story –	__________	10	bush –	__________
11	moth –	__________	12	letter –	__________
13	box –	__________	14	phone –	__________
15	life –	__________	16	safe –	__________
17	idea –	__________	18	toy –	__________
19	bath –	__________	20	song –	__________
21	church –	__________	22	tomato –	__________
23	cup –	__________	24	zoo –	__________
25	brush –	__________			

Practice More I

C 다음 명사의 복수형이 잘못 짝지어진 것을 고르시오.

1 ① friend – friends ② sheep – sheeps
③ fish – fish ④ fly – flies
⑤ hour – hours

2 ① tooth – teeth ② woman – women
③ child – childs ④ deer – deer
⑤ foot – feet

3 ① ox – oxes ② goose – geese
③ insect – insects ④ leaf – leaves
⑤ half – halves

4 ① lady – ladies ② city – cities
③ tomato – tomatoes ④ bush – bushes
⑤ clay – claies

D 다음 문장의 밑줄 친 부분을 바르게 고치시오.

1 I want to have some moneys. *money*

2 Chan and I bought some coffees. ________

3 Loves is the most valuable thing in the world. ________

4 She needs cup to drink water. ________

5 My grandfather has a wisdom. ________

6 There are lots of monkies in the zoo. ________

7 How many brushs do you have? ________

8 Please pass me the salts. ________

9 I have two daughter. ________

10 Daniel needed more axs. ________

Answer Keys p. 23~24

E 다음 우리말 해석에 맞게 문장의 빈칸을 채우시오.

1 나에게는 아들이 세 명 있다.
➡ I have ___*three sons*___.

2 그녀는 목이 마르기 때문에 마실 물을 원한다.
➡ Because she is thirsty, she needs ____________ to drink.

3 Alex는 양 세 마리와 케이크 두 개를 샀다.
➡ Alex bought ____________________________.

4 그들은 캔디 다섯 개와 샌드위치 세 개를 가져왔다.
➡ They brought ____________________________.

5 Ryan은 13세 소년이다.
➡ Ryan is a __________________ boy.

6 나는 구슬 다섯 개를, 너는 구슬 열 개를 가지고 있다.
➡ I have ______________ and you have ______________.

7 우리는 지금 핫도그 열 개도 먹을 수 있을 것 같다.
➡ We might eat ______________ now.

8 우리 우정 변치 말자.
➡ Let's hold on to our ______________ forever.

9 그녀는 약간의 커피를 마시고 싶어한다.
➡ She wants to drink some ______________.

10 그들은 우리에게 막대사탕 두 개를 주었다.
➡ They gave us ______________.

Note
- hold on ~을 유지하다
- lollipop 막대사탕

Point Check Ⅱ

◆ **명사의 수량 표현 :** 셀 수 있는 명사는 한 개, 두 개 등으로 셀 수 있지만 셀 수 없는 명사는 담는 용기로 양을 표현한다.

◆ **명사의 소유격 :** 명사 뒤에 「's / '」 또는 'of + 명사'의 형태로 '~의' 뜻을 나타낸다.

1. 명사의 수량 표현

	조금, 약간	많은	거의 없는
셀 수 없는 명사의 수량	a little	much	little
셀 수 있는 명사의 수량	a few	many	few
모두 사용하는 수량	some	a lot of, lots of, plenty of	–

(1) 셀 수 없는 명사는 '조금' 또는 '많은'이라는 뜻으로 해석되어도 셀 수 없기 때문에 항상 단수 취급한다.

There is **a little** water in the bottle.

(2) '거의 없는'은 결국 조금이라도 있다는 뜻이므로 복수 취급한다.

There are **few** pencils in my pencil case.

2. 셀 수 없는 명사의 수량 표현

단수	복수	명사
a piece of	two (three…) pieces of	bread, cake, cheese, cloth, paper, advice
a bottle of	two (three…) bottles of	beer, ink, juice, milk
a cup of	two (three…) cups of	coffee, tea
a glass of	two (three…) glasses of	water, milk, juice

3. 명사의 소유격

(1) **생명체의 소유격: 's 또는 '를 붙인다.**

① 's를 붙이는 경우: 대부분의 명사

② '를 붙이는 경우: s로 끝나는 복수 명사

(2) **무생물체의 소유격: of + 명사**

4. 명사의 동격: ',(콤마)'로 표시해준다.

• This is **my coach, Mr. Smith.**

Lesson 4-3

주의해야 할 명사의 수량

• 셀 수 있는 명사와 셀 수 없는 명사에 대해 많거나 적은 수량을 나타낼 수 있다.

1. 명사의 수량 표현

	조금, 약간	많은	거의 없는
셀 수 없는 명사 수량	a little	much	little
셀 수 있는 명사 수량	a few	many	few

(1) 셀 수 없는 명사
- Jane doesn't have **much** money.
- There is **a little** scratch in this furniture.
- There is **little** water in my bottle.

(2) 셀 수 있는 명사
- Tom has **many** friends.
- There are **a few** candies in his pocket.
- There are **few** girls in the classrom.

2. 셀 수 없는 명사와 셀 수 있는 명사에 모두 사용하는 수량 표현

(1) some: 조금, 약간
- My little brother has **some** apples. **(= a few)**
- We have **some** orange juice. **(= a little)**

(2) a lot of, lots of, plenty of: 아주 많은
- There are **a lot of** bananas in the basket. **(= many)**
- There is **lots of** water in my bucket. **(= much)**

Check up!

Answer Keys p. 24

A 다음 괄호 안에서 알맞은 말을 고르시오.

1 The rich man has (much / many) money.

2 There is (many / much) time to study.

3 There are (a little / a few) things in the box.

4 Cindy has (a few / a little) hope.

5 There was (little / few) chance of success.

6 He has (a few / a little) sugar in his jar.

7 We have (little / few) milk to drink.

Check up!

Answer Keys p. 24

B 다음 괄호 안의 우리말을 참고하여 빈칸에 들어갈 알맞은 말을 보기에 골라 쓰시오.

보기
some   much   any   a lot of   many

1 You always have ___*much*___ (많은) water in your bottle.

2 Jack and I have __________ (약간) money to buy it.

3 Jessy prepared __________ (매우 많은) candies and I prepared __________ (약간) cookies.

4 My mother made __________ (많은) paper flowers for us.

5 They got __________ (조금) bread from their neighbors.

6 In the autumn, __________ (매우 많은) leaves fall from the trees.

7 He didn't bring __________ (조금) gifts to the concert.

C 다음 문장에서 명사의 수량 표현과 복수형이 잘못된 것을 찾아 바르게 고치시오.

1 We have much friends around us.
➡ ___*much friends*___ ➡ ___*many friends*___

2 She makes any candy for her children.
➡ __________ ➡ __________

3 The movie star has a lot of fan all over the world.
➡ __________ ➡ __________

4 Any thieves tried to escape the jail.
➡ __________ ➡ __________

5 I got many information about the test from my seniors.
➡ __________ ➡ __________

Note
- chance 기회
- paper flower 종이꽃
- all over the world 전 세계에
- escape 탈출하다
- senior 선배, 상급생
- prepared 준비했다

Lesson

4-4 셀 수 없는 명사의 수량 표현

• 셀 수 없는 명사는 뚜렷한 모양이 없거나 정확히 수를 셀 수 없기 때문에 '한 개, 두 개' 등으로 세지 못한다. 그래서 이들을 담는 용기를 이용하여 양을 표시한다.

단수	복수 표현	명사
a piece of	two (three…) pieces of	bread, cheese, cloth, paper, advice
a bottle of	two (three…) bottles of	beer, ink, juice, milk
a cup of	two (three…) cups of	coffee, tea
a glass of	two (three…) glasses of	water, milk, juice
a slice of	two (three…) slices of	bread, cheese, meat, pizza
a pound of	two (three…) pounds of	sugar, meat, beef, pork
a bar of	two (three…) bars of	soap, chocolate
a bowl of	two (three…) bowls of	soup, rice
a sheet of	two (three…) sheets of	paper
a loaf of	two (three…) loaves of	bread
a spoonful of	two (three…) spoonfuls of	sugar, salt

• Tom bought **a loaf of** bread.
• We ordered **two glasses of** grape juice.

Check up!

Answer Keys p. 24

A **우리말 해석에 맞게 빈칸에 알맞은 말을 쓰시오.**

1 나에게 소금 두 스푼이 필요하다.
= I need _*two spoonfuls of*_ salt.

2 빵 두 조각과 커피 한 잔을 사 와.
= You buy ______________ bread and ______________ coffee.

3 Samuel에게 피자 한 조각을 전해 주세요.
= Please give Samuel ______________ pizza.

4 그는 와인 두 병과 초콜릿 한 개를 샀다.
= He bought ______________ wine and ______________ chocolate.

5 나에게 종이 세 장이 필요해.
= I need ______________ paper.

Lesson

4-5 명사의 소유격

• **명사의 소유격:** 명사 뒤에 's 또는 of + 명사를 사용하여 '~의'라는 소유의 의미를 나타낸다.
※ **'**는 apostrophe라고 한다.

1. 사람 또는 동물 등 생명체의 소유격: 's 또는 '로 표현

's를 하는 경우	• 대부분 명사의 소유격을 표현할 때는 명사 뒤에 's를 붙인다. Jane's wish a frog's life cycle children's dream women's average weight
'를 하는 경우	• s로 끝나는 복수 명사 Seoul Girls' Middle School boys' restroom
	• s로 끝나는 단수 명사, 신의 이름, 유명 인물의 이름 a princess' shoes Achilles' heel Socrates' achievement
예외	※ 일반적인 사람 이름의 경우에는 's를 붙인다. Thomas's novels Jobs's Apple

2. 무생물체의 소유격: of + 명사

• the legs **of a table**
• the quality **of the furniture**

3. 시간, 거리, 가격, 무게: 's나 '를 붙인다.

• today**'s** news [시간]
• 20 kilometers**'** distance [거리]
• one million dollars**'** worth [가격]
• a pound**'s** weight [무게]

Check up!

Answer Keys p. 24

A 다음에서 알맞은 위치에 '(apostrophe)를 넣으시오.

1 Jim's dream
2 a dogs life span.
3 a womans bathroom
4 a kings crown
5 Platos theory
6 Edisons invention
7 mens average height
8 a teachers ring
9 Socrates words
10 Venus love

Check up!

Answer Keys p. 24

B 다음 빈칸에서 알맞은 말을 고르시오.

1 There's much news in (todays' / today's) paper.

2 (The legs of the chair / Chair's legs) are green.

3 (The title of the novel / The novel's title) is "The Black House."

4 (Lucas's wife / Wife of Lucas) is Helen.

5 I want to know (tomorrow's weather / weather of tomorrow).

6 One of the (wheels of the cart / the cart's wheels) is broken.

7 Jenny wonders how (wings of a bird / a bird's wings) move up and down.

8 We are so excited about (today's news / news of today).

9 The picture has (ten million dollars' / ten million dollars of) worth.

10 It is so important the (quality of the furniture / furniture's quality).

Lesson

4-6 명사의 동격

• **명사의 동격:** 명사나 대명사를 보충 설명하기 위하여 콤마(,)와 다른 명사(구)를 쓰는 것을 말한다.

• This is my litte **sister, Jane.**
(my sister = Jane)

• **Ms. Brown, the best teacher in my school,** talked to me.

Check up!

Answer Keys p. 25

A 다음 문장에서 명사의 동격을 찾아 밑줄을 치시오.

1 Chloe, <u>my niece</u>, is very beautiful.

2 This is my husband, John.

3 Mrs. White, the tallest woman in our office, laughed at me.

4 I think Helen, my best friend, can solve the problem.

5 They are Bob and Linda, a recently married couple.

6 This film, Harry Potter, is so exciting.

7 I hate that girl, Jessica.

8 I take a picture of Daniel, the most famous actor in Britain.

9 Please show me that paper, Amy's letter.

10 I love this flower, a rose.

B 다음 문장을 우리말로 바르게 옮겨 쓰시오.

1 Mary, my best friend, will move to Seoul next month.
➡ *나의 가장 친한 친구인 Mary는 다음 달에 서울로 이사를 간다*.

2 The girl was my sister, Emily that you met yesterday.
➡ ______________________.

3 Mrs. Green, my history teacher, always cheers me up.
➡ ______________________.

4 Do you think they, Isabella and Jackson, are your good friends?
➡ ______________________?

5 Will you come to my party with your sister, Jessy?
➡ ______________________?

Note

• **laugh at** ~을 비웃다
• **just married** 갓 결혼한
• **take a picture** 사진을 찍다
• **move to~** ~로 이사가다
• **cheer ~ up** ~을 격려하다, 기분 좋게 하다

Practice More II

Answer Keys p. 25

A 다음 문장의 괄호 안에서 알맞은 것을 고르시오.

1 Linda has ((many) / much) friends.

2 I need (a few / a little) time to study.

3 John gives (many / much) love to his daughter.

4 There is (little / few) pepper on the table.

5 He drinks too (much / many) coffee.

6 There are (few / little) minutes for Lisa to finish her her homework.

7 He sent her (a few / a little) books.

8 We have (few / little) questions about the menu.

9 I ate too (many / much) bread.

10 Andrew has (a few / a little) pens in his bag.

B 다음 우리말 해석에 맞게 빈칸을 채우시오.

1 나는 우리 팀을 위해 차 세 잔을 샀다.
= I bought ___*three cups of*___ tea for our team.

2 아침마다 한 스푼의 올리브 오일을 먹는 것은 유익하다.
= It is useful to drink ______________ olive oil every morning.

3 Seon은 수학 시험에 대해서 정보 두 가지를 갖고 있다.
= Seon has ______________ information about the math test.

4 나는 만날 친구가 거의 없다.
= I have __________ friends to meet.

5 그녀는 치즈 세 조각과 고기 2파운드를 구입했다.
= She bought ______________ cheese and ______________ meat.

6 진열장 안에 약 네 병이 있다.
= There are ______________ medicine in the cabinet.

7 배가 고파서 그는 피자 네 조각을 먹었다.
= He ate ______________ pizza because he was hungry.

8 나의 동생 Lisa는 빨간 치마를 입고 있다.
= ________________, Lisa, is wearing a red skirt.

9 우리에게는 그녀를 기다릴 시간이 거의 없다.
= We have ___________ time to wait for her.

10 나는 한국에서 가장 유명한 배우 중 한 명인 Mr. Kim의 사인을 받았다.
= I got Mr. Kim's autograph, ____________________________.

C 다음 문장에서 어법상 어색한 것을 찾아 바르게 고치시오.

1 There are many sheeps in the farm.
sheeps ➡ *sheep*

2 Julia drinks eight glasses of waters a day.
________________ ➡ ________________

3 I go to the girl's shoes store.
________________ ➡ ________________

4 They bring three loafs of bread.
________________ ➡ ________________

5 The desk's legs are green.
________________ ➡ ________________

6 That car is your's.
________________ ➡ ________________

7 He bought a pair of glove.
________________ ➡ ________________

8 Give me three piece of paper.
________________ ➡ ________________

9 Shes' beautiful.
________________ ➡ ________________

10 I know name of the boy.
________________ ➡ ________________

Answer Keys p. 25

서술형 연습 **D** **다음 주어진 단어를 이용하여 우리말에 맞게 영작하시오.**

1 Linda는 주스 두 잔을 주문했다.
(two, juice, Linda, glasses of, ordered)
➡ *Linda ordered two glasses of juice.*

2 그녀는 Mason의 책을 가져왔다. (book, Mason's, brought, she)
➡ ______________________

3 나는 오늘 뉴스를 볼 수 없었다. (news, I, see, today's, couldn't)
➡ ______________________

4 Dorothy는 딸의 가방과 안경을 가져왔다.
(glasses, Dorothy, her daughter's, and, brought, bags)
➡ ______________________

5 그 방에는 읽을 책이 별로 없다.
(in the room, to read, there, few, are, books)
➡ ______________________

6 저 탁자의 다리는 금속으로 만들어졌다.
(are made from, the table, metal, legs, of, the)
➡ ______________________

E **다음 문장을 우리말로 바르게 옮겨 쓰시오.**

1 Today's weather is so hot.
➡ 오늘의 날씨는 아주 덥다.

2 John is looking for his socks.
➡ ______________________

3 We should take care of children's health.
➡ ______________________

4 I don't like the color of the shirts.
➡ ______________________

Point Check Ⅲ

◆ **부정관사 a/an:** 단수 명사 앞에 붙어 '하나'의 의미 외에 '~마다', '종족 전체'를 나타낼 때도 사용한다.

◆ **정관사 the:** 단수/복수 명사에 모두 사용하며, 특정한 것이나 반복적인 것을 가리킬 때 사용한다.

1. 부정관사 a/an

자음으로 시작하는 명사 앞 'a'	모음으로 시작하는 명사 앞 'an'
She has a pink ribbon. ※ 철자는 모음이지만 발음이 자음으로 시작하는 단어의 경우 'a'를 사용한다. You should wear a uniform.	He is not an engineer. ※ 철자는 자음이지만 발음이 모음으로 시작하는 단어의 경우 'an'을 사용한다. We only have an hour left.

2. 'a/an'의 의미

one (하나)	A year has twelve months.
per (~마다)	I go to art class twice a week.
종족 전체 대표	A pig is a useful animal.

3. 'the'의 쓰임

앞에 언급된 명사가 반복될 때	We have a dog. The dog is so cute.
상황상 서로가 무엇을 가리키는지 알고 있을 때	Can you turn on the light?
가리키는 대상이 정확할 때	The cookie on the table is for you.
유일한 것일 때	The sun rises in the east.
서수, 최상급 앞에 쓰일 때	She is the tallest girl in the class.
악기 이름 앞에 쓰일 때	We can play the piano.
종족 전체를 대표할 때	The polar bear lives in the Arctic.

4. 'the'가 쓰이지 않는 경우

(1) 식사, 운동, 질병 앞에 쓰일 때
- Neil and his friends are playing **baseball**.

(2) 건물, 기구가 본래 목적으로 쓰일 때
- go to **church**.
- go to **bed**

Lesson 4-7

관사

부정관사 a/an

• a / an : '하나'의 뜻을 가졌으며 셀 수 있는 단수 명사 앞에 붙는다.
첫 소리가 자음일 때 'a'를, 모음일 때 'an'을 붙인다.

1. 부정관사 a/an의 쓰임

첫 소리가 자음일 경우	첫 소리가 모음일 경우
(1) a + 명사 a pen, a house, a teacher	(1) an + 명사 an apple, an engineer, an athlete
(2) a + 형용사 + 명사 a red bean, a new tie	(2) an + 형용사 + 명사 an old lady, an ugly doll
※ 철자는 모음이지만 발음이 자음인 경우에도 a를 사용한다. a uniform, a universe	※ 철자는 자음이지만 발음이 모음인 경우에는 an을 사용한다. an hour, an honest man

2. 'a/an'

(1) 'one (하나)'
An hour is 60 minutes. **(= one)**

(2) 'per (~마다)'
Tom eats cake three times **a** month. **(= per)**

(3) 종족 전체 대표
A dog is a loyal animal. **(dog 전체를 의미)**

Check up!

Answer Keys p. 25

A 다음 괄호 안에서 알맞은 것을 고르시오.

1 Leo has (a / an) brother.
2 There is (an / a) orange on the table.
3 It will arrive in (an / a) hour.
4 He is (an / a) great musician.
5 What (an / a) lovely girl she is!
6 You should wear (a / an) uniform here.
7 I want to be (an / a) famous athlete.
8 Jejudo is (an / a) island in Korea.

Lesson

4-8 정관사 the

• the : 특정한 것 또는 이미 언급하였거나 알고 있는 명사를 가리킬 때 쓴다.
단수/복수 명사에 모두 사용할 수 있다.

1. 정관사 the의 사용

(1) 앞에 언급된 명사가 반복될 때
I have a watch. **The watch** is new.

(2) 상황상 서로가 무엇을 가리키는지 알고 있을 때
Would you please close **the door**?

(3) 구나 절에 의해 수식을 받아 가리키는 대상이 정확할 때
The black pen on the desk is yours.

(4) 유일한 것일 때
The sun goes down in the west.

(5) 서수, 최상급 앞에 쓰일 때
Their company is on **the fifth** floor of that building.

(6) 악기 이름 앞에 쓰일 때
He can play **the drums** very well.

(7) 종족 전체를 대표할 때
The ostrich cannot fly.

Check up!

Answer Keys p. 25

A **다음 빈칸에 a, an, the 중 알맞은 말을 골라 채우시오.**

1 Maria can play ___*the*___ piano.

2 Look at ________ girl! She is so pretty.

3 I want to eat ________ apricot.

4 The earth moves around ________ sun.

5 I'm ________ tallest person in our club.

6 She has ________ brother and three sisters.

7 They work eight hours ________ day.

8 I want to meet ________ boy in the picture.

9 A woman is crying. ________ woman must be sad.

10 Helen should get on ________ last train.

11 There are 24 hours in ________ day, and 7 days in ________ week.

Lesson 4-9 'the'가 쓰이지 않는 경우

• the : 명사 앞에 붙어서 명사의 의미를 한정 짓는 역할을 하는 'the'를 사용하지 않는 몇 가지 경우가 있다.

1. 식사, 운동, 질병 앞에 쓰일 때
• I don't have breakfast every day.
• His grandfather had cancer.

2. 건물, 기구가 본래 목적으로 쓰일 때
• go to church
• go to bed
• go to school
※ 'go to the school'은 공부하러 학교에 가는 것이 아니라 다른 목적으로 학교에 간 상황을 말한다.
Jane and Maria go to the school to play badminton.

Grammar Plus +

관사를 쓰지 않는 경우
- 물질명사와 추상명사 앞: coffee, tea, art, life
- 'by + 교통수단' : by train, by bus
- 사람 이름, 소유격 앞: Jack, my teacher

Check up!

Answer Keys p. 26

A 다음 빈칸에 정관사 the가 필요하면 쓰고, 필요하지 않으면 X 표시를 하시오.

1 He goes to office by ___X___ bus.
2 She got an okay score on ________ test.
3 He usually plays ________ guitar for his mother.
4 My sister doesn't have ________ dinner every day.
5 Selena goes to ________ school to meet her brother.
6 I go to ________ gym to exercise.
7 I want to learn how to play ________ flute.
8 Jane contacted him by ________ email.
9 Will you close ________ blinds, please?
10 You should go to ________ bed early.
11 My grandmother goes to the park by ________ bicycle.
12 Sam lives on ________ fifth floor.
13 Mark and I wear ________ same pants today.
14 We often play ________ baseball.
15 They go to ________ church on Sundays.

Practice More Ⅲ

A 다음 빈칸에 알맞은 말을 쓰시오.

1 Put your homework on ___the___ table.

2 _______ hour is 60 minutes.

3 I think you are _______ best driver in the company.

4 Tina goes hiking twice _______ month.

5 I started to play _______ drum last week.

6 There is _______ old lady. She was a nurse 30 years ago.

7 Alex wears _______ red shirt. I like _______ shirt.

8 John, can you turn off _______ light? I have to sleep now.

9 Linda goes to _______ hospital to meet Alex.

10 There are eight planets in _______ solar system.

B 다음 문장의 밑줄 친 부분을 바르게 고치시오.

1 There is the Eiffel Tower in a France. ___France___

2 I go to the school to study. _______________

3 John is first person to come in. _______________

4 He is looking for old man wearing black hat. _______________

5 I want to eat a apple. _______________

6 I know a girl. A girl is a popular singer. _______________

7 A chair was painted black. _______________

8 Christina can play a piano. _______________

9 She's a smartest girl in our class. _______________

10 A boys are dancing on the street. _______________

Answer Keys p. 26

C 다음 문장의 빈칸에 a/an이나 the 중 알맞은 것을 쓰고, 필요 없는 곳에는 X 표시를 하시오.

1 I got ___an___ idea about what to do.

2 We had ________ lunch in the restaurant.

3 My sister will enter ________ middle school next year.

4 Could you pass me ________ pepper?

5 I went to ________ school again to bring my textbook.

6 The baby sleeps 12 hours ________ day.

7 They got off ________ last subway.

8 Lina can play ________ piano and ________ tennis.

9 ________ month has 30 days.

10 My grandmother has ________ lung cancer.

11 I know ________ girl. ________ girl lived next door to us.

12 Look at ________ building! It looks like a dragon.

13 We don't have to go to ________ bed early tonight.

14 Kate and I wore ________ same hat today.

15 ________ penguin can swim well.

Practice More Ⅲ

서술형 연습 **D** 다음 우리말 해석에 맞게 주어진 단어를 이용하여 문장을 완성하시오.

1 서울은 한국의 수도다. (is, of, Seoul, the, Korea, capital)
➡ *Seoul is the capital of Korea.*

2 Sally는 초등학생이다.
(is, Sally, elementary school student, an)
➡ ______________________

3 Andrew는 우리 반에서 가장 축구를 잘 한다.
(in our class, is, best, soccer player, Andrew, the)
➡ ______________________

4 내 남동생은 플루트 연주를 잘 한다.
(flute, my brother, is good at, playing, the)
➡ ______________________

Note
• be good at ~을 잘하다

5 그 집에 있는 방들은 크다. (the, big, are, in the house, rooms)
➡ ______________________

E 다음을 우리말로 해석하시오.

1 I am the only child in my family.
➡ *나는 외동이다.*

2 Our office is on the fourth floor in the building.
➡ ______________________

3 Tom always eats breakfast every morning.
➡ ______________________

4 I went to church to give flowers to my girlfriend.
➡ ______________________

5 Everyone knows that the earth is round.
➡ ______________________

중간 기말고사 예상문제

Answer Keys p. 26

내신 최다 출제 유형

01 다음 밑줄 친 부분 중 어법상 올바른 것을 고르시오. [출제 예상 80%]

① Here is a pretty dresses.
② My mother and aunt are sister.
③ Harry needs a MP3 player.
④ Insu always borrows an eraser.
⑤ I'd like to buy a pencils.

02 다음 밑줄 친 부분 중 어법상 바르게 쓰인 것 두 개를 고르시오. [출제 예상 90%]

① She has many water in her glass.
② I drink much milk every morning.
③ Are there much animals and plants?
④ There are a lot of people in the hall.
⑤ The store has many paper.

03 다음 중 어법상 표현이 올바르지 않은 것을 모두 고르시오. [출제 예상 95%]

① Would you like some more tea?
② I got some beautiful postcards from Paris.
③ Everybody can answer the questions.
④ Is there any restaurants near here?
⑤ There isn't not salt in this food.

04 다음 밑줄 친 복수명사가 바르지 않은 것을 고르시오. [출제 예상 80%]

① The farmer bought two sheeps.
② There is some juice in the bottle.
③ I have much money to buy a car.
④ He has a lot of books.
⑤ There are many women in the market.

05 다음 빈칸에 알맞은 것을 모두 고르시오. [출제 예상 80%]

There are __________ in the room.

① the wooden table ② a window
③ young men ④ lots of children
⑤ an old lady

06 다음 문장 중 빈칸에 들어갈 a(n)의 뜻이 다른 하나를 고르시오. [출제 예상 80%]

① The company brought __________ bunch of bananas.
② They are having __________ great time.
③ __________ dog is friendly.
④ There is __________ cup of tea on the table.
⑤ Sam has __________ sister and two brothers.

07 다음 문장 중 빈칸에 the가 들어갈 수 없는 것을 고르시오. [출제 예상 95%]

① __________ earth goes around the sun.
② __________ milk in the bottle is just for me.
③ I can play __________ the cello.
④ Mickey and Jack play __________ soccer.
⑤ She is in __________ kitchen.

중간 기말고사 **예상문제**

[01~05] 다음 중 명사의 복수형이 잘못된 것을 고르시오.

01 ① bus – buses ② photo – photoes ③ church – churches ④ woman – women ⑤ tooth – teeth

02 ① girl – girls ② half – halves ③ boy – boys ④ belief – believes ⑤ cliff – cliffs

03 ① wolf – wolves ② box – boxes ③ goose – gooses ④ leaf – leaves ⑤ foot – feet

04 ① monkey – monkeies ② kite – kites ③ family – families ④ fish – fish ⑤ ant – ants

05 ① doll – dolls ② bag – bags ③ knife – knives ④ wife – wives ⑤ deer – deers

[06~08] 다음 문장의 빈칸에 알맞지 않은 것을 고르시오.

06

> Harry has many __________.

① dolls ② notebooks ③ toy cars ④ milk ⑤ tomatoes

07

> We bought a pair of __________.

① shoes ② pants ③ jeans ④ socks ⑤ skirts

08

> They want to take a __________.

① piece of cake ② sheet of blanket ③ pound of meat ④ loaves of bread ⑤ slice of cheese

[09~10] 다음 문장 중 밑줄 친 부분이 어법상 올바른 것을 고르시오.

09
① People are sitting on the benchs.
② Her foots are very small.
③ I learned about the war heros.
④ My mom bought some potatoes.
⑤ Six gooses are flying in the sky.

Answer Keys p. 27~28

10 ① The rich has a lot of <u>moneys</u>.
② My friend, Lisa brought three <u>puppys</u>.
③ I am worried about their <u>health</u>.
④ You drank a lot of <u>waters</u> today.
⑤ There are five heavy <u>boxs</u>.

[11~12] 다음 중 밑줄 친 관사의 쓰임이 바르지 <u>않은</u> 것을 고르시오.

11 ① The man has <u>an</u> idea about that.
② It's <u>a</u> rainy day.
③ There is <u>an</u> university in this city.
④ I saw <u>a</u> cute girl in the bus.
⑤ It's <u>an</u> important part for our holiday.

12 ① I am practicing <u>the</u> piano in my room.
② We put some flowers on <u>the</u> table.
③ Can I open <u>the</u> window?
④ They traveled around <u>the</u> world.
⑤ John likes to play <u>the</u> soccer.

[13~14] 다음 문장의 빈칸에 알맞지 <u>않은</u> 것을 고르시오.

★★★
13

That is an ________.

① apple ② orange
③ umbrella ④ honest boy
⑤ uniform

14

We are playing ________.

① baseball ② tennis
③ table tennis ④ flute
⑤ hockey

[15~16] 다음 문장 중 문법적으로 <u>틀린</u> 것을 고르시오.

15 ① She is 15 years old.
② The river is 10 kilometers long.
③ The hole is 30 feets deep.
④ The mountain is 3,000 meters high.
⑤ Jasmine is 165 centimeters tall.

16 ① Jack wants to buy a pair of shoes.
② Peter gave me a bunches of roses.
③ She sent him a pair of gloves.
④ There are beggars on the street.
⑤ Biology is my favorite subject.

[17~18] 다음 주어진 문장의 빈칸에 공통으로 들어갈 말을 고르시오.

17

A I need to buy ________ of bread. What about you?
B I want to buy ________ of cheese.

① a piece ② a bowl
③ a glass ④ a cup
⑤ a bottle

18

- Jack bought __________ of meat.
- I have to sell __________ of sugar.

① a bunch ② a bar ③ a pound
④ a sheet ⑤ a cup

[19~20] 다음 문장의 밑줄 친 부분 중 생략이 불가능 한 것을 고르시오. (답이 여러개 일 수 있음)

★★★
19 ① This is Jane's house.
② Suzie has been at her parents' place.
③ I went to the dentist's office.
④ I like to read Emily Bronte's books.
⑤ This book is my father's book.

20 ① Joe works at Mark's grocery store.
② Mary had her sister's birthday party.
③ My dad and I dropped by a barbershop.
④ That building is Jennifer's house.
⑤ I want to work at Jane's bakery.

[21~22] 다음 문장 중 문법적으로 틀린 것을 고르시오.

21 ① There are much stars in the night sky.
② There is plenty of water in the river.
③ There is some snow on the roof.
④ I didn't drink any milk.
⑤ She always drinks some coffee.

22 ① My sister can play the piano very well.
② I saw an elephant at the zoo.
③ The woman has two daughters.
④ Mr. Rich has many energy.
⑤ They play basketball after school.

[23~25] 다음 문장 중 문법적으로 올바른 것을 모두 고르시오.

★★★
23 ① We saved a lot of money.
② Please give me some a pound of beef.
③ There is much teas on the shelf.
④ This food are very bad.
⑤ They gave some money to an old lady.

24 ① He doesn't have some comic books.
② We forgot that we had many homework.
③ We saw a great deal of fish in the river.
④ My little brother brushes his teeth well.
⑤ This is my friend' favorite pen.

25 ① She is wearing a pair of earrings.
② They didn't know where the books is.
③ We have any water.
④ We looked at the geese flew away.
⑤ You've got the emails.

Answer Keys p. 27~28

[26~27] 다음 문장 중 밑줄 친 부분이 틀린 것을 고르시오.

26 ① It's good to know the friends's dreams.
② Those men's arms are strong.
③ The women's thoughts are difficult for laymen to understand.
④ Jessy is reading today's news.
⑤ Those are Paul's sticks.

27 ① I picked up some leaves.
② He saved much oil.
③ Cut the bread in halfs.
④ There are many cars on the road.
⑤ Mom washes the dishes.

28 ① We watched a monkeys eating bananas.
② There is much tomato juice.
③ My aunt has three babies.
④ John always drinks two bottles of milk.
⑤ She puts three teaspoons of sugar in her tea.

[29~31] 다음 문장 중 문법적으로 올바른 것을 고르시오.

29 ① Suzie has a little bread.
② I have a little friends.
③ We want to drink any milk.
④ Sally has much toy cars.
⑤ I'm collecting much stamps.

30 ① We should listen to the doctors's advice.
② I am so proud of his's success.
③ Jenny understands his behavior.
④ Mom wanted to be teachers.
⑤ He go to the hraidresser's.

31 ① Lucy sing songs very well.
② They play the hockey on the ice.
③ I learn to speak a Chinese.
④ Jack's sister fought with his.
⑤ I saw some birds flying in the sky.

★★★
32 다음 문장 중 빈칸에 the가 필요 없는 것을 고르시오.

① She was ________ first girl to come.
② ________ laptop is not mine.
③ Mrs. Lee plays ________ piano very well.
④ Can I close ________ door?
⑤ Sam and Jerry go to school by ________ subway.

33 다음 문장의 밑줄 친 부분과 바꿔 쓸 수 있는 것으로 짝지어진 것을 고르시오.

> • I need a lot of money to buy a sports car.
> • After party, he washed lots of dishes for me.

① some – many　② many – much
③ much – many　④ lots of – any
⑤ some – any

중간 기말고사 예상문제

34 다음 우리말에 맞게 빈칸에 들어갈 알맞은 것끼리 짝지어진 것을 고르시오.

> ________ students like reading books ________ hard.

① Some – a few　② Some – a little
③ Any – few　④ Some – many
⑤ Any – Some

◇◇◇◇◇◇◇◇◇◇◇ **서술형 평가** ◇◇◇◇◇◇◇◇◇◇◇

[35~37] 다음 문장의 빈칸에 우리말에 맞도록 알맞은 단어를 써 넣으시오.

35

> Emily와 나는 한 나이 든 여성분을 도와드렸다.

➡ Emily and I helped ________.

36

> 우리는 아침 식사 전에 물 한 잔을 마신다.

➡ We drink ________ before breakfast.

37

> 나와 Phillip은 일주일에 한 번 영화를 본다.

➡ Phillip and I watch movies ________.

[38~39] 다음 그림을 보고 상황에 맞게 주어진 단어를 배열하여 문장을 완성하시오.

38

(She / a bowl of / eats / mushroom soup / morning / every)

➡ ________

39

(They / drink / pizza / black tea / eat / two pieces of / two cups of / and)

➡ ________

[40~41] 다음 주어진 단어들을 이용하여 우리말에 맞게 영작하시오.

★★★
40

> 그들은 그것의 중요성을 강조하였다.
> (They / importance / it / of / the / emphasized)

➡ ________

Answer Keys p. 27~28

41

Jane과 나는 택시를 타고 집에 갔다.
(Jane / went / and / I / by taxi / home)

➡ ______________________

[42~43] 다음 글을 읽고 물음에 답하시오.

Jessy is ⓐ a Australian. She likes Korean food so much.
I am good at cooking, so I cook for her ⓑ twice a week.
She especially likes Korean cucumber cold soup called *Ohyinanguk*.
To Make it, we need ⓒ any chopped cucumber, (A) 물 한 병, ⓓ some ice, sugar, and salt.
If you like sour food, add ⓔ a spoonful of vinegar.

★★★

42 윗 글의 ⓐ~ⓔ에서 어법상 틀린 것을 찾아 바르게 고쳐 쓰시오.

➡ ______________________

____

43 윗글 (A)의 단어를 영어로 쓰시오.

➡ ______________________

44 Where does Jessy come from?

➡ ______________________

★★★

45 다음 우리말과 뜻이 같도록 빈칸에 알맞은 단어를 쓰시오.

Joe 삼촌은 농장에 오리 다섯 마리, 양 세 마리, 그리고 젖소 열 마리를 가지고 계신다. 그는 매달 치즈 10파운드와 우유 30병을 생산한다.

➡ Uncle Joe has five ducks, __________, and ten cows.
He produces ______________ cheese and thirty bottles of __________ every month.

[46~47] 다음 중 어법상 어색한 부분을 찾아 문장을 다시 쓰시오.

★★★

46 Jennifer washes her hands, tooths and foots before dinner.

➡ ______________________

____

★★★

47 I bought two pack of milk, three bottle of orange juice, and two bunch of grapes.

➡ ______________________

____

Note

05

Chapter
대명사

Point Check I

◆ **대명사 :** 명사를 대신하여 사용하는 말로 인칭대명사, 소유대명사, 재귀대명사가 있다.

1. 대명사의 종류

수	인칭	인칭대명사			소유대명사	재귀대명사
		주격	소유격	목적격		
단수	1인칭	I	my	me	mine	myself
	2인칭	you	your	you	yours	yourself
	3인칭	he	his	him	his	himself
		she	her	her	hers	herself
		it	its	it	–	itself
복수	1인칭	we	our	us	ours	ourselves
	2인칭	you	your	you	yours	yourselves
	3인칭	they	their	them	theirs	themselves

2. 비인칭 주어 'it' : '그것'이라고 해석하지 않는다.

- It is five o'clock. [시간]
- It is December 24th. [날짜]
- It is Sunday. [요일]
- It is cloudy today. [날씨]
- It is too far from here. [거리]
- It is spring. [계절]

3. 지시대명사

(1) this / these

- 가까운 곳에 있는 것을 가리킬 때

  This is an orange.

  These are oranges.

- 소개하거나 전화상에서 사람을 말할 때

  This is my friend, Tom.

  Hello, **this** is Amy. Can I speak to Ron?

(2) that/those : **먼 곳에 있는 것을 가리킬 때**

- **That** is a new book.
- **Those** are new books.

Lesson 5-1

대명사의 종류

- **대명사**: 명사를 대신해서 사용하는 말이다.
- **인칭대명사는(I, you, we, they, he, she, it)**: 문장 안의 위치에 따라 목적격, 소유격, 소유대명사로 구분하여 사용한다.
- **소유대명사**: 소유대명사는 '소유격 + 명사'를 줄인 형태이다.

◈ 대명사의 종류

수	인칭	인칭대명사			소유대명사
		주격	소유격	목적격	
단수	1인칭	I	my	me	mine
	2인칭	you	your	you	yours
	3인칭	he	his	him	his
		she	her	her	hers
		it	its	it	–
복수	1인칭	we	our	us	ours
	2인칭	you	your	you	yours
	3인칭	they	their	them	theirs

1. **주격과 목적격 대명사**: 주격대명사는 주어로, 목적격 대명사는 목적어로 쓰인다.

- **Tom** likes **orange juice.** ➡ **He**(주어) likes **it**(목적어).
- **Anna and I** bought **apples.** ➡ **We**(주어) bought **them**(목적어).

2. **소유격과 소유대명사**: 소유격의 뒤에는 명사가 오지만 소유대명사 뒤에는 명사가 오지 않는다.

- This is **my toy car.** ➡ This toy car is **mine.**
- That is **her pencil.** ➡ That pencil is **hers.**
- Those are **your books.** ➡ Those books are **yours.**

3. **명사의 소유격과 소유대명사**: 고유명사 또는 일반명사의 소유격과 소유대명사는 형태가 같다.

- This is **Tom's** new pencil case. ➡ This new pencil case is **Tom's.**

Check up!

Answer Keys p. 29

A 다음 밑줄 친 부분을 알맞은 인칭대명사로 바꾸어 쓰시오.

1 This is <u>my book</u>. *mine*

2 <u>Sandra and her mom</u> love grapes. ____________

3 <u>Joe</u> likes milk a lot. ____________

4 <u>The boy</u> sings well. ____________

5 <u>The dog</u> is black. ____________

6 This is <u>my father's</u> invention. ____________

7 <u>Jina's and my</u> cars are red. ____________

8 Grandmother welcomed <u>Sue and me</u>. ____________

9 That is <u>her new coat</u>. ____________

10 <u>The rabbit's</u> ears are long. ____________

11 These are <u>Tom's</u> shirts. ____________

12 <u>The boy</u> works at a café. ____________

13 This is Helen. <u>Helen</u> is a painter. ____________

14 I love <u>Barbara's bag</u>. ____________

15 Minho gave books to <u>Brian and Susan</u>. ____________

Answer Keys p. 29

B 괄호 안에 주어진 단어를 알맞은 형태로 바꾸어 빈칸을 채우시오.

1 This is ___my___ pen. (I)

2 She likes to fly kites. That's _________ hobby. (she)

3 The blue pants are _________. (he)

4 Minji made tomato juice for _________. (we)

5 The yellow hat is _________. (you)

6 You have a nice coat! I love _________ color. (it)

7 This room is _________. (we)

8 Billy bought flowers for _________. (she)

9 Father fixed _________ bikes. (we)

10 There are some melons on the table. Are these _________? (you)

11 I know the girl. _________ name is Linda. (she)

12 These books are _________. I bought _________ yesterday. (I / they)

13 They should wash _________ hands after going to school. (they)

14 _________ dreams are the same. They want to be an actor in the future. (they)

15 You have many great pictures. Can you show _________ them? (I)

Lesson

5-2 재귀대명사

• **재귀대명사:** 인칭대명사에 -self나 -selves를 붙인 것으로 '자신'을 가리키는 말이다. 재귀대명사는 '~자신'을 표현할 때 사용한다.

◈ 재귀대명사

인칭대명사	재귀대명사	인칭대명사	재귀대명사
I	myself	we	ourselves
you	yourself	you	yourselves
he	himself	they	themselves
she	herself		
it	itself		

➡ 재귀대명사는 재귀용법과 강조용법으로 나뉜다.

1. **재귀용법:** 문장의 주어와 목적어가 같을 때 사용하며, 재귀용법으로 사용되었을 경우 생략이 불가능하다.

• **She** is looking at **herself**. (She = herself)

• **They** are proud of **themselves**. (They = themselves)

2. **강조용법:** 주어, 보어, 목적어를 강조할 때 사용하며, 강조하는 말 바로 뒤 또는 문장의 맨 끝에 쓴다. 이때 재귀대명사는 생략이 가능하다.

• We made it **(ourselves)**.
• He fixed it **(himself)**.

3. 재귀대명사 숙어

• **enjoy oneself** 즐기다
• **by oneself** 홀로, 혼자 힘으로
• **help oneself** 마음껏 먹다
• **say(talk) to oneself** 혼잣말 하다
• **for oneself** 혼자 힘으로
• **make oneself at home** 편히 쉬다

Check up!

Answer Keys p. 29

A 괄호 안에 주어진 단어에서 알맞은 것을 찾으시오.

1 He feels proud of (him / himself).

2 I love (me / myself).

3 Sandra made a dress for (she / herself).

4 Let me introduce (I / myself).

5 Nick enjoyed (his / himself) over the weekend.

6 She (her / herself) finished the project.

7 Help (yours / yourself)!

8 He used to talk to (his / himself).

9 I made it by (myself / mine).

10 They are angry with (themselves / theirs)

B 밑줄 친 부분을 생략할 수 있으면 O, 생략할 수 없으면 X 표시를 하시오.

1 She can make kimchi herself. [○]

2 They decided to go to the concert themselves. [ ]

3 She thought of herself. [ ]

4 They helped themselves to lunch. [ ]

5 I don't know myself. [ ]

6 Mark's mother likes cooking herself. [ ]

7 He can repair his computer himself. [ ]

8 Minji hurt herself. [ ]

9 People take care of themselves. [ ]

10 We painted the wall ourselves last week. [ ]

C 다음 문장에서 재귀대명사를 쓰고, 용법과 생략이 가능한지 못한지를 밝히시오.

1 The kid sometimes talks to ___*himself*___.

➡ ___*재귀용법, 생략 불가능*___

2 Jane packs the boxes ________.

➡ ________________

3 You always study English ________.

➡ ________________

4 The cat looks at ________ in the mirror.

➡ ________________

5 The man ________ draws a picture.

➡ ________________

Lesson

5-3 비인칭 주어 'it'

• **비인칭 주어 'it'**: 주로 사물, 동물을 가리키는 대명사로 사용되지만 시간, 날짜, 요일, 계절, 날씨, 거리, 명암 등을 표현할 때 주어로 사용되며, 이때 'it'은 해석하지 않는다.

1. 비인칭 주어 'it'

(1) **시간**

What time is **it**? **It** is 7 o'clock.

(2) **날짜**

What date is **it** today? **It** is May 15th.

(3) **요일**

What day is **it** today? **It** is Friday.

(4) **계절**

It is summer now.

(5) **날씨**

It is raining heavily.

(6) **거리**

How far is **it** from here to the church? **It** is about one kilometer.

(7) **명암**

It is so dark here.

2. 대명사 it: 대명사로 쓰일 경우 '그것'이라고 해석한다.

There is **a laptop** on the table. **It** is my brother's. (**a laptop = it**)

Check up!

Answer Keys p. 29

A 다음 밑줄 친 it이 대명사인지 비인칭 주어인지 구별하시오.

1 It is Monday. Let's go to the park for a picnic. _비인칭 주어_

2 I will buy it tomorrow. ____________

3 It's two o'clock. I will be late. ____________

4 It is my brother's car. ____________

5 It is so cold outside. ____________

6 What date is it today? It is March 13th. ____________

7 Look at the new camera! I love it. ____________

Lesson

5-4 지시대명사

• **지시대명사**: 정해진 사람이나 사물, 동물 등을 가리킨다.

1. this / these

(1) 가까이에 있는 사람이나 사물을 가리킬 때 쓰인다.

(2) 'this'는 단수, 'these'는 복수를 나타낸다.

• **This** is my father's car.

• **These** are my new textbooks.

2. that / those

(1) 멀리 있는 사람이나 사물을 가리킬 때 쓰인다.

(2) 'that'은 단수, 'those'는 복수를 나타낸다.

• **That** is his new English teacher.

• **Those** are her kittens.

3. 누군가를 소개하거나, 전화상에서 사용

지시대명사 'this'는 상대방에게 소개를 하거나 전화상에서 '나'를 가리킬 때 사용한다.

• Tom, **this** is my sister, Catherine.

• Hello, **this** is David. Who's calling, please?

Check up!

Answer Keys p. 29

A 다음 괄호 안에서 알맞은 말을 고르시오.

1 (Those / This) puppies are white.

2 (This / These) is for you.

3 (These / This) is Sam speaking. Who's calling, please?

4 (These / That) house is so big.

5 I don't know (this / these) people so well.

6 (These / This) is my new watch.

7 (That/ Those) books are interesting.

8 (This / These) is Max's hat.

9 (These / That) man is a dentist.

10 (Those / This) is my nephew, Sangeun.

Practice More I

A 다음 문장의 밑줄 친 부분을 바르게 고치시오.

1 What's <u>you</u> name? ___your___

2 <u>It's</u> tail is so long. ________

3 I often welcomed <u>they</u>. ________

4 Thank <u>your</u> very much. ________

5 <u>That's</u> sunny today. ________

6 <u>This</u> are my toys. ________

7 <u>She</u> hair is gold. I like it. ________

8 <u>These</u> is my new car. ________

9 <u>I</u> grandmother loves me. ________

10 <u>That</u> was great to meet you. ________

11 That book was <u>me</u>. ________

12 <u>Them</u> are doing their homework. ________

13 <u>It</u> is Mike speaking. ________

14 We prepared a lot of food. Help <u>you</u>! ________

15 He made some cookies by <u>him</u>. ________

B 주어진 단어를 이용하여 빈칸에 알맞은 말을 쓰시오.

1 My teacher scolded ___me___ for being late. (I)

2 My dog is as big as ________. (you)

3 Mom is always on ________ side. (I)

4 ________ acting is really impressive. (he)

5 Yoonsuk lived by ________ for a year. (he)

6 Look at the skirt. I like ________ color. (it)

7 How far is it from here to ________ office? (they)

8 Oprah is thinking about ________ mom. (she)

Answer Keys p. 30

9 Her skirt is as long as ___________. (you)

10 This is Matthew's bag. I will let ___________ know. (he)

11 I made this house for ___________. (I)

12 Our teacher told ___________ that we should study hard. (we)

13 These are ___________ dogs. Kate and I love them. (we)

14 That ring isn't ___________. My ring is round. (my)

15 They feel proud of ___________. (they)

C 다음 그림을 보고, 주어진 빈칸에 this, those, that, these 중 알맞은 말을 쓰시오

1 ____*This*____ cat is mine. Its name is Cindy.

2 Look at ___________ dogs!

3 ___________ are my favorite books.

4 ___________ man is my private tutor.

5 ___________ is John speaking.

Practice More I

Answer Keys p. 30

서술형 연습 **D** **다음 우리말 해석에 맞게 주어진 단어를 바르게 배열하시오.**

1 내일은 맑을 것이다. (tomorrow, will, it, sunny, be)
= *It will be sunny tomorrow*.

2 저 여자를 봐! 그녀는 30년 전에 유명한 여배우였어.
(look, that, at, lady)
= ____________________! She was a famous actress 30 years ago.

3 Cindy는 그와 그의 딸들을 만났다.
(Cindy, his daughters, met, and, him)
= ____________________.

4 그건 너의 잘못이 아니다. (fault, it's, your, not)
= ____________________.

5 Linda는 자신의 시험 결과를 걱정했다.
(about, Linda, test results, worried, her)
= ____________________.

6 Steven은 벽에 걸린 그림을 좋아한다. 그는 그것을 사고 싶어한다.
(likes, on the wall, picture, that, Steven)
= ____________________. He wants to buy it.

7 이 파스타를 너 혼자 만들었니? (did, by, this, make, pasta, you, yourself)
= ____________________?

8 만나서 반가워. 내 소개를 할게. (me, myself, introduce, let)
= Nice to meet you. ____________________.

9 저 책은 나의 것이 아니다. 내 책은 과학책이다.
(that, mine, book, isn't)
= ____________________. My book is about science.

10 나는 Helen의 가족들을 위해 이 차를 샀어.
(for, bought, I, Helen's family, bought, car, this)
= ____________________.

Point Check Ⅱ

◆ **부정대명사 :** 특별히 정해지지 않는 사람이나 사물을 가리키는 대명사를 가리킨다.

1. one, another : 불특정한 명사를 대신하는 말로 단수 취급한다.

- My jacket is too old. I want a new **one**.
- David read a book. He wants **another**.

2. others, the others

- I think some of my friends are kind, **others** are not so kind.
- There are a lot of foods. Some foods are very delicious, **the others** are very bad.

3. some, any : 'some'은 주로 긍정문에, 'any'는 부정문과 의문문에 사용된다.

- **Some** of the students are absent.
- You didn't want **any** apples.

4. each, every

- **Each** of the girls is wearing a yellow ribbon.
- **Every** school has its own uniform.

5. -thing, -one, -body

(1) something, someone, somebody
- **Someone(= Somebody)** is behind you.
- He has **something** mystical.

(2) anything, anyone, anybody
- We didn't do **anything** all day.
- **Anyone(=Anybody)** else over here?

(3) everything, everyone, everybody
- **Everything** was perfect.
- **Everyone(=Everybody)** has to wear black shoes.

(4) nothing, none
- There is **nothing** special at the party.
- **None** of the men want to go fishing.

Lesson

5-5 부정대명사_one / another

- **one**: 앞에서 말한 명사와 같은 종류의 것이지만 정해지지 않은 대상이 하나일 경우 사용한다.
- **another**: '또 다른 하나'를 가리킬 때 사용한다.

1. one과 it

(1) **one**: 불특정한 명사를 대신한다.

- My watch is broken. I want to buy a new **one.** (one = watch: 언급한 시계와 똑같은 것이 아닌 그 종류의 어떤 시계)
- Do you prefer blue **ones** more than those? (ones = those)

➡ 불특정 명사가 복수일 경우 'ones'를 사용한다.

(2) **it**: 앞에서 언급한 특정한 명사를 대신한다.

My cellphone is old-fashioned. I don't like **it.** (it = my cellphone: 언급한 휴대전화)

2. another: 단수 명사와 사용되며 단수 취급한다.

This hat's color is not good. Show me **another.** (another: 다른 모자를 가리 킴)

3. one과 another: 하나 이상의 사람이나 사물이 있을 경우 차례대로 말할 때 사용한다.

- There are two flowers. **One** is a red rose and **another** is a pink carnation.
- The girls are talking with **one another.**

➡ 셋 이상일 경우 'one another는 '서로'라는 뜻으로 사용한다.

Check up!

Answer Keys p. 30

A 다음 빈칸에 알맞은 것을 one, it, ones, another 중에서 골라 쓰시오.

1 He lost his helmet. He needs a new ___one___.

2 My friends are talking with __________.

3 This is __________ good example.

4 Do you prefer red __________ than those?

5 I don't like this shirt. Can you show me __________?

6 Harry's pants are torn. He should buy new __________.

7 She has two dogs. __________ is Jerry and __________ is Tom.

8 This cup is broken. Do you have __________?

9 Coke is my favorite beverage. I drink __________ every day.

Lesson

5-6 부정대명사_others/the other(s)

- **others/the other(s)**: 전체에서 일부를 뺀 나머지에 대해 말할 때 사용할 수 있으며, 특별히 정해진 것을 이야기할 때는 'the'를 붙여 쓴다.

1. **some ~ others...**: 몇몇은~, 다른 사람(것)들은··· ['나머지 일부'를 뜻함]

   Some people are kind, **others** are unkind.
   (= other people)

2. **some ~ the others...**: 몇몇은~, 다른 사람(것)들은··· ['나머지 전부'를 뜻함]

   Some of the students did homework, **the others** did not do it.
   (= the other students)

3. **one ~ the other...**: 하나는~ 다른 하나는··· [나머지 하나]

   There are two girls. **One** is Angela and **the other** is Julie.

4. **one ~, another..., the other–**: 하나는~ 다른 하나는···, 나머지 하나는 –

   There are three colors. **One** is blue, **another** is green, and **the other** is purple.

Check up!

Answer Keys p. 30

A 괄호 안에 주어진 말 중 알맞은 것을 고르시오.

1 Some people wear a red shirt, but (other / others) wear a blue shirt.

2 He has a lot of fruit. Some of them are melons and (other / the others) are cherries.

3 I have two pens. One is yellow and (the other / others) is gray.

4 Nick has four children. Two of them are daughters, and (the others / other) are sons.

5 I think Timmy doesn't think of (others / the other).

6 (Some / One) like to play baseball, but (others / another) like to play soccer.

7 He bought four notebooks. One was five dollars, and (the others / some) were three dollars.

Lesson

5-7 부정대명사_some / any

• **some / any**: 'some'은 긍정문과 제안하는 의문문에 주로 쓰이고, 'any'는 부정문과 의문문에 쓰인다.

1. some

• **Some** of the students got good grades.
• Would you have **some** more?

2. any

• I want to buy some bread. Do you have **any (bread)**?
• **A** Can you lend me some paint?
B Sorry, but I don't have **any (paint)**, either.

Check up!

Answer Keys p. 30

A 다음 빈칸에 some과 any 중 맞는 것을 골라 쓰시오.

1 ___Some___ of us are invited to Helen's party.
2 She doesn't have ________ time to study English.
3 Do you have ________ questions?
4 Lucas wants ________ bread because he didn't eat breakfast.
5 Can you lend me ________ money?
6 Are there ________ books to read?
7 You should get ________ rest today. You look so tired.
8 We don't have ________ time for a picnic. We are so busy these days.
9 I need ________ water. I'm really thirsty.
10 Are you playing ________ sports today?
11 If you have ________ time, please visit me.
12 There are ________ important reasons to study English.

Lesson

5-8 부정대명사_each / every

• **each/every**: 우리말의 해석은 다르지만, 'each, every' 모두 단수 취급하여 사용한다.

1. **each**: '각자, 각기, 각각'의 뜻으로 명사를 수식하며 단수 취급한다.

   • **Each** class has 25 students.

   → 'each other'는 사람이 둘 일 때 '서로'라는 뜻으로 쓰인다.

   • They are different from **each other**.

2. **every**: '모든'의 뜻으로 명사를 수식하며 단수 취급한다.

   • **Every** child is our future.

Check up!

Answer Keys p. 30

A 다음 문장에서 어법상 어색한 것을 찾아 바르게 고치시오.

1 Every men has his goal. *men* ➡ *man*

2 Each classes has two teachers. ________ ➡ ________

3 Everything are alright. ________ ➡ ________

4 I think each presents should be wrapped.

________ ➡ ________

5 Each student go to school by bus.

________ ➡ ________

6 Everyone need to be quiet in the library.

________ ➡ ________

7 Tom eats pizza and coke every nights.

________ ➡ ________

8 Every moments are important.

________ ➡ ________

9 People should respect each others.

________ ➡ ________

10 Everyone are going to watch movies.

________ ➡ ________

Lesson

5-9 부정대명사_-thing/-one/-body

• **-thing/-one/-bod**: 'some, any, every'와 함께 여러 가지 뜻의 부정대명사가 된다.
모두 단수로 취급한다.

• **-thing**: 주로 사물을 표현하는 데 사용한다.

• **-one/-body**: 사람을 표현하는 데 사용한다.

1. **something, someone, somebody**: 긍정문에 주로 쓰이며, 단수 취급한다.

• **Someone(= Somebody)** is standing at the front door.

• **Something** is moving in the box.

2. **anything, anyone, anybody**: 부정문과 의문문에 주로 쓰이며, 단수 취급한다.

We don't need **anything**.

➡ any/anybody(anyone): 긍정문에 쓰이면 강한 뜻이 된다.

They think that **anybody(=anyone)** loves it.

3. **everything, everyone, everybody**: 단수 취급한다.

Evelyn is so polite. **Everybody(=Everyone)** likes her.

4. **nothing, none**: 자체가 부정을 뜻하므로 'not'을 함께 쓰지 않는다.

(1) **nothing**: 단수로 취급한다.

Nothing is more important than my family.

(= **Anything** is **not** more important than my family.)

➡ 부정의 뜻을 가진 'nothing'은 'anything ~ not'으로 바꿔 쓸 수 있다.

(2) **none**: 단수와 복수로 취급한다.

• **None** of the students are in the classroom.

• **None** of the lesson is easy to understand.

Check up!

Answer Keys p. 31

A **괄호 안에 주어진 말 중 알맞은 것을 고르시오.**

1 Somebody (is / are) singing in front of my house.

2 The singer says everybody (loves / love) him.

3 Nothing (is / isn't) happier than having a baby.

4 None of the students (is / are) studying math.

5 He thinks he doesn't need (something special / special something).

6 Everybody (celebrates / celebrate) Korean culture all over the world.

7 Please, someone (call / calls) the doctor! That boy is injured.

8 Anyone who (want / wants) to visit my house should just call me.

9 (Nothing / Something) is more interesting than watching SF movies.

10 Everybody (reads / read) this book because it's very useful for studying English.

B 다음 문장에서 어색한 부분을 찾아 바르게 고쳐 쓰시오.

1 There is anybody in my house.

anybody ➡ *somebody*

2 Larry doesn't need something to drink.

________ ➡ ________

3 We have beautiful something.

________ ➡ ________

4 Non of the animals are on the farm.

________ ➡ ________

5 Anybody visited my house. He was my uncle.

________ ➡ ________

6 No thing is more precious than our family.

________ ➡ ________

7 Anyone helped the sick people.

________ ➡ ________

8 I saw anyone in the theater but I didn't remember who she was.

________ ➡ ________

9 Jennifer doesn't need nothing to eat.

________ ➡ ________

10 She is beautiful. Anyone likes her.

________ ➡ ________

Practice More Ⅱ

A 다음 빈칸에 보기 에서 알맞은 말을 골라 써 넣으시오.

보기

one it ones another the other some others

1 I lost my cellphone yesterday. I should buy a new ___one___.

2 I have a black hat. You can borrow ________.

3 Sally has glasses. My sister wants to have the same ________.

4 I went to Busan last week. ________ is one of the most beautiful cities in Korea.

5 There are two pens. ______________ is a black pen and ______________ is a red pen.

6 I don't like this shirt. Can you show me ________?

7 We bought two flowers. ________ is a rose, and the other is a lily.

8 He has a box of apples. ________ of apples are fresh, ________ are not.

9 Some students are tall, ________ are short.

10 If you don't like it, you can choose ________.

B 괄호 안에 주어진 말 중 알맞은 것을 고르시오.

1 There are five cups on the table. Some are red and (the others / other) are blue.

2 Some flowers are white and (the other / others) are yellow.

3 There are three girls. One is Korean, another is Japanese, and (the other / other) is American.

4 This coffee smells good. Can I have (another/ the other)?

5 There are six letters. One is from Lisa and (the others / other) are from Max.

6 (Some / The other) speak English fluently, but (other / others) don't.

7 Some computers in the room are new, but (the other / the others) are not.

8 She brings three dolls. (One / Some) is for me and the others are for her daughter.

Answer Keys p. 31

C 다음 문장에서 어법상 어색한 것을 찾아 바르게 고치시오.

1 I can feel anyone is behind me.

anyone ➡ someone

2 Every children has to be protected from danger.

__________ ➡ __________

3 Would you please give me any water?

__________ ➡ __________

4 Suzie picked up anything on the street.

__________ ➡ __________

5 Each class in the elementary school have about 25 students.

__________ ➡ __________

6 No of the students wear their school uniforms today.

__________ ➡ __________

7 Some students like math. Other don't like it.

__________ ➡ __________

8 My brother's bike is too old. So he wants to buy new ones.

__________ ➡ __________

D 다음 주어진 우리말과 뜻이 같도록 빈칸에 알맞은 말을 쓰시오.

1 어떤 사람들은 빨간색을 좋아하고, 또 어떤 사람들은 파란색을 좋아한다.

➡ Some people like red and others like blue.

2 나는 10개의 반지가 있다. 이것들 중 일부는 유리이고, 나머지 전부는 플라스틱이다.

➡ I have ten rings. __________ of them are made of glass, but __________ are made of plastic.

3 두 마리의 강아지가 공원에 있다. 한 마리는 잠을 자고 있고, 다른 한 마리는 놀고 있다.

➡ There are two puppies. __________ is sleeping and __________ is playing.

4 Jack은 파란색 신발을 좋아하지 않는다. 그는 하얀색 신발을 좋아한다.

➡ Jack doesn't like blue shoes. He likes white __________.

5 나는 지우개가 없어. 나에게 하나를 빌려줄 수 있니?

➡ I didn't have an eraser. Can you borrow me __________?

Point Check Ⅲ

◆ **의문대명사 :** 어떤 대상을 가리키며 의문을 나타내는 대명사를 말한다.

◆ **타동사 + (대)명사 + 부사 :** 목적어가 명사이면 타동사와 부사 사이 혹은 뒤에 올 수 있지만, 목적어가 대명사일 경우 반드시 타동사와 부사 사이에 넣어야 한다.

1. 부정대명사 : so / same / such

(1) **so** : 아주, 그렇게

A This math quiz is **so** difficult.

B I think **so** too.

(2) **same** : 같은 (항상 정관사 the와 함께 쓰인다.)

The color of these bags is **the same**.

(3) **such** : 그러한 ('~와 같은'이라는 'such as' 로 많이 쓰인다.)

I like tropical fruits **such as** pineapples, bananas, and coconuts.

2. 의문대명사

(1) who(누구), whose(누구의, 누구의 것), whom(누구를)

- **Who** is that pretty woman? [주격]
- **Whose** pencil is this? [소유격]
- **Whose** is this Smartphone? [소유대명사]
- **Who(m)** does he like? [목적격]

(2) what(무엇)

- **What** does she want to do?
- **What** color do you like?

(3) which(어느 것)

- **Which** is better, a puppy or a kitten?
- **Which** bread do you want to buy?

3. 타동사 + (대)명사 + 부사 : '이어 동사'라고도 한다.

(1) **'타동사 + 부사'에서 대명사** : 타동사와 부사 사이에 와야 한다.

She remembered to call **him** up.

(2) **'타동사 + 부사'에서 일반 명사** : 타동사와 부사 사이 또는 뒤에 위치할 수 있다.

They tried **the dress** on. = They tried on **the dress**.

Lesson 5-10 부정대명사_so/same/such

- **so**: '그렇게'라는 뜻으로 앞에 나온 긍정의 문장을 대신한다.
- **same**: '같은'이라는 뜻으로 항상 정관사 'the'와 함께 사용한다.
- **such**: '그러한 것'이라는 뜻으로 앞에 나온 단어, 구, 절을 받는다.

1. so: 'think, suppose, believe, expect, hope, say, tell'의 목적으로 주로 사용된다.

- **A** I think she will be happy.
  B I hope **so**.

2. same

- The length of those pencils is **the same**.
- My sister and his brother go to **the same** school.
  ➡ 'same'은 형용사로도 쓰인다.

3. such

- **Such** was its effect.

4. 숙어 표현

- **the same as~**: ~와 같은
  The shoes are **the same as** Jimmy's.
- **such as~**: ~와 같은 그런
  We like light colors **such as** sky blue.

Check up!

Answer Keys p. 31

A 다음 우리말 해석에 맞게 빈칸을 완성하시오.

1 그는 멋있어. / 나는 그렇게 생각하지 않아.
= He is awesome! / I don't think ___so___.

2 나는 그가 곧 돌아 올 것이라고 믿어. / 나도 그렇게 생각해.
= I believe he will come back soon. / I believe ___________.

3 Tom은 초콜릿과 같은 달콤한 것들을 좋아한다.
= Tom likes something sweet ___________ chocolate.

4 그 셔츠는 나의 남동생의 것과 같다.
= That shirt is ___________ my brother's.

5 Woody와 Kim은 같은 학년이다.
= Woody and Kim are in ___________ grade.

Lesson

5-11 의문대명사

• **의문대명사**: 의문을 나타내며 물어보는 대명사를 말한다. 사람을 가리키는 who, whose, whom 과 사물을 가리키는 what(which)이 있다.

1. **who**: 사람의 이름이나 관계 등을 물을 때 사용된다.

(1) 주격: 누구(~은/는/이/가)

Who is this man?

(2) 소유격: 누구의

Whose cellphone is this?

➡ 'whose + 명사'에서 whose는 who의 소유격으로 '누구의'라는 뜻을 가지지만, whose가 명사 없이 혼자 나올 경우에는 소유대명사로서 '누구의 것'이라는 뜻이다

➡ **Whose** is this cellphone?

(3) 목적격: 누구(~을/를/~에게)

Whom did Amy meet yesterday?

→ 목적격 whom이 혼자서 앞으로 오는 경우, 'm'을 생략하고 'who'를 사용하기도 한다.

2. **what**: 동물이나 사물, 사람의 직업이나 신분을 물을 때 사용된다.

• **What** did you make?
• **What** does your mother do?

3. **which**: 동물이나 사물을 가리킬 때 사용하지만, 선택의 범위 내에서 '어느 것'인지 물을 때 사용된다.

Which is looks better, red or pink?

4. **'what + 명사', 'which + 명사'**: 명사를 수식하는 의문형용사로 사용된다.

• **What color** does he like?
• **Which food** did you eat for breakfast?

Check up!

Answer Keys p. 31

A **다음 문장의 빈칸에 who, whose, whom 중 알맞은 것을 찾아 쓰시오.**

1 ___*Who*___ is that pretty girl?

2 __________ did you talk to yesterday?

3 __________ are these shoes?

Answer Keys p. 31

4 __________ is your favorite actor?

5 __________ did you play last week?

6 __________ makes you happy?

7 __________ car is that?

8 __________ are you?

9 __________ did Jieun meet?

10 __________ teaches your science class?

B 주어진 괄호 안에서 알맞은 것을 고르시오.

1 (Which / What) pen did you buy this morning?

2 (What / Which) is your favorite movie?

3 (What / Which) does John like?

4 (Whom / Which) is bigger, red or black?

5 Which color is looks better, blue (or / nor) green?

6 (What / Which) did you do last night?

7 Linda doesn't know (what / which) she should choose.

8 (What / Which) makes you worry?

9 (Which / What) season do you like?

10 (Which / What) happened to his parents?

C 다음 밑줄 친 부분이 어떤 문장 요소인지 쓰시오.

1 What color do you like? ➡ 의문형용사

2 Who is that handsome boy? ➡ __________

3 Which subject does she like? ➡ __________

4 What does your brother do? ➡ __________

5 Whose is that white puppy? ➡ __________

Lesson 5-12 타동사 + (대)명사 + 부사 (이어 동사)

• 타동사 + 부사: '타동사+부사'로 이루어진 동사는 목적어가 명사인지 또는 대명사인지에 따라 위치가 달라진다. 이 동사를 '이어 동사'라고 한다.

1. **'타동사 + 부사'에서 목적어가 대명사**: 타동사와 부사 사이에 와야 한다.

• I forgot to wake **him** up. (O)
I forgot to wake up him. (X)

2. **'타동사 + 부사'에서 목적어가 명사**: 타동사와 부사 사이 또는 뒤에 위치할 수 있다.

• I can pick **the kids** up at school. (O)
I can pick up **the kids** at school. (O)

3. **'타동사 + 부사' 숙어 표현**

• **call up**	부르다, 전화하다	• **carry out**	수행하다
• **give up**	포기하다	• **pick up**	줍다, 차로 데리러 가다
• **put away**	치우다	• **put down**	진압하다, 내려놓다
• **put on**	입다	• **put off**	연기하다, 미루다
• **see off**	배웅하다	• **take off**	벗다, 이륙하다
• **throw away**	내버리다	• **turn in**	제출하다
• **turn down**	소리를 낮추다, 거절하다	• **turn on**	켜다
• **turn off**	끄다	• **try on**	시험 삼아 해보다, 옷을 입어보다
• **use up**	다 써버리다		

4. **'자동사 + 전치사'**: 일반명사와 대명사 모두 전치사 뒤에 위치해야 한다.

• Look at **her**. (O) Look her at. (X)
• Tom talks with **Anna**. (O) Tom talks Anna with. (X)

5. **'자동사 + 전치사' 숙어 표현**

• **agree to**	(제안을) 받아들이다	• **care for**	~을 돌보다, 좋아하다
• **agree with**	(사람에) 동의하다	• **get on**	~에 타다
• **apply for**	~에 지원하다	• **listen to**	~을 듣다
• **ask for**	~을 요구하다	• **look at**	~을 쳐다보다
• **believe in**	~을 믿다	• **talk to/with**	~와 대화하다
• **care about**	~을 신경 쓰다	• **wait for**	~을 기다리다

Check up!

Answer Keys p. 32

A 다음 문장에서 어법상 어색한 것을 찾아 바르게 고치시오.

1 Don't give up it. You can do it.

up it ➡ *it up*

2 I can pick it to up. ________ ➡ ________

3 Carl likes to care his baby for.

________ ➡ ________

4 Sarah sees off him in the airport.

________ ➡ ________

5 Was she waiting him for? ________ ➡ ________

6 Just throw away it. It's too dirty.

________ ➡ ________

7 Look it at! It's snowing outside.

________ ➡ ________

8 Do you like it? Just try on it. ________ ➡ ________

9 He wants to apply this position for.

________ ➡ ________

10 Mary doesn't care it about. ________ ➡ ________

11 My hobby is listening music to.

________ ➡ ________

12 Cindy calls up him. ________ ➡ ________

13 John agrees her idea to. ________ ➡ ________

14 Don't use up them. ________ ➡ ________

15 Will you pick up it? I'm so busy now.

________ ➡ ________

16 Tim tried to put on it, but it was too big.

________ ➡ ________

17 You don't agree Suzie with, do you?

________ ➡ ________

18 You should carry out it. ________ ➡ ________

19 He forgot to put away them. ________ ➡ ________

20 I can't remember when I handed in it.

________ ➡ ________

Practice More Ⅲ

A 다음 문장의 괄호 안에서 알맞은 것을 고르시오.

1 (Who / What) is your favorite color?

2 I didn't think (such / so).

3 (Whom / Who) did you meet at that restaurant?

4 (Which / What) is smaller, that blue one or the red one?

5 Please (turn it off / turn off it).

6 The prices are (the / a) same.

7 (Whose / Which) bike is this?

8 I can (carry out it / carry it out).

9 My skirt is (the same as / such as) yours.

10 I like fruit (such as / the same) grapes and apples.

B 다음 질문에 알맞은 답을 찾아 바르게 연결하시오.

① Which color do you like? •	• ⓐ They are my brothers.
② Who are they? •	• ⓑ He helped his grandmother.
③ Whose laptop is this? •	• ⓒ It's mine.
④ What does your mother do? •	• ⓓ Blue is my favorite color.
⑤ Whom did Chris help? •	• ⓔ She is a nurse.

⑥ Which season do you like the most? •	• ⓕ This is John.
⑦ Whom did they talk about? •	• ⓖ It's Helen's.
⑧ What do you want to eat? •	• ⓗ I want to eat something sweet.
⑨ Whose jacket is this? •	• ⓘ They talked about their teacher.
⑩ Who's calling, please? •	• ⓙ I like winter.

Answer Keys p. 32

C 다음 문장에서 어법상 어색한 것을 찾아 바르게 고치시오.

1 A Tom will come back soon.
B I hope to. ___to___ ➡ ___so___

2 Kate and I don't look a same. ______ ➡ ______

3 Same was her excuse for the mistake.
______ ➡ ______

4 What is bigger, A or B? ______ ➡ ______

5 Whose did you talk to? ______ ➡ ______

6 I like Korean food same as galbi.
______ ➡ ______

7 What dictionary is this? ______ ➡ ______

8 Look her at! She is good at dancing.
______ ➡ ______

9 I bought the such as bag as yours.
______ ➡ ______

10 You have to turn in it by five. ______ ➡ ______

서술형 연습

D 다음 우리말 해석에 맞게 주어진 단어를 알맞게 배열하시오.

1 너는 어제 누구를 만났니?
(meet, did, whom, you, yesterday)
➡ ___Whom did you meet yesterday___?

2 Jack은 누구랑 얘기 중이니? (talk to, does, whom, Jack)
➡ ______________________?

3 너는 Kate와 같은 음악 장르를 좋아해?
(Kate, do, like, you, music genre, the sam, as)
➡ ______________________?

4 선생님의 설명은 그러했다.
(explanation, such, teacher's, was, the)
➡ ______________________.

5 그와 나는 같은 자동차를 갖고 있다.
(car, he, the same, I, and, have)
➡ ______________________

6 그것을 창문 밖에 던지면 안 된다.
(you, the window, throw, don't, it, out)
➡ ______________________

7 이것은 누구의 컴퓨터이니? (is, whose, this, computer)
➡ ______________________

8 Sara는 약속을 다음으로 연기했다.
(Sara, appointment, put, the, off)
➡ ______________________

9 그들 각자 사과를 그곳에서 몇 개 샀다.
(of, them, bought, some apples, there, each)
➡ ______________________

10 Jenny는 점심으로 무엇을 먹어?
(which, lunch, food, does, eat, Jenny, for)
➡ ______________________

E **다음 문장을 바르게 해석하여 쓰시오.**

1 Helen forgot to see him off.
➡ *Helen은 그를 배웅해야 하는 것을 잊었다.*

2 Do you believe the rumor?
➡ ______________________

3 You should agree to the proposal.
➡ ______________________

4 I used them up.
➡ ______________________

5 What do you want to be in the future?
➡ ______________________

중간 기말고사 예상문제

Answer Keys p. 32

내신 최다 출제 유형

01 다음 빈칸에 공통으로 들어갈 알맞은 단어를 고르시오. [출제 예상 85%]

> • I was angry. So I did nothing for ________ hour.
> • My watch is very old. I want a new ________.

① an ② one ③ that ④ it ⑤ this

02 다음 빈칸에 들어갈 말이 바르게 짝지어진 것을 고르시오. [출제 예상 90%]

> • Hello, everyone. Let me introduce ________.
> • They have to do it ________.

① myself – them
② himself – herself
③ myself – you
④ yourself – theirselves
⑤ myself – themselves

03 다음 밑줄 친 부분의 쓰임이 나머지 넷과 다른 것을 고르시오. [출제 예상 95%]

① It's sunny today.
② What date is it today?
③ It is too far from here to your house.
④ Turn on the light. It's dark.
⑤ It's my favorite flower.

04 다음 문장 중 어법상 올바른 것을 고르시오. [출제 예상 90%]

① The clock in the living room is correct.
② I can play piano so well.
③ She didn't give me some food.
④ You can't find nobody in this room.
⑤ They have any water.

05 다음 중 문법상 틀린 것을 고르시오. [출제 예상 85%]

> **A** ① Is this ② your pencil case?
> **B** Oh, yes. It's ③ mine.
> **A** ④ Mine friend found it in the art room.
> **B** Wow, good. ⑤ Thank you so much.

06 다음 빈칸에 들어갈 알맞은 말을 고르시오. [출제 예상 80%]

> I didn't have an eraser, so Sumi gave me ________.

① hers ② her ③ his
④ him ⑤ herself

중간 기말고사 예상문제

[01~02] 다음 중 어법상 올바른 문장을 고르시오.

01
① His is a good man.
② Her is a kind teacher.
③ He's mother is a math teacher.
④ My name's is Kevin.
⑤ Our new teacher is Mrs. Smith.

02
① Jason has he book.
② Jenny and Minsu did their homework.
③ I didn't want to meet he's sister.
④ It's legs are so small.
⑤ Hers family is very kind.

03 다음 중 문법적으로 틀린 문장을 고르시오.

① She doesn't meet me.
② I don't like him.
③ Her name is Jamie Brown.
④ You look like you're mother.
⑤ I'd like to drink it.

04 다음 밑줄친 her의 용법이 다른 하나를 고르시오.

① Ben is her best friend.
② Paul sings a song for her.
③ Her sister is so beautiful.
④ She always shares her food.
⑤ Jina will go to her party.

05 다음 글의 빈칸에 알맞은 단어를 고르시오.

> Look over there. She is so pretty. What's ________ name?

① hers ② his ③ your
④ her ⑤ my

[06~07] 각 문장의 빈칸에 들어갈 말이 보기 의 밑줄 친 단어와 같은 것을 고르시오.

06

> 보기
> Mary has a handsome boyfriend. His name is Jack.

① I like this toy. What's ________ name?
② Julie has a cute pet. ________ name is Toto.
③ She lost her key. But I found ________ key.
④ Jerry bought a book. It is in ________ bag.
⑤ Wendy talked with Mr. White. Mr. White is ________ homeroom teacher.

07

> 보기
> I have a cute kitten. Its eyes are shining.

① Tony has a kind sister. ________ name is Sara.
② Sora is a good girl. She takes care of ________ little brother well.
③ I want to buy a new phone. ________ shape is so cool.
④ Jack and Tony are sports players. They like ________ team.
⑤ Harry has a girlfriend. But anybody doesn't know________.

Answer Keys p. 33~34

[08~09] 다음 문장 중 어법상 틀린 문장을 모두 고르시오.

08 ① You sometimes forget you're things.
② They have a plan to build their house.
③ It's his new jacket.
④ This is my favorite food.
⑤ That is a her pencil.

09 ① Jessy's family lives in a small house.
② They are my best friends.
③ English is he's favorite subject.
④ We met our grandparents at noon.
⑤ She really doesn't like he.

[10~11] 다음 문장 중 어법상 맞는 문장을 모두 고르시오.

10 ① Jennifer got their own car.
② Phillip looks like his mother.
③ Her is very kind to people.
④ My name is Minsu Gang.
⑤ We need to buy ours house.

★★★
11 ① The actor doesn't have her own waiting room.
② I was surprised when I checked mine grade.
③ Yours notebook was under the desk.
④ Our house has a pretty garden.
⑤ James prays for his son.

[12~13] 다음 대화를 보고 물음에 답하시오.

A Hello. ⓐ Who's calling, please?
B Hello. ⓑ I am Woody. May I speak to Jessie?
A Hi, Woody. ⓒ This is she speaking. What's the matter?
B ⓓ I have two movie tickets. Will you go with me?
A (A) 물론이지. ⓔ I will.

12 윗글의 ⓐ ~ ⓔ 중에서 틀린 문장을 고르시오.

① ⓐ ② ⓑ ③ ⓒ ④ ⓓ ⑤ ⓔ

13 윗글의 (A)를 바르게 영작한 것을 고르시오.

① Of course ② Sorry
③ Thank you ④ Course
⑤ Alright

14 다음 글의 빈칸에 들어갈 말이 순서대로 짝지어진 것을 고르시오.

Hello, mom and dad.
This is Ellen. How are you? I'm so good.
I made many Korean friends.
__________ are so kind to me.
I want to introduce __________ to you.
Here are __________ pictures.

① They – them – they
② Their – them – their
③ They – them – their
④ Their – they – them
⑤ Them – they – their

★★★
15 다음 문장 중 밑줄 친 단어를 생략할 수 있는 것을 고르시오.

① We are new here ourselves.
② Take care of yourself.
③ Tony is proud of himself.
④ Wendy did it for herself.
⑤ You should respect yourself more.

[16~17] 다음 밑줄 친 it의 용법이 다른 하나를 고르시오.

16 ① It is their life.
② It is not easy to learn Japanese.
③ I will not take it.
④ It is my new bag.
⑤ Everyone wants to take it.

17 ① It is cloudy and chilly.
② It is summer in Canada.
③ It is eleven o'clock.
④ It is dark outside.
⑤ It is one of the cats.

[18~19] 다음 중 어법상 틀린 문장을 고르시오.

★★★
18 ① This is my friend, Jamie.
② That is your brother, Harry.
③ Those women is so beautiful.
④ These pictures are not for you.
⑤ This is your final exam score.

19 ① Someone is calling my name.
② She can't take care of her brothers.
③ Nobody doesn't know what it means.
④ He has nothing to eat.
⑤ None of them are sad.

20 다음 대화의 빈칸에 알맞은 질문을 고르시오.

A ____________________________?
B She is my English teacher.

① Who do you like better?
② What is her name?
③ What does she do?
④ Who is that woman over there?
⑤ Whom do you talk with?

[21~22] 다음 문장들의 빈칸에 알맞은 단어끼리 짝지어 진 것을 고르시오.

★★★
21

• Sam bought a new sweater yesterday, but he still wears an old __________.
• Sam bought a new sweater yesterday, but he still hasn't worn __________.

① one – one ② ones – it
③ other – ones ④ one – it
⑤ one – that

22

• Phillip wanted to have new gloves, but his mother didn't buy __________.
• I don't want this. Show me __________.

① them – another ② others – another
③ ones – another ④ another – one
⑤ them – one

23 다음 두 문장의 의미가 다른 하나를 고르시오.

① This is my new hat.
= This hat is mine.
② That is Jenny's pencil.
= That pencil is Jenny's.
③ This is your old dress.
= This old dress is yours.
④ This is not my computer.
= This computer is not yours.
⑤ That is your toy bear.
= That toy bear is yours.

[24~26] 다음 빈칸에 공통으로 들어갈 알맞은 단어를 고르시오.

24

- __________ a wonderful day!
- __________ do you want to do after school?

① What ② Where ③ How
④ When ⑤ Who

25

- __________ do you go there?
- __________ is the weather?

① What ② Where ③ When
④ How ⑤ Who

26

- __________ spring here.
- __________ very warm and sunny in Paris these days.

① It is ② They are ③ That is
④ This is ⑤ These are

27 다음 글에서 her가 나타내는 것을 고르시오.

There is an old woman in this town. She is poor and she has no kids.
She is so kind to everyone. She likes to share her things with her neighbors. Everyone likes her. So my friend, Jessica, will have a party for her.

① kids ② neighbors
③ everyone ④ an old woman
⑤ Jessica

28 다음 글의 흐름상 잘못 쓰인 것을 고르시오.

Mr. Barnes is ① a history teacher. He ② teaches us history of the world. ③ He is so nice.
④ Every students like him so much. ⑤ He likes us, too.

[29~30] 다음 글의 빈칸에 들어갈 알맞은 단어들로 짝지어진 것을 고르시오.

29

__________ young people buy all their goods on the Internet.
But __________ young people don't want to buy them on the Internet.

① Some – others ② One – others
③ Some – other ④ One – some
⑤ One – another

30

Jack has two kittens. __________ is white and __________ is black.

① One – other ② One – the other
③ Some – others ④ Some – the other
⑤ Some – the others

31 다음 중 소유대명사로 바꾸었을 때 잘못된 것을 고르시오.

① her computer – hers
② my hat – mine
③ Jason's glasses – Jason's
④ Socrates' theory – Socrates'
⑤ his shirts – his'

◇◇◇◇◇◇◇◇◇◇◇ 서술형 평가 ◇◇◇◇◇◇◇◇◇◇◇

32 다음 대화에서 우리말과 같은 뜻이 되도록 빈칸에 알맞은 말을 쓰시오.

A Hello, can I speak to Tony?
B Who's calling, please?
A __________ Maria.
(저는 Maria입니다.)

[33~34] 우리말과 같은 뜻이 되도록 주어진 단어를 배열하여 문장을 완성하시오.

33

이것은 나의 오빠의 새 가방이다.
(this / brother's / bag)

➡ ______________________________

34

Jenny는 아침 몇 시에 학교에 갑니까?
(What / does / Jenny / time / school / go / to)

➡ ______________________________ in the morning?

[35~38] 다음 주어진 그림과 일치하도록 빈칸에 알맞은 단어를 쓰시오.

35

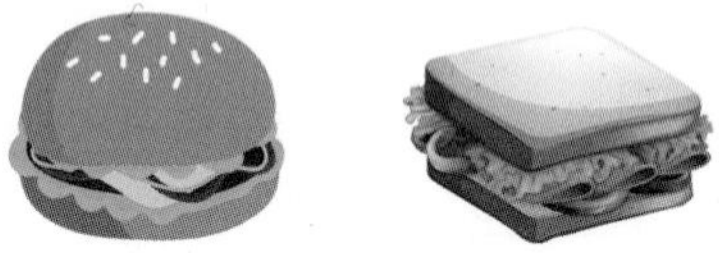

__________ is a hamburger and __________ is a sandwich.

★★★
36

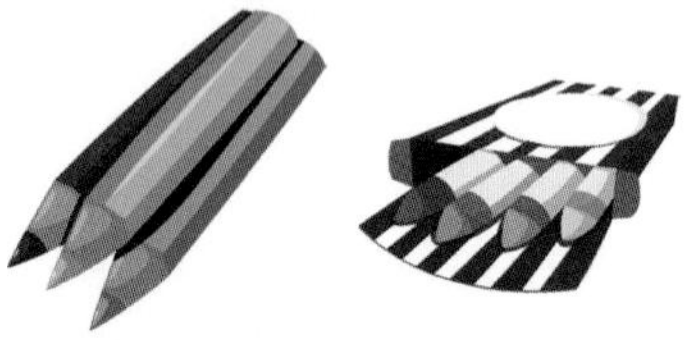

__________ are crayons and __________ are colored pencils.

★★★
37

__________ is a rose, __________ is a lily, and __________ is a carnation.

38

__________ are blue and
__________ are red.

[39~40] 다음 글을 읽고 물음에 답하시오.

It is very cold in Montreal, Canada. Many people go skiing in the mountains in winter. It's snowing today.
___ⓐ___ children are making snowmen, ___ⓑ___ are sledding on the ice.
The old people are cleaning the snow in front of their houses.

39 What are the old people doing today? (대명사를 이용하여 답하시오.)

➡ __________ are cleaning the snow in front of their house.

40 윗글의 밑줄 친 부분이 다음 우리말과 같도록 할 때 ⓐ, ⓑ에 들어갈 알맞은 말을 쓰시오.

어떤 아이들은 눈사람을 만들고, 다른 아이들은 얼음 위에서 썰매를 탄다.

➡ ⓐ __________ ⓑ __________

[41~43] 다음 주어진 문법을 사용하여 지시어대로 문장을 만들어 쓰시오.

★★★
41 소유대명사 사용하기 (2개 문장 만들기)

➡ ______________________________

____

★★★
42 oneself (강조용법)

➡ ______________________________

____

★★★
43 some ~ the others

➡ ______________________________

____

Note

06

Chapter
형용사

Point Check I

◆ **형용사:** 사람이나 사물의 성질, 모양, 상태 등을 나타내며 명사나 대명사를 꾸며준다.
명사의 앞이나 뒤에 위치하여 주격보어나 목적격보어로 쓰이기도 한다.

1. 형용사의 용법 및 위치

(1) **한정적 용법: [형용사 + 명사]**

• My grandmother gave me a **blue** sapphire.

• I like my **white** puppy, Nana.

(2) **서술적 용법**

1) [be동사 (또는 감각동사) + 형용사] ➡ 주격 보어

• She is **ugly**.

• That clown looks **funny**.

➡ (look, sound, smell, feel, taste) ➡ 감각동사 뒤에는 반드시 형용사가 나온다.

2) [목적어 + 형용사] ➡ 목적격보어

The teddy bear makes her children **happy**.

2. 수량 형용사

많은	조금의, 약간의	거의 없는	명사
many	a few	few	+ 셀 수 있는 명사
much	a little	little	+ 셀 수 없는 명사
a lot of, lots of	some, any	–	+ 셀 수 있는 명사, 셀 수 없는 명사

➡ 권유나, 부탁, 제안을 하는 의문문에는 'some'을 사용한다.

Would you like **some** cold water?

➡ 긍정문에 쓰이는 'any'는 '어느 것이든, 어떤 ~라도'의 뜻으로 사용된다.

You can get **any** jobs if you study hard.

3. 기타 형용사

(1) **-one, -body** + 형용사

(2) **every + 숫자**: 매~, ~마다

(3) **not any (= no)**: 조금도(아무것도) ~없는

Lesson 6-1 형용사의 쓰임

• **형용사:** 사람이나 사물의 성질, 모양, 상태 등을 나타내는 말이다.
명사의 앞이나 뒤에서 꾸며주며, 주격보어나 목적격 보어로 쓰인다.

1. 한정적 용법: 명사의 바로 앞 또는 뒤에서 꾸며준다.

(1) 형용사 + 명사

They have a **wonderful** time.

(2) 명사 + 형용사: -thing, -one, -body 등의 부정대명사와 쓰일 때 형용사는 뒤에 온다.

Mary saw something **strange**.

2. 서술적 용법: 주어나 목적어의 상태가 어떠한지를 나타낸다.

(1) 주격보어

This book is **interesting**. [형용사 interesting이 주어 this book을 설명]

(2) 목적격보어

John made us **scared**. [형용사 scared가 목적어 us를 설명]

Check up!

Answer Keys p. 35

A 문장에서 형용사를 찾아 동그라미 하고 수식되는 명사에 밑줄을 그으시오.

1 I think your dress is beautiful.
2 We have a good time.
3 Tim wears a red shirt today.
4 I have a serious problem.
5 Lilly wants to be a good actress.
6 She is so lovely.
7 What a wonderful place!
8 Your sister is cute. How old is she?
9 This lecture is so boring.
10 Tim wants to do something exciting.

형용사의 위치

• **형용사의 위치:** 주격보어로 쓰일 경우 동사 뒤에 나오고, 목적격보어로 쓰일 경우 목적어 뒤에 위치한다. 또 명사 앞에 관사나 소유격 대명사가 있는 경우 관사나 소유격 뒤에 위치한다.

1. **명사의 수식:** [a/an, the + 형용사 + 명사]

• a **red** diamond
• the **beautiful** girls

2. **소유형용사 + 형용사 + 명사:** 소유격의 인칭대명사 (my, your, our, their, his, her, its)를 수식

• my **lovely** baby
• their **new** shoes

→ 소유격 인칭 대명사를 '소유 형용사'라고 한다.

3. **주어나 목적어의 서술:** 주격보어로 쓰일 때는 동사 뒤에, 목적격보어로 쓰일 때는 목적어 뒤에 위치

• She is **happy**.
• We think her **polite**.

Check up!

Answer Keys p. 35

A 다음 우리말 해석과 같도록 주어진 단어를 배열하여 문장을 완성하시오.

1 그들은 하와이에서 멋진 시간을 보냈다. (time, a, great)
= They had ___a great time___ in Hawaii.

2 사람들은 그녀가 아름답다고 생각한다. (is, she, beautiful)
= People think ____________________.

3 그녀는 우리의 새 영어 선생님이다. (new, our, teacher, English)
= She is ____________________.

4 Tom은 자기의 사랑스런 아기 Ann과 함께 잠이 들었다. (lovely, baby, his, Ann)
= Tom slept with ____________________.

5 그 커다란 공연장은 사람들로 붐볐다. (the, hall, concert, big)
= ____________________ was crowded with people.

6 John의 연기는 사람들을 행복하게 해준다. (makes, happy, people)
= John's acting ____________________.

7 정말 귀여운 고양이야! (cute, cat, a)
= What ____________________!

Lesson

6-3 수량형용사_many/much

- many/much: 명사의 수나 양을 나타 낼 수 있는 표현으로, 'many'는 셀 수 있는 명사에 쓰이고, 'much'는 셀 수 없는 명사에 쓰인다.
- a lot of: 셀 수 있는 명사와 셀 수 없는 명사에 모두 사용할 수 있다.

1. many + 셀 수 있는 명사

We have **many** old books.

2. much + 셀 수 없는 명사

Mary has **much** work to do.

3. a lot(= lots) of + 명사 (셀 수 있는 명사, 셀 수 없는 명사)

- There are **a lot of (lots of)** animals in the zoo.
- We have **a lot of (lots of)** food.

4. how many/how much

(1) How many + 셀 수 있는 명사
How many people live in Korea?

(2) How much + 셀 수 없는 명사
How much money do you have?

Check up!

Answer Keys p. 35

A 다음 빈칸에 알맞은 말을 보기 에서 골라 쓰시오.

보기

many much how many how much

1 ___Many___ people think exercising regularly is important.

2 Susan bought ________ flowers for her boyfriend.

3 Thank you very ________ for your help.

4 I have ________ friends from all over the world.

5 He can't buy this car because he doesn't have ________ money.

6 ___________ cars do you have?

7 ___________ money does Tim spend on clothes?

8 ___________ water do they need?

Lesson

6-4 수량형용사_(a) few / (a) little

• (a)few/(a)little: '조금, 약간'의 의미를 가지고 있다.
'(a) few'는 셀 수 있는 명사 앞에, '(a)little'은 셀 수 없는 명사 앞에 붙는다.

1. a few/few + 셀 수 있는 명사

• They have **a few** tomatoes.

• She has **few** friends here.

2. a little/little + 셀 수 없는 명사

• There is **a little** work to be done.

• There is **little** milk in the glass.

➡ 'few'와 'little'은 '거의 없는'의 뜻으로 사용되며 부정적 의미를 지니고 있다.

Grammar Plus +

a few / few

• a few : 조금, 약간 (=긍정문: some, 부정문/의문문: any)

• few : 거의 없는 ('거의 없는'의 뜻을 가지지만 아주 조금이라도 있다는 의미가 되기 때문에 명사의 복수형과 함께 사용한다.)

Check up!

Answer Keys p. 35

A 괄호 안에서 알맞은 것을 고르시오.

1 Billy knows (a few / a little) Korean proverbs.

2 I had (a little / little) spaghetti for dinner.

3 Today is holiday. So, there are (few / little) people in town.

4 I'm so tired. I want to take (a few / a little) nap.

5 There is (a little / a few) time to study.

6 Anna can speak (a little / a few) languages.

7 They visited (a few / a little) cities in Italy.

8 I drank (a few / a little) milk.

9 In (a few / a little) minutes, the train will arrive.

10 There is (a little / a few) trouble between Kate and John.

11 There is (a few / a little) water in the pot.

12 Sam has (few / little) friends to talk with.

13 They should finish their project in (a few / a little) days.

14 There is (little / few) air in the room.

15 Erica has (a little / a few) work to do.

Lesson

6-5 수량형용사_some / any

• some / any: '조금의, 약간의' 뜻을 가지며, 셀 수 있는 명사와 셀 수 없는 명사에 모두 사용할 수 있다. 'some'은 긍정문에, 'any'는 부정문과 의문문에 사용한다.

1. some

• They want to buy **some** strawberries.

➡ 권유나 부탁, 제안을 하는 의문문에는 'some'을 사용한다.

• Would you like **some** coffee?

• Do you want to eat **some** sandwiches?

2. any

• Do you have **any** stamps?

• She does not have **any** coins.

➡ 긍정문에 쓰이는 'any'는 '어느 것이든, 어떤 ~라도'의 뜻으로 사용된다.

If there are **any** problems with the oven, just call us.

Check up!

Answer Keys p. 35

A 다음 빈칸에 some, any 중 알맞은 말을 쓰시오.

1 The doctor said he should take ___*some*___ rest.

2 Do you have ________ questions?

3 I don't have ________ time to go hiking.

4 There are still ________ rooms in the dormitory.

5 Are there ________ tickets?

6 Do you want ________ more chickens?

7 If you miss me, you can come to my house at ________ time.

8 Joe bought ________ beautiful flowers for the party.

9 Do they prepare ________ special activities for the festival?

10 Would you like ________ pasta?

11 She promised that she didn't spend ________ money.

12 Harry wrote ________ books about baseball.

13 Do you have ________ ideas for the trip?

14 I have ________ time before I leave here.

15 I don't have ________ medicine for a cold.

Lesson 6-6 기타 형용사

1. -thing, -one, -body + 형용사

- Let's not do **something** bad for others.
- John is looking at **someone** beautiful.
- There is **nobody** in the room.

2. every + 숫자: 매~, ~마다

- We go shopping **every three days.** [every + 기수 + 복수명사]
  = We go shopping **every third day.** [every + 서수 + 단수명사]
  → every 뒤에 명사가 올 경우에는 단수가 온다.
  Every child likes to play outside. [every + 단수명사]

3. not any (= no): 조금도(아무것도) ~없는

- There are**n't any children** at the playground.
  = There are **no children** at the playground.
- I do**n't** know **anything** about it.
  = I know **nothing** about it.

Check up!

Answer Keys p. 35

A 다음 괄호 안에서 알맞은 것을 고르시오.

1 I want to eat (something sweet / sweet something).

2 Let's do exercise every (fourth / four) days.

3 Does she have (anything else / else anything)?

4 She changes her hair every (two / twice) months.

5 The researchers discovered (something important / important something).

6 Do you need (anything cold / cold anything) to drink?

7 Would you like (drink something / something to drink)?

8 There is (nobody else / else nobody) in the room.

9 He discovered (something wrong / wrong something) in his report.

10 Do (good something / something good) for your class.

Answer Keys p. 35

B

보기 와 같이 짝지어진 두 문장의 의미가 같도록 빈칸을 채우시오.

> 보기
>
> Max doesn't have anything to say.
> = Max has nothing to say.

1 They have nothing to worry about.
= They don't have __________ to worry about.

2 There isn't anyone in the class.
= There is __________ in the class.

3 I don't have anything to wear.
= I have __________ to wear.

4 I cannot eat anything without kimchi.
= I can eat __________ without kimchi.

5 Sally has no time to meet Tim today.
= Sally __________ time to meet Tim today.

6 We couldn't see anything in this village.
= We could see __________ in this village.

7 There is nothing to tell you.
= There isn't __________ to tell you.

8 He doesn't have any water to drink.
= He has __________ to drink.

9 I have nothing special planned this weekend.
= I don't have __________ special planned this weekend.

10 She has no time to do exercise.
= She doesn't have __________ time to do exercise.

Practice More I

A 다음 문장에서 형용사에 동그라미 하시오.

1 I have a (great) time in LA.

2 It's so delicious.

3 There are a few people in the hall.

4 He is a nice son.

5 Mr.Kim is a famous actor in Korea.

6 This cookie is so sweet.

7 Helen is so beautiful girl. Everyone think she is also kind.

8 We had a wonderful dinner tonight.

B 아래의 수량형용사 다음에 들어갈 수 있는 명사를 보기 에서 골라서 모두 쓰시오.

보기

money baby deer coffee dog friend water

1 many ➡ *baby, deer, dog, friend*

2 much ➡ ____________________

3 a few ➡ ____________________

4 lots of ➡ ____________________

5 little ➡ ____________________

6 any ➡ ____________________

7 few ➡ ____________________

C 괄호 안의 형용사를 알맞은 위치에 넣어 문장을 다시 쓰시오.

1 Sally is a student. (diligent)

➡ *Sally is a diligent student*.

2 I have a book. (interesting)

➡ ____________________.

3 There is a boy. (tall)

➡ ____________________.

Answer Keys p. 36

4 I have nothing to say for her. (special)

➡ ______________________________.

5 Tim has talent. (artistic)

➡ ______________________________.

6 Father gave me a puzzle. (difficult)

➡ ______________________________.

7 He has a sense of humor. (nice)

➡ ______________________________.

8 I love your smile. (beautiful)

➡ ______________________________.

9 I don't have time. (much)

➡ ______________________________.

D 다음 문장에서 어법상 어색한 것을 찾아 바르게 고치시오.

1 Tim has a few ink.

a few ➡ *a little*

2 She is a beautifully woman.

__________ ➡ __________

3 I have few money.

__________ ➡ __________

4 Would you like any coffee?

__________ ➡ __________

5 That music sounds terribly.

__________ ➡ __________

6 He had much chances to win.

__________ ➡ __________

7 I want to do interesting something.

__________ ➡ __________

8 He will be a well student.

__________ ➡ __________

9 She exercises every two day.

__________ ➡ __________

Practice More I

Answer Keys p. 35

서술형 연습 **E** **다음 우리말 해석에 맞게 주어진 단어들을 배열하여 문장을 완성하시오.**

1 그의 얼굴이 창백해졌다. (pale, turned, face, his)

➡ *His face turned pale.*

2 그녀는 좋은 엄마가 될 것이다. (mother, she, will, a, good, be)

➡ ______________________________

3 차가운 음료 좀 드릴까요?
(would, to drink, you, something, like, cold)

➡ ______________________________

4 Kelly에게는 쿠키 몇 개와 물이 약간 필요했다.
(Kelly, water, a few, a little, cookies, needed, and)

➡ ______________________________

5 그 단체는 병든 강아지들을 돕는다.
(The organization, the sick, helps, dogs)

➡ ______________________________

6 새로운 집은 꽤 크다. (new, big, the, house, is, so)

➡ ______________________________

7 나는 뭔가 빠른 걸 원해. (I, fast, something, want)

➡ ______________________________

8 그 노래는 나를 우울하게 해. (gloomy, the song, me, makes)

➡ ______________________________

9 어항 안에는 물고기가 몇 마리 있다.
(are, in the fishbowl, there, fish, a few)

➡ ______________________________

10 소풍 가는 데 얼마나 많은 돈을 썼니?
(much, going on a picnic, spend on, you, how, did, money)

➡ ______________________________

Point Check Ⅱ

◆ **기수와 서수:** 일반적으로 개수를 나타내는 숫자를 '기수'라고 하고, 순서를 나타내는 숫자를 '서수'라고 한다.

1. 기수와 서수

기수 뒤에 'th'를 붙이면 서수가 되며, 보통 서수는 'the'와 함께 사용한다.

기수		서수 (the ~)	
1	one	1st	first
2	two	2nd	second
3	three	3rd	third
4	four	4th	fourth
5	five	5th	fifth
6	six	6th	sixth
7	seven	7th	seventh
8	eight	8th	eighth
9	nine	9th	ninth
10	ten	10th	tenth

2. 기수와 서수를 이용한 숫자 읽기

- 427 = four hundred (and) twenty-seven
- 203–1647 = two oh three, one six four seven
- 12.39 = twelve point three nine
- 0.05 = (zero) point zero five
- $\frac{1}{2}$ = a half / one half
- $\frac{3}{4}$ = three fourths / three quarters
- 1976 = nineteen seventy-six
- 2014 = two thousand (and) fourteen
- 32℃ = thirty-two **degrees Celsius**
- 85℉ = eighty-five **degrees Fahrenheit**
- 1979년 8월 5일 (월/일/연도 순으로 읽음) = August (the) fifth, nineteen seventy-nine
- ₩8,236 = eight thousand, two hundred (and) thirty-six won

3. 시각 표현

- 09 : 00 = nine o'clock
- 07 : 30 = half past seven

4. 형용사의 관용표현

- dozens of~, scores of : 수십의
- hundreds of~ : 수백의

Lesson 6-7

기수와 서수

• **기수와 서수:** 기수는 '개수'를 나타내고, 서수는 '순서'를 나타내는 말이다.
보통 서수는 앞에 'the'와 함께 사용하며 기수 뒤에 'th'를 붙여서 만든다.

◈ 기수와 서수

기수			
1	one	19	nineteen
2	two	20	twenty
3	three	21	twenty-one
4	four	22	twenty-two
5	five	23	twenty-three
6	six	24	twenty-four
7	seven	25	twenty-five
8	eight	30	thirty
9	nine	40	forty
10	ten	50	fifty
11	eleven	80	eighty
12	twelve	90	ninety
13	thirteen	100	one hundred
14	fourteen	1,000	one thousand
15	fifteen	1,000,000	one million

서수			
1st	first	19th	nineteenth
2nd	second	20th	twentieth
3rd	third	21st	twenty-first
4th	fourth	22nd	twenty-second
5th	fifth	23rd	twenty-third
6th	sixth	24th	twenty-fourth
7th	seventh	25th	twenty-fifth
8th	eighth	30th	thirtieth
9th	ninth	40th	fortieth
10th	tenth	50th	fiftieth
11th	eleventh	80th	eightieth
12th	twelfth	90th	ninetieth
13th	thirteenth	100th	one hundredth
14th	fourteenth	1,000th	one thousandth
15th	fifteenth	1,000,000th	one millionth

Check up!

Answer Keys p. 36

A 다음을 서수로 바꿔 쓰시오.

1 nine ➡ ninth
2 one ➡ ________
3 two ➡ ________
4 fifteen ➡ ________
5 one thousand ➡ ________
6 three ➡ ________
7 forty ➡ ________
8 seven ➡ ________
9 ten ➡ ________
10 twenty-two ➡ ________
11 thirty ➡ ________
12 eighteen ➡ ________
13 ninety-nine ➡ ________
14 twenty ➡ ________
15 seventeen ➡ ________
16 eight ➡ ________
17 eleven ➡ ________
18 four ➡ ________
19 sixty-seven ➡ ________
20 five ➡ ________
21 one hundred ➡ ________
22 twenty-three ➡ ________
23 seventy-four ➡ ________
24 sixty-six ➡ ________
25 fifty-one ➡ ________
26 thirty-three ➡ ________

B 괄호 안의 숫자를 서수 형태로 바꾸어 쓰시오.

1 My second daughter will get married summer. (2)
2 Today is our parents' ________ wedding anniversary. (20)
3 He is in his ________ year of high school. (3)
4 May ________ is Children's Day. (5)
5 Helen's birthday is on March the ________. (13)
6 My office is on the ________ floor. (1)
7 This is my ________ trip to Japan. (4)

Lesson

6-8 기수와 서수를 이용한 숫자 읽기 (1)

1. **정수:** 3자리씩 끊어 읽는다. hundred 뒤의 and는 생략이 가능하다.
   - 427 = four hundred (and) twenty-seven
   - 2,745 = two thousand, seven hundred (and) forty-five
   - 32,759 = thirty-two thousand, seven hundred (and) fifty-nine

2. **전화번호:** 한 자리씩 읽는다. 같은 숫자가 두 개 나오는 경우 double을 이용한다.
   숫자 '0'은 'zero' 또는 'oh'라고 읽는다.
   - 938–7885 = nine three eight, seven eight eight five (= seven double eight five)
   - 203–1647 = two oh three, one six four seven

3. **소수:** 소수점은 'point'로 읽고, 소수점 이하는 한 자리씩 읽는다.
   - 7.25 = seven point two five
   - 12.39 = twelve point three nine
   - 0.05 = (zero) point zero five

4. **분수:** 분자부터 읽고 분모를 읽는다. 분자는 기수로, 분모는 서수로 읽는다.
   분자가 2 이상일 경우 분모에 복수를 뜻하는 '-s'를 붙여준다.
   - $\frac{1}{3}$ = a third / one third
   - $\frac{6}{7}$ = six seventh**s**
   - $\frac{3}{4}$ = three fourth**s** / three quarter**s**
   - $2\frac{3}{5}$ = two and three fifth**s**

Check up!

Answer Keys p. 36~37

A **다음 숫자 표현들을 영어로 읽으시오.**

1 428 ➡ *four hundred twenty-eight*

2 32,850 ➡ ____________________

3 7,789 ➡ ____________________

4 660 ➡ ____________________

5 9.87 ➡ ____________________

6 9,807 ➡ ______________________

7 658 ➡ ______________________

8 2,580 ➡ ______________________

9 $\frac{5}{6}$ ➡ ______________________

10 748 ➡ ______________________

11 530 ➡ ______________________

12 0.98 ➡ ______________________

13 $2\frac{1}{3}$ ➡ ______________________

14 66 ➡ ______________________

15 19,487 ➡ ______________________

16 6.589 ➡ ______________________

17 $\frac{1}{2}$ ➡ ______________________

18 21,203 ➡ ______________________

19 1,004 ➡ ______________________

20 0.078 ➡ ______________________

B 다음 전화번호를 영어로 읽으시오.

1 732-1717 ➡ *seven three two, one seven one seven*

2 2948-8903 ➡ ______________________

3 4588-9748 ➡ ______________________

4 112 ➡ ______________________

5 018-6914-8154 ➡ ______________________

6 1-847-985-2035 ➡ ______________________

7 2015-4875 ➡ ______________________

Lesson 6-9 기수와 서수를 이용한 숫자 읽기 (2)

1. **연도:** 보통 두 자리씩 끊어 읽는다.
   - 1976 = nineteen seventy-six
   - 1700 = seventeen hundred (= one thousand, seven hundred)
   - 2002 = two thousand (and) two
   - 2013 = two thousand (and) thirteen (= twenty hundred and thirteen/twenty thirteen)

2. **날짜**
   - 5월 8일 = May (the) fifth (= the fifth of May)
   - 2015년 10월 5일 (월 / 일 / 연도 순으로 읽음)
     = October (the) fifth, twenty-fifteen (= the fifth of October, twenty-fifteen)
     ※ '2015'의 다른 표기: two thousand fifteen

3. **금액:** 미화는 dollar와 cent를 사용하여 읽고, 원화는 won을 사용하여 읽는다.
   - $52.72 = fifty-two dollars (and) seventy-two cents (= fifty-two, seventy-two)
   - ₩8,236 = eight thousand, two hundred (and) thirty-six won

4. **온도:** 섭씨는 Celsius, 화씨는 Fahrenheit를 사용하여 읽는다.
   - 35℃ = thirty-five degrees Celsius
   - 79℉ = seventy-nine degrees Fahrenheit

5. **기타**
   - 1950's = the nineteen fifties
   - 18세기 = the eighteenth century
   - 21세기 = the twenty-first century

Check up!

Answer Keys p. 37

A 다음 연도와 날짜를 영어로 읽으시오.

1 2018 ➡ *two thousand eighteen*

2 3월 21일 ➡ ______

3 1997 ➡ ______

4 1월 25일 ➡ ______

5 10월 12일 ➡ ______

6 1989 ➡ ______

7 11월 22일 ➡ ______

8 1999년 3월 17일 ➡ ______

9 12월 13일 ➡ ______

10 2015년 7월 10일 ➡ ______

B 다음 금액을 영어로 읽으시오

1 $30.85 ➡ *thirty dollars(and) eighty-five cents*

2 $15.74 ➡ ______

3 ₩8,648 ➡ ______

4 $95.74 ➡ ______

5 $74.18 ➡ ______

6 ₩84,510 ➡ ______

C 다음 온도를 영어로 읽으시오

1 69℃ ➡ *sixty nine degrees Celsius*

2 17℉ ➡ ______

3 648℃ ➡ ______

4 174℉ ➡ ______

5 211.85℃ ➡ ______

6 147.655℉ ➡ ______

7 0.145℉ ➡ ______

Lesson

6-10 시각 표현

1. 정각: 'o'clock'을 붙여 읽는다.

- 10 : 00 = ten o'clock
- 03 : 00 = three o'clock

2. 시간과 분

(1) 일반적으로 읽기

- 05 : 20 = five twenty
- 03 : 37 = three thirty-seven
- 11 : 25 = eleven twenty-five

(2) 전치사를 사용하여 읽기 : 'after ~을 지나서', 'to ~전에'

- 07 : 05 = five after seven
- 07 : 10 = ten after seven
- 07 : 15 = a quarter after seven/a quarter past seven
- 07 : 20 = twenty after seven
- 07 : 25 = twenty-five after seven
- 07 : 30 = half past seven
- 07 : 35 = twenty-five to eight
- 07 : 40 = twenty to eight
- 07 : 45 = fifteen to eight
- 07 : 50 = ten to eight
- 07 : 55 = five to eight

➡ 'a quarter, half'를 쓰면 after 대신에 'past'를 사용한다.

3. 시간을 물어보는 표현

- What time is it (now)?
- Do you have the time?

Check up!

Answer Keys p. 37

A 다음 시각을 영어로 읽으시오.

1 5 : 35 ➡ *five thirty-five*　　2 9 : 23 ➡ ____________

3 1 : 29 ➡ ____________　　4 12 : 37 ➡ ____________

5 4 : 26 ➡ ____________　　6 12 : 06 ➡ ____________

7 11 : 02 ➡ ____________　　8 4 : 28 ➡ ____________

9 3 : 04 ➡ ____________　　10 5 : 57 ➡ ____________

Check up!

Answer Keys p. 37

B 다음 시각을 after(past) 또는 to를 사용하여 영어로 읽으시오.

1 10 : 25 ➡ *twenty-five after ten*

2 07 : 45 ➡ ______________

3 09 : 40 ➡ ______________

4 11 : 30 ➡ ______________

5 05 : 15 ➡ ______________

6 11 : 25 ➡ ______________

7 8 : 50 ➡ ______________

8 3 : 15 ➡ ______________

9 1 : 55 ➡ ______________

10 2 : 10 ➡ ______________

11 4 : 40 ➡ ______________

12 6 : 45 ➡ ______________

13 1 : 20 ➡ ______________

14 5 : 35 ➡ ______________

15 12 : 15 ➡ ______________

16 1 : 35 ➡ ______________

17 1 : 10 ➡ ______________

18 2 : 20 ➡ ______________

19 3 : 35 ➡ ______________

20 4 : 45 ➡ ______________

21 11 : 15 ➡ ______________

22 6 : 55 ➡ ______________

23 7 : 05 ➡ ______________

24 8 : 25 ➡ ______________

25 9 : 50 ➡ ______________

Lesson

6-11 형용사의 관용 표현

• 숫자를 이용한 표현 중에 'hundreds(thousands, millions, dozens, scores) of'는 구체적인 수가 아닌 막연한 수를 나타낼 때 쓰며, of 뒤에는 복수명사가 온다.

(1) **dozens of, scores of:** 수십의

Mary bought **dozens (scores) of eggs** at the market.

(2) **hundreds of:** 수백의

Hundreds of mice begin to run.

(3) **thousands of:** 수천의

Thousands of people cheer for the team.

(4) **tens of thousands of:** 수만의

Tens of thousands of soldiers were died in the war.

(5) **millions of:** 수백만의

People cut down **millions of** trees every year.

Check up!

Answer Keys p. 38

A **다음 우리말 해석과 같은 뜻이 되도록 문장을 완성하시오.**

1 나는 수십 장의 우표를 수집했다.
= I have collected ___*dozens of*___ stamps.

2 수천명의 사람들이 콘서트홀에 모였다.
= ______________ people gathered in the concert hall.

3 이 왕궁은 수백 년 전에 지어졌다.
= This palace was built ______________ years ago.

4 Tim은 어제 수십 장의 편지를 받았다.
= Tim received ______________ letters.

5 수만의 병사들이 전쟁에 참여했다.
= ______________ soldiers took part in the war.

6 극장에는 수백 개의 좌석이 있다.
= There are ______________ seats in the theater.

7 그 단체는 매년 수백 그루의 나무를 심는다.
= The organization plants ______________ trees every year.

8 수백 만 명의 사람들이 김연아의 피겨 스케이트 경기를 보고 있다.
= __________ people are watching Yuna Kim's figure skating.

Practice More Ⅱ

Answer Keys p. 38

A 다음 괄호 안의 숫자를 문맥에 맞게 기수 또는 서수로 고쳐서 빈칸에 쓰시오.

1 She has ___*four*___ babies. (4)

2 Tim lives on the __________ floor in this building and he has __________ dogs. (3 / 2)

3 There are __________ people in the hall. (15)

4 Go straight __________ blocks and turn left. (2)

5 Saturday is the __________ day of the week. (6)

6 John got the __________ place in an English speaking contest. (1)

7 She has lived in LA for __________ years. (9)

8 My birthday is the __________ day of March. (13)

9 It's __________ kilometers from here to my school.(70)

10 Sally is __________ years old. (24)

11 Today is my parents' __________ wedding anniversary. (14)

12 She is still teaching English although she is __________ years old. (60)

13 I spent __________ dollars on my son's birthday party. (10,000)

14 Kid's wear is on the __________ floor. (5)

15 Ann usually drinks __________ cups of coffee in a day. (5)

B 다음 여러 가지 숫자와 날짜 표현을 영어로 읽으시오.

1 2581 ➡ ___*two thousand five hundred (and) eighty-one*___

2 3월 27일 ➡ ______________________________

3 0.293 ➡ ______________________________

4 1989년 ➡ ______________________________

5 1,000,000 ➡ ______________________________

6 3.591 ➡ ______________________________

7 2005년 1월 26일 ➡ ______________________________

8 $88.19 ➡ ______________________________

9 $\frac{4}{7}$ ➡ ______________________________

10 2015년 6월 12일 ➡ ______________________________

11 13세기 ➡ ______________________________

12 $6\frac{4}{5}$ ➡ ______________________

13 138.17 ➡ ______________________

14 1730's ➡ ______________________

15 ₩7,459 ➡ ______________________

C 다음 시간을 past 또는 to를 사용하여 영어로 읽으시오.

1 8:30 ➡ *It's half past eight*　　2 3:15 ➡ ______________

3 10:15 ➡ ______________　　4 5:45 ➡ ______________

5 2:10 ➡ ______________　　6 11:30 ➡ ______________

서술형 연습 **D** 다음 우리말에 맞게 빈칸에 알맞은 말을 쓰시오.

1 내 여동생은 이 중학교의 3학년이다.
➡ My sister is in *the third* grade at this middle school.

2 Helen의 전화번호는 010-732-1717이다.
➡ Helen's phone number is ______________________.

3 Mr. Kim의 사무실은 이 건물 16층입니다.
➡ Mr. Kim's office is on ______________ of this building.

4 수업은 9시 15분 전에 시작한다.
➡ The class starts at ______________.

5 오늘은 섭씨 33도다.
➡ It's ______________ today.

6 수 백 명의 사람들이 그의 콘서트에 갔다.
➡ ______________ went to his concert.

7 Tim은 665장의 우표를 모았다.
➡ Tim collected ______________________.

8 200만 명의 사람들이 그 영화를 보았다.
➡ ______________ saw the movie.

9 오늘은 6월 19일이다.
➡ Today is ______________________.

10 그는 수십 권의 책을 썼다.
➡ He wrote ______________ books.

중간 기말고사 예상문제

Answer Keys p. 38

내신 최다 출제 유형

01 다음 중 어법상 올바른 것끼리 짝지어진 것을 고르시오. [출제 예상 85%]

ⓐ I need some help.
ⓑ They don't have some milk.
ⓒ Jack has many money.
ⓓ Would you like to eat some cherries?
ⓔ Much birds fly in the sky.

① ⓐ, ⓓ ② ⓑ, ⓓ ③ ⓒ, ⓔ
④ ⓑ, ⓐ ⑤ ⓒ, ⓑ

02 다음 문장의 밑줄 친 부분이 어색한 것을 고르시오. [출제 예상 80%]

① Would you like to eat some pizza?
② We didn't see any cute boys.
③ There are a little bananas in the basket.
④ You have some money to buy this hamburger.
⑤ Mary has much homework to do.

03 다음 문장의 빈칸에 올 수 없는 형태의 단어를 고르시오. [출제 예상 80%]

Anna and I wanted to buy something ________.

① special ② beautiful ③ cute
④ love ⑤ unique

04 다음 문장에서 어색한 부분을 찾아 고치시오. [출제 예상 80%]

There isn't many water in the bottle.

________ ➡ ________

[05~06] 다음 글을 읽고 물음에 답하시오. [출제 예상 90%]

ⓐ Many teenagers have their own smartphone. They always carry them. ⓑ How many time do they spend using their smartphone a day? Sometimes teenagers forget ⓒ to study, do homework, even ⓓ eat meals. A smartphone is ⓔ not bad. However, it is not good for their health if (A) teenagers use smartphones too much.

05 윗글의 ⓐ~ⓔ 중 어법상 어색한 것을 고르고, 바르게 고치시오.

➡ ________________

06 윗글의 밑줄 친 (A)에서 대명사로 바꿀 수 있는 것을 모두 바꾸어서 다시 쓰시오.

➡ ________________

07 다음 문장의 밑줄 친 부분을 같은 뜻이 되도록 다른 말로 고쳐 쓰시오. [출제 예상 80%]

There isn't anyone else in my house.

➡ ________

중간 기말고사 예상문제

[01~02] 다음 문장의 빈칸에 들어갈 단어로 적당하지 않은 것을 고르시오.

01

Jessy is a __________ woman.

① poor ② lovely ③ smart
④ friend ⑤ pretty

02

His voice sounds __________ now.

① funny ② husky ③ nicely
④ strange ⑤ high

03 다음 문장 중 밑줄 친 부분이 어법상 올바른 것을 고르시오.

① Phillip is a handsome boy.
② This cloth feels softly.
③ Is there warm anything to eat?
④ The show makes me happily.
⑤ Your hands are looks dirty.

04 다음 문장 중 문법적으로 올바른 것을 고르시오.

① Those flowers smells sweet.
② I watched a movie funny yesterday.
③ She is so kind to her friends.
④ There is lots of people.
⑤ They bought hot something to drink.

[05~06] 다음 중 나머지 넷과 성격이 다른 하나를 고르시오.

05 ① pretty ② nice ③ happily
④ tall ⑤ fat

06 ① ugly ② late ③ sad
④ glad ⑤ cloud

[07~08] 다음 짝지어진 단어가 바르지 않은 것을 고르시오.

07 ① one – first ② twenty – twentieth
③ three – threeth ④ fifteen – fifteenth
⑤ thirty – thirtieth

08 ① four – fourth
② twenty-one – twentieth first
③ two – second
④ thirty-one – thirty first
⑤ nine – ninth

[09~10] 다음 빈칸에 들어갈 수 없는 단어를 고르시오.

09

There are __________ problems in this city.

① many ② a few ③ lots of
④ few ⑤ much

Answer Keys p. 39~40

10

Helen has __________ pretty dresses.

① a little ② a few ③ many
④ a lot of ⑤ few

[10~11] 다음 빈칸에 들어갈 알맞은 단어를 고르시오.

11

Jack __________ nice today.

① smells ② look ③ has
④ looks ⑤ were

12

We __________ the delicious food.

① are ② looks ③ smell
④ were ⑤ smells

[13~15] 다음 중 숫자를 영어로 읽은 것 중 잘못된 것을 고르시오.

13
① 1985년 – nineteen eighty-five
② 2007년 – two thousand seven
③ 256년 – two fifty-six
④ 1900년 – nineteen hundred
⑤ 1979년 – one nine hundred seventy-nine

14
① 57 – five-seven
② 489 – four hundred and eighty-nine
③ 1,748 – one thousand, seven hundred (and) forty-eight
④ 50,000 – fifty thousand
⑤ 75,379 – seventy-five thousand, three hundred (and) seventy-nine

15
① $\frac{1}{5}$ – a fifth
② $\frac{1}{2}$ – one half
③ $\frac{4}{8}$ – four eighths
④ $2\frac{3}{4}$ – two and three fourth
⑤ $\frac{1}{4}$ – a quarter

[16~18] 다음 주어진 문장과 바꿔 쓸 수 있는 표현을 고르시오.

16

It's a quarter to ten.

① It's nine forty-five.
② It's eleven fifteen.
③ It's ten fifteen.
④ It's ten forty-five.
⑤ It's nine fifteen.

17

It's June (the) thirteenth.

① They're June thirteenth.
② That's the thirteenth of June.
③ It's the thirteenth of June.
④ It's June thirteen.
⑤ It's thirteen, June.

18

It's May the ninth, nineteen eighty-six.

① It's May, nine, nineteen eighty-six.
② It's nine of the May, nineteen eighty-six.
③ It's nineteen eighty-six, ninth of May.
④ It's the ninth of May, nineteen eighty-six.
⑤ It's nineteen eighty-six of May ninth.

[19~20] 다음 문장의 밑줄 친 부분과 바꾸어 쓸 수 있는 단어를 고르시오.

19

Suah and I drink <u>a lot of</u> coffee everyday.

① few ② much ③ any
④ many ⑤ a few

20

We could see <u>lots of</u> beautiful flowers at Versailles Palace.

① much ② few ③ some
④ plenty of ⑤ any

[21~22] 다음 밑줄 친 부분을 영어로 바르게 바꾼 것을 고르시오.

21

A When is Jane's birthday?
B It's <u>12월 28일</u>.

① twenty-eighth December
② December of twenty-eighth
③ twenty-eighth of December
④ December twenty-eighth
⑤ December, two eight

22

A: What is todays date?
B: It's <u>8월 31일</u>.

① the August of thirty - first
② the thirty - first of August
③ eight thirty - first
④ thirty - one of August
⑤ August, thirty - oneth

[23~24] 다음 문장 중 문법적으로 맞는 것을 <u>모두</u> 고르시오.

23
① How many honey do you have?
② Jacky has few friends.
③ Would you like some more ice cream?
④ We don't have some water.
⑤ Jennifer wants a few advice from you.

24
① There is a few Chinese students in the class.
② She made much mistakes in the speech contest.
③ We are looking for any pets.
④ There is a little water in the pale.
⑤ He didn't have much time to exercise.

[25~26] 다음 문장 중 밑줄 친 부분이 <u>어색한</u> 것을 <u>모두</u> 고르시오.

25
① Can I have <u>some</u> cheese?
② You didn't bring <u>anything</u> to eat.
③ She doesn't have <u>some</u> money.
④ There isn't <u>any</u> milk in the pack.
⑤ Would you like to have <u>any</u> cookies?

26 ① She was so confusing.
② We were very exciting.
③ The movie was sad.
④ I feel tired with hard work.
⑤ Little kids are scared of thunder.

[27~28] 주어진 우리말에 맞게 빈칸에 들어갈 알맞은 단어를 고르시오.

27

수천 명의 사람들이 그를 보기 위해 모였다. ➡ __________ ________ people gathered to see him.

① Hundreds of ② Lots of
③ Most of ④ Thousands of
⑤ Dozens of

28

나의 할머니는 며칠 전 매우 슬퍼 보였다. ➡ My grandmother looked very sad __________ ago.

① a few days ② a little days
③ few days ④ some days
⑤ any days

29 다음 중 시간 표현이 잘못된 것을 고르시오.

① 12:35 – twelve thirty-five
② 3:47 – three forty-seven
③ 7:50 – ten to eight
④ 6:45 – a quarter past five
⑤ 12:00 – twelve o'clock

[30~31] 다음 빈칸에 들어갈 단어의 형태로 올바른 것을 고르시오.

30

We were very __________ that Sam had an accident.

① surprising ② have surprised
③ surprised ④ to surprise
⑤ be surprised

31

The night view of Namsan Tower is so __________.

① to be amazed ② amazing
③ amazed ④ being amazed
⑤ amazes

★★★
32 다음 대화의 빈칸에 들어갈 단어가 순서대로 바르게 나열된 것을 고르시오.

A Did you have fun at the amusement park? **B** Yes. Everything was __________ and wonderful. We felt Especially __________ to see the parade. It was fantastic that pretty and cute characters were __________. **A** That sounds fun!

① grateful – amazed – move
② great – amazing – moved
③ great – amazed – moving
④ greatest – be amazed – move
⑤ great – amazed – be moving

33 다음 문장 중 밑줄 친 부분이 어색한 것을 고르시오.

① Lots of person go skiing in winter.
② She has two tomatoes for lunch.
③ The baby drank a lot of milk.
④ Can I have some chicken?
⑤ There are some rules at school.

34 다음 빈칸에 들어갈 수 없는 단어를 고르시오.

> How many ________ does she want?

① flowers ② apples ③ erasers
④ boxes ⑤ water

35 다음 빈칸에 들어갈 알맞은 단어를 고르시오.

> I studied very hard with my mom last night.
> But I can't remember ________. What should I do?

① nothing ② anything
③ something ④ all
⑤ every

36 다음 밑줄 친 nice의 쓰임이 다른 하나를 고르시오.

① That is a nice movie.
② This is a nice picture.
③ They had a nice holiday.
④ She is really nice and kind.
⑤ We found a nice hat.

◇◇◇◇◇◇◇◇◇◇ 서술형 평가 ◇◇◇◇◇◇◇◇◇◇

[37~38] 다음 주어진 두 문장이 같은 뜻이 되도록 빈칸에 알맞은 말을 쓰시오

37 The lady is very pretty.

➡ She is ____________________

38 That picture is really fantastic.

➡ It is ____________________

[39~40] 다음 문장에서 틀린 단어를 찾아 고친 후 문장을 다시 쓰시오.

39

> The clown looks very sadly.

➡ ____________________

40

> This is a very excited ride.

➡ ____________________

[41~42] 다음 중 어법상 틀린 것을 2개 골라 차례대로 고쳐 쓰세요.

> ① There is few rain in Africa.
> ② Would you like any cold water?
> ③ I don't want anything.
> ④ How many monkeys are in the zoo?
> ⑤ I was so bored by his long talk.

★★★
41 ____________________

Answer Keys p. 39~40

★★★
42 ______________________

[43~44] 다음 글을 읽고 물음에 답하시오.

> It was sunny yesterday. I went to the amusement park with my friends.
> We enjoyed ⓐ much rides. They were very ⓑ exciting. We watched a parade.
> The parade was ⓒ fantastic. There were ⓓ a lot of people came to see it.
> And we went a haunted house. Oh, my! It was really ⓔ scaring.
> We bought (A) 약간의 souvenirs. They were (B) 3,000원 each.

43 윗글의 ⓐ ~ ⓔ에서 어법상 틀린 것을 찾아 고쳐 쓰시오.

➡ ______________________

44 윗글의 밑줄 친 (A)와 (B)를 영어로 알맞게 쓰시오.

(A) ______________________

(B) ______________________

★★★
45 다음 날짜를 영어로 알맞게 쓰시오.

> 1976년 3월 23일

➡ ______________________

[46~48] 다음 우리말을 영어로 바르게 영작 하시오.

46 Gijoon의 생일은 1998년 5월 24일이야.

➡ ______________________

____

47 이곳은 섭씨 36도입니다.

➡ ______________________ here.

48 그는 운동할 어떤 시간도 없다.

➡ ______________________

Note

07

Chapter
부사

Point Check I

◆ **부사:** 부사는 다른 말을 도와서 더 자세한 내용을 나타내는 말로서 문장 안에서 동사, 형용사, 부사 또는 문장 전체를 설명한다.

1. 부사의 역할

(1) **동사 수식**
We have to follow the rules **well**.

(2) **형용사 수식**
They are **very** funny.

(3) **부사 수식**
I swim **pretty** well.

(4) **문장 전체 수식**
Luckily, I got an average grade on the test.

2. 부사의 종류

장소	here, there, inside, outside, upstairs, abroad
시간	today, yesterday, tomorrow, now, then
빈도	always, often, usually, sometimes, never, once
강조, 정도	very, so , quite, too, pretty

3. 형용사를 부사로 바꾸는 방법

대부분의 형용사	-ly	quick 빠른	➡	quickly 빠르게
		large 큰	➡	largely 크게
		safe 안전한	➡	safely 안전하게
'자음+y'로 끝나는 경우	y를 i로 바꾸고 -ly	easy 쉬운	➡	easily 쉽게
		happy 행복한	➡	happily 행복하게

4. 부사와 형용사의 형태가 같은 단어들

단어	의미	단어	의미
fast	형 빠른, 신속한 / 부 빨리	**early**	형 이른, 초기의 / 부 일찍
hard	형 열심인, 어려운 / 부 열심히	**late**	형 늦은 / 부 늦게
long	형 긴 / 부 길게	**well**	형 훌륭한 / 부 잘
high	형 높은 / 부 높게	**pretty**	형 예쁜 / 부 꽤
low	형 낮은 / 부 낮게	**daily**	형 매일의 / 부 매일

Lesson **7-1**

부사의 역할

• **부사:** 부사는 다른 말을 도와서 더 자세히 알려주는 말로서, 부사는 문장 안에서 동사, 형용사, 다른 부사 또는 문장 전체를 설명한다.

1. 동사 수식

We must **study hard.**

2. 형용사 수식

He is **very handsome.**

3. 부사 수식

My sister runs **very fast.**

4. 문장 전체 수식

Fortunately, I didn't hurt at the accident.

Grammar Plus +

부사가 꾸며주는 동사는 일반동사이다.
be동사 또는 감각동사 뒤에는 반드시 형용사가 나와야 한다.

Check up!

Answer Keys p. 41

A 다음 문장에서 부사를 찾아 밑줄 치시오.

1 She drives carefully.

2 Sue smiles happily.

3 Thank you very much.

4 My sister can run fast.

5 I'm really sorry.

6 I want to speak English fluently.

7 He was very handsome.

8 I certainly don't want to be with you.

9 The test was quite difficult.

10 The accident happened suddenly.

B 다음 문장에서 표시된 부사가 수식하는 말을 찾아 동그라미 치시오.

1 John solves the problem easily.

2 I usually wake up early.

3 She studies hard to pass the exam.

4 Tim looks so tired.

Lesson

7-2 부사의 종류

• **부사의 종류:** 방법, 장소, 시간, 횟수, 강조, 정도, 의문을 나타내는 부사들이 있으며, 대개의 부사는 '형용사 + ly'의 형태로 만들어진다.

1. '방법, 방식'의 부사

• Mr. Brown walks **fast**.
• It snowed **heavily**.

2. '장소, 시간'의 부사

장소	here, there, inside, outside, upstairs, abroad
시간	today, yesterday, tomorrow, now, then

• Let's go **outside**.
• John and she did homework together **yesterday**.

3. '빈도, 강조, 정도'의 부사

빈도	always, often, usually, sometimes, never, once
강조, 정도	very, so, quite, too, pretty

• You **always** misunderstand me.
• She is **too** silly.

Check up!

Answer Keys p. 41

A 우리말 해석에 맞게 빈칸에 알맞은 부사를 쓰시오.

1 위층으로 올라가보자.
➡ Let's go ___upstairs___.

2 오늘 시간 있니?
➡ Are you free ____________?

3 Joe와 Sally는 어제 공원에서 조깅을 했다.
➡ Joe and Sally jogged in the park ____________.

4 나는 가끔 나의 강아지와 산책한다.
➡ I ____________ walk my dog.

5 Mr. Kim은 다음 주에 해외로 떠난다.
➡ Mr. Kim will go ____________ next week.

6 어제는 눈이 많이 왔다.
➡ It snowed ____________ yesterday.

Lesson 7-3

형용사를 부사로 바꾸는 방법 (1)

• 대부분의 경우 '형용사 + ly'의 형태로 부사를 만들 수 있다.

◈ 형용사를 부사로 바꾸기

대부분의 형용사	-ly	quick 빠른 – quickly 빠르게 large 큰 – largely 크게 safe 안전한 – safely 안전하게 kind 친절한 – kindly 친절하게 clear 맑은 – clearly 맑게 nice 멋진, 훌륭한 – nicely 멋지게, 훌륭하게
'자음 + y'로 끝나는 경우	y를 i로 바꾸고 -ly	easy 쉬운 – easily 쉽게 happy 행복한 – happily 행복하게 lucky 운이 좋은 – luckily 운 좋게 angry 화난 – angrily 화내어

Check up!

Answer Keys p. 41

A 다음 형용사의 부사형을 쓰시오.

1 nice ➡ *nicely*　　2 new ➡ ________
3 easy ➡ ________　　4 close ➡ ________
5 loud ➡ ________　　6 usual ➡ ________
7 real ➡ ________　　8 great ➡ ________
9 quick ➡ ________　　10 angry ➡ ________
11 happy ➡ ________　　12 beautiful ➡ ________
13 glad ➡ ________　　14 sudden ➡ ________
15 quiet ➡ ________　　16 clear ➡ ________
17 wonderful ➡ ________　　18 brave ➡ ________
19 sad ➡ ________　　20 poor ➡ ________
21 safe ➡ ________　　22 similar ➡ ________
23 various ➡ ________　　24 main ➡ ________
25 possible ➡ ________　　26 busy ➡ ________
27 bad ➡ ________　　28 sure ➡ ________
29 strong ➡ ________　　30 strange ➡ ________

Lesson 7-4

형용사를 부사로 바꾸는 방법 (2)

• 부사와 형용사의 형태가 같은 단어들이 있다. 이러한 단어는 문장 안에서의 뜻에 따라 부사와 형용사로 구분된다.

1. 가장 많이 쓰이는 '부사 = 형용사'의 형태

(1) **fast** ㊒ 빠른, 신속한 / ㊑ 빨리
- I have a **fast** horse.
- My horse can run very **fast**.

(2) **hard** ㊒ 열심인, 어려운 / ㊑ 열심히
- She gave me a **hard** quiz.
- I will practice **hard** every day.

(3) **early** ㊒ 이른, 초기의 / ㊑ 일찍
- In the **early** 2000s, cell phones are not common.
- I don't want to wake up **early**.

(4) **late** ㊒ 늦은 / ㊑ 늦게
- We said sorry for being **late**.
- They studied **late** every night.

2. 그 외 부사와 형용사의 형태가 같은 단어들

- long 긴, 길게
- high 높은, 높게
- low 낮은, 낮게
- well 훌륭한, 잘
- pretty 예쁜, 꽤
- daily 매일의, 매일

Check up!

Answer Keys p. 41

A 문장에서 밑줄 친 부분이 부사인지 형용사인지 구별하시오.

1 Max can jump high. 부사
2 Don't be late for English class. ____________
3 In the early 90's, there were few smartphones. ____________
4 The plan was pretty good. ____________
5 Tim wants to leave early. ____________
6 Helen had fast food for dinner. ____________
7 My brother can run fast. ____________
8 They had a good time. ____________
9 This line is too long. I want to cut it by 10 centimeters. ____________
10 John didn't sing well. ____________

Practice More Ⅰ

Answer Keys p. 41

A 다음 문장에서 형용사의 부사형을 쓰시오.

1 weak ➡ weakly
2 soft ➡ ________
3 calm ➡ ________
4 terrible ➡ ________
5 serious ➡ ________
6 polite ➡ ________
7 heavy ➡ ________
8 sensible ➡ ________
9 special ➡ ________
10 huge ➡ ________
11 important ➡ ________
12 rich ➡ ________
13 surprising ➡ ________
14 different ➡ ________
15 equal ➡ ________
16 wise ➡ ________
17 cold ➡ ________
18 dangerous ➡ ________

B 다음 괄호 안에서 알맞은 것을 고르시오.

1 Mr. Joe worked (lately / late) last night.
2 He can sing (good / well).
3 This movie was (real / really) exciting!
4 Kate smiled (happily / happy).
5 I can jump (highly / high).
6 Hana envies Helen's (long / longly) hair.
7 My teacher said that students should study (hardly / hard).
8 My brother can run (fast / fastly).
9 Maria can speak English (fluent / fluently).
10 (Fortunate / Fortunately), I passed the math exam.

C 다음 우리말 해석에 맞게 알맞은 부사를 쓰시오.

1 다행히도, 영어 시험 날짜가 변경되었다.
➡ Luckily, the English test date was changed.

2 그 강아지는 빠르게 나에게 달려왔다.
➡ The puppy ran up to me ________.

3 그는 조심스럽게 운전한다.
➡ He drives ________.

4 어제는 눈이 심하게 내렸다.
➡ Yesterday, it snowed ________.

Answer Keys p. 41

5 그녀는 좋은 점수를 받기 위해 열심히 공부했다.
➡ She studied __________ to get a good grade.

6 나는 내일 아침에 일찍 일어날 필요가 없다.
➡ I don't have to get up __________ tomorrow morning.

7 그 시험은 꽤 어려웠다.
➡ The test was __________ difficult.

8 그들은 40분 늦게 도착했다.
➡ They arrived 40 minutes __________.

9 Jack과 Jane은 함께 오랫동안 행복하게 살았다.
➡ Jack and Jane lived together __________ for a long time.

10 조금만 기다려보자. 그녀가 곧 올 거야.
➡ Wait a moment. She will come __________.

서술형 연습 **D** **다음 보기 와 같이 문장을 고쳐 쓰시오.**

> 보기
> Andrew is a careful driver. ➡ Andrew drives carefully.

1 Julia is a good dancer. ➡ *Julia dances well.*

2 Eric is a quick starter. ➡ ______________________

3 Sam is a slow worker. ➡ ______________________

4 My father is a heavy smoker. ➡ ______________________

5 He is a fast runner. ➡ ______________________

6 Tim is a strange actor. ➡ ______________________

7 They are loud talkers. ➡ ______________________

8 He is an amazing soccer player. ➡ ______________________

9 She is a good pianist. ➡ ______________________

10 It was a sudden change. ➡ ______________________

Point Check Ⅱ

◆ **빈도부사:** 어떤 일의 빈도, 즉 횟수나 정도를 나타내는 부사를 말한다.

◆ **의문부사:** 의문사가 부사처럼 쓰이는 말을 가리킨다.

1. 빈도부사의 의미

always 항상	100%
usually 보통, 대개	90%
often 자주, 종종	70%
sometimes 가끔씩, 때때로	50%
never 결코 ~아닌	0%

2. 빈도부사의 위치

(1) **일반동사 앞:** We **always** listen to music.

(2) **be동사/조동사 뒤**

- She is **usually** having breakfast.
- He can **sometimes** make monkey sounds.

3. 의문부사: where, when, why, how

Where do you live?
When do you feel happy?
Why are you so angry?
How did you complete this project?

- How long~ 얼마나 오랫동안~
- How often~ (횟수) 얼마나 자주~
- How much~ (가격이) 얼마나~
- How old~ (나이가) 얼마나~
- How far~ (거리) 얼마나 멀리~

4. 시간을 나타내는 부사 표현

(1) 전치사가 없는 시간 부사

- this morning 오늘 아침에
- every weekend 주말마다
- this year 올해, 이번 해에
- the day after tomorrow 모레

(2) 전치사가 있는 시간 부사

- in the morning 아침에
- at noon 정오에
- on Sunday, on Monday··· 일요일에, 월요일에···
- in September 9월에
- in summer 여름에
- on my birthday 나의 생일에

Lesson

7-5 빈도부사의 종류와 의미

• **빈도부사:** 어떤 일의 빈도, 즉 횟수나 정도를 나타내는 부사를 말한다.

◈ **빈도부사의 의미**

always 항상	100%
usually 보통, 대개	90%
often 자주, 종종	70%
sometimes 가끔씩, 때때로	50%
never 결코 ~아닌	0%

	Mon	Tue	Wed	Thu	Fri	Sat	Sun
Mary	○	○	○	○	○	○	○
John	○	×	○	○	○	○	○
Anna	○	○	×	○	×	○	○
Tom	×	○	×	○	×	○	×
Ron	○	×	×	×	×	×	○
I	×	×	×	×	×	×	×

• Mary **always** does her homework.
• John **usually** does his homework.
• Anna **often** does her homework.
• Tom **sometimes** does his homework.
• Ron **rarely** does his homework.
• I **never** do my homework.

Check up!

Answer Keys p. 42

A 우리말과 같은 뜻이 되도록 알맞은 빈도부사를 쓰시오.

1 나는 항상 아침을 먹는다.
➡ I ___*always*___ eat breakfast in the morning.

2 Sam의 가족들은 종종 야구를 한다.
➡ Sam's family __________ plays baseball together.

3 John과 나는 거의 영화를 보러 가지 않는다.
➡ John and I __________ go to the movies.

4 그녀는 결코 채소를 먹지 않는다.
➡ She __________ eats vegetables.

5 그는 때때로 부인을 위해 꽃을 산다.
➡ He __________ buys flowers for his wife.

6 Andrew의 아버지는 종종 그에게 편지를 쓴다.
➡ Andrew's father __________ writes letters to Andrew.

7 나는 결코 Tom을 용서하지 않을 것이다.
➡ I will __________ forgive Tom.

Grammar Plus +

거의~하지 않는 이라는 뜻으로 rarely 또는 hardly를 사용하기도 한다.
※ hardly는 hard의 부사형이 아니다.

Lesson 7-6

빈도부사의 위치

1. **일반동사 앞:** always, usually, often, sometimes, never + 일반동사
   - They **always** play soccer.
   - He **usually** practices the piano five hours a day.
   - I **never** learned how to swim.

2. **be동사 뒤:** be동사(am, are, is) + always, usually, often, sometimes, never
   - I am **sometimes** sad.
   - We are **often** taking care of sick animals.
   - Candy is **never** late.

3. **조동사 뒤**

   (1) can, will + always, usually, often, sometimes, never
   - I can **always** trust you.
   - He will **usually** be there.

   (2) have(has) + always, usually, often, sometimes, never + 과거분사
   - She has **never** eaten kimchi.
   - They have **often** been to Japan.

Check up!

Answer Keys p. 42

A 다음 괄호 안에서 알맞은 것을 고르시오.

1 They (sing often / often sing) songs.

2 It (seldom rains / rains seldom) in this city.

3 Helen's room (is always / always is) clean.

4 My grandfather (rarely watches / watches rarely) TV.

5 You (should never / never should) cheat on a test.

B 다음 주어진 단어를 사용하여 문장을 다시 쓰시오.

1 The baby sleeps 17 hours a day. (usually)

➡ *The baby usually sleeps 17 hours a day.*

2 The English class starts 8: 30 a.m. (always)

➡ ______________________________

3 John and I go to school by bus. (often)

➡ ______________________________

4 I will leave without saying goodbye. (never)

➡ ______________________________

Lesson **7-7**

의문부사

• **의문부사:** 의문사가 부사처럼 쓰이는 말을 가리킨다.

1. 장소, 시간, 이유, 방법

(1) **where** 어디에(서)

Where are you going? I'm going fishing.

(2) **when** 언제

When does *Larva* start? It starts at five thirty.

(3) **why** 왜

Why did she leave last night? Because there isn't any public transporttation this morning.

(4) **how** 어떻게

How did you make this kite? My father taught me.

2. How+형용사/부사: 얼마나 ~한

(1) **How long~** 얼마나 오랫동안~

How long have you lived here? I've lived here for seven years.

(2) **How old~** (나이가) 얼마나~

How old is your new teacher? He's in his early forties.

(3) **How often~** (횟수) 얼마나 자주~

How often do they watch movies? They watch movie two times a week.

(4) **How far~** (거리) 얼마나 멀리~

How far is the museum from here? It's about 300 meters.

(5) **How much~** (가격이) 얼마나~

How much is this oven? It's 500 dollars.

Check up!

Answer Keys p. 42

A 다음 문장의 빈칸에 알맞은 의문부사를 쓰시오.

1 A ___Where___ is my key?
  B I saw it on the table.

2 A __________ will Tom get up tomorrow?
  B He will get up at eight tomorrow.

3 A __________ will you stay in this country?
  B Two months.

4 A ___________ did they come from?
B They came from Italy.

5 A ___________ is the weather today?
B It's sunny. Let's go on a picnic!

6 A ___________ did Sujin call you?
B Because she wanted to ask me how to make corn bread.

7 A ___________ did you eat dinner?
B I ate dinner at Herin's house.

8 A ___________ do you take walks?
B I walk three times a week.

9 A ___________ are you crying?
B Because I saw a sad movie.

10 A ___________ did John finish his homework?
B At about five o'clock.

11 A ___________ is your teacher?
B He is about 55 years old.

12 A Your watch looks awesome. ___________ was it?
B It was almost 10 thousand won.

13 A ___________ is your car dirty?
B Because I drove through a dust storm yesterday.

14 A ___________ dogs do you have?
B I have four dogs. They always make me happy.

15 A ___________ is the next bus for Seoul?
B It leaves at 3:45.

16 A ___________ are you going over winter vacation?
B I'm going to visit my uncle.

17 A ___________ have you been waiting for Dennis?
B For 15 minutes.

18 A ___________ are you so late?
B Because I forgot to set my alarm clock. I'm so sorry.

19 A ___________ do you exercise?
B Two days a week.

20 A ___________ is it from your home?
B It is three kilometers.

Lesson

7-8 시간을 나타내는 부사표현

1. 전치사가 없는 시간 부사

- this morning 오늘 아침에
- yesterday morning 어제 아침에
- tomorrow morning 내일 아침에

- this afternoon 오늘 오후에
- yesterday afternoon 어제 오후에
- tomorrow afternoon 내일 오후에

- tonight 오늘 밤에
- last night 지난밤에, 어젯밤에
- tomorrow night 내일 밤에

- every Friday 매주 금요일에
- every weekend 주말마다
- every week / each week 매주

- the day before yesterday 그저께

- this Saturday 이번 토요일에
- last Saturday 지난 토요일에
- next Saturday 다음 토요일에

- this week 이번 주에
- last week 지난주에
- next week 다음 주에

- this month 이번 달에
- last month 지난달에
- next month 다음 달에

- this year 올해, 이번 해에
- last year 작년에
- next year 내년에, 다음 해에

- the day after tomorrow 모레

2. 전치사가 있는 시간 부사

*** 하루**

- in the morning 아침에
- in the afternoon 오후에
- in the evening 저녁에
- at night 밤에
- at noon 정오에
- at midnight 한밤중에, 자정에
- in the middle of the night 한밤중에

*** 요일**

- on Sunday 일요일에
- on Sundays 일요일마다

*** 월, 계절, 연도**

- in September 9월에
- in summer 여름에
- in 1998 1998년에
- in the 21st century 21세기에

*** 특정일**

- on my birthday 나의 생일에
- on New Year's Day 설날에
- on Thanksgiving Day 추수감사절에
- on December 25 12월 25일에

Check up!

Answer Keys p. 42

A 우리말 해석과 같은 뜻이 되도록 빈칸에 알맞은 말을 쓰시오.

1 너는 오늘 아침에 무엇을 먹었니?
➡ What did you eat breakfast _this morning_?

2 John은 지난밤에 무엇을 했니?
➡ What did John do ____________?

3 나의 남동생은 올해 이탈리아에 갈 예정이다.
➡ My brother is going to visit Italy ____________.

4 그들은 5월에 LA에서 공연을 했다.
➡ They had a performance in LA ____________.

5 나는 추수감사절에 고향에 다녀왔다.
➡ I went to my hometown ________________.

6 Tom은 어제 밤 늦게까지 영어 공부를 했다.
➡ Tom studied English late ____________.

7 나의 부모님은 2003년에 결혼하셨다.
➡ My parents married ____________.

8 다음 주에 여름 방학이 시작될 것이다.
➡ Summer vacation will start ____________.

9 주말마다 우리 집에서 모이자.
➡ Let's hang out at my house ____________.

10 오늘 오후에 수학 시험이 있어.
➡ I have a math test ____________.

11 한밤 중에 TV를 보지 마라.
➡ Don't watch TV ____________.

12 Jane은 내년에 중학교에 입학할 것이다.
➡ Jane will enter middle school ____________.

13 나는 가을에 태어났다.
➡ I was born ____________.

14 부모님께서는 매주 일요일에 한강에 가신다.
➡ My parents go to Han River ________________.

15 5월에 장미가 필 것이다.
➡ The rose will bloom ____________.

16 Cathy는 설날에 친구들과 일출을 보았다.
➡ Cathy saw the sunrise ______________.

Practice More Ⅱ

A 우리말과 같은 뜻이 되도록 알맞은 빈도부사를 빈 칸에 쓰시오.

1 Paul은 종종 엄마와 영화를 보러 간다.
➡ Paul ___often___ goes to the theater with his mother.

2 나는 매일 아침마다 등산을 한다.
➡ I __________ hike in the morning.

3 Tom은 절대 그녀를 잊지 못할 것이다.
➡ Tom will __________ forget her.

4 John은 자기 여자친구와 가끔 테니스를 친다.
➡ John __________ plays tennis with his girlfriend.

5 Tiffany는 때때로 일본 여행을 간다.
➡ Tiffany __________ travels to Japan.

6 Chris는 일요일 저녁에는 늘 집에 있는다.
➡ Chris is __________ at home Sunday evening.

B 다음 괄호 안의 빈도부사를 알맞은 곳에 넣어 문장을 완성하시오.

1 He plays tennis on Sunday morning. (usually)
➡ ___He usually plays tennis___ on Sunday morning.

2 I am busy in the afternoon. (sometimes)
➡ __________________________ busy in the afternoon.

3 He is late for his appointment. (never)
➡ __________________________ for his appointment.

4 You stay here. (often)
➡ You __________________________ here.

5 John eats breakfast in the morning. (always)
➡ __________________________ in the morning.

6 Does she take a taxi? (usually)
➡ Does she __________________________ a taxi?

7 We will forget you. (never)
➡ We __________________________ you.

8 I eat healthy food. (always)
➡ I __________________________ healthy food.

Answer Keys p. 42

C 다음 대화에 어울리는 의문부사를 알맞게 쓰시오.

1 A ___Where___ are you from?
  B I'm from Korea.

2 A __________ does she go to the concert hall?
  B She goes to the concert hall by bus.

3 A __________ was she angry?
  B Because of her brother. He broke her chair.

4 A __________ do you feel today?
  B I feel good today. The weather makes me happy.

5 A __________ is your mother's birthday?
  B March 13th.

6 A John, __________ are you going to go paragliding?
  B Well, next Friday.

7 A __________ do you like this shirt?
  B Oh, it's not good.

서술형 연습

D 다음 우리말 해석과 같도록 주어진 단어를 알맞게 배열하시오.

1 너는 어제 저녁에 왜 전화를 했니?
(call, last night, why, you, did, me)
➡ ___Why did you call me last night?___

2 Susan은 매주 금요일마다 파티를 연다.
(Susan, on Fridays, has, parties)
➡ ______________________________

3 그 학교는 얼마나 멀어? (the school, far, is, how)
➡ ______________________________

4 Alice는 대개 저녁을 8시에 먹는다.
(eats, at, Alice, dinner, 8 o'clock, usually)
➡ ______________________________

5 우리는 내일모레 양을 보러 목장에 간다.
(sheep, we, to see, will, a farm, go to, the day after tomorrow)
➡ ______________________________

6 프랑스에 간 지 얼마나 되셨습니까?
(France, have, been to, how long, you)
➡ ______________________________

중간 기말고사 예상문제

내신 최다 출제 유형

01 다음 중 어법상 올바른 것을 고르시오. [출제 예상 85%]

① I always am busy.
② What is your math teacher?
③ You usually go to the park to play tennis.
④ She never play soccer.
⑤ I don't has any ideas.

02 다음 밑줄 친 빈도부사의 위치가 어색한 것을 고르시오. [출제 예상 80%]

① She always acts like a comedian.
② I can never find my watch.
③ My brother sometimes comes home at six.
④ We often are late for school.
⑤ She usually goes to bed at 11:30.

03 다음 주어진 문장의 빈칸에 들어갈 수 있는 단어를 고르시오. [출제 예상 80%]

> Sometimes, I really don't want to get up __________.

① lately ② hardly ③ early
④ yesterday ⑤ good

04 다음 문장에서 'never'가 들어갈 위치로 알맞은 곳을 고르시오. [출제 예상 80%]

> Jack ① is so ② lazy. He ③ cleans his room ④ by ⑤ himself.

05 다음 밑줄 친 well이 나머지 넷과 다른 것을 고르시오. [출제 예상 85%]

① Anna is a so well woman.
② Mr. Brown teaches very well.
③ She speaks English pretty well.
④ I can play the flute as well as you.
⑤ He flies a kite very well.

06 다음 밑줄 친 곳의 쓰임이 바르지 않은 것을 고르시오. [출제 예상 90%]

① Mary drives fast.
② My sister runs very slowly.
③ You are very beautifully.
④ He plays badminton very well.
⑤ You have to use it carefully.

07 Which is incorrect among the underlined words? [출제 예상 85%]

> Helen ① goes usually to school by bike. She ② sometimes takes the school bus. Paul ③ always goes to work ④ on foot. It is ⑤ very close from his house to his office.

Answer Keys p. 43~44

[01~03] 두 단어의 관계가 보기 와 다른 것을 고르시오.

보기

kind – kindly

01 ① safe – safely ② nice – nicely ③ friend – friendly ④ simple – simply ⑤ quick – quickly

02 ① lucky – luckily ② easy – easily ③ happy – happily ④ clear – clearly ⑤ love – lovely

03 ① large – largely ② late – lately ③ angry – angrily ④ calm – calmly ⑤ careful – carefully

[04~05] 다음 중 형용사를 부사로 고친 것 중 틀린 것을 고르시오.

★★★

04 ① smooth – smoothly
② hard – hardly
③ good – well
④ fast – fast
⑤ complete – completely

05 ① beautiful – beautifully
② sad – sadly
③ glad – gladly
④ bad – worse
⑤ high – high

[06~08] 다음 빈칸에 들어갈 수 있는 단어를 고르시오.

06

- __________ cute! Is this your kitten?
- __________ is it going?

① What ② How ③ Who ④ When ⑤ Why

07

- How __________ is that building?
- The bird flew __________ in the sky.

① highs ② highly ③ high ④ height ⑤ higher

08

- __________ is the weather like?
- __________ does she do?

① When ② Why ③ How ④ Who ⑤ What

09 다음 문장에서 'never'가 들어갈 알맞은 위치를 고르시오.

Jennifer ① goes to ② travels ③ abroad ④ alone ⑤.

10 다음 문장에서 'usually'가 들어갈 알맞은 위치를 고르시오.

> Mike and Jane ① are ② doing ③ their homework ④ in the library ⑤.

11 다음 대화의 밑줄 친 부분과 바꾸어 쓸 수 있는 단어를 고르시오.

> A <u>What time</u> do you usually get up?
> B I get up at 6:45.

① What ② When ③ Who
④ Where ⑤ Which

[12~13] 다음 중 밑줄 친 부분의 쓰임이 <u>잘못된</u> 것을 고르시오.

12 ① What do you <u>usually</u> do after school?
② Mr. Black <u>never</u> is angry.
③ Harry <u>sometimes</u> eats carrots.
④ Jessy <u>often</u> comes at six.
⑤ I <u>always</u> use a pencil and an eraser.

13 ① They <u>sometimes</u> study in the library.
② She is <u>always</u> kind to us.
③ I laugh <u>sometimes</u> at other people.
④ Do you <u>often</u> write letters to your friends?
⑤ Mrs. Pink <u>usually</u> smiles at them.

[14~15] 다음 중 밑줄 친 단어의 쓰임이 나머지 넷과 <u>다른</u> 것을 고르시오.

★★★
14 ① Your grade is <u>pretty</u> excellent this time.
② Jenny is <u>pretty</u> tall in our class.
③ He is a <u>pretty</u> nice man.
④ They played the piano <u>pretty</u> well.
⑤ Sara bought a <u>pretty</u> dress.

15 ① He always studies <u>hard</u>.
② It is <u>hard</u> to be accepted to a good university.
③ I knew Jane tried very <u>hard</u>.
④ I work <u>hard</u> day and night.
⑤ It rained <u>hard</u> last night.

[16~17] 다음 중 어법상 올바르지 <u>않은</u> 것을 <u>모두</u> 고르시오.

★★★
16 ① We should get up early.
② Thank you so much.
③ Ellen studies always hard.
④ The school bus arrived very lately.
⑤ I carried them carefully.

17 ① Sam and Mary sing very good.
② My puppy is very noisy.
③ Tom often goes to school on foot.
④ You are a pretty girl, too.
⑤ I stay usually up late at night.

Answer Keys p. 43~44

[18~20] 다음 대화의 빈칸에 들어갈 말로 알맞은 것을 고르시오.

18

A How often does Jack go to the movies?
B ______________________________.

① One time.
② He goes there three times a month.
③ He went to there last week.
④ He always goes to school.
⑤ Two time a week.

19

A Excuse me. How do I get to COEX?
B ______________________________.

① Sure.
② Of course, you can.
③ Don't worry. You can go.
④ Take subway line number two.
⑤ Yes, you can.

20

A How far is it from here to City Hall?
B ______________________________.

① They are only one feet.
② It takes a bus.
③ They are three kilometer.
④ It is here.
⑤ It's only 500 meters.

[21~22] 다음 대화의 빈칸에 들어갈 단어가 바르게 짝 지어진 것을 고르시오.

21

A __________ is the church from here?
B It's three or four blocks.
A __________ I go there?
B You can take a bus.

① How far – How can
② How often – How to
③ How much – How long
④ How can – How far
⑤ How many – How can

22

A __________ was she absent?
B Because she had a high fever.
A Oh, that's too bad. __________ do you know that?
B Her dad called me in the morning.

① Why – what
② Why – how
③ What – how
④ Who – why
⑤ Why – which

23 다음 글의 괄호 안에 들어갈 영어 표현이 바르게 짝 지어진 것을 고르시오.

My nephew, Sunny was born (3개월 전). There's a party to celebrate his 100 days (이번 주 토요일에).

① three month later – this weekend
② after three months – next Saturday
③ three months – this Saturday
④ three months ago – this Saturday
⑤ third month ago – this Saturday

[24~25] 다음 중 어법상 올바른 것을 모두 고르시오.

24
① We're going to Sam's party at night.
② My dad always jogs at the morning.
③ In 2002, all the Koreans were happy to cheer for the soccer team.
④ I have to leave for Tokyo in Wednesday.
⑤ Jessy came back late in Jim's birthday.

★★★
25
① I read usually a book before bed.
② My dad can swim very fast.
③ The runners ran fast at the marathon.
④ She is very lovely and sweet.
⑤ Thank you for invited me.

26 다음 문장의 밑줄 친 부분을 한 단어로 바꿀 때 나머지와 다른 것을 고르시오.

① My farm produces a lot of milk.
② A lot of birds are flying in the sky.
③ We took a lot of pictures at the park.
④ She likes to meet a lot of people.
⑤ A lot of bakers participated the contest.

[27~28] 다음 대화의 밑줄 친 부분 중 어법상 어색한 것을 고르시오.

27

A The Spanish test ① was not ② easy.
B Yes. I didn't ③ answer some ④ very ⑤ hardly questions.

28

A What do you ① usually do ② on the weekends?
B Well, I surf ③ usually the Internet and write emails. ④ But last weekend, I met my friends and went ⑤ shopping.

★★★
29 다음 중 밑줄 친 fast의 쓰임이 나머지 넷과 다른 것을 고르시오.

① I finished my homework fast.
② Jack can run so fast.
③ Can you swim fast?
④ Cheetahs are fast animals.
⑤ They usually eat really fast.

30 다음 빈칸에 알맞은 것을 모두 고르시오.

There are __________ fresh vegetables in the market.

① much　② lots of　③ a little
④ some　⑤ little

★★★
31 다음 빈칸에 알맞지 않은 단어를 고르시오.

Ally will __________ from school.

① pick up me　② pick her up
③ pick Jack up　④ pick me up
⑤ pick up her son

32 다음 주어진 문장을 부정문으로 바꿨을 때 가장 올바른 것을 고르시오.

Ben finished his work on time.

① Ben not finished his work on time.
② Ben wss not finish his work on time.
③ Ben never dind't finish his work on time.
④ Ben finished never his work on time.
⑤ Ben never finished his work on time.

33 다음의 대답에 어울리는 질문으로 알맞은 것을 고르시오.

A ______________________________?
B I sometimes play the guitar.

① What time do you play the guitar?
② How often do you play the guitar?
③ How much do you play the guitar?
④ How many do you play the guitar?
⑤ How are is it?

★★★
34 다음 문장 중 어법상 옳은 것을 고르시오.

① That drama finishes usually at 11 o'clock.
② He always is strong and healthy.
③ She sometimes do the dishes.
④ We often go to the amusement park.
⑤ I came back home safe.

35 다음 문장 중 어법상 잘못된 것을 고르시오.

① They will leave for LA early in the morning.
② My kitten was hurt badly.
③ We were so sad in the morning.
④ I answered his question very well.
⑤ He drinks sometimes hot chocolate before bed.

◇◇◇◇◇◇◇◇◇◇◇ 서술형 평가 ◇◇◇◇◇◇◇◇◇◇◇

[36~37] 다음 두 문장의 뜻이 같도록 빈칸에 알맞은 말을 써 넣으시오.

36

• Jenny's uncle is a good cook.
= Jenny's uncle cooks __________.

➡ __________

37

• Miran is a fast runner.
= Miran runs __________.

➡ __________

[38~39] 다음 글을 읽고 물음에 답하시오.

Paul has ____ⓐ____ (많은) pets. He (A)(of / care / always / takes) a puppy, a kitten, some fish, and a bird. ____ⓑ____ (아침마다), he feeds all his pets first. He ____ⓒ____ (보통) goes for a walk with his pets on weekends. He wants to buy more pets.

38 윗글의 빈칸 ⓐ~ⓒ에 우리말에 맞게 알맞은 단어를 쓰시오.

ⓐ: ______________
ⓑ: ______________
ⓒ: ______________

39 윗글의 (A)를 문맥에 맞게 배열하여 문장을 완성하시오.

(A): ______________

Answer Keys p. 43~44

40 다음 표를 보고 빈도를 나타내는 단어를 사용하여 빈칸을 채우시오.

	Mon.	Tue.	Wed.	Thu.	Fri.	Sat.	Sun.
Jenny	O	O	O	O	O	O	O
Sam	X	O	X	O	O	X	O
I	O	X	O	X	X	X	X

➡ Jenny __________ exercises, Sam __________ does, and I __________ do.

[41~42] 다음 대답을 보고 빈칸에 알맞은 질문을 쓰시오.

41

A ______________________________?
B Thomas was born in 1989.

➡ ______________________________

★★★
42

A ______________________________?
B I lived in Beijing for three years.

➡ ______________________________

43

A ______________________________?
B He plays football three times a week.

➡ ______________________________

[44~46] 다음 주어진 문장의 밑줄 친 부분을 부사로 바꿔서 문장을 다시 쓰시오.

44

Jenny is a very <u>fast</u> swimmer.

➡ ______________________________

45

I am a <u>slow</u> speaker.

➡ ______________________________

46

Billy Elliot is a <u>good</u> dancer.

➡ ______________________________

[47~48] 다음 괄호 안의 단어를 우리말에 맞게 배열하여 문장을 완성하시오.

47

Sam은 피아노 연습을 거의 하지 않는다.
(Sam / piano / the / rarely / practices)

➡ ______________________________

48

그들은 매주 산에 올라간다.
(They / week / mountains / every / climb)

➡ ______________________________

08

Chapter
비교구문

Point Check I

◆ **원급 :** 형용사나 부사의 원래 형태를 원급이라 한다.

◆ **비교급 :** 형용사나 부사에 '-er' 또는 'more'를 붙여 '더 ~한'이라는 뜻을 나타낸다.

◆ **최상급 :** 형용사나 부사에 '-est' 또는 'most'를 붙여 '가장 ~한'이라는 뜻을 나타낸다.

1. 비교급과 최상급의 규칙 변화

구분	규칙	원급	비교급	최상급
1음절의 경우	-er / -est	young	younger	youngest
'e'로 끝나는 경우	-r / -st	nice	nicer	nicest
'자음+y'로 끝나는 경우	y를 i로 고치고 '-er' / '-est'	easy	easier	easiest
'단모음+단자음'으로 끝나는 경우	자음을 한 번 더 쓰고 '-er' / '-est'	big	bigger	biggest
2음절 이상의 형용사/부사	more / most	difficult	more difficult	most difficult
분사 형태의 형용사		excited	more excited	most excited
'형용사+ly' 형태의 부사		quickly	more quickly	most quickly

2. 비교급과 최상급의 불규칙 변화

원급	비교급	최상급
good/well	better	best
bad/ill	worse	worst
many/much	more	most
few	fewer	fewest
little	less	least
far	farther	farthest
	further	furthest
late	later	latest
	latter	last
old	older	oldest
	elder	eldest

Lesson 8-1

비교급과 최상급의 규칙 변화 (1)

• **원급**: 형용사나 부사의 원래 형태를 원급이라 한다.

• **비교급**: 형용사나 부사에 '-er' 또는 'more'를 붙여 '더 ~한'이라는 뜻을 나타낸다.

• **최상급**: 형용사나 부사에 '-est' 또는 'most'를 붙여 '가장 ~한'이라는 뜻을 나타낸다. 최상급을 표현할 때는 단어 앞에 'the'를 꼭 붙여준다.

◈ 비교급과 최상급 만들기 1

구분	규칙	원급	비교급	최상급
1음절의 경우	• -er • -est	tall short smart	taller shorter smarter	tallest shortest smartest
'e'로 끝나는 경우	• -r • -st	fine large safe	finer larger safer	finest largest safest
'자음+y'로 끝나는 경우	• y를 i로 고치고 '-er' • y를 i로 고치고 '-est'	dry pretty funny	drier prettier funnier	driest prettiest funniest
'단모음+단자음'으로 끝나는 경우	• 자음을 한 번 더 쓰고 '-er' • 자음을 한 번 더 쓰고 '-est'	thin hot fat	thinner hotter fatter	thinnest hottest fattest

Check up!

Answer Keys p. 45

A 다음 형용사나 부사의 비교급과 최상급을 쓰시오.

1 large – *larger* – *largest*

2 weak – ______ – ______

3 hard – ______ – ______

4 wise – ______ – ______

5 mild – ______ – ______

6 dirty – ______ – ______

7 clean – ______ – ______

8 loud – ______ – ______

9 strong – ______ – ______

10 pretty – ______ – ______

11 small – ______ – ______

12 poor – ______ – ______

13	fat	–	________	– ________	14	happy	–	________	– ________
15	safe	–	________	– ________	16	cheap	–	________	– ________
17	low	–	________	– ________	18	noisy	–	________	– ________
19	polite	–	________	– ________	20	easy	–	________	– ________
21	friendly	–	________	– ________	22	busy	–	________	– ________
23	close	–	________	– ________	24	tall	–	________	– ________
25	soon	–	________	– ________	26	brave	–	________	– ________
27	lucky	–	________	– ________	28	fast	–	________	– ________
29	thin	–	________	– ________	30	long	–	________	– ________
31	high	–	________	– ________	32	cold	–	________	– ________
33	light	–	________	– ________	34	heavy	–	________	– ________
35	great	–	________	– ________	36	warm	–	________	– ________
37	hungry	–	________	– ________	38	wet	–	________	– ________
39	strict	–	________	– ________	40	angry	–	________	– ________
41	near	–	________	– ________	42	funny	–	________	– ________
43	strange	–	________	– ________	44	early	–	________	– ________
45	thick	–	________	– ________	46	tasty	–	________	– ________
47	short	–	________	– ________	48	lovely	–	________	– ________
49	ugly	–	________	– ________	50	soft	–	________	– ________

Lesson 8-2

비교급과 최상급의 규칙 변화 (2)

• 비교급과 최상급을 만들 때 '-er'과 '-est'를 붙인다. 그러나 2음절, 3음절 이상의 형용사와 부사에는 'more'와 'most'를 붙여 사용한다.

◈ 비교급과 최상급 만들기 2

구분	규칙	원급	비교급	최상급
대부분의 2음절 이상의 형용사 (-y로 끝나는 단어 제외)	more most	useful hopeless foolish famous patient handsome diligent important expensive	more useful more hopeless more foolish more famous more patient more handsome more diligent more important more expensive	most useful most hopeless most foolish most famous most patient most handsome most diligent most important most expensive
분사 형태의 형용사		interesting tired surprised	more interesting more tired more surprised	most interesting most tired most surprised
'형용사+ly' 형태의 부사		quickly easily seriously	more quickly more easily more seriously	most quickly most easily most seriously

Check up!

Answer Keys p. 45

A 다음 형용사나 부사의 비교급과 최상급을 쓰시오.

1 hopeful – *more hopeful* – *most hopeful*

2 ridiculous – ________ – ________

3 critical – ________ – ________

4 rare – ________ – ________

5 interesting – ________ – ________

6 quickly – ________ – ________

7 pleasing – ________ – ________

8 exciting – ________ – ________

9 quiet – ________ – ________

10 expensive – ________ – ________

11 careful – ______________ – ______________

12 important – ______________ – ______________

13 complicated – ______________ – ______________

14 creative – ______________ – ______________

15 alone – ______________ – ______________

16 awesome – ______________ – ______________

17 familiar – ______________ – ______________

18 convenient – ______________ – ______________

19 positive – ______________ – ______________

20 afraid – ______________ – ______________

21 colorful – ______________ – ______________

22 famous – ______________ – ______________

23 beautiful – ______________ – ______________

24 tired – ______________ – ______________

25 clever – ______________ – ______________

26 boring – ______________ – ______________

27 special – ______________ – ______________

28 useful – ______________ – ______________

29 difficult – ______________ – ______________

30 delicious – ______________ – ______________

31 different – ______________ – ______________

32 hopeless – ______________ – ______________

33 foolish – ______________ – ______________

34 bright – ______________ – ______________

35 popular – ______________ – ______________

36 curious – ______________ – ______________

37 slowly – ______________ – ______________

38 ashamed – ______________ – ______________

39 excellent – ______________ – ______________

40 nutritious – ______________ – ______________

Lesson 8-3

비교급과 최상급의 불규칙 변화

• 비교급과 최상급을 만들 때 '-er'과 '-est'를 붙이는 대신에 불규칙적으로 변하는 형용사와 부사들이 있다.

◈ 비교급과 최상급의 불규칙 변화

원급		비교급	최상급
good	형 좋은	better	best
well	형 건강한, 부 잘		
bad	형 나쁜	worse	worst
ill	형 아픈, 나쁜		
many	형 수가 많은	more	most
much	형 양이 많은, 부 매우		
few	형 수가 적은	fewer	fewest
little	형 양이 적은, 부 약간	less	least
far	형 거리가 먼	farther	farthest
	형 정도가 큰	further	furthest
late	형 시간이 늦은	later	latest
	형 순서가 나중인	latter	last
old	형 나이 든	older	oldest
	형 손위의, 연상의	elder	eldest

➡ 2, 3음절 이상의 형용사와 부사에 붙는 'more, most' 뒤에는 형용사 또는 부사가 나온다. 하지만, 'more, most' 뒤에 바로 명사가 올 때는 'many, much'의 비교급과 최상급의 불규칙 변화로 이해하면 된다.

➡ 'old'의 비교 · 최상급 표현이 'elder – eldest'의 경우는 형제간의 손위를 나타낼 때 사용한다.

Answer Keys p. 46

A 다음 형용사나 부사의 비교급과 최상급을 쓰시오.

1 late (늦은) – *later* – *latest*

2 ill – ________ – ________

3 good – ________ – ________

4 old (손위의) – ________ – ________

5 few – ________ – ________

6 bad – ________ – ________

7 similar – ________ – ________

8 much – ________ – ________

9 far (정도가 큰) – ________ – ________

10 many ________ ________

11 well – ________ – ________

12 old (나이 든) – ________ – ________

13 costly – ________ – ________

14 slim – ________ – ________

15 far (거리가 먼) – ________ – ________

16 little – ________ – ________

17 useless – ________ – ________

18 patient – ________ – ________

19 late (순서가 나중인) – ________ – ________

20 deep – ________ – ________

Practice More I

Answer Keys p. 46

A 다음 단어들의 비교급과 최상급을 쓰시오.

1 slim – *slimmer* – *slimmest*

2 slow – ________ – ________

3 fast – ________ – ________

4 long – ________ – ________

5 low – ________ – ________

6 well – ________ – ________

7 ridiculous – ________ – ________

8 ill – ________ – ________

9 large – ________ – ________

10 old – ________ – ________

11 mild – ________ – ________

12 hot – ________ – ________

13 tasty – ________ – ________

14 hopeless – ________ – ________

15 important – ________ – ________

16 few – ________ – ________

17 easy – ________ – ________

18 tired – ________ – ________

19 tough – ________ – ________

20 lovely – ________ – ________

B 다음 괄호 안의 단어를 이용하여 비교급을 쓰시오.

1 Tom is ___*taller*___ than Inho. (tall)

2 Helen looks ____________ than a flower. (beautiful)

3 Today is ____________ than yesterday. (hot)

4 Cooperation is ____________ than competition. (important)

5 My car is ____________ than hers. (new)

6 Sam works ____________ than Alex does. (hard)

7 This hole is ____________ than that one. (deep)

8 Mt. Everest is ____________ than Halla Mountain. (high)

9 I think pasta is ____________ than pizza. (delicious)

10 Yellow is ____________ than black. (bright).

11 Young people should respect ____________ people. (old)

12 I think baseball is ____________ than basketball. (interest)

13 He usually wakes up ____________ than his son. (early)

14 This computer is ____________ than that one. (expensive)

15 I have ____________ cookies than John. (many)

16 A mouse is ____________ than a tiger. (small)

17 Studying math is ____________ than studying English. (difficult)

18 Jim drives ____________ than his wife. (slow)

19 I finished my homework ____________ than Hansu did. (quickly)

20 Linda looks ____________ than her sister. (old)

Answer Keys p. 46

C 다음 우리말 해석에 맞게 문장을 완성하시오.

1 2월은 3월보다 더 짧다.
➡ February is ___shorter___ than March.

2 그 빨간 치마는 Jina의 것보다 길다.
➡ The red skirt is ____________ than Jina's.

3 내가 오빠보다 더 똑똑하다.
➡ I am ____________ than my brother.

4 Dean은 나보다 적게 먹는다.
➡ Dean eats ____________ than I do.

5 그녀의 집은 Ava의 집보다 크다.
➡ Her house is ____________ than Ava's.

6 사자는 토끼보다 힘이 세다.
➡ A tiger is ____________ than a rabbit.

7 그는 자기 아버지보다 더 잘생겼다.
➡ He is ______________ than his father.

8 Sara는 Joe보다 나이가 많다.
➡ Sara is ____________ than Joe.

9 추리 소설이 로맨스 소설보다 재미있다.
➡ The detective story is ______________ than the romantic novel.

10 Hyunwoo는 Jack보다 한국에서 더 유명하다.
➡ In Korea Hyunwoo is ____________ than Jack is.

Point Check Ⅱ

◆ **원급의 비교 :** 형용사와 부사의 원급을 사용하여 두 개의 대상을 비교하는 것을 말한다.

◆ **비교급의 비교 :** 두 개의 대상을 '-er than'을 사용하여 비교하는 것을 말한다.

◆ **최상급의 비교 :** 세 개 이상의 대상을 'the -est'를 사용하여 비교하는 것을 말한다.

1. 원급의 비교

(1) **[as + 원급 + as]** …만큼 ~한
She is **as diligent as** her mom.

(2) **[not as (so) + 원급 + as]** …만큼 ~하지 않은
He is **not as (so) tall as** his big brother.

(3) **[배수사 + as + 원급 + as A]** A보다 …배 ~한
Your chocolate bar is **twice as big as** mine.

2. 비교급의 비교

(1) **[-er than / more + 원급 + than]** …보다 더 ~한
A roller coaster is **more exciting than** a merry-go-round.

(2) **[비교급 + and + 비교급]** 점점 더 ~한
It is getting **worse and worse**.

(3) **비교급의 강조**
The blue jeans are **even** nicer than the black jeans.

3. 최상급의 비교

(1) **[the + 최상급]** 가장 ~한
The smartest student in our school is Jenny.

(2) **[the + 최상급 + of (in)]** ~에서 가장 ~한
- Her hair is **the longest** in our class. [장소]
- The blue whale is **the largest** of all animals. [집단]

(3) **[one of the + 최상급 + 복수명사]** 가장 ~한 것들 중 하나
Skiing is **one of the most popular sports** in winter.

Lesson

8-4 원급의 비교

• 원급 비교: '…만큼 ~한' 이라는 뜻으로 비슷한 것이나 같은 것들을 비교한다.

1. as + 원급 + as: …만큼 ~한

• Anna is **as tall as** Mary.

• They can play baseball **as well as** we can.

(= us) ➡ 'as' 뒤에 오는 '주어+동사'는 목적어로 바꾸어 쓸 수 있다.

➡ as와 as 사이에는 형용사나 부사의 원형이 들어간다.

2. not as (so) + 원급 + as: …만큼 ~하지 않은

• He is **not as (so) smart as** you are. (= you)

• Red roses **are not as (so) beautiful as** white roses.

3. 배수사 + as + 원급 + as A: A보다 …배 ~한

➡ 원급 비교 구문에 twice, three times, four times 등과 같이 배수의 숫자를 이용하여 비교를 나타낸다.

• I have **twice as much work as** you.

• This house is **three times as large as** that house.

Check up!

Answer Keys p. 46

A 다음 문장의 괄호 안에서 알맞은 것을 고르시오.

1 John is as (smart / smarter) as his brother.

2 My room is as (smaller / small) as yours.

3 He is (not so / so not) handsome as Joe.

4 I can memorize as (many / best) English words as you can.

5 We can run as (fast / fastly) as they can.

6 David is (not as / as not) busy as you.

7 Literature is as (interesting / interested) as science.

8 The dress is (not as / as not) beautiful as mine.

9 I ate (twice / two) as much as you.

10 Today is as (colder / cold) as yesterday.

11 My car is as (new / newly) as yours.

12 I collect as (better / many)stamps as Tina.

13 Dorothy is (not as / as not) pretty as her mom.

14 Jina is (three / three times) as old as her daughter.

Lesson

8-5 비교급의 비교

• **비교급 비교:** 대상이 둘일 때 사용하며, 비교급은 '-er(more) than'으로 표현한다.

1. -er than / more + 원급 + than: …보다 더 ~한

• My father gets up **earlier than** my mother does. (=my mother)

• 'Harry Potter' is **more interesting than** 'The Lord of the Rings.'

2. 비교급 + and + 비교급: 점점 더 ~한

주로 'become, get, grow, turn'처럼 '~이 되다'라는 뜻을 지닌 동사와 함께 쓰인다.

• My grades became **better and better.**

• It's getting **warmer and warmer.**

3. 비교급의 강조

부사 'even, much, still, far, a lot'은 비교급 앞에 쓰여 '훨씬, 더욱'의 뜻으로 사용된다.

• That pickup is **even** worse than this one.

• This pie is **still** better than that one.

Check up!

Answer Keys p. 47

A 다음 괄호 안의 단어를 사용하여 알맞은 비교급을 쓰시오.

1 My bike is *more expensive* than yours. (expensive)

2 He is ____________ than John. (tall)

3 I am ____________ than my boyfriend. (old)

4 English is ____________ than math. (interesting)

5 It's getting ____________. (cold)

6 I get up ____________ than you. (early)

7 She finished the homework ____________ than Tim did. (quickly)

8 Two hands are ____________ than one. (good)

9 Mr. Park is ____________ than Thomas. (young)

10 My computer is ____________ than yours. (new)

11 A bear is ____________ than a tiger. (big)

12 Tim is ____________ than his brother. (careful)

13 It is ____________ than before. (long)

14 Your picture is ____________ than mine. (colorful)

15 He became ____________ and ____________. (rich)

16 Korea is ____________ than China. (small)

17 John is ____________ than others. (popular)

18 She feels ____________ than she did last week. (good)

19 I love him ____________ than you. (much)

20 The hole became ____________ and ____________. (deep)

B 다음 문장에서 어법상 어색한 것을 찾아 바르게 고치시오.

1 My book is thicker as yours. ___as___ ➡ ___than___

2 That bag is more cheap than mine. ________ ➡ ________

3 Tigers are strong than rabbits. ________ ➡ ________

4 Fiona is fatter to her sister. ________ ➡ ________

5 This coat is even bad than that one. ________ ➡ ________

6 He is still kind than I am. ________ ➡ ________

7 Linda became richer and rich. ________ ➡ ________

8 My diary is thin than yours. ________ ➡ ________

9 Sam is taller than yours. ________ ➡ ________

10 I can run a lot fast than him. ________ ➡ ________

11 Kevin studied more then last week. ________ ➡ ________

12 He feels many and many sick. ________ ➡ ________

13 Cookies are a lot expensive than candies. ________ ➡ ________

14 He wants to be strong than his father. ________ ➡ ________

15 This rule is more strict than that one. ________ ➡ ________

Lesson 8-6 최상급의 비교

• **최상급 비교:** 셋 이상의 대상을 비교할 때 사용하며 'the -est(most)'로 표현한다.

1. the + 최상급: 형용사의 최상급 앞에는 항상 정관사 'the'를 붙여준다.

• **The shortest** student in our class is Jessie.

• The Nile is **the longest** river.

2. the + 최상급 + of (in)

(1) **the + 최상급 in:** (한 장소에서) 가장 ~한

His bag is **the heaviest in** our class.

(2) **the + 최상급 of:** (한 집단에서) 가장 ~한

You are **the most intelligent girl of** my friends.

3. one of the + 최상급 + 복수명사: 가장 ~한 것들 중 하나

• A pizza is **one of the most popular foods** in the world.

• London is **one of the largest cities** in the world.

Check up!

Answer Keys p. 47

A 괄호 안의 단어를 이용하여 알맞은 최상급을 쓰시오.

1 The black note is *the thinnest* of the four. (thin)

2 Suji is ______________ girl in our school. (powerful)

3 It was ______________ movie I've ever seen. (good)

4 Mt. Everest is ______________ mountain in the world. (high)

5 Eric is ______________ of us. (old)

6 February is ______________ month of the 12 months. (short)

7 Her song is ______________ song in our class. (famous)

8 Chohee is ______________ player of her team. (valuable)

9 You are ______________ boy of our community. (diligent)

10 Today is ______________ day of this week. (cold)

Check up!

Answer Keys p. 47

B 다음 문장을 보기 와 같이 'one of the 최상급'의 형태로 바꾸시오.

> 보기
>
> Sam is the tallest boy in our class.
>
> ➡ Sam is one of the tallest boys in our class.

1 Tim is the happiest person I've ever met.

➡ ____________________

2 The ring is the most expensive thing in my room.

➡ ____________________

3 Sujin is the most talented student in our class.

➡ ____________________

4 John is the bravest man in the group.

➡ ____________________

5 He is the heaviest boy in our village.

➡ ____________________

C 다음 괄호 안의 단어를 사용하여 우리말을 바르게 영작하시오.

1 Jack은 반에서 가장 키가 크다. (in class)

➡ *Jack is the tallest in class.*

2 Laura는 그녀의 나라에서 가장 인기가 많다. (most, in her country)

➡ ____________________

3 나의 오빠는 세상에서 제일 상냥한 남자이다. (mild, in the world)

➡ ____________________

4 Hong Kong은 제일 바쁜 도시들 중 하나 이다. (one of, busy)

➡ ____________________

5 T-Rex는 가장 사나운 공룡들 중 한 마리이다. (dinosaurs, fierce)

➡ ____________________

Practice More Ⅱ

A 다음 문장의 괄호 안에서 알맞은 것을 고르시오.

1 The book is as (thinner / thin) as yours.

2 I'm not as (tall / taller) as Serena.

3 She is (the most famous / famous) singer in America.

4 My car is (faster / fast) than yours.

5 Sara spent twice as (much / more) as Jina did.

6 Inho is (the most / more) important student in our class.

7 Kate is (more prettier / prettier) than her sister.

8 I can run (fastest / faster) than you.

9 Wonbin is one of the most handsome (actor / actors).

10 Tim is as (fat / fatter) as Nick.

B 다음 문장에서 어법상 어색한 것을 찾아 바르게 고치시오.

1 She has less money then you. *then* ➡ *than*

2 This model is the cheaper in this store. ________ ➡ ________

3 My grade is not the better than yours. ________ ➡ ________

4 Hyunsoo is one of the best soccer player. ________ ➡ ________

5 I'm old than you. ________ ➡ ________

6 Today is coldest than yesterday. ________ ➡ ________

7 My wallet is expensivier than Tom's. ________ ➡ ________

8 Ted is as tall than Minsu. ________ ➡ ________

9 It's the most late version. ________ ➡ ________

10 Sandra is the most lovely baby in town. ________ ➡ ________

Answer Keys p. 47~48

C 다음 두 문장을 괄호 안의 표현을 이용하여 한 문장으로 바꾸시오.

1 Barbara is taller than Jim. (배수사, as~as)
➡ Jim is ___not as tall as___ Barbara.

2 I am younger than Minhyuk. (as~as)
➡ Minhyuk is ______________ I.

3 Mijin's hair is 30 centimeters long. Suzy's hair is also 30 centimeters long. (as~as)
➡ Mijin's hair is ______________ Suzy's hair.

4 The red skirt is bigger than the yellow one. (as~as)
➡ The yellow skirt is ________________ the red one.

5 The bear is the biggest animal in the zoo. (as~as)
➡ The other animals are ______________ the bear in the zoo.

D 다음 두 문장을 비교 표현을 이용하여 한 문장으로 바꾸시오.

1 I have five dollars. Yujin has ten dollars.
➡ Yujin has ___twice as much as me___.

2 Mia is 27 years old. Her professor is 50 years old.
➡ Mia is ______________ her professor.

3 The green building is 150 meters high. The gray building is 180 meters high.
➡ The green building is ______________ the gray building.

4 There are many beautiful flowers in the garden. A rose is one of them.
➡ A rose is ____.

5 Black is the darkest color.
➡ The other colors are ___________________.

Practice More Ⅱ

서술형 연습 **E** **다음 우리말 해석과 같도록 주어진 단어를 배열하여 문장을 완성하시오.**

1 Jina는 Linda만큼 똑똑하다. (Linda, as, Jina, smart, is, as)

➡ *Jina is as smart as Linda.*

2 야구는 한국에서 인기 있는 스포츠 중 하나이다.
(baseball, in Korea, is, the most popular, one of, sports)

➡ ____________________

3 내 의자는 너의 의자만큼 새 것이다. (as, yours, my chair, new, is, as)

➡ ____________________

4 Samantha는 반에서 제일 우등생이다. (Samantha, in our class, the best, is, student)

➡ ____________________

5 Lily는 자기 남편보다 세 배 더 많은 옷을 가지고 있다.
(her husband, Lily, as many as, clothes, three times, has)

➡ ____________________

6 서울은 세계에서 가장 아름다운 도시들 중 하나이다.
(Seoul, the most beautiful, in the world, is, one of, cities)

➡ ____________________

7 Jane의 가방은 Jim의 것만큼 작다.
(Jim's, Jane's bag, as, is, small, as)

➡ ____________________

서술형 연습 **F** **다음 주어진 문장을 우리말로 바르게 해석하시오.**

1 Mary cooks as well as her mom.

➡ *Mary*는 엄마만큼 요리를 잘한다.

2 He was not as brave as Tom.

➡ ____________________

3 They are the best dancers all over the country.

➡ ____________________

4 Hamburger is the least healthy food.

➡ ____________________

5 I'm more honest than Tina.

➡ ____________________

중간 기말고사 예상문제

Answer Keys p. 48

내신 최다 출제 유형

01 다음 중 어법상 어색한 것을 고르시오. [출제 예상 85%]

① He feels happy than yesterday.
② It looks nicer than that one.
③ This soup is sweeter than that soup.
④ The green pants are bigger than the blue pants.
⑤ He is taller than his younger brother.

02 다음 글의 ⓐ ~ ⓒ의 빈칸에 들어갈 말이 바르게 짝지어진 것을 고르시오. [출제 예상 80%]

> Sea horses are the ____ⓐ____ fish. They move only two meters an hour. Blue whales are the ____ⓑ____ animals. They grow up to 100 feet long. They are ____ⓒ____ than two buses.

① slower – hugest – longer
② slowest – hugest – longest
③ slowest – hugest – longer
④ slow – huge – long
⑤ slowest – huger – longer

03 다음 중 어법상 올바른 것을 고르시오. [출제 예상 90%]

① Tina is not as so tall as Jack.
② We are as cute as they.
③ She is fat than Jenny.
④ You are the shortest in the class.
⑤ I am the faster than Kelly.

04 다음 중 밑줄 친 부분의 쓰임의 나머지 넷과 다른 것을 고르시오. [출제 예상 90%]

① I am the most intelligent of them.
② She is the most famous scientist in the world.
③ Jack has most bananas among us.
④ The diamond is the most expensive jewel.
⑤ Kevin is the most handsome in the class.

05 다음 글을 읽고 어법상 틀린 것을 고르시오. [출제 예상 90%]

> Ms. White is a teacher. She wants to make children ① happy. So, she surfed the Internet to get some ② gooder ideas. There was a website that was ③ more interesting website than others. It shows what ④ teenagers wrote about their future dreams. It's ⑤ more exciting than other websites that show images or photographs.

06 다음 우리말과 같은 의미가 되도록 괄호 안의 단어를 바르게 배열하여 문장을 쓰시오. [출제 예상 80%]

> 코모도 드래곤은 가장 큰 도마뱀이다.
> (the / biggest / is / lizard)

➡ The Komodo dragon ______________.

중간 기말고사 예상문제

[01~03] 다음 중 '원급-비교급-최상급'의 연결이 <u>잘못된</u> 것을 고르시오.

01
① mild – milder – mildest
② long – longer – longest
③ fat – fatter – fattest
④ little – littler – littlest
⑤ smart – smarter – smartest

02
① beautiful – more beautiful – most beautiful
② big – biger – bigest
③ dirty – dirtier – dirtiest
④ old – older – oldest
⑤ difficult – more difficult – most difficult

03
① quickly – more quickly – most quickly
② strange – stranger – strangest
③ excited – more excited – most excited
④ pretty – prettier – prettiest
⑤ foolish – foolisher – foolishest

[04~06] 다음 문장을 한 문장으로 바꿀 때 빈칸에 들어갈 알맞은 것을 고르시오.

04

• Jack is 167 centimeters tall. Sue is 170 centimeters tall.
➡ Sue is __________ than Jack.

① old ② tall ③ taller
④ long ⑤ longer

05

• Jessica got a 95 at the English test. Saewon got a 95 at the English test, too.
➡ Jessica is as __________ as Saewon.

① smarter ② smartest ③ same as
④ the same ⑤ smart

06

• Harry is fat. Jack is fatter.
➡ Harry is not as __________ as Jack.

① fatter ② fat ③ fattest
④ short ⑤ thin

[07~08] 다음 우리말을 영어로 옮길 때 빈칸에 알맞은 것을 고르시오.

07

• Jane은 우리 반에서 세 번째로 키가 작다.
➡ Jane is the third __________ in our class.

① short ② smaller ③ shortest
④ shorter ⑤ smallest

08

• 그녀는 가장 유명한 화가들 중 한 명이다.
➡ She is one of the __________ painters.

① famousest ② most famousest
③ more famous ④ famouser
⑤ most famous

09 다음 중 빈칸에 들어갈 말이 바르게 연결된 것을 고르시오.

A What is the __________ animals?
B A cheetah is __________ than any other animals.

① longest – longer ② fastest – faster
③ slowest – slower ④ scariest – scarier
⑤ heaviest – heavie

10 다음 표와 일치하지 않는 것을 고르시오.

	Jaejoon	Gieun
Age	17	16
Height	175	177

① Jaejoon is older than Gieun.
② Gieun is taller than Jaejoon.
③ Jaejoon is not older than Gieun.
④ Gieun is younger than Jaejoon.
⑤ Gieun is not shorter than Jaejoon.

[11~13] 다음 문장 중 어법상 올바른 것을 모두 고르시오.

11 ① An airplane is fast than a taxi.
② A snake is more longer that an earthworm.
③ She is the most beautiful person in the world.
④ This building is the most tallest.
⑤ I am as strong as John.

12 ① Jack is as taller as Harry.
② He is not as slow you.
③ Christine is as pretty as Jane.
④ Rihannd is one of the most popular singers.
⑤ Red is powerfuler than yellow.

13 ① It's getting cold and cold.
② This book is more heavy than that one.
③ You are the prettier than Anne.
④ This Smartphone is even better than that one.
⑤ She works twice as hard as you.

[14~16] 다음 문장 중 어법상 어색한 것을 고르시오.

14 ① Linda is not as cute as Jane.
② He is the best kindest man.
③ We want to eat the best food in this restaurant.
④ Harry is the smartest boy in my class.
⑤ Minsu is more honest than Jaedong.

15 ① Wendy can run faster than Jane can.
② I am not older than her.
③ You are not as fast as I am.
④ My computer is not newer than yours.
⑤ Tommy's grades became gooder and gooder

16 ① Ellen is the busyiest girl in our class.
② Science is not more difficult than math.
③ I like soccer better than baseball.
④ This rope is not as long as that one.
⑤ French is as difficult as German.

[17~18] 괄호 안의 우리말과 같은 형태의 영어 표현 중 잘못된 것을 고르시오.

17

Mina's playing is becoming (점점 더 ~한).

① worse and worse ② faster and faster
③ nicer and nicer ④ better
⑤ better and better

18

The gag concert is (~배) as popular as the music concert.

① twice ② three times
③ third ④ four times
⑤ five times

[19~20] 주어진 우리말과 같은 뜻이 되도록 빈칸에 알맞은 단어를 고르시오.

19

나의 이모는 엄마보다 아름답지 않다.
➡ My aunt is not ________ than my mother.

① younger ② pretty
③ more beautiful ④ beautiful
⑤ prettier

20

그는 자기 엄마보다 훨씬 일찍 일어난다.
➡ He gets up ________ than his mom.

① earlier ② much earlier
③ more earlier ④ not earlier
⑤ not so earlier

[21~22] 다음 두 단어의 관계가 나머지 넷과 다른 것을 고르시오.

21 ① big – bigger ② run – runner
③ tall – taller ④ hot – hotter
⑤ late – later

22 ① young – younger ② few – fewer
③ well – better ④ quiet – quieter
⑤ light – lighter

23 다음 중 밑줄 친 부분이 바르게 쓰인 것을 모두 고르시오.

① Sue is very shorter than Jane.
② The boy grows stronger and stronger.
③ Pumpkin pie is still better than apple pie.
④ You are as lazy as so your cousin, Jack.
⑤ He is not as thinner as her.

[24~25] 우리말을 영어로 바르게 옮긴 것을 고르시오.

24

민수는 Phillip보다 두 배 더 열심히 공부한다.

① Minsu studies than Phillip.
② Phillip doesn't study as hard as Minsu.
③ Minsu studies twice as hard as Phillip.
④ Minsu doesn't study than Phillip.
⑤ Minsu study twice as hard as Phillip.

Answer Keys p. 48~49

25

저 차는 이 차보다 훨씬 더 느리다.

① That car is slower than this car.
② This car is faster than that car.
③ This car is not fast than that one.
④ That car is not slow as this one.
⑤ That car is even slower than this one.

[26~27] 주어진 영어 문장을 우리말로 바르게 해석한 것을 고르시오.

26

'The Hobbit' is the most interesting film.

① '호빗'은 모든 영화들 중에서 가장 재미없다.
② '호빗'은 가장 재미있는 영화이다.
③ '호빗'은 가장 재미있는 영화 중 하나다.
④ '호빗'은 영화들 중 재미있는 편이다.
⑤ '호빗'은 모든 영화들과 함께 가장 재미있다.

27

Bali island is one of the most beautiful islands in the world.

① 발리 섬은 세계에서 가장 아름다운 섬들 중 하나이다.
② 발리 섬은 아름다운 섬들이다.
③ 세계에서 가장 아름다운 섬은 발리 섬이다.
④ 세계에서 가장 아름다운 것들 중 하나는 발리 섬이다.
⑤ 발리 섬의 하나는 세계에서 가장 아름답다.

28 **다음 중 보기의 문장과 뜻이 같은 것을 고르시오.**

Dictionaries are thicker than other books.

① Dictionaries are not thicker than the other books.
② Dictionaries are thinner than the other books.
③ The other books are not as thick as dictionaries.
④ Dictionaries are the thickest books.
⑤ The other books are as thick as dictionaries.

29 **다음 중 문장의 의미가 나머지 넷과 다른 것을 고르시오.**

① Susan is the best dancer in our school.
② No other dancer is better than Susan in our school.
③ Susan dances much better than any other in our school.
④ No other dancer is as good as Susan in our school.
⑤ Susan is one of the best dancers in our school.

[30~32] 다음 글을 읽고 물음에 답하시오.

Ted and Tina are twins. Tina was born later than Ted by about five minutes. (A) Tina is 162 centimeters tall and Ted is 157 centimeters tall. (B) Ted는 Tina보다 더 빨리 달립니다. They like English. (C) So they are both good at speaking English.

30 윗글의 밑줄 친 (A)를 한 문장으로 올바르게 표현한 것을 모두 고르시오.

① Tina is not taller than Ted.
② Tina is as tall as Ted.
③ Tina is taller than Ted.
④ Ted is taller than Tina.
⑤ Ted is shorter than Tina.

31 윗글의 밑줄 친 (B)를 영어로 바르게 표현한 것을 모두 고르시오.

① Ted is running faster than Tina.
② Tina runs as fast as Ted.
③ Tina doesn't run so fast as Ted.
④ Ted runs faster than Tina.
⑤ Tina is faster than Ted.

32 윗글의 밑줄 친 (C)를 'as ~ as' 구문으로 바꿔 쓰시오.

➡ ____________________

◇◇◇◇◇◇◇◇◇◇ **서술형 평가** ◇◇◇◇◇◇◇◇◇◇

[33~34] 우리말과 같은 뜻이 되도록 괄호 안의 단어를 알맞은 형태로 바꾸어 쓰시오.

33

겨울에는 낮이 점점 짧아진다.
➡ In winter, the daytime gets ________________. (short)

➡ ____________________

34

다이아몬드는 보석 중에서 가장 비싸다.
➡ The diamond is ________________ of jewels. (expensive)

➡ ____________________

35 괄호 안에 주어진 단어를 알맞은 형태로 바꾸어 쓰시오.

① My little sister, Jade is the __________ in my family. (young)
② My father is the __________ in my family. (strong)
③ My mother is the __________ in my family. (diligent)
④ My elder brother is the __________ in my family. (tall)

① __________ ② __________
③ __________ ④ __________

Answer Keys p. 48~49

[36~37] 괄호 안의 단어를 우리말에 맞게 배열하여 문장을 완성하시오.

36

중국은 한국보다 훨씬 더 크다.
(China / larger / Korea / much / than / is)

➡ ______________________

37

너는 그녀만큼이나 못생기지 않았어.
(you / her / are / ugly / as / not / as)

➡ ______________________

[38~40] 주어진 영어 문장을 우리말로 해석하시오.

38

Winter is the coldest of the four seasons.

➡ ______________________

39

Shakespeare is one of the greatest authors in the world.

➡ ______________________

40

Smartphones are more convenient than computers.

➡ ______________________

[41~43] 다음 주어진 문법을 사용하여 원하는 문장을 만들어 보세요.

41 원급 비교: 'as ~ as' 또는 'not as (so) ~ as'

➡ ______________________

42 비교급 비교: '-er / more than'

➡ ______________________

43 최상급 비교: 'the + -est / most + in / of'

➡ ______________________

Note

09

Chapter
부정사

Point Check I

◆ **부정사 :** 부정사는 동사원형 앞에 'to'가 있거나 동사원형만 있는 형태를 말한다.

◆ **to부정사 :** 'to'가 있는 것을 'to부정사'라고 하며 형태는 'to+동사원형'이다.

◆ **원형부정사 :** 'to'가 없는 것을 '원형부정사'라고 하며 형태는 '동사원형'이다.
'to부정사'는 문장 안에서 명사, 형용사, 부사처럼 사용된다.

1. 부정사의 명사적 용법

(1) **주어 역할**: ~하는 것, ~하기
To write a diary in English is not easy.

(2) **보어 역할**: ~하는 것(이다)
Her hobby is **to collect** dried flowers.

(3) **목적어 역할**: ~하는 것을, ~하기를
His parents want **to go** abroad with him.

2. 부정사의 형용사적 용법

(1) **형용사 역할**: ~할, ~해야 할
There is some paper here **to make** something.

(2) **'to부정사' 뒤에 전치사가 오는 경우**: 전치사를 빠뜨리지 않도록 주의
He left some paper **to write on**.

3. 부정사의 부사적 용법

(1) **목적**: ~하기 위하여, ~하려고
We volunteered **to help** many sick animals.

(2) **감정의 원인**: ~해서, ~하니
They were so proud **to hear** the news.

(3) **결과**: …해서 ~하다
I hope **to pass** the difficult exam.

(4) **이유/판단의 근거**: ~하는 것을 보니, ~하다니
He must be honest **to tell** the truth all the time.

4. 의문사 + to부정사

- They didn't know **when to play** the music.
- My math teacher taught me **how to solve** the problem.

Lesson

9-1 부정사의 형태

- **to부정사:** 'to + 동사원형'의 형태로 문장 안에서 명사, 형용사, 부사처럼 사용된다.
- **원형부정사:** 'to' 없이 동사원형으로만 이루어진 부정사를 원형부정사라고 하며, 몇몇 동사의 목적격보어로 사용된다.

1. 부정사의 형태

(1) **to부정사**: [to + 동사원형]

- sing → to sing
- eat → to eat
- told → to tell
- was / were → to be

(2) **원형부정사**: [동사원형]

They made me **change** my plan.

(3) **원형부정사를 목적격보어로 취하는 동사**

사역동사	let have make
지각동사	see feel hear smell watch

2. 부정사의 역할: 동사의 특징을 가지면서도 명사, 형용사, 부사로 사용된다.

(1) **명사 역할**: ~하는 것은

To speak English is not easy.

(2) **형용사 역할**: ~할

John has a lot of homework **to do.**

(3) **부사 역할**: ~을 위해, ~하게 되어

She became a doctor **to help** many poor people.

Grammar Plus +

to 부정사 부정문: not + to부정사

My boss made me **not to work** anymore.

Check up!

Answer Keys p. 50

A 다음 문장에서 to부정사의 역할을 구분하시오.

1 To eat breakfast is important. ___명사적 용법___

2 He has a lot of work to do. ________

3 She went to the store to buy fruits. ________

4 Tom was happy to meet you. ________

5 To wake up early is so hard. ________

6 I need something to drink. ________

Check up!

Answer Keys p. 50

B 다음 문장에서 어법상 어색한 것을 찾아 바르게 고치시오.

1 To playing baseball is fun. ___playing___ ➡ ___play___

2 Teachers made students being quiet. ________ ➡ ________

3 Linda wants to eating spicy food. ________ ➡ ________

4 I have many things to doing. ________ ➡ ________

5 Jack's hobby was to collected stamps. ________ ➡ ________

6 Mom made me to clean my room. ________ ➡ ________

7 We want to winning the game. ________ ➡ ________

8 My dream is to being an English teacher. ________ ➡ ________

9 Today's homework is to taking dictation. ________ ➡ ________

10 To saving money is important. ________ ➡ ________

C 다음 우리말과 뜻이 같도록 괄호안의 단어를 이용하여 빈칸을 채우시오.

1 내 여동생의 소원은 캔디를 많이 먹는 것이다. (eat)
➡ My sister's wish ___is___ ___to___ ___eat___ a lot of candies.

2 내가 가장 좋아하는 활동은 오후에 산책하는 것이다. (go)
➡ My favorite activity ________ ________ ________ for a walk in the afternoon.

3 나는 그녀에게 언제 돌아 올건지 물었다. (come)
➡ I asked her when ________ ________ back.

4 그들에게 마실 것 좀 주어라. (drink)
➡ Give them something ________ ________.

5 Jennifer는 파티에 입고 갈 새 드레스를 살 것이다.
➡ Jennifer will buy a new dress ________ ________ to the party.

Lesson

9-2 to부정사의 명사적 용법

• **명사적 용법:** 'to부정사'가 명사처럼 주어, 보어, 목적어의 역할을 한다.

1. 주어 역할: '~하는 것', '~하기' – 주어로 쓰이며, 동사는 항상 단수형을 사용한다.

• **To learn** new things is not easy.
• **To be** a nice person is not difficult.

2. 보어 역할: '~하는 것(이다)' – 보어로 사용한다.

• My dream is **to go** all around the world. [주격보어]
• We want her **to try**. [목적격보어]

3. 목적어 역할: '~하는 것을', '~하기를' – 동사 뒤에 위치하며, 목적어로 사용된다.

• He wants **to be** an entertainer.
• They like **to play** basketball.

4. 의문사 + to부정사: 주로 목적어 역할을 하며, 의문사에 따라 의미가 달라진다.

• We don't know **what to do**.
• Can you tell me **how to write** an email?

Check up!

Answer Keys p. 50

A 다음 문장에서 to부정사의 역할을 구분하시오.

1 To help poor people is a very good thing. 주어

2 I don't want Tina to go. ____________

3 To learn a new language is not easy. ____________

4 Sam wants to be a painter. ____________

5 My favorite activity is to play soccer. ____________

6 Sophia promised not to go out late at night. ____________

Check up!

Answer Keys p. 50

B 우리말 해석에 맞게 빈칸에 알맞은 의문사를 쓰시오.

1 그는 다음에 무엇을 해야 할지 말하지 않았다.
➡ He didn't tell me ___what___ to do next.

2 그녀는 그것을 어떻게 사용할지 알고 있다.
➡ She knows ________ to use it.

3 이 컵을 어디에 두면 될지 말해줘.
➡ Tell me ________ to put this cup.

4 Jinju는 언제 숙제를 시작할지 아직 결정하지 않았다.
➡ Jinju hasn't decided ________ to start doing her homework.

5 그들은 방학에 무엇을 할지 얘기 중이다.
➡ They are talking about ________ to do on vacation.

6 나는 어떻게 호두파이를 만드는지 알고 싶다.
➡ I want to know ________ to make a walnut pie.

7 Sally는 언제 잘지 모른다.
➡ Sally doesn't know ________ to sleep.

C 다음 빈칸에 알맞은 말을 보기 에서 찾아 골라 쓰시오.

보기
go eat buy visit ride

1 Does she want ___to___ ___buy___ a new car?

2 My friends planned ________ ________ to Jeju island next month.

3 Billy likes ________ ________ ice cream.

4 Peter decides ________ ________ Anna's house next week.

5 I learned ________ ________ a bike last year.

Lesson 9-3

to부정사의 형용사적 용법

• **형용사적 용법:** 'to부정사'가 형용사처럼 명사를 꾸며준다.

1. 형용사 역할: '~해야 할', '~할' – 명사나 대명사를 뒤에서 꾸며준다.

• She doesn't have enough paper **to write** a letter.

2. 'to부정사' 뒤에 전치사가 오는 경우: 전치사를 빠뜨리지 않도록 주의한다.

• He has many good friends **to talk with.**

Grammar Plus +

to부정사와 함께 쓰이는 전치사

• to write on ~ 위에 써야 할
• to write with ~로 써야 할
• to talk to (with) ~와 이야기할
• to live in ~에서 살
• to live with ~와 함께 살
• to take care of ~을 돌보아야 할
• to put on ~을 입을
• to cut with ~을 자를

Check up!

Answer Keys p. 50

A 다음 중 형용사 역할을 하는 것에 밑줄을 그으시오.

1 I need something to drink.

2 She doesn't have time to study English.

3 Sumi has a lot of work to do.

4 They need a pen to write with.

5 Jenny bought a house to live in.

6 I have nothing to tell you.

7 I want something to eat.

8 He has five dogs to take care of.

9 Jessica wants a handsome guy to fall in love with.

10 They are looking for a room to study in.

Check up!

Answer Keys p. 50

B 다음 괄호 안에서 알맞은 것을 고르시오.

1 Give me some (candies to eat / to eat candies).

2 She told me some facts (to remember / remember to).

3 I need some (to breathe air / air to breathe).

4 It's time (to say / saying) goodbye.

5 Victoria has something important (to talk / to talk about).

6 He gives Tim a chair (to sit / to sit on).

7 My family doesn't have time (to exercise / to exercise in)

8 We have many tests (to study for / study)

9 I want to have a beautiful house (to live / to live in).

10 Zoe has no friends (to talk with / talk with to).

C 다음 우리말과 뜻이 같도록 빈칸에 알맞은 말을 쓰시오.

1 나는 지금 무언가 먹을 것을 원한다.
➡ I want something __to eat__ now.

2 우리들은 오늘 해야 할 숙제가 너무 많다.
➡ We have much homework ________ today.

3 그는 더 이상 그들과 캠핑을 가고 싶어 하지 않는다.
➡ He doesn't want ________ camping with them anymore.

4 Jerry는 이번 주에 읽을 많은 책들이 있다.
➡ Jerry has a lot of books ________ this week.

5 당신은 그곳에 가는 방법을 알고 있나요?
➡ Do you know the way ________ there?

Lesson 9-4

to부정사의 부사적 용법

• **부사적 용법**: 'to부정사'가 부사처럼 동사, 형용사, 다른 부사 또는 문장 전체를 꾸며준다.

1. 목적: ~하기 위하여, ~하려고

We went to the theater **to watch** the movie.

Grammar Plus +

to부정사 부사적 용법의 '목적'

'~하기 위하여' 라는 목적의 의미를 나타낼 경우 **'in order to + 동사원형'** 과 바꿔 쓸 수 있다.

Jack hurried up **to catch** the bus. ➡ Jack hurried up **in order to catch** the bus.

Jack은 버스를 잡기 위해 서둘렀다.

2. 감정의 원인: ~해서, ~하니

She was so surprised **to hear** about my accident.

3. 결과: …해서 ~하다

She grew up **to become** a famous model.

4. 이유/판단의 근거: ~하다니, ~하는 것을 보니

They must be kind **to help** poor people.

Grammar Plus +

to부정사를 이용하여 두 문장을 한 문장으로 만들기

	I was happy. I got a new dress.
① 첫 문장을 그대로 옮긴다.	I was happy.
② 둘째 문장의 주어를 삭제한다.	got a new dress
③ 둘째 문장의 목적어가 명사일 경우 동사 앞에 to를 붙여준다.	got ➡ to get
	➡ **I was happy to get a new dress.**

Check up!

Answer Keys p. 50

A 다음 밑줄 친 to부정사의 쓰임을 목적, 원인, 결과, 근거로 구분하시오.

1 I was sad <u>to hear</u> the news. ___원인___

2 Eric and I went to the library <u>to study</u> math. ________

3 She must be a genius <u>to solve</u> the problem. ________

4 My daughter grew up <u>to be</u> a nurse. ________

5 They must be tired <u>to look</u> sleepy. ________

6 She goes to the store <u>to buy</u> some apples. ________

7 My grandmother lived <u>to be</u> 100 years old. ________

8 You must be crazy <u>to say</u> that. ________

9 I'm happy <u>to see</u> you again. ________

10 He came <u>to join</u> the club. ________

B 주어진 두 문장을 한 문장으로 만드시오.

1 I went to the park. I want to run.
➡ *I went to the park to run.*

2 Joe studies hard. He wants to pass the exam.
➡ ________________

3 Camilla must be a fool. Because she loves him.
➡ ________________

4 They are disappointed. They lose the soccer game.
➡ ________________

5 Samuel must be kind. He did such a thing.
➡ ________________

Practice More I

Answer Keys p. 51

A 다음 문장의 밑줄 친 to부정사를 주어, 목적어, 보어로 구분하시오.

1 To be an actress is my new ambition. 주어

2 Alex's hobby is to collect old coins. ______

3 She wants to buy a red sweater. ______

4 To answer this question is very difficult. ______

5 I hope to meet you again. ______

6 I want her to go. ______

7 To learn math is difficult. ______

8 Tim is trying to buy that car. ______

9 We like to play baseball. ______

10 His wish is to live happily together. ______

B 다음 밑줄 친 to부정사의 쓰임을 명사, 형용사, 부사로 구분하시오.

1 He came to see her. 부사

2 I decided to accept the proposal. ______

3 She has no place to go. ______

4 They were surprised to see him. ______

5 I hope to get an A on the test. ______

6 I was happy to meet you again. ______

7 They don't have enough water to drink. ______

8 Max lived to be 88 years old. ______

9 My dream is to be a writer. ______

10 She needs a chair to sit on. ______

Practice More I

C 다음 문장에서 어법상 어색한 것을 찾아 바르게 고치시오.

1 Be an English teacher is my dream. ___Be___ ➡ ___To be___

2 She decided going to a concert with John.
__________ ➡ __________

3 Would you like to something drink? __________ ➡ __________

4 My sister's hobby is to riding a bike. __________ ➡ __________

5 Jacob wants to not eat carrots. __________ ➡ __________

6 I want to being a doctor. __________ ➡ __________

7 To playing soccer is fun. __________ ➡ __________

8 There is a bad news to telling you. __________ ➡ __________

9 It is time to gone to bed. __________ ➡ __________

10 Her dream is to buying a new car. __________ ➡ __________

11 Ann decided to not become a teacher. __________ ➡ __________

12 I should buy clothes wearing. __________ ➡ __________

13 Joe decided going to school by bus. __________ ➡ __________

14 Stanley wishes to went to the park. __________ ➡ __________

15 I need a pen to writing with. __________ ➡ __________

D 다음 괄호 안에서 알맞은 것을 고르시오.

1 I have many friends to talk (on / (to)).

2 Andrew's dream was to buy a house to live (in / to).

3 He bought a pen to write (with / on).

4 John has many toys to play (to / with).

5 Can you give me some paper to write (with / on)?

Answer Keys p. 51

E 다음 우리말 해석에 맞게 주어진 단어를 알맞게 배열하시오.

1 나는 그 소식을 듣고 유감이었다. (to, the news, hear)
➡ I was sorry ___to hear the news___.

2 해가 뜨기 시작했다. (to, began, rise)
➡ The sun ______________________.

3 나는 매일 30분씩 걸으려고 노력한다.
(30 minutes, for, try, walk, to)
➡ I ______________________ everyday.

4 John은 그녀를 다시 만나 행복했다.
(again, happy, to, her, meet)
➡ John was ______________________.

5 Sandra는 새로운 영화를 찍기로 결심했다.
(to, a new movie, make, decided)
➡ Sandra ______________________.

6 그들은 축구경기에서 이기기 위해 열심히 연습했다.
(win, the soccer, to, game)
➡ They practiced hard ______________________.

7 Mr. Kim은 99세까지 살았다. (old, be, 99 years, to)
➡ Mr. Kim lived ______________________.

8 우리는 무언가 달콤한 먹을 것이 필요하다.
(to, something, sweet, eat)
➡ We need ______________________.

9 나는 매일 긍정적으로 생각하기 위해 노력한다.
(think, try, positively, to)
➡ I ______________________ everyday.

10 그는 식료품을 사기 위해 가게로 갔다.
(groceries, the store, went, to, buy, to)
➡ He ______________________.

Note
- **rise** 뜨다
- **again** 다시
- **practice** 연습하다
- **try to** ~하기위해 노력하다
- **positively** 긍정적으로
- **grocery** 식료품

Point Check Ⅱ

◆ **사역동사:** 누구에게 '~을 하도록 시키다'의 뜻을 가진 동사로서 'let, have, make'가 있다.

◆ **지각동사:** '감각을 느끼다'라는 의미를 갖는 동사로, 목적격보어로 원형부정사가 온다.
지각동사에는 'see, hear, taste, feel, touch, smell' 등이 있다.

1. 사역동사와 지각동사

사역동사: let have make (help) 지각동사: feel hear smell watch see touch	+	목적어	+	동사원형

※ help: 준사역동사이며 원형부정사와 to부정사를 모두 사용할 수 있다.

- I **help** my mom **to clean** the house.
  = I **help** my mom **clean** the house.
- They **had** the children **eat** some vegetables.
- I **watched** Mary **walk** along the river.

2. to부정사의 관용 표현

too + 형용사 + to + 동사원형: 너무 …해서 ~할 수 없는	That old man is too old to walk alone.
형용사 + enough to + 동사원형 …할 만큼 충분히 ~한	This young man is handsome enough to be an actor.
enough + 명사 + to + 동사원형 ~하기에 충분한	We have enough money to buy our teacher's present.

Grammar Plus +

동명사만을 목적어로 사용하는 동사	enjoy 즐기다 finish 끝내다	keep 유지하다 practice 연습하다	mind 꺼리다 give up 포기하다
to부정사만을 목적어로 사용하는 동사	want 원하다 hope 희망하다	plan 계획하다 wish 바라다	decide 결정하다 would like ~하고 싶다
동명사, to부정사 모두를 사용하는 동사	begin 시작하다 start 시작하다	continue 계속하다 love 사랑하다	like 좋아하다 hate 미워하다

Lesson

9-5 사역동사+목적어+원형부정사

• **사역동사:** 사역동사는 누구에게 '~을 하도록 시키다'라는 뜻을 가진 동사로 'let, have, make, help'가 있다. 5형식 문장에서 동사가 사역동사일 경우 목적격보어로 원형부정사가 온다.

1. **let**

They **let** their children **wash** their hands.

2. **have**

She **had** us **stand** in line.

3. **make**

Our parents **make** us **write** in our diaries every night.

4. **help**: 준사역동사로 부르며, 원형부정사와 to부정사 모두를 사용할 수 있다.

She **helps** me **(to) do** the dishes.

Check up!

Answer Keys p. 51

A 보기 와 같이 우리말 해석에 맞게 문장을 완성하시오.

보기

그는 나를 행복하게 느끼도록 만든다.

➡ He __makes__ me __feel happy__.

1 그들은 내게 벽을 칠하게 시켰다.

➡ They ________ me ________ the wall.

2 내가 너에게 좋은 예를 보여줄게.

➡ ________ me ________ you good examples.

3 엄마가 나에게 방을 청소하게 시켰다.

➡ Mom ________ me ________ my room.

4 내가 너에게 Helen을 소개시켜 줄게.

➡ ________ me ________ Helen to you.

Check up!

Answer Keys p. 51

5 제발 제가 자도록 해주세요.
➡ Please __________ me __________.

6 그녀는 나의 숙제를 도와준다.
➡ She __________ me __________ my homework.

7 아빠는 내게 매일 밤 일기를 쓰게 했다.
➡ Father __________ me __________ a diary every night.

8 그는 나를 미소 짓게 한다.
➡ He __________ me __________.

9 내 스마트폰은 내가 음악 듣는 것을 도와준다.
➡ My smartphone __________ me __________ to music.

10 그 선생님은 우리에게 책상을 닦도록 시켰다.
➡ The teacher __________ us __________ our desks.

B **다음 괄호 안에서 알맞은 것을 고르시오.**

1 My homeroom teacher had me (to do / (do)) my homework.

2 Let me (try / to try) the game again.

3 He helped his father (to clean / cleaning) his car.

4 Let him (hold / holds) your bag.

5 I had my little brother (read / reads) books every night.

6 Ellie helps her mom (to do / doing) the shopping.

7 They made us (finish / to finish) our project early.

8 Wind helps a kite (fly / flying) well.

9 Linda had her daughters (stop / stopping) fighting.

10 I had my hair (to cut / cut).

Lesson

9-6 지각동사 + 목적어 + 원형부정사

• **지각동사:** 감각기관을 통해 느끼는 것을 표현하는 동사이다. 목적격보어로 원형부정사가 오며, 'see, hear, taste, feel, touch, smell' 등이 있다.

1. **see**: ~하는 것을 보다

I **saw** Maria **cross** the street.

2. **hear**: ~하는 것을 듣다

They **heard** me **sing**.

3. **feel**: ~하는 것을 느끼다

She **felt** her bag **vibrate**.

➡ 동작이 진행 중인 것을 강조할 때는 원형부정사 대신에 현재분사(-ing)를 사용하기도 한다.

He **heard** her playing the drums.

Check up!

Answer Keys p. 51

A 다음 괄호 안에서 알맞은 것을 고르시오.

1 He saw Sally (dance / to dancing) in the room.

2 I heard the choir (sing / to sing) in the church.

3 Harry watched her (to jog / jogging) in the park.

4 Mother had me (to do / do) my homework.

5 Mr. Kim could feel the house (to shake / shaking) heavily.

6 I saw the dog (running / ran) after me.

7 They saw a man (stole / steal) their car.

8 I could feel something (touched / touch) my shoulder.

9 William can't hear her (talking / to talk).

10 I saw the boys (playing / to play) soccer.

11 They watched me (to go / going) out.

12 Can you hear the cat (to cry / crying)?

13 Have you ever seen Christian (shout / to shout)?

14 He could feel the wind (blow / to blow) through the window.

15 I can hear her (calling / to call) my name.

Lesson

9-7 too... to~ / enough to~

- to부정사가 부사 'too'와 쓰이면 부정의 뜻을 갖는다.
- to부정사가 부사 'enough'와 쓰이면 '정도'의 뜻을 갖는다.

1. too + 형용사 + to + 동사원형: 너무 ~해서 …할 수 없는

This box is **too** heavy **to** lift.

= [so + 형용사 + that + 주어 + can't/couldn't + 동사원형]

This box is **so** heavy **that** I **can't** lift it.

➡ that절 이하의 시제는 주절의 동사 시제와 일치시켜야 한다.

2. 형용사 + enough to + 동사원형: ~할 만큼 충분히 …한

He is strong **enough to** bring the rock.

= [so + 형용사 + that + 주어 + can/could + 동사원형]

He is **so** strong **that he can** bring the rock.

3. enough + 명사 + to + 동사원형: ~하기에 충분한

We have **enough** paint **to** draw several pictures.

Check up!

Answer Keys p. 52

A 다음 괄호 안에서 알맞은 것을 고르시오

1 My little brother is (so / too) young to go to preschool.

2 Tim is too tiny (to / that) ride a roller coaster.

3 He was kind (enough / that) to help weak children.

4 She was (so / too) sick that she couldn't go to school last week.

5 I think Daniel is tall enough (reaching / to reach) the ceiling.

6 Sara was so tired that she (couldn't / could) meet Suji.

7 He has enough time (to travel / travel) all around the world.

8 It was sharp enough (to cut / cutting) the thick cable.

9 Lily has (so / too) little money that she can't buy that necklace.

10 They are (enough smart / smart enough) to answer all the questions.

Check up!

Answer Keys p. 52

B 다음 두 문장의 뜻이 같도록 빈칸을 채우시오.

1 Lisa is so young that she cannot understand the lecture.
➡ Lisa is ___too___ young ___to___ understand the lecture.

2 This Mexican food is too spicy to eat.
➡ This Mexican food ________ spicy ________ I can't eat.

3 The book is easy enough to read.
➡ The book is ________ easy ________ I can read.

4 He is so clever that he can solve the problem.
➡ He is ________ to solve the problem.

5 They have enough time to study English and math.
➡ They have ________ much time ________ they can study English and math.

C 다음 문장에서 어법상 어색한 것을 찾아 바르게 고치시오.

1 He was so tired that he can finish his homework.
___can___ ➡ ___couldn't___

2 Father is enough strong to move the furniture.
________ ➡ ________

3 You are too small to going to the concert alone.
________ ➡ ________

4 Luciana is so busy that she can go to the meeting.
________ ➡ ________

5 I was to impatient too wait for someone.
________ ➡ ________

Practice More Ⅱ

A 다음 괄호 안에서 알맞은 것을 고르시오.

1 We can see him (cross / to cross) the street.

2 Let me (introduce / to introduce) my brother to you.

3 I saw Tim (smile / to smile) at her.

4 He is too big (to / that) get out of the manhole.

5 I saw the boys (togather / gather) on the stage.

6 Jack was (too / to) tired to carry the backpack.

7 Let us (tell / telling) him something.

8 She has (enough time / time enough) to go back home.

9 I had her (to clean / clean) the wet floor.

10 The teacher let us (to turn in / turn in) homework until tomorrow.

11 They watched Patricia (go / going) out of town.

12 Matthew made his daughter (eat / ate) some healthy food.

13 He saw the dog (barking / barked) at strangers.

14 Let him (to solve / solve) his problem on his own.

15 My parents didn't allow me (to play / play) computer games at night.

B 다음 주어진 단어들을 순서대로 바르게 배열해 문장을 완성하시오.

1 My brother is (too,watch, young, to) horror movies.
➡ My brother is ___too young to watch___ horror movies.

2 Isabella was (smart, that, so) she could graduate early.
➡ Isabella was ________________ she could graduate early.

3 He is (enough, kind, show, to) us the way to the museum.
➡ He is ________________ us the way to the museum.

4 He was (sad, couldn't, he, so, anything, that, do).
➡ He was ________________.

Answer Keys p. 52

5 We have (much, luggage, to carry, too).
➡ We have ______________________.

6 She is (enough, tall, reach, to).
➡ She is ______________________ the shelf.

7 It was (early, to, go, too) camping.
➡ It was ______________________ camping.

C 다음 문장에서 어법상 어색한 것을 찾아 바르게 고치시오.

1 This strange ball is too heavy throw.
throw ➡ to throw

2 She helped us solving the difficult problem.
__________ ➡ __________

3 Helen is to weak to move the refrigerator.
__________ ➡ __________

4 He is enough brave to catch the robber.
__________ ➡ __________

5 Have you ever seen her laughed?
__________ ➡ __________

6 He is so little that he can join the soccer team.
__________ ➡ __________

7 Did his father let Sam going hiking?
__________ ➡ __________

8 Mr. Park is enough rich to buy the jewelry.
__________ ➡ __________

9 The woman saw a boy stolen some money.
__________ ➡ __________

10 Let me to show you some examples.
__________ ➡ __________

Note

- rise 뜨다
- again 다시
- practice 연습하다
- try to ~하기위해 노력하다
- positive 긍정적인
- grocery 식료품

Practice More Ⅱ

D **다음 우리말 해석에 알맞게 주어진 단어들을 바르게 배열하시오.**

1 이 책상은 너무 무거워서 옮길 수 없다.
(so, it, can't, I, heavy, move, that)
➡ This desk is *so heavy that I can't move it.*

2 그 교수는 내게 그의 오래된 책들을 읽는 것을 허락했다.
(his old books, let, read, me)
➡ The professor ______________________

3 Helen은 누군가 자기의 머리 위에 손을 올려 놓는 것을 느꼈다.
(someone, put, felt, his hand, on her head)
➡ Helen ______________________

4 엄마는 나에게 짧은 치마를 입지 못하게 했다.
(not, a short skirt, wear, had, me)
➡ Mom ______________________

5 그녀의 음식은 나에게 예전의 기억들을 떠올리게 했다.
(old memories, me, bring back, made)
➡ Her food ______________________

6 너는 미식축구 하는 소녀들을 보았니?
(football, see, playing, the girls)
➡ Did you ______________________

7 Jack은 자기의 아들에게 앞마당을 청소하지 않도록 했다.
(clean, his son, had, the front yard, not)
➡ Jack ______________________

8 그 소녀는 이 강의를 이해하기에는 너무 어리다.
(understand, too, the lecture, to, young)
➡ The girl is ______________________

9 Hana는 너무 졸려서 숙제를 할 수 없었다.
(too, her, sleepy, homework, do, to)
➡ Hana was ______________________

10 Bora는 욕실에서 그가 노래하는 것을 들었다.
(in the bathroom, sing, heard, him)
➡ Bora ______________________

Note
- **professor** 교수
- **bring back** 떠올리다
- **memory** 기억, 추억
- **front yard** 앞마당
- **football** 미식축구(럭비)
- **lecture** 강의
- **sleepy** 졸린

중간 기말고사 예상문제

Answer Keys p. 52

내신 최다 출제 유형

01 다음 중 밑줄 친 부분이 나머지 넷과 다른 하나를 고르시오. [출제 예상 85%]

① I am so tired that I want to sleep more.
② He begins to read books in the school cafeteria.
③ Sophia likes to play ping-pong very much.
④ John went to the park to play basketball with his friends.
⑤ My sister wants to be a professional violinist.

02 다음 중 어법상 올바른 문장을 고르시오. [출제 예상 85%]

① Thomas decided to learn Japanese.
② Do you want have enough money to buy that picture?
③ She wished to getting new shoes.
④ Mr. Black planned make a huge kite with his students.
⑤ I begin to learning how to dance today.

03 다음 중 어법상 올바른 것을 고르시오. [출제 예상 90%]

① It starting to snow.
② I planned to learning Chinese.
③ Jane wishes going to Brazil.
④ Jack likes to meet new people.
⑤ Jerry and Lucas love read comic books.

04 다음 밑줄 친 부분의 쓰임이 보기 와 같은 것을 고르시오. [출제 예상 85%]

보기
> My grandparents want to see me and my sister.

① It is not easy to use chopsticks.
② His hobby is to play the piano.
③ My wish is to meet him soon.
④ Jerry decided to go to England this summer vacation.
⑤ To learn something is good for us.

05 다음의 우리말과 같은 뜻이 되도록 빈칸에 알맞은 말을 고르시오. [출제 예상 80%]

> 당신은 무언가 마실 것을 원합니까?
> ➡ Would you like __________?

① drink ② to drink
③ to something ④ something to drink
⑤ drink something

06 다음 밑줄 친 부분 중 'to부정사'로 바꿀 수 없는 것을 고르시오. [출제 예상 80%]

① Jack stopped the car in order to pick up the phone.
② It starts raining.
③ Jennifer likes playing hide-and-seek.
④ I jogged every morning in order to lose weight.
⑤ He enjoys singing very loudly.

중간 기말고사 예상문제

[01~02] 다음 빈칸에 공통으로 들어갈 알맞은 단어를 고르시오.

01

- In winter, I like ________ make snowmen.
- I'm going ________ go on a date with you.

① to ② for ③ at ④ in ⑤ of

02

- Can you tell me ________ to get to the Joe's restaurant?
- She will learn ________ to swim this summer.

① what ② which ③ when
④ how ⑤ where

[03~04] 다음 밑줄 친 부분 중 잘못된 것을 고르시오.

03

① Your hobby is ② go for a ③ walk with your sister and ④ play badminton ⑤ in the evening.

04

① This office is very ② hot. ③ Would you like to ④ opens the ⑤ window?

[05~07] 다음 주어진 문장의 밑줄 친 부분과 쓰임이 다른 것을 고르시오.

05

Isabella wanted to be a movie actress.

① She wants to meet the actor.
② I like to play soccer.
③ His dream is to travel all around the world.
④ They learn how to ride a bike.
⑤ I heard you decided to marry her.

06

Jane has many things to do.

① We are very nice to see you.
② I have nothing to drink.
③ You have no paper to write on.
④ We don't have any books to read.
⑤ There aren't any chairs to sit on.

07

To see is not everything.

① To do yoga is good for your health.
② It isn't always good to have a lot of money.
③ To read many books is good.
④ You'll be sad to leave here alone.
⑤ It is very good to have a hobby.

[08~10] 다음 빈칸에 들어갈 말로 알맞은 것을 고르시오.

08

You don't need ________ some new clothes for him.

① to buy ② will buy ③ buy
④ buy to ⑤ buys

Answer Keys p. 53~54

09

> Jean was very glad ________ it again in front of everyone.

① do ② to do ③ did
④ does ⑤ will do

10

> We saw you ________ volleyball at the beach.

① play ② to play ③ playing
④ plays ⑤ played

[11~12] 다음 중 어법상 어색한 것을 고르시오.

11
① He wants to live in London.
② Jasmine and Victoria love go shopping.
③ You like to wear a long dress.
④ I don't want to leave here.
⑤ They planned to visit New York.

12
① I have a lot of homework to finish by tomorrow.
② She has something to give you.
③ You will go shopping to buy a new jacket.
④ I don't want to watching the movie with you.
⑤ He listens to music to relax.

13 다음 주어진 단어를 우리말에 맞게 배열한 것을 고르시오.

> 너는 그들에게 무엇을 만들어 주고 싶니?
> What (you / want / to / make / do) for them?

① What do you want to make for them?
② What do you want make to for them?
③ What do you make want to for them?
④ What you do want to make for them?
⑤ What you want to do make for them?

[14~15] 다음 문장 중 어법상 올바른 것을 고르시오.

14
① I wish to being a famous singer.
② To play games is so exciting.
③ Sometimes, to eating out is good.
④ It is not easy to speaking English well.
⑤ He won't goes there to help people.

15
① She wants something to eating.
② It is not good to be waste your time.
③ You are pretty enough to participate in the beauty contest.
④ I don't have much time do homework.
⑤ It is hard make him happy.

16 다음 중 어법상 옳은 것끼리 짝지어진 것을 고르시오.

ⓐ I like to riding in-line skates.
ⓑ I've got the mail to pass the examination.
ⓒ He will goes to America next month.
ⓓ They were happy seeing me.
ⓔ You have many friends to play with.

① ⓐ, ⓓ ② ⓒ, ⓔ ③ ⓑ, ⓔ
④ ⓒ, ⓓ ⑤ ⓑ, ⓐ

Note examination : 시험 (=exam)

[17~18] 다음 중 밑줄 친 to의 쓰임이 나머지 넷과 다른 것을 고르시오.

17
① I want to meet you tomorrow.
② Phillip needs to help me.
③ Sara and Taylor go to school.
④ Harry likes to play the drum.
⑤ I will invite them to have a party.

18
① Jack has a lot of letters to send.
② I want something to drink.
③ I raised my hand to ask a question.
④ Maria has many friends to help her.
⑤ There is nothing to eat on the table.

[19~20] 다음 주어진 우리말과 같은 뜻이 되도록 빈칸에 알맞은 말을 고르시오.

19

그들은 첫 기차를 타기 위해 5시에 일어났다.
➡ They got up at five o'clock ________.

① to catch the first train
② catching first train
③ to caught the first train
④ catches the first train
⑤ caught the first train

20

하루 종일 스마트폰을 사용하는 것은 나쁘다.
➡ It is bad for you ________ a Smartphone all day.

① use ② uses ③ to use
④ used to ⑤ used

21 다음 문장들 중 빈칸에 to를 쓸 수 없는 것을 고르시오.

① It is hard ______ solve this problem alone.
② It is not difficult ______ make cookies.
③ I wish ______ visit London someday.
④ He had me ______ wash the dishes.
⑤ The old lady is kind enough ______ help other people.

22 다음 문장들 중 빈칸에 to를 쓸 수 있는 것을 고르시오.

① Jessie watched me ______ dance on the stage.
② My friend helped me ______ do my homework.
③ You may feel the ground ______ shake.
④ They didn't let me ______ go outside.
⑤ He heard his teacher ______ call his name.

[23~25] 다음 주어진 문장의 밑줄 친 부분과 쓰임이 같은 것을 고르시오.

23

> Tommy was very happy to see her again.

① To work on the farm is good for me.
② I don't have any paper to draw on.
③ We have much homework to do.
④ To know is the real power.
⑤ I was so glad to get many birthday presents.

24

> His grandmother lived to be ninety-two years old.

① His hobby is to play the drums.
② They're glad to come and help me.
③ She grew up to be a famous architect.
④ It's very hard to ride a bike to me.
⑤ I like to climb a tree.

25

> Mary went to a shopping mall to buy a new dress.

① I turn on the TV to watch the news.
② My little brother decided to learn letters.
③ To sing in a band is a new experience.
④ I want to read comic books all day.
⑤ Rachel has a lot of work to do.

[26~27] 다음 빈칸에 들어갈 알맞은 말을 두 개 고르시오.

26

> Phillip은 내가 길을 건너는 것을 보았다.
> ➡ Phillip saw me ________ the street.

① cross ② to cross ③ crossed
④ crossing ⑤ is crossing

27

> 나는 네가 추위로 떨고 있는 것을 느꼈다.
> ➡ I felt you ________ with cold.

① to shiver ② are shiver
③ shiver ④ shivered
⑤ shivering

[28~30] 다음 빈칸에 들어갈 알맞은 단어를 고르시오.

28

> Would you please give me some paper to write ________?

① to ② of ③ in ④ with ⑤ on

29

Someday, I will build a big house to live ________.

① in ② of ③ with
④ to ⑤ on

30

He needs some friends to talk ________.

① in ② of ③ with
④ for ⑤ on

[31~33] 다음 빈칸에 공통으로 들어갈 알맞은 말을 고르시오.

31

• She grew up ________ a famous writer.
• My grandfather lived ________ 80 years old.

① be ② to be ③ to being
④ became ⑤ being

32

• My sister has a lot of homework ________.
• She always tells me ________ my best.

① do ② doing ③ to do
④ did ⑤ doing

33

• What do you want ________ in the future?
• Leah hopes ________ a famous ballerina.

① being ② been ③ be
④ to do ⑤ to be

34 다음 중 어법상 옳은 것들끼리 묶은 것을 고르시오.

ⓐ To save water is important.
ⓑ Teachers made students being noisy.
ⓒ My dream is go to around the world.
ⓓ Linda wants to eat spicy food.

① ⓐ,ⓓ ② ⓑ,ⓒ ③ ⓒ,ⓓ
④ ⓐ,ⓒ ⑤ ⓐ,ⓑ

[35~37] 다음 중 어법상 잘못된 것을 고르시오.

35
① The book is light enough to handle.
② She decided to tell the truth.
③ Jack has a small house to live in.
④ I noticed them to get out of the classroom.
⑤ He wished to be a famous actor.

36
① I saw her dog running at the park.
② You will let me to know the truth.
③ He watched a girl crossing the street.
④ She heard me singing a song alone.
⑤ I told him to call me tonight.

Answer Keys p. 53~54

37 ① Olivia loves go shopping with her mom.
② They saved some money to buy their parents a gift.
③ I want to live in a house near a lake.
④ To speak a foreign language is difficult.
⑤ You don't have to spend much time to work for him.

[38~40] 다음 문장 중 어법상 올바른 것을 고르시오.

38 ① I could hear someone cry loudly.
② He want to live in a big house.
③ She likes to wearing jeans.
④ The man is too old to walking.
⑤ Do you want something drink?

39 ① I got a new radio to listening to music.
② The boy decided to studies hard.
③ The old woman needs a chair to sit on.
④ There is a lot of food to eating.
⑤ Rita watched me to dance with Jack.

40 ① She is so young that she can't entering the school.
② These jeans are too bigger to wear.
③ She made her kids to play a computer game.
④ They are so kind that they can to help other people
⑤ You can order something to eat.

서술형 평가

[41~42] 다음 주어진 두 개의 문장을 하나로 만들 때 빈칸에 알맞은 말을 쓰시오.

41

I don't have enough money. So I can't buy a car.

➡ I don't have enough money ________.

42

Eat breakfast every morning. It is good for your health.

➡ ________________ is good for your health.

[43~45] 다음 주어진 우리말과 같은 뜻이 되도록 괄호 안의 단어를 알맞게 배열하여 쓰시오.

43

그녀는 어디로 이사 갈지 정해야 한다. (should / decide / move / to / where / she)

➡ ________________

44

John은 무엇을 살지 모른다. (doesn't / John / buy / to / what / know)

➡ ________________

Answer Keys p. 53~54

45

그들은 어떻게 책을 읽는지 가르친다.
(teach / how / read / to / they / a / book)

➡ ______________________________

[46~47] 다음 두 개의 문장이 서로 같은 뜻이 되도록 빈칸에 알맞은 말을 쓰시오.

46

This new book is too heavy to carry.

➡ This new book is ________ heavy ________ carry it.

47

She is beautiful enough to be a popular actress.

➡ She is ________ beautiful ________ a popular actress.

[48~50] 다음 주어진 우리말에 맞게 빈칸에 알맞은 말을 쓰시오. (각 칸에 한 단어씩 써야 함)

48

우리에게 몇 시간 동안 읽기에 충분한 책들이 있다.

➡ We ________ ________ books ________ ________ for several ________.

49

나는 내 아이들이 숙제 후에 배드민턴을 칠 수 있도록 했다.

➡ I ________ my children ________ ________ after doing their ________.

50

그녀는 자신이 바랐던 것처럼 자라서 나이팅게일 같은 훌륭한 간호사가 되었다.

➡ She ________ up ________ ________ a great ________ like Nightingale as ________ ________.

10
Chapter
동명사

Point Check I

◆ **동명사 :** '동사원형 + ing'의 형태로, '~하는 것', '~하기'로 해석한다.
동사의 성질을 그대로 가지고 있으면서 명사 역할을 한다.

1. 동명사의 규칙

(1) **동명사는 단수로 취급된다.**

- **Reading** is his way to learn English.

(2) **동명사를 부정할 경우 앞에 'not'이 붙는다.**

- She hates not **trying** at all.

(3) **명사의 소유격 또는 목적격으로 사용된다.**

- I like his/him **working** so hard.

2. 동명사의 역할

(1) **주어의 역할**

- **Recycling** is necessary to our lives.

(2) **보어의 역할**

- Their dream is **traveling** around the world some day.

(3) **타동사의 목적어 역할**

- Fiona enjoys **studying** English.

(4) **전치사의 목적어 역할**

- I was worried about **doing** my homework.

3. 동명사와 to부정사의 동사

동명사만을 목적어로 사용하는 동사	enjoy practice	finish mind	keep give up
to부정사만을 목적어로 사용하는 동사	want wish	hope decide	plan would like
동명사, to부정사를 모두 사용하는 동사	begin love	start like	continue hate

4. 동명사의 관용표현

- **How (What) about + -ing** ~하는 게 어때?
- **be busy + -ing** ~하느라 바쁘다
- **spend + 시간/돈 + -ing** ~하는 데 시간/돈을 소비하다
- **feel like + -ing** ~하고 싶다
- **keep (on) + -ing** 계속~하다
- **keep (stop) A from + -ing** A가 ~하는 것을 막다
- **go + -ing** ~하러 가다
- **be (get) used to + -ing** ~하는 데 익숙하다
- **look forward to + -ing** ~하는 것을 기대하다
- **cannot help + -ing** ~하지 않을 수 없다

Lesson

10-1 동명사의 규칙

• **동명사:** 동사에 '-ing'가 붙은 형태로 동사와 명사의 성질을 가지고 있으며, 문장 안에서는 명사의 역할을 한다.

1. 동명사의 규칙: [동사+ing]

• cook ➡ cooking
• play tennis ➡ playing tennis
• watch TV ➡ watching TV

2. 동명사의 쓰임

(1) 주어: 단수 취급을 한다.

• **Collecting stamps** is her hobby.
• **Reading comic books** is funny.

(2) 부정문: 동명사 앞에 'not'을 붙인다.

• She apologized me for not **telling** the truth.
• I was angry about them not **inviting** me.

(3) 의미상의 주어: 명사의 소유격 또는 목적격을 사용한다.

• They really mind my (me) **leaving** here.
• Do you mind her **opening** the doorway?

Check up!

Answer Keys p. 55

A 다음 괄호 안에서 알맞은 것을 고르시오.

1 Watching funny movies (is / are) my hobby.
2 Jane and I started (swim / swimming) yesterday.
3 (Exercise / Exercising) regularly makes me healthy.
4 Do you mind (her / she) coming to our home?
5 Writing a letter to parents (is / are) not easy.
6 Does she mind (he / him) borrowing her pen?
7 Telling the truth about yourself (is / are) very important.
8 He was angry about (not calling / calling not) him.
9 Do you mind (walking / walk) to school on foot?
10 Playing tennis with her (is / are) very fun.

Lesson 10-2 동명사의 역할

• **동명사**: 문장에서 주어, 보어, 목적어의 역할을 한다.

1. 주어 역할

• **Riding** a roller coaster is so fun.
• **Being** a nice person is not easy.

2. 보어 역할

• My future dream is **becoming** a dentist.
• Her favorite hobby is **taking** pictures in nature.

3. 타동사 목적어 역할

• Anya and I enjoyed **playing** computer games.
• He needs to start **exercising** right now.

4. 전치사의 목적어 역할

• We learned a lot about **gardening**.
• Thank you for **coming** to see me.

Check up!

Answer Keys p. 55

A 다음 밑줄 친 부분을 어법상 알맞은 형태로 고쳐 쓰시오.

1 Lisa enjoys __reading__ romance novels. (read)

2 His new hobby is ________ pictures of birds. (take)

3 I like ________ wild flowers. (draw)

4 ________ a car for the first time is fun. (drive)

5 His job is ________ all the machines. (repair)

6 Mina is good at ________. Her food is delicious. (cook)

7 He should quit ________ to them now. (talk)

8 ________ to classical music makes me comfortable. (listen)

9 Their main goal is ________ the writing contest. (win)

Answer Keys p. 55

10 __________ new people sometimes makes me nervous. (meet)

11 Thank you for __________ our tour of Europe. (join)

12 He is tired of __________. He wants to sleep. (work)

13 I'm so bad at __________ essays. (write)

14 There is no easy road to __________ a foreign language.(learn)

15 I'm sorry for not __________ you earlier. (tell)

16 Tim has just finished __________ his homework. (do)

17 Mom says that __________ vegetables keeps me healthy. (eat)

18 She began __________ the piano at the age of 10. (play)

19 He gave no reason for __________ so suddenly. (leave)

20 John's dream is __________ a world-famous doctor. (become)

B **다음 우리말과 뜻이 같도록 괄호안의 단어를 이용하여 빈칸을 채우시오.**

1 나는 새 차를 사는 것을 포기했다. (give up)
➡ I ___*gave*___ ___*up*___ ___*buying*___ a new car.

2 어린이들은 웃기 시작했다. (start, laugh)
➡ The children __________ __________.

3 Peter는 밤낮으로 기타를 연습했다. (practice, play)
➡ Peter __________ __________ the guitar day and night.

4 Lina의 엄마는 한국 음식을 요리하는 것을 매우 좋아한다. (love, cook)
➡ Lina's mother __________ __________ Korean food.

5 그녀는 캠프에서 춤추는 것을 즐겼다. (enjoy, dance)
➡ She __________ __________ at the camp.

Note
- **nervous** 긴장된
- **tour** 관광
- **be tired of** ~에 싫증 내다, 지겨워하다
- **suddenly** 갑자기
- **give up** 포기하다
- **laugh** (소리 내어) 웃다
- **practice** 연습하다
- **day and night** 밤낮으로

Lesson 10-3 동명사와 to부정사의 동사

• 어떤 동사는 동명사나 to부정사 중 하나만 목적어로 사용할 수 있지만, 목적어로 동명사나 to부정사를 모두 사용할 수 있는 동사도 있다.

1. 동명사를 목적어로 취하는 동사

enjoy	**finish**	**keep**	**mind**	**practice**	**give up**

• I **enjoy** listening to K-pop music.
• They **finished** doing their homework.
• She **practices** playing the violin every day.

2. to부정사를 목적어로 취하는 동사

want	**hope**	**plan**	**wish**	**decide**	**would like**

• We **want** to buy some new clothes.
• I **decided** to meet my ex-girlfriend again.

3. 동명사, to부정사를 모두 취하는 동사

begin	**start**	**like**	**love**	**hate**	**continue**

• My brother **likes** to make model cars.
= My brother **likes** making model cars.

Grammar Plus +

to부정사와 동명사를 모두 사용하지만 뜻이 달라지는 동사

(1) try + to부정사: ~하려고 노력하다 / try + 동명사: ~하려고 시도하다
➡ She **tries to make** spaghetti.
She **tries making** spaghetti.

(2) stop + to부정사: ~하기 위해 멈추다 / stop + 동명사: ~하는 것을 멈추다
➡ The gentleman **stopped to take a** bus.
The gentleman **stopped taking** a bus.

Check up!

Answer Keys p. 55

A 다음 괄호 안의 단어를 알맞은 형태로 바꾸어 쓰시오.

1 He wants ___*to live*___ in the countryside. (live)

2 I can't finish ___________ my homework until tonight. (do)

3 Would you mind ___________ my picture? (take)

4 We decided ___________ hiking tomorrow. (go)

5 Jack enjoys ___________ games every night. (play)

6 Do you want ___________ with us? (go out)

7 We plan ___________ the dance festival. (participate in)

8 I wish to be good at ___________ English someday. (speak)

9 I would like ___________ to Canada with my friends. (travel)

10 Tim wants ___________ this red shirt. (buy)

11 Sara practices ___________ the violin on Sundays. (play)

12 I hope ___________ Paris in the future. (visit)

13 I'd like ___________ something sweet. (eat)

14 Linda needs ___________ home because she has a cold. (stay)

15 He avoided ___________ about that rumor. (talk)

B 다음 문장과 같은 뜻이 되도록 문장을 완성하시오.

1 Helen started to exercise regularly.
➡ Helen started ___*exercising*___ regularly.

2 She didn't like to eat vegetables.
➡ She didn't like ___________ vegetables.

3 Father loves going fishing on Saturdays.
➡ Father loves ___________ fishing on Saturdays.

4 They like to sing that song again and again.
➡ They like ___________ that song again and again.

5 She continues using her digital camera.
➡ She continues ___________ her digital camera.

6 Lucas started studying English to go to America.
➡ Lucas started ___________ English to go to America.

Note

- countryside 시골
- would you mind~? ~해도 될까요?
- decide to ~을 결정하다
- go out 외출하다
- participate in ~에 참가하다
- avoid 피하다, 회피하다
- rumor 소문
- regularly 규칙적으로, 정기적으로
- again and again 몇 번이고, 되풀이해서

Lesson

10-4 동명사의 관용 표현

• 동명사의 관용 표현은 오랫동안 써와 굳어진 말들로 동명사가 들어있는 것들이다.

1. '동명사 + 명사'의 주요 표현

sleeping car	침대차	sleeping bag	침낭
waiting room	대기실	smoking room	흡연실
washing machine	세탁기	dressing room	분장실
walking stick	지팡이	sleeping pill	수면제
swimming suit	수영복	swimming pool	수영장

2. 동명사의 관용표현

(1) **[How (What) about + 동명사]** ~하는 게 어때?

• **How (What) about drawing** some trees?

※ 'How (What) about -ing?'는 상대방의 의견을 물어보거나 제안을 하는 표현으로, 'Let's~'로 바꾸어 쓸 수 있다. 이때 '-ing'형의 동사는 '동사원형'으로 바꾸어 줘야 한다.

• **How (What) about going** outside? = **Let's go** outside.

(2) **[be busy + 동명사]** ~하느라 바쁘다

• I **am busy cooking** for my mom's birthday.

(3) **[spend + 시간/돈 + 동명사]** ~하는 데 시간/돈을 소비하다

• I **spent my time reading** books.

• He **spent much money buying** the musical instrument.

(4) **[feel like + 동명사]** ~하고 싶다

• Her sister **felt like going** to the baseball stadium.

(5) **[keep (on) + 동명사]** 계속 ~하다

• It **keeps snowing** all day long.

(6) **[keep (stop) A from + 동명사]** A가 ~하는 것을 막다

• His teacher **kept him from going** back home early.

(7) **[go + 동명사]** ~하러 가다

• Shall we **go skating**?

(8) **[be (get) used to + 동명사]** ~하는 데 익숙하다

• I **am used to keeping** my diary.

(9) **[look forward to + 동명사]** ~하는 것을 기대하다

• We **look forward to hearing** from you soon.

(10) **[cannot help + 동명사]** ~하지 않을 수 없다

• I **cannot help waiting** for them.

Check up!

Answer Keys p. 55

A 다음 괄호 안의 단어를 알맞은 형태로 바꾸어 쓰시오.

1 Sophia는 다음 주에 야영하러 갈 것이다. (go, camp)
➡ Sophia is going to ___go camping___ next week.

2 그들은 밤에 숙제를 하는 것에 익숙하다. (do homework)
➡ They ____________ homework at night.

3 우리는 뉴욕으로 여행을 떠날 것을 기대했다. (travel)
➡ We ____________ to New York.

4 나는 John을 사랑하지 않을 수 없다. (love)
➡ I ____________ John.

5 Emma는 어제 설거지를 하느라 바빴다. (do the dish)
➡ Emma was ____________ the dishes yesterday.

6 나와 Ted는 야구를 보느라 많은 시간을 보냈다. (watch)
➡ Ted and I ________ much time ________ the baseball game.

7 Linda는 친구들과 음악회에 가고 싶다. (go)
➡ Linda ____________ to a concert with her friends.

8 학생들은 컴퓨터 게임을 하는 데 너무 많은 시간을 쓴다. (play)
➡ Students ________ too much time ________ computer games.

9 그는 계속 교수님과 얘기 중이다. (talk to)
➡ He ____________ his professor.

10 그 소음이 밤새 내가 자는 것을 방해했다. (sleep)
➡ The noise ____________ all night.

11 나는 낮잠을 자고 싶다. (feel like)
➡ I ________ taking a nap.

12 그들은 프로젝트를 끝내는 데 한달을 보냈다. (finish)
➡ They ________ a month ________ the project.

13 그녀는 그를 한 시간 동안 계속 기다리고 있는 중이다. (wait for)
➡ She kept ____________ him for an hour.

14 선생님은 학생들의 질문에 대답하고 싶지 않았다. (answer)
➡ The teacher ____________ his students' questions.

15 간식을 좀 먹는 건 어때? (eat)
➡ ____________ some snacks?

Note

- go camping 야영하러 가다
- be used to –ing ~하는데 익숙하다
- look forward to –ing ~하는 것을 고대하다
- do (wash) the dishes 설거지하다
- all night 밤새
- wait for ~을 기다리다

Practice More Ⅰ

A 다음 주어진 단어들을 알맞은 동명사 형태로 바꾸시오.

1 Thank you for ___inviting___ me. (invite)

2 Charles is good at ______ sit-ups. (do)

3 She could pass the exam by ______ hard. (study)

4 He likes ______ tricks on his friends. (play)

5 My hobby is ______ to rock music. (listen)

6 ______ how to speak Korean is fun. (learn)

7 Victoria left without ______ goodbye. (say)

8 I'm interested in ______ a horse. (ride)

9 You should stop ______ TV. (watch)

10 Do you mind ______ loudly? (laugh)

B 다음 밑줄 친 동명사의 쓰임을 주어, 목적어, 보어로 구분하시오.

1 Playing tennis is a good exercise. ___주어___

2 My hobby is watching SF movies. ______

3 Tim likes jogging near his home. ______

4 I'm sorry for being late. ______

5 My favorite activity is dancing. ______

6 Seeing the sights in Seoul is thrilling. ______

7 He stopped eating unhealthy food. ______

8 Driving a tractor is not difficult. ______

9 Linda gave up buying a new coat. ______

10 Ann's good habit is exercising regularly. ______

Answer Keys p. 56

C 다음 문장에서 어법상 어색한 것을 찾아 바르게 고치시오.

1 She wants to living with her family.

living ➡ *live*

2 The team gave up to participate in the contest.

________ ➡ ________

3 Lim is interested in learn how to bake.

________ ➡ ________

4 I enjoy to write handwritten letters.

________ ➡ ________

5 They kept played computer games all night.

________ ➡ ________

6 My little sister would like eating spicy food.

________ ➡ ________

7 Thank you for to help us to solve the problem.

________ ➡ ________

8 Minhee is good at play the cello.

________ ➡ ________

9 Her job is make a TV program.

________ ➡ ________

10 Reading many books are better than watching TV.

________ ➡ ________

Practice More I

D 다음 우리말과 같은 뜻이 되도록 주어진 단어를 사용하여 문장을 완성하시오.

1 Kevin은 계속 Chloe를 기다리는 중이다. (wait for)
➡ Kevin keeps ___*waiting for*___ Chloe.

2 다음 토요일에 스키 타러 가실래요? (go, ski)
➡ Would you like to ______________ next Saturday?

3 그들은 Jack의 생일 파티를 준비하느라 바쁘다.
(busy, prepare for, birthday party)
➡ They are ______________________________.

4 나는 너를 사랑하지 않을 수 없다. (cannot help, love)
➡ I __________________ you.

5 나는 오늘 밤에 낚시를 가고 싶다. (feel like, go fishing)
➡ I __________________ tonight.

6 부모님은 내가 밤에 혼자 나가는 것을 막으신다.
(keep from, go out alone)
➡ My parents ______________________ at night.

7 공원에서 테니스를 치는 게 어때? (how about, play tennis)
➡ ____________________ in the park?

8 그는 어제 자기 아버지와 함께 사냥하러 갔다. (go, hunt)
➡ He ______________ with his father yesterday.

9 Joe는 사진 찍는 데 많은 돈을 썼다.
(spend, a lot of money, take pictures)
➡ Joe ____________________________.

10 그녀는 그 뮤지컬을 보러 가는 것을 기대하고 있다. (look forward to, go)
➡ She ______________________ to the musical.

중간 기말고사 예상문제

Answer Keys p. 56

내신 최다 출제 유형

01 다음 대화의 빈칸에 알맞은 말을 고르시오.

[출제 예상 95%]

> A Do you ________ my sitting here?
> B Not at all.

① mind ② plan ③ decide
④ hope ⑤ want

02 다음 문장의 빈칸에 알맞은 것을 모두 고르시오.

[출제 예상 85%]

> ________ something new is very exciting.

① Learn ② Learns ③ Learned
④ To learn ⑤ Learning

03 다음 밑줄 친 단어의 쓰임이 올바른 것을 고르시오.

[출제 예상 90%]

① I like ride a skateboard.
② She likes drawing wild flowers.
③ Would you mind take a picture for me?
④ My uncle's hobby is play video games.
⑤ I can't finish do my chores.

[04~05] 다음 문장 중 문법적으로 올바른 것을 고르시오.

[출제 예상 85%]

04 ① They all felt something touched them.
② He practices speaking English a lot.
③ I want be a movie star.
④ I don't like she coming here.
⑤ My little brother tried to drawing a house.

05 ① Mr. Smith enjoys teach his students.
② Jenny needs to staying home.
③ Would you mind sing in this room?
④ I like making pretty dolls.
⑤ She plans to traveling by bike.

06 다음 글의 빈칸 ⓐ~ⓓ에 알맞은 말을 보기에서 골라 올바른 형태로 고쳐 쓰시오. [출제 예상 80%]

보기
> exercise watch play do

> My sister, Anna is a very lively girl. She does ___ⓐ___ every day. She enjoys ___ⓑ___ tennis and ___ⓒ___ the tennis game on TV. She wants to ___ⓓ___ something interesting.

ⓐ ________ ⓑ ________
ⓒ ________ ⓓ ________

07 다음 주어진 문장과 뜻이 같도록 빈칸에 알맞은 말을 쓰시오. [출제 예상 85%]

> Jennifer loves to play the violin with her best friend, Mina.

➡ ________ ________ ________ the violin with her best friend, Mina.

중간 기말고사 예상문제

[01~05] 다음 빈칸에 알맞은 말을 고르시오.

01

Jack and Isabella went ________ yesterday.

① swims ② to swimming
③ swimming ④ swam
⑤ for swimming

02

Many students are busy ________ for the final exam.

① prepare ② prepared
③ prepared to ④ preparing
⑤ to prepare

03

Would you mind ________ on the air conditioner?

① turn ② turned
③ to turn ④ for turning
⑤ turning

Note air conditioner: 에어컨

04

I look forward to ________ him soon.

① meet ② meeting ③ met
④ meet to ⑤ meets

05

________ English is very interesting.

① Learning ② Learn ③ Of learn
④ Learns ⑤ Learnings

[06~07] 다음 빈칸에 들어갈 말이 순서대로 바르게 짝지어진 것을 고르시오.

06

• I expected ________ to the opera with my sister.
• He keeps ________ a diary.

① going – write ② to go – to write
③ to go – writing ④ go – write
⑤ going – writing

07

• We couldn't stop ________.
• The traveler stopped ________ under a tree.

① running – sitting ② to run – to sit
③ to run – sitting ④ running – to sit
⑤ running – sit

[08~09] 다음 밑줄 친 부분이 바르게 쓰인 것을 고르시오.

08 ① How about <u>playing</u> the clarinet?
② She keeps <u>to run</u> at the park.
③ <u>Use</u> the Internet makes people smarter.
④ Thank you for <u>join</u> us.
⑤ I enjoy <u>read</u> other person's blogs.

09 ① I and my sister started <u>exercise</u> last week.
② He is sorry for not <u>tell</u> you earlier.
③ She gave up <u>to jump</u> rope.
④ We enjoy <u>playing</u> chess after dinner.
⑤ My friend, Cindy is good at <u>sing</u>.

Answer Keys p. 56~57

[10~11] 다음 우리말과 같은 뜻이 되도록 빈 칸에 알맞은 말을 고르시오.

10

그는 걸음을 멈추고 한 여자를 쳐다보았다.
➡ He stopped ________ and looked at a woman.

① walk ② walking ③ take a walk
④ walked ⑤ walks

11

영화 '쥬라기 월드' 보러 가는 것은 어때?
➡ What about ________ the movie 'Jurassic World'?

① watching ② to watch ③ watch
④ watched ⑤ go watching

[12~13] 다음 빈칸에 들어갈 말로 알맞지 <u>않은</u> 것을 고르시오.

12

My family ________ watching movies.

① likes ② enjoys ③ loves
④ hopes ⑤ continues

13

We ________ putting the puzzle together.

① wanted ② gave up ③ stopped
④ finished ⑤ enjoyed

[14~16] 다음 문장의 밑줄 친 부분의 쓰임이 나머지 넷과 <u>다른</u> 것을 고르시오.

★★★
14
① <u>Taking</u> a walk is good for your diet.
② Jasmine finished <u>writing</u> a message.
③ Jack avoided <u>sitting</u> too long.
④ I don't mind <u>waiting</u> for you.
⑤ She likes <u>watching</u> movies.

★★★
15
① My job is <u>fixing</u> the machine.
② His hope is <u>becoming</u> a great composer.
③ Harry is <u>listening</u> to classical music.
④ Her dream is <u>passing</u> the mid-term exam.
⑤ My boyfriend's hobby is <u>collecting</u> comic books.

★★★
16
① I hate <u>making</u> the same mistakes.
② My puppy loves <u>taking</u> a walk at the park with me.
③ I don't like <u>using</u> a public transportation during rush hour.
④ They can't give up <u>eating</u> at night.
⑤ I and my sister are <u>going</u> hiking.

17 다음 대화의 밑줄 친 부분 중 어법상 올바른 것을 고르시오.

A What does Maria ① <u>want do this weekend</u>?
B She ② <u>was going to</u> ③ <u>go swimming</u>?
A What ④ <u>do you going to do</u>?
B I'm going to ⑤ <u>go to fishing</u>.

18 다음 문장들의 의미가 같도록 할 때 빈칸에 들어갈 알맞은 말로 바르게 짝지어진 것을 고르시오.

> • Kelly ________ to buy a new bag.
> = Kelly ________ to buy a new bag.
> = Kelly ________ buying a new bag.

① hopes – likes – would like
② hopes – wants – feels like
③ would like – wants – wants
④ wants – enjoys – tries
⑤ wants – hopes – wants

19 다음 밑줄 친 부분의 뜻이 어색한 것을 고르시오.

① I feel like playing the piano. (연주하고 싶다)
② How about going on a picnic? (가는 것은 어때?)
③ My mom is busy cooking dinner. (요리하느라 바쁘다)
④ She tried breaking the thick ice. (시험 삼아 깨뜨려보다)
⑤ He looks forward to eating the Italian food. (먹는 것을 보다)

20 다음 글의 밑줄 친 동사의 형태가 바르지 않은 것을 고르시오.

> My uncle ① is a cook. He really likes ② cooking food.
> He usually ③ visits children's homes.
> He loves to ④ playing soccer with the children and ⑤ cook a great meal for them.

[21~22] 다음 중 문법적으로 틀린 문장을 모두 고르시오.

★★★
21 ① I hope visit Japan this summer vacation.
② She likes talking about herself.
③ What about catch a ball?
④ They wanted to eat some pizza.
⑤ Sarah planned to learn Spanish.

★★★
22 ① My brother wanted to be an architect.
② Living in the country is not easy.
③ People dreamed about flying in the sky.
④ She enjoys teach her students.
⑤ I usually practice sing for three hours.

23 다음 문장의 밑줄 친 부분을 대신 사용할 수 있는 알맞은 인칭대명사를 고르시오.

> They really mind us climbing on Mount Everest.

① we ② ours ③ our
④ ourselves ⑤ I

24 다음 문장 중 올바른 것을 고르시오.

① She apolpgized me for playing not here.
② Reading comic books are funny.
③ Do you mind open the window?
④ I was angry about not calling me.
⑤ They want to go in-line skate.

Answer Keys p. 56~57

25 다음 글의 빈칸에 들어갈 알맞은 말을 고르시오.

> Maria and her friends are going to go _________ to Greece this weekend.

① traveling ② travel ③ travels
④ traveled ⑤ to traveling

★★★
26 다음 주어진 문장의 밑줄 친 부분과 쓰임이 같은 것을 고르시오.

> My focus is on <u>becoming</u> a doctor.

① We studied about <u>fixing</u> radios.
② Her favorite hobby is <u>drawing</u> pictures.
③ Thank you for <u>coming</u> to meet me.
④ I enjoyed <u>playing</u> the drums.
⑤ She should continue <u>exercising</u>.

27 다음 주어진 문장의 밑줄 친 부분과 쓰임이 <u>다른</u> 것을 고르시오.

> <u>Being</u> a kind person is not difficult.

① <u>In–line skating</u> is interesting.
② <u>Watching</u> movies is my favorite hobby.
③ <u>Taking</u> a walk is not boring.
④ <u>Driving</u> a car too fast is not good.
⑤ Positive <u>thinking</u> makes us nicer people.

[28~30] 다음 우리말을 바르게 영작한 것을 고르시오.

28

> 그는 그 소문에 대해 말하는 것을 피했다.

① He avoids to talk about the rumor.
② He avoided to talk about the rumor.
③ He avoids talk about the rumor.
④ He avoided talking about the rumor.
⑤ He avoided to talk about the rumor.

29

> Esther는 무대에서 노래 부르는 것을 꿈꾼다.

① Esther is dreaming about sing on the stage.
② Esther's dream is singing on the stage.
③ Esther dreams about singing on the stage.
④ Esther dreamed about singing on the stage.
⑤ Esther dreams about sing on the stage.

30

> Harry는 그녀와 다시 만나기로 결정했다.

① Harry decided to meet her again.
② Harry decides to meet her again.
③ Harry deciding to meet her again.
④ Harry decided meeting her again.
⑤ Harry is decided meeting her again.

Answer Keys p. 56~57

◇◇◇◇◇◇◇◇◇◇◇ 서술형 평가 ◇◇◇◇◇◇◇◇◇◇◇

[31~33] 다음의 주어진 문장의 밑줄 친 부분을 알맞은 형태로 고치시오.

31

I and Jessica like to go <u>skate</u> and skiing in winter.

➡ ____________

32

How about <u>meet</u> in front of the Jamsil Stadium?

➡ ____________

★★★

33 다음 빈 칸에 공통으로 들어갈 주어진 철자로 시작하는 알맞은 단어를 쓰시오.

- __________ in the morning is good for your health.
- His dream is __________ a flower shop.
- Let's catch the __________ pig with pink ribbon.

➡ r____________

[34~38] 다음 우리말과 같도록 괄호 안의 단어를 바르게 배열하여 문장을 완성하시오.

34

그는 자신의 어릴 적 이야기들을 하는 것을 즐긴다.
(enjoys / stories / his / childhood / he / telling / about)

➡ ____________

35

매일 걷는 것은 건강에 좋다.
(every day / health / your / is / good / walking / for)

➡ ____________

36

그는 집을 사는 데 많은 돈을 썼다.
(he / his / house / a lot of / buying / money / spent)

➡ ____________

37

Philip은 겨울마다 스키를 타러 간다.
(winter / Philip / goes / every / skiing)

➡ ____________

38

나는 아침 일찍 일어나는 것이 익숙하지 않다.
(I'm / in the morning / not / getting / early / up / used to)

➡ ____________

11
Chapter 수동태

Point Check I

◆ **수동태:** '어떤 일이 일어났는가'에 초점이 맞춰져 있는 문장으로, 대부분 스스로 행동할 수 없는 사물이 주어가 된다.

1. 수동태의 형태: [be동사 + 과거분사 + by 목적격] …에 의해 ~되었다

- This movie **is made** by Steven Spielberg.

2. 수동태를 사용하는 경우

(1) 주어가 행동을 받거나 당하는 경우

- The actors in *Iron Man* are loved **(by people)**.

(2) 행동을 하는 주체가 중요하지 않거나 알려지지 않은 경우

- My headset was stolen **(by someone)**.

3. 능동태를 수동태로 바꾸기

(1) 능동태의 목적어는 수동태의 주어가 된다.

(2) 능동태의 동사는 수동태에서 'be동사 + 과거분사'의 형태로 바뀐다.

(3) 능동태의 주어는 수동태에서 'by + 목적격'으로 바뀐다.

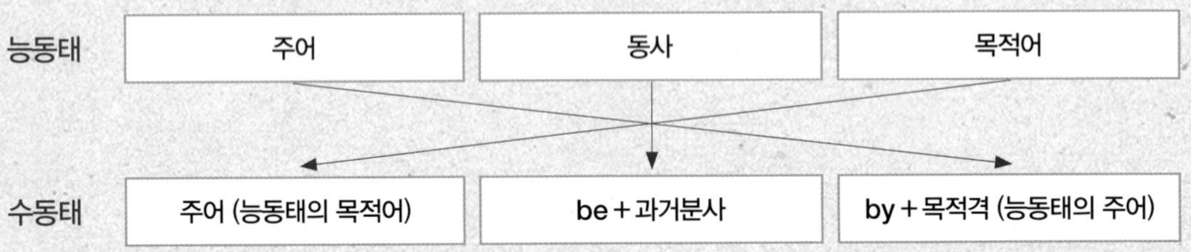

- Mary baked the chocolate cake.
  ➡ The chocolate cake **was baked by Mary**.

4. 'by + 목적격'의 생략: 행위자가 분명하지 않거나 밝힐 필요가 없을 경우 생략한다.

- **People** enjoy listening to music throughout the world.
  = Listening to music **is enjoyed (by people)** throughout the world.

5. 수동태의 현재와 과거

(1) 수동태의 현재형: [am/are/is+과거분사]

- The puppy **bites** my little sister. ➡ My little sister **is bitten** by the puppy.

(2) 수동태의 과거형: [was/were+과거분사]

- My father **opened** the trunk. ➡ The trunk **was opened** by my father.

Lesson 11-1 수동태의 사용

• **수동태:** 수동태 문장은 어떤 일이 어떻게 일어나게 되었는지를 나타내는 문장으로, 스스로 행동할 수 없는 사물이 주어로 올 때 사용된다.

1. 수동태의 형태: [be동사 + 과거분사 + by 목적격] …에 의해 ~되다

• The seascape **was drawn** by the painter.
• This book **was written** by Jane Austen.

2. 수동태를 사용하는 경우

(1) 주어가 행동을 받거나 당하는 경우
• J.K. Rowling **is loved** by many people.

(2) 행동을 하는 주체가 중요하지 않거나 알려지지 않은 경우
• This stone tower **was built** long ago.
➡ 누가 지었는지 행위자가 확실하지 않을 경우 'by + 행위자'는 생략이 가능하다.

Check up!

Answer Keys p. 58

A 다음 문장이 능동태 문장인지 수동태 문장인지 쓰시오.

1 I painted the wall. 능동
2 John loves his mother. ________
3 The book is written by Mr. Brown. ________
4 Mother planted flowers in her garden. ________
5 The street was cleaned by many people. ________
6 A serious storm destroyed the building. ________
7 The door was closed by the wind. ________
8 This school was built in 2008. ________
9 Mia sends a letter to her best friend. ________
10 The airplane was invented by the Wright brothers. ________
11 Jane likes detective stories. ________
12 Tim was invited to the party by Helen. ________
13 Ann makes chocolate cookies. ________
14 The cup was broken by my grandmother. ________
15 This MP3 player was made in Korea. ________

Lesson 11-2

수동태에 많이 쓰이는 불규칙 동사

• 수동태의 동사는 'be동사 + 과거분사'로 나타내며, 과거와 과거분사의 형태가 불규칙적인 동사들이 있다.

◈ 불규칙 동사의 변화

원형	과거형	과거분사형	원형	과거형	과거분사형
be	was/were	been	lose	lost	lost
bear	bore	born	make	made	made
bite	bit	bitten	read	read	read
blow	blew	blown	ride	rode	ridden
break	broke	broken	say	said	said
bring	brought	brought	see	saw	seen
build	built	built	set	set	set
buy	bought	bought	sell	sold	sold
catch	caught	caught	send	sent	sent
do	did	done	sing	sang	sung
draw	drew	drawn	speak	spoke	spoken
drink	drank	drunk	spend	spent	spent
eat	ate	eaten	steal	stole	stolen
find	found	found	take	took	taken
fly	flew	flown	teach	taught	taught
forget	forgot	forgotten	tell	told	told
get	got	got(ten)	think	thought	thought
give	gave	given	throw	threw	thrown
hold	held	held	understand	understood	understood
keep	kept	kept	wake	woke	woken
know	knew	known	wear	wore	worn
lay	laid	laid	write	wrote	written

Check up!

Answer Keys p. 58

A 다음 동사의 과거형과 과거분사형을 쓰시오.

1	eat – ate – eaten		2	give – ______ – ______	
3	tell – ______ – ______		4	think – ______ – ______	
5	be – ______ – ______		6	blow – ______ – ______	
7	cook – ______ – ______		8	hit – ______ – ______	
9	do – ______ – ______		10	write – ______ – ______	
11	use – ______ – ______		12	speak – ______ – ______	
13	get – ______ – ______		14	fly – ______ – ______	
15	hold – ______ – ______		16	throw – ______ – ______	
17	find – ______ – ______		18	lay – ______ – ______	
19	come – ______ – ______		20	lose – ______ – ______	
21	make – ______ – ______		22	read – ______ – ______	
23	break – ______ – ______		24	draw – ______ – ______	
25	agree – ______ – ______		26	carry – ______ – ______	
27	cry – ______ – ______		28	choose – ______ – ______	
29	fix – ______ – ______		30	ride – ______ – ______	
31	take – ______ – ______		32	kill – ______ – ______	
33	build – ______ – ______		34	know – ______ – ______	
35	bear – ______ – ______		36	send – ______ – ______	
37	teach – ______ – ______		38	sing – ______ – ______	
39	mean – ______ – ______		40	steal – ______ – ______	
41	worry – ______ – ______		42	feed – ______ – ______	
43	destroy – ______ – ______		44	saw – ______ – ______	
45	visit – ______ – ______		46	keep – ______ – ______	
47	spend – ______ – ______		48	wake – ______ – ______	
49	clean – ______ – ______		50	put – ______ – ______	
51	bite – ______ – ______		52	begin – ______ – ______	
53	invite – ______ – ______		54	dry – ______ – ______	
55	drive – ______ – ______		56	understand – ______ – ______	
57	plan – ______ – ______		58	hide – ______ – ______	

Lesson

11-3 능동태를 수동태로 바꾸기

• 주어가 동작을 행하는 문장을 능동태라고 하고, 주어가 동작의 대상이 되는 문장을 수동태라고 한다.

1. 수동태를 능동태로 바꾸기: [be동사 + 과거분사 + by 목적격] …에 의해 ~되다

(1) 능동태의 목적어는 수동태의 주어가 된다.

(2) 능동태의 동사는 'be동사 + 과거분사'의 형태로 바뀐다.

(3) 능동태의 주어는 'by + 목적격'으로 바뀐다.

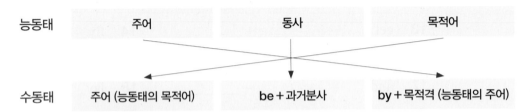

능동태	주어	동사	목적어
수동태	주어 (능동태의 목적어)	be + 과거분사	by + 목적격 (능동태의 주어)

• The explorer **discovered** a new treasure.
➡ A new treasure **was discovered** by the explorer.

Check up!

Answer Keys p. 58

A 다음 우리말과 같도록 빈칸을 알맞게 채우시오.

1 Sam invites them to the party.
➡ They ___*are invited*___ to the party by Sam.

2 Wilson sends an email.
➡ An email ____________ by Wilson.

3 He collects many stamps.
➡ Many stamps ____________ by him.

4 Hanna visits her grandmother twice a month.
➡ Her grandmother ____________ by Hanna twice a month.

5 He opened the cabinet door.
➡ The cabinet door ____________ by him.

6 She made these pies.
➡ These pies ____________ by her.

7 My mother fixes my doll.
➡ My doll ____________ by my mother.

Lesson

11-4 'by + 목적격'의 생략

• 능동태의 주어가 'you, we, they, people'처럼 일반적인 사람일 때는 'by + 목적격'을 생략할 수 있다. 또 행위자가 분명하지 않거나, 굳이 밝히지 않아도 알거나 혹은 알릴 필요가 없을 경우에도 생략된다.

• **People** speak English all over the world.
= English is spoken **(by people)** all over the world.
➡ 일반적인 사람들을 지칭하므로 생략이 가능하다.

• **Mark Twain** wrote the novel, 'The Adventures of Huckleberry Finn'.
= The novel, 'The Adventures of Huckleberry Finn' was written by **Mark Twain**.
➡ 행위자가 확실하기 때문에 생략이 불가능하다.

Check up!

Answer Keys p. 58

A 다음 능동태 문장을 수동태로 바꾸시오. 단, 알 수 없거나 중요하지 않은 일반인 (we, you, they, somebody, people 등)이 'by + 목적격'으로 바뀔 경우 괄호로 표시하시오.

1 They published many books.
➡ *Many books were published (by them)*.

2 People take photos here.
➡ ______________________.

3 Someone broke the cup.
➡ ______________________.

4 He wrote these letters.
➡ ______________________.

5 They sell fresh vegetables in the store.
➡ ______________________.

6 The students elected Sujin class president.
➡ ______________________.

7 People visit the park every day.
➡ ______________________.

8 Lily makes a jar of apple jam.
➡ ______________________.

9 People consider the dove a symbol of peace.
➡ ______________________.

Lesson 11-5 'by' 이외의 전치사를 사용하는 수동태

• 감정을 나타내는 표현은 원인이 되는 일에 의해 감정이 느껴지기 때문에 수동태 문장으로 많이 표현하며, 'by' 이외의 다양한 전치사들을 사용한다.

◈ 전치사를 사용하는 수동태

• be pleased with	~에 즐거워하다	• be tired of	~에 지치다, 피곤하다
• be covered with	~로 덮이다	• be worried about	~에 대해 걱정하다
• be filled with	~로 가득 차다	• be interested in	~에 흥미가 있다
• be bored with	~에 지루해하다	• be surprised at	~에 놀라다
• be scared of (at)	~에 두려워하다	• be excited at	~에 흥분하다
• be made of	~로 만들어지다 (재료의 성질에 변화가 없는 경우)	• be made from	~로 만들어지다 (재료가 화학적으로 변화된 경우)

• I **am scared of** the snakes.
• She **was surprised at** the news.
• Cheese **is made from** milk.
• The earth **is made of** water and land.
• We **were pleased with** our new house.

Check up!

Answer Keys p. 59

A 다음 우리말 해석에 맞게 빈칸에 알맞은 말을 쓰시오.

1 그녀는 개를 무서워한다.
➡ She ___is scared of___ the dogs.

2 나는 수학 공부를 하는 것이 지루하다.
➡ I ______________ studying math.

3 Lewis는 그녀의 사고에 놀랐다.
➡ Lewis ______________ her accident.

4 그 컵은 오렌지 주스로 가득 차있다.
➡ The cup ______________ orange juice.

5 Samantha는 요즘 글쓰기에 흥미가 있다.
➡ Samantha ______________ writing these days.

6 거리는 낙엽으로 뒤덮여 있다.
➡ The street ______________ leaves.

7 France는 에펠 탑으로 유명하다.
➡ France ______________ the Eiffel Tower.

8 이 빵은 옥수수로 만들어진다.
➡ This bread ______________ corn.

Lesson 11-6 수동태의 현재와 과거

• 수동태의 be동사가 현재형일 때는 'am/are/is'를 사용하며, 과거형일 때는 'was/were'를 사용한다.

1. 수동태의 현재형: [am/are/is + 과거분사]

능동태의 동사가 현재형이면 수동태의 be동사도 현재형으로 나타낸다.

• Dorothy **sings** the song 'Moon River.' = The song 'Moon River' **is sung** by Dorothy.

2. 수동태의 과거형: [was/were + 과거분사]

능동태의 동사가 과거형이면 수동태의 be동사도 과거형으로 나타낸다.

• I **wrote** a love letter to Phillip. = A love letter to Phillip **was written** by me.

Grammar Plus +

과거에 이미 끝난 일에 대해 수동태 문장으로 만들 경우 be동사의 과거형을 써준다.
The tower of Pisa **was built** in Italy. ➡ 과거에 지어졌기 때문에 수동태 과거형을 썼음.

Check up!

Answer Keys p. 59

A **다음 우리말 해석에 맞게 빈칸에 알맞은 말을 쓰시오.**

1 She sends this book to Jim.
➡ This book ___*is sent*___ to Jim by her.

2 Samuel washed his bike.
➡ His bike ______________ by Samuel.

3 Mr. Jang recommends this chair.
➡ This chair ______________ by Mr. Jang.

4 Mom made this sauce.
➡ This sauce ______________ by mom.

5 The city builds a new park.
➡ A new park ______________ by the city.

6 Cindy invited her friends to her party.
➡ Cindy's friends ______________ to her party.

7 The woman delivers pizza.
➡ Pizza ______________ by the woman.

8 Students broke plates and cups.
➡ Plates and cups ______________ by students.

9 Minju used my library card.
➡ My library card ______________ by Minju.

Practice More I

A 다음 문장의 괄호 안에서 알맞은 것을 고르시오.

1 Scott is interested (in / by) reading detective novels.

2 She was surprised (to / at) seeing him.

3 The window was broken (by / at) him.

4 Kate is bored (by / with) studying English.

5 My sister was scared (of / to) spiders.

6 The seminar is held (by / to) one of the musical groups.

7 Many people are shocked (by / in) the surprising news.

8 The red dress was made (by / with) a famous designer.

9 Tom was tired (of / by) running.

10 I was excited (at / by) playing computer games with Taylor.

11 Alex is pleased (with / at) his exam result.

12 This novel was not written (by / with) her.

B 다음 문장을 수동태 문장으로 전환할 때 빈칸에 알맞은 말을 쓰시오.

1 Graham Bell invented the first phone.
➡ The first phone *was invented* by Graham Bell.

2 She washed the dog.
➡ The dog ____________ by her.

3 He scolded his daughter for telling a lie.
➡ His daughter ____________ by him for a telling a lie.

4 The artist drew a vase.
➡ A vase ____________ by the artist.

5 The cat ate the salmon.
➡ The salmon ____________ by the cat.

6 The rumor surprised me.
➡ I ____________ the rumor.

Answer Keys p. 59

7 My father caught the fish in the lake.
➡ The fish ____________ by my father in the lake.

8 Jay fixed the radio.
➡ The radio ____________ by Jay.

9 He wrote two letters.
➡ Two letters ____________ by him.

10 They saw many dancers in the street.
➡ Many dancers ____________ by them in the street.

C 다음 문장의 밑줄 친 부분을 바르게 고치시오.

1 The pumpkin pie is ate by my brother.
➡ *is eaten*

2 A dancing girl are saw by me.
➡ ____________

3 The pink dress with a red ribbon was chose by an actress.
➡ ____________

4 The flowers is withered by the strong sunshine.
➡ ____________

5 The portrait was paint by Gogh himself.
➡ ____________

6 The holiday tasks were finish by Luna.
➡ ____________

Note
- **wither** (식물이) 시들다
- **paint(take) a portrait** 초상화를 그리다
- **task** 일, 업무

Practice More I

D 다음 우리말 해석에 알맞게 주어진 단어들을 이용하여 문장을 완성하시오.

1 그 음악은 그 연주가에 의해 연주되었다. (by, be, play).
➡ The music ___was played by___ the musician.

2 50여 명의 직원들이 채용되었다. (adapt, be, by).
➡ About 50 workers ______________ the company.

3 그는 나의 여행 계획에 흥미가 있다. (in, be, interest).
➡ He ______________ my travel plan.

4 많은 책이 Mr. Han에 의해 쓰여졌다. (be, by, write).
➡ Many books ______________ Mr. Han.

5 그 창문은 자동으로 열린다. (be, open).
➡ The window ______________ automatically.

E 다음 문장을 수동태로 바꿔 쓰시오.

1 He composed many songs.
➡ ___Many songs were composed by him.___

2 The dog bit my brother.
➡ ______________________________

3 My grandfather grows strawberries.
➡ ______________________________

4 The thief stole the expensive diamonds.
➡ ______________________________

5 She took care of the baby.
➡ ______________________________

중간 기말고사 예상문제

Answer Keys p. 59

내신 최다 출제 유형

01 다음 중 어법상 올바른 것을 고르시오. [출제 예상 90%]

① She was bitten by a mosquito.
② The tulip is picked by I.
③ That car is park by its driver.
④ A lot of trees are cut by they.
⑤ The meeting was hold in London.

02 다음 밑줄 친 부분 중 어법상 잘못된 것을 고르시오. [출제 예상 80%]

① This book was written by Julie.
② The vase is broken by my little sister.
③ I am worried about my grades.
④ The fruit pie is make by me.
⑤ She is surprised at my patience.

03 다음 밑줄 친 부분 중 생략할 수 있는 것을 고르시오. [출제 예상 85%]

① Mother Teresa was looked up to by many Indians.
② This diary is written by Jane.
③ The window was broken by somebody.
④ An email is sent by Jenny's teacher.
⑤ Some fish are caught by my uncle.

04 다음 문장 중 어법상 바른 것을 고르시오. [출제 예상 85%]

① The book is become a best seller.
② My room made a mess by my sister.
③ Many things are known about the moon.
④ The table is setted by his wife.
⑤ The bucket was filled of water.

05 다음 주어진 문장을 수동태로 바르게 고친 것을 고르시오. [출제 예상 90%]

Elsa built an ice castle on top of the mountain.

① An ice castle was built by Elsa on top of the mountain.
② An ice castle is built by Elsa on top of the mountain.
③ An ice castle built by Elsa on top of the mountain.
④ An ice castle was built on top of the mountain.
⑤ An ice castle is built on top of the mountain.

[06~07] 다음 글을 읽고 물음에 답하시오. [출제 예상 90%]

Stella is a mean girl. (A) She always laughs at other students. One day, she lost her new watch. The new watch ⓐ was buy by her father as a birthday gift. She was very sad. But her friends ⓑ decided to help her. So, the new watch ⓒ was found by her friends. Stella ⓓ was very sorry about laughing at them. Now, Stella ⓔ likes her friends very much.

06 윗글의 ⓐ~ⓔ에서 어법상 어색한 것을 골라 기호를 쓰고, 바르게 고치시오.

➡ ______________

07 윗글의 밑줄 친 (A)를 수동태 문장으로 고치시오.

➡ ______________________________

중간 기말고사 예상문제

[01~03] 다음 중 동사원형과 과거분사형이 올바른 것을 고르시오.

01 ① keep – keeped ② ride – rode
③ break – broke ④ bear – bear
⑤ know – known

02 ① am – was ② do – did
③ wake – woke ④ fly – flown
⑤ bite – bit

03 ① give – gave ② write – written
③ sing – sang ④ swim – swam
⑤ wear – wore

[04~06] 다음 우리말과 같은 뜻이 되도록 빈칸에 알맞은 말을 고르시오.

04

> 가구는 나무로 만들어진다.
> ➡ The furniture is ________ of wood.

① make ② making ③ made
④ to make ⑤ maded

05

> 그 산의 꼭대기는 눈으로 뒤덮여 있다.
> ➡ The top of the mountain is ________ with snow.

① covered ② cover covering
③ covered of ④ covers
⑤ to be covered

06

> 그 바구니는 장미꽃으로 가득 차 있다.
> ➡ The basket is ________ with roses.

① fill ② filled ③ filling
④ fills ⑤ to fill

[07~08] 다음 두 문장이 같은 뜻이 되도록 빈칸에 들어갈 알맞은 말을 고르시오.

07

> Jason broke the toy car.
> = The toy car ________ by Jason.

① is broken ② broken ③ was broken
④ to break ⑤ is breaking

08

> Angelina sings a theme song of *Carmen*.
> = A theme song of *Carmen* ________ by Angelina.

① was sang ② is sang ③ sung
④ was sung ⑤ is sung

[09~10] 다음 문장에서 밑줄 친 단어를 바르게 고친 것을 고르시오.

09

> Hamlet <u>wrote</u> by Shakespeare.

① was written ② is written
③ is wrote ④ was wrote
⑤ written

Answer Keys p. 60~61

10

A baby kangaroo <u>calls</u> Joey.

① called ② is calling ③ is called
④ was call ⑤ was called

[11~12] 다음 문장 중 어법상 바르지 <u>않은</u> 것을 고르시오.

★★★
11
① Fresh vegetables are sold in the market.
② Milk and cheese are produced by my father.
③ Jack is drew a still-life picture.
④ A picture of apples is painted by me.
⑤ The grand piano is played by Harry.

Note still-life picture 정물화

★★★
12
① My laptop is used by my sister.
② Chocolate cake was baked by my mom.
③ Jenny's wallet was stolen by somebody.
④ Phillip's video player was broke by me.
⑤ The dirty teddy bear was washed by me.

[13~15] 다음 능동태 문장을 수동태로 올바르게 바꾼 것을 고르시오.

13

Thomas Edison invented the light bulb.

① The light bulb is invented by Thomas Edison.
② The light bulb was invented by Thomas Edison.
③ The light bulb invented by Thomas Edison.
④ The light bulb was inventing by Thomas Edison.
⑤ The light bulb was invented.

★★★
14

Sometimes, the Greens hold a garage sale on their garden.

① Sometimes, a garage sale was held by the Greens on their garden.
② Sometimes, a garage sale held by the Greens on their garden.
③ Sometimes, a garage sale is helded by the Greens on their garden.
④ Sometimes, a garage sale is held by the Greens on their garden.
⑤ Sometimes, a garage sale is hold by the Greens on their garden.

15

I watered the flowers.

① The flowers were watered by me.
② The flowers was watered by me.
③ The flowers are watered by me.
④ The flowers has watered by me.
⑤ The flowers is watered by me.

[16~18] 다음 빈칸에 들어갈 말로 알맞은 것을 고르시오.

16

The ball ________ by Jack.

① throws ② was thrown ③ threw
④ is throw ⑤ was threw

17

The email message ________ by my coach.

① is send ② are send ③ were sent
④ sent ⑤ was sent

18

This yummy brownie __________ by mom.

① were baked ② baking
③ bakes ④ was baked
⑤ baked

[19~20] 다음 빈칸에 순서대로 들어갈 말이 알맞게 짝 지어진 것을 고르시오.

19

• The love letter was __________ by Harry.
• The telephone was __________ by his brother.

① written – broken
② wrote – broke
③ writing – breaking
④ write – break
⑤ written – broke

★★★
20

• The water ballet is __________ by many people.
• Young dolphins were __________ by two fishermen.

① watching – catching
② watch – catch
③ watched – caught
④ watches – caught
⑤ watched – catch

[21~24] 다음 두 문장이 같은 뜻이 되도록 빈칸에 알맞은 말을 고르시오.

21

A scientist discovered a new cure for cancer.
= A new cure for cancer __________ by a scientist.

① discover ② was discovered
③ discovering ④ is discovered
⑤ to discover

22

Tobby broke the vase.
= The vase was __________ by Tobby.

① break ② broke ③ breaking
④ breaks ⑤ broken

23

Many people watched the dolphin show.
= The dolphin show __________ by many people.

① watched ② was watched
③ watching ④ is watched
⑤ to watch

24

The blue yacht was sailed by a young boy.
= A young boy __________ the blue yacht.

① sails ② sailing ③ sailed
④ to sail ⑤ sail

[25~27] 다음 빈칸에 들어갈 전치사로 바르게 짝지어진 것을 고르시오.

25

- This muffin is covered ________ sugar powder.
- Fred is really tired ________ studying medicine.

① with – at ② of – with ③ with – of
④ at – for ⑤ by – of

Note study medicine 의학을 연구하다

26

- Jennifer is pleased ________ the new service.
- They were surprised ________ the wild waves at sea.

① with – of ② with – at ③ at – with
④ at – for ⑤ for – at

27

- Maria is bored ________ the documentary movie.
- We are worried ________ the math quiz on Monday.

① in – of ② of – to
③ with – about ④ of – about
⑤ about – with

[28~30] 다음 우리말을 영어로 바르게 옮긴 것을 고르시오.

28

우리는 어린이날에 그 나무들을 심었습니다.

① We plant the trees on Children's Day.
② We planted the trees Children's Day.
③ We planted the trees on Children's Day.
④ We were planted the trees on Children's Day.
⑤ We are planted the trees on Children's Day.

Note children's Day 어린이 날

★★★
29

나는 그의 제안에 매우 흥미가 있습니다.

① I was very interested in his suggestion.
② I am very interested his suggestion.
③ I am interest in his suggestion.
④ I am very interested in his suggestion.
⑤ I am very interested in suggestion.

30

한글은 세종대왕에 의해 창제되었습니다.

① Hangul is created by King Sejong.
② Hangul created by King Sejong.
③ King Sejong creating Hangul.
④ Hangul was creating by King Sejong.
⑤ Hangul was created by King Sejong.

[31~33] 다음 중 어법상 옳은 문장을 모두 고르시오.

★★★
31 ① English and French are both spoken in Canada.
② Merry-go-round is rode by many children.
③ The paper is made from wood.
④ The popcorn is poped in the frypan.
⑤ The expressway is blocking by a landslide.

★★★
32 ① Susan's purse was stole from the restaurant.
② Mr. Black's doorbell were broken.
③ Yellow ribbons is tied in the trees.
④ The movie *Frozen* was loved by all kinds of people.
⑤ This grammar book was written by a famous author.

★★★
33 ① Peanut butter is sell out.
② This pretty vase was made in China.
③ The Barbie Doll is known all over the world.
④ The old computers was sent to other countries.
⑤ Those comic book were read by you.

[34~36] 다음 중 문법적으로 틀린 문장을 모두 고르시오.

★★★
34 ① A beautiful song was hearing in the classroom.
② Some flies were catch by my father.
③ The ice cream cake was made by aunt Amelia.
④ This quilt is sewed by my grandmother.
⑤ This pink keyboard was bought by me.

★★★
35 ① Some popular songs were written by Eric.
② A bunch of red roses are given to Minho.
③ The blue sweater was knit by my mom.
④ A pinwheel is spinned by the wind.
⑤ A lot of balloons were brought by his fans.

★★★
36 ① The horrible story was told by a narrator.
② The drum were played by the band.
③ The information is included in the announcement.
④ Mickey Mouse was drown by Disney.
⑤ The information is included in the announcement.

Answer Keys p. 60~61

◇◇◇◇◇◇◇◇◇◇◇ 서술형 평가 ◇◇◇◇◇◇◇◇◇◇◇

[37~38] 다음 문장의 밑줄 친 부분을 바르게 고쳐 쓰시오.

37

The Olympic <u>is hold</u> every four years.

➡ ________________

38

A red sports car is washed <u>of Eddie</u>.

➡ ________________

[39~40] 다음 빈칸에 알맞은 전치사를 쓰시오.

39

Glasses are made ________ mud.

➡ ________________

40

The lake is covered ________ ice.

➡ ________________

[41~42] 다음 두 문장이 같은 뜻이 되도록 빈칸에 알맞은 말을 쓰시오.

41

Many accidents are caused by careless driving.
= Careless driving ________ many accidents.

➡ ________________

42

My father planted these seeds on my first birthday.
= These seeds ________ by my father on my first birthday.

➡ ________________

[43~44] 다음 문장을 수동태로 고쳐 쓰시오.

★★★
43

A programmer developed the computer program.

➡ ________________

★★★
44

Leonardo drew the outline of the picture.

➡ ________________

[45~46] 다음 우리말을 영어로 바르게 옮겨 쓰시오.

★★★
45

이 멋진 탑은 이탈리아의 한 예술가에 의해 만들어졌다.

➡ ________________

★★★
46

그 주스는 나의 남동생에 의해 쏟아졌다.

➡ ________________

Note

12

Chapter
분사

Point Check I

◆ **분사:** 동사원형에 '-ing'나 '-ed'가 붙어서 현재분사나 과거분사가 된 것이다. 분사는 명사를 수식하거나 주어와 목적어의 상태를 알려주는 형용사 역할을 한다.

1. 분사의 종류와 형태

	현재분사	과거분사
형태	동사원형+ing	동사원형+ed/ 불규칙동사
해석	진행 또는 능동	완료 또는 수동
역할	~하고 있는, ~하게 되는	~하여진(당한), ~한

(1) 현재분사: Everyone is **waiting** for the Halloween parade.

(2) 과거분사: Mt. Everest is **covered** with snow.

2. 현재분사 vs. 과거분사

현재분사	과거분사
[능동] I'm having lunch with my friends.	[수동] This is a book written in Chinese.
[진행] The smiling woman is my teacher.	[완료] Some roses are planted in our garden.
[주격보어] My sister and I are not watching TV.	[주격보어] My mirror was broken by my younger sister.
[목적격보어] I can find her swimming.	[목적격보어] I found the ring lost.

3. 분사의 쓰임

(1) 진행형: be동사+현재분사
- We **are going** to the park.

(2) 완료형: have+과거분사
- I **have been** to Tokyo.

(3) 수동태: be동사+과거분사
- Many piano pieces **were composed** by Chopin.

Lesson 12-1

분사의 종류와 형태

• **분사**: '동사에서 갈라져 나온 말'이라는 의미에서 붙여졌다. 분사는 명사를 수식하거나, 주어나 목적어의 상태를 나타내는 형용사 역할을 한다.

◈ 분사의 종류

	현재분사	과거분사
형태	동사원형+ing	동사원형+ed / 불규칙동사
역할	진행 또는 능동	완료 또는 수동
의미	~하고 있는, ~하게 되는	~하여진(당한), ~한
예	[진행] a burning house [능동] interesting novels	[완료] a burned house [수동] interested people

Grammar Plus +

• 분사가 **명사만을 수식**하면 명사 앞에 위치한다.
• **구와 함께 명사를 수식**할 경우에는 명사의 뒤에 위치한다.
• 주어와 주격보어, 목적어와 목적격보어와의 관계가 **능동**일 경우 현재분사를 사용한다.
• 주어와 주격보어, 목적어와 목적격보어와의 관계가 **수동**일 경우 과거분사를 사용한다.

• **[with+(대)명사+분사]**
(대)명사와의 관계가 능동이면 현재분사를, 수동이면 과거분사를 사용한다.
Yuran usually goes for a walk **with her puppy following her.** [능동]
Max sat on the sofa **with his eyes closed.** [수동]

Check up!

Answer Keys p. 62

A 우리말과 같은 뜻이 되도록 빈칸에 알맞은 말을 쓰시오.

1 지루한 영화 ➡ a *boring* movie
2 미소 짓는 소녀 ➡ a __________ girl
3 떨어지는 나뭇잎 ➡ __________ leaves
4 부서진 창문 ➡ a __________ window
5 잊혀진 남자 ➡ a __________ man
6 떠오르는 태양 ➡ a __________ sun
7 잠자는 개 ➡ a __________ dog
8 우는 아기 ➡ a __________ baby
9 흥미로운 장난감 ➡ an __________ toy
10 닫힌 문 ➡ a __________ door

Lesson 12-2 현재분사

• **현재분사**: 형용사처럼 명사를 꾸며주며 보어로 사용된다.
'~하고 있는, ~하는'의 뜻을 가진 현재분사는 진행과 능동의 뜻을 가졌으며, be동사와 함께 진행형으로 쓰인다.

1. 명사의 앞뒤에서 꾸며주는 역할

(1) 능동: We watched an **exciting movie**.

(2) 진행: Mary saw the **boy dancing** in front of the school.

2. 보어

(1) 주격보어
My mom and I are **shopping**.

(2) 목적격보어
He saw you **singing** at the concert.

Check up!

Answer Keys p. 62

A 다음 괄호 안에 단어 중 알맞은 것을 고르시오.

1 The (running / run) dog looks happy.

2 I read an (interesting / interested) novel last weekend.

3 The man (standing / stood) in front of the door is my father.

4 Look at the bird (flying / flew) in the sky.

5 Tim heard (surprising / surprised) news.

6 Does she remember the man (crossed / crossing) the street?

7 I know the boy (eating / ate) colorful ice cream.

8 He takes care of his (sleeping / slept) nephew.

9 The teacher (taking / taken) pictures of flowers is Mr. Evans.

10 Who is that girl (singing / sang) on the stage?

Check up!

Answer Keys p. 62

B 다음 문장에서 어법상 어색한 것을 찾아 바르게 고치시오.

1 Helen looks at the boy cleaned the classroom.

cleaned ➡ cleaning

2 Billy loves the girl sat next to Hana.

______ ➡ ______

3 I saw Tina crossed the bridge.

______ ➡ ______

4 We had our bike washing.

______ ➡ ______

5 Sam is played the guitar.

______ ➡ ______

6 The unsatisfied girl is cried.

______ ➡ ______

7 The stars are shone in the sky.

______ ➡ ______

8 He and I are had lunch in the restaurant.

______ ➡ ______

9 Mom is cooked in the kitchen.

______ ➡ ______

10 The boat is floated on the river.

______ ➡ ______

Lesson

12-3 과거분사

• **과거분사**: 형용사처럼 명사를 꾸며주기도 하고, 보어로도 사용된다.
'~되어진, ~로 된'이라는 뜻을 가진 과거분사는 have와 함께 완료의 의미로 쓰이거나,
be동사와 함께 수동의 의미로 쓰인다.

1. 명사의 앞뒤에서 꾸며주는 역할

(1) 수동: I saw the **actor respected** by people.

(2) 완료: There are many **closed stores** early in the evening.

2. 보어

(1) 주격보어
The window was **broken** by some boys.

(2) 목적격보어
I heard your name **called** in the distance.

Check up!

Answer Keys p. 62

A 다음 문장에서 과거분사에 밑줄을 긋고 꾸며주는 명사에 동그라미를 하시오.

1 I want to read a (novel) written in English.

2 I want to exchange my broken chair.

3 She found her lost dog.

4 Is this the picture drawn by your mom?

5 The money spent on Children's Day is too much.

B 다음 괄호 안에서 알맞은 것을 고르시오.

1 Helen had her watch (repairing / (repaired)).

2 Tim is a (beloved / beloving) actor.

3 My car was (broken / breaking) into last week.

4 The boy (naming / named) Robert wrote me a letter.

5 Father had his car (washed / washing).

Lesson **12-4**

분사의 쓰임

• 분사는 동사와의 관계에 따라 진행형, 완료형, 수동태로 사용된다.

1. 진행형: [be동사 + 현재분사]

• They **are doing** their homework.
• We **were playing** hide-and-seek at school.

2. 완료형: [have + 과거분사]

• I **have lived** here for three years.
• She **has been** to Chicago.

3. 수동태: [be동사 + 과거분사]

• The baseball game **was stopped** by rain.
• This poem **was written** by a firefighter.

Check up!

Answer Keys p. 62

A 다음 문장의 괄호 안에서 알맞은 것을 고르시오.

1 What is he (looking / looked) for?
2 The cup was (broken / breaking) by Minwoo.
3 They are (having / had) lunch together.
4 Tim was (practicing / practiced) the violin.
5 Have you ever (being / been) to France before?
6 Children are (running / ran) on the ground.
7 I'm (preparing / prepared) some food for the party.
8 She is (listening / listened) to music.
9 The game was (canceled / canceling) due to rain.
10 Sally is (waiting / waited) for her mom.
11 Three trees are (planted / planting) in our garden.
12 They have (lived / living) here since 1995.
13 He is (watching / watched) TV.
14 My father was (born / bearing) in Europe.
15 You have (done / doing) this work for two weeks.

Note

• **look for** ~을 찾다
• **prepare** 준비하다
• **cancel** 취소하다
• **plant** 심다
• **be born** 태어나다

Practice More I

Answer Keys p. 62~63

A 다음 괄호 안에서 알맞은 것을 고르시오.

1 This is the most (boring / bored) story in the world.

2 The girl (holding / held) a glass of water is my sister.

3 He has heard (surprising / surprised) news.

4 The concert was (exciting / excited) for many tourists.

5 Can you see them (climb / climbing) the mountain?

6 A very (interesting / interested) idea just entered my mind.

7 I know the boy (crossing / crossed) the road.

8 Sally wants to read a book (written / writing) in Chinese.

9 The money (spent / spending) on the graduation party was too much.

10 A (rolled / rolling) stone gathers no moss.

B 주어진 단어를 알맞은 형태로 바꾸어 빈칸에 쓰시오.

1 The _running_ man is my friend, John. (run)

2 One of my friends is __________ to music. (listen)

3 They are __________ with the news. (please)

4 The boy was __________ in Korea. (bear)

5 She found a __________ child on the street. (miss)

6 This is the book __________ in English. (write)

7 I met him again the __________ year. (follow)

8 Nick found his rare bag that was __________. (steal)

9 Have you __________ to Germany? (be)

10 My mother had her bracelet __________. (repair)

Answer Keys p. 62~63

C 다음 문장에서 어법상 어색한 것을 찾아 바르게 고치시오.

1 Playing in a soccer game is so excited.

excited ➡ exciting

2 The man chewed gum is my father.

______ ➡ ______

3 Look at the flew bird in the sky.

______ ➡ ______

4 I know the man sat on the bench.

______ ➡ ______

5 John had his room cleaning.

______ ➡ ______

6 Has he playing the piano for seven years?

______ ➡ ______

7 We are lived in Seoul right now.

______ ➡ ______

8 I saw Jack walked down the street.

______ ➡ ______

9 Sue was shocking because of the news.

______ ➡ ______

10 The superheroes in the movie have amazed powers.

______ ➡ ______

D 다음 우리말 해석에 맞게 주어진 단어들을 알맞게 배열하시오.

1 저 울고 있는 아기를 봐. (look at, baby, that, crying).

= Look at that crying baby.

2 줄넘기를 하고 있는 여자가 내 동생이야.
(the girl, my sister, jumping, is, rope).

= ______________________.

3 아침에 신나는 얘기를 들었어.
(I, the morning, an, story, exciting, heard, in)

= ______________________.

Note

- chew (껌을) 씹다
- look at ~을 보다
- walk down the street 길을 걷다
- because of ~ 때문에
- jump rope
  명 줄넘기
  동 줄넘기를 하다

Practice More Ⅰ

Answer Keys p. 62~63

4 우리는 그의 사고에 대해 듣고서 충격을 받았다.
(We, of, his accident, were, to, shocked, hear)
= ____.

5 Joe는 여자 친구로부터 받은 코트를 입고 있다.
(given, Joe, his girlfriend, a coat, wears, to, him, by)
= ____.

6 나는 Nick이 언덕 위에 서있는 것을 보았다.
(I, on the hill, Nick, saw, standing)
= ____.

7 그녀는 꽃들로 둘러싸여 앉아 있다.
(the flowers, she, by, surrounded, sits)
= ____.

8 Mr. Lee는 늘 피곤해 보인다.
(tired, always, Mr.Lee, looks)
= ____.

9 그녀는 하루 종일 책을 읽으며 빈둥거린다.
(she, all day, reading, around, lies, books)
= ____.

10 나는 시험에 통과하지 못해서 실망했다.
(I, pass, didn't, was, the exam, disappointed, because, I)
= ____.

Note

- **be shocked** 충격을 받다
- **accident** 사고
- **hill** 언덕
- **surround** 둘러싸다, 에워싸다
- **lie around** 빈둥거리다
- **all day** 하루 종일
- **disappointed** 실망한
- **pass** 통과하다

Point Check Ⅱ

◆ **현재분사 :** '~하고 있는'의 뜻으로 명사의 동작이나 상태를 설명하는 형용사 역할을 한다.

◆ **동명사 :** '~하기 위한'이라는 뜻으로 용도나 목적을 나타내며, 명사 역할을 하면서 주어, 목적어, 보어로 쓰인다.

◆ **분사구문 :** 현재분사를 이용하여 부사절을 부사구로 나타낸 표현으로, '이유, 양보, 때, 조건, 동시동작' 등의 다양한 의미를 나타낸다.

1. 현재분사와 동명사

현재분사	동명사
현재분사 + 명사 a dancing girl = a girl who is dancing	동명사 + 명사 dancing shoes = shoes for dancing
be동사 + 현재분사 We are walking on the street. (We ≠ walking)	be동사 + 동명사 His plan is traveling around the world. (His plan = traveling)

2. 감정을 나타내는 분사

감정 동사	현재분사 (동사 + ing ~하게 하는)		과거분사 (동사 + ed ~하게 느끼는)	
excite	exciting	흥분하게 하는	excited	흥분을 느끼는
interest	interesting	재미있게 하는	interested	재미있게 느끼는
satisfy	satisfying	만족스럽게 하는	satisfied	만족스러운
shock	shocking	충격을 주는	shocked	충격을 느끼는

3. 분사구문

(1) **접속사를 생략한다.**

(2) **주어를 생략한다.**

(3) **동사를 '동사원형 + ing'의 형태로 바꾼다.**

Because I **lost** my wallet, I couldn't buy her dinner.
(Because I: 생략, lost: lose + ing)

➡ **Losing** my wallet, I couldn't buy her dinner.

Lesson 12-5 현재분사와 동명사

• 현재분사와 동명사는 모두 '동사원형 + ing'의 형태로 헷갈리기 쉽기 때문에 문장 안에서 쓰인 의미와 역할로 구분해야 한다.

◈ 현재분사와 동명사의 구분

현재분사	동명사
현재분사 + 명사 • a dancing girl = a girl who is dancing • a sleeping baby = a baby who is sleeping ➡ 명사의 상태나 현재 진행 중인 동작을 나타낸다.	동명사 + 명사 • dancing shoes = shoes for dancing • a sleeping bag = a bag for sleeping ➡ 명사의 용도나 목적을 나타낸다.
be동사 + 현재분사 We are running in the marathon. (We ≠ running) ➡ '~하고 있다, ~하는 중이다'의 뜻으로 진행을 나타낸다.	be동사 + 동명사 Her job is hosting the main event. (Her job = hosting) ➡ '…은 ~하는 것이다'의 뜻으로 동명사가 주격보어 역할을 한다.

Check up!

Answer Keys p. 63

A 다음 밑줄 친 부분이 현재분사인지 동명사인지 구분하여 쓰시오.

1 The baby is sleeping in the room. 현재분사

2 Her hobby is taking pictures. ________

3 Look at the girl who is reading the book. ________

4 His task is writing a book. ________

5 They are dancing in the street. ________

6 I know that dancing boy on the stage. ________

7 Sue needs drinking water. ________

8 My wish is buying a new coffee machine. ________

9 He is playing soccer game. ________

10 I want to have a swimming pool at my house. ________

Lesson 12-6 감정을 나타내는 분사

• 감정을 나타내는 분사는 형용사로 사용된다. 이때 사물을 꾸며주거나 사물이 주어이면 현재분사를 사용한다. 사람이 주어일 경우에는 과거분사를 사용한다.

◈ 감정을 나타내는 현재분사와 과거분사

감정 동사	현재분사(동사+ing ~하게 하는)		과거분사(동사+ed ~하게 느끼는)	
excite	exciting	흥분하게 하는	excited	흥분을 느끼는
interest	interesting	재미있게 하는	interested	재미있게 느끼는
satisfy	satisfying	만족스럽게 하는	satisfied	만족스러운
shock	shocking	충격을 주는	shocked	충격을 느끼는
confuse	confusing	혼란스럽게 하는	confused	혼란스러운
disappoint	disappointing	실망스럽게 하는	disappointed	실망한
tire	tiring	피곤하게 하는	tired	피곤한
annoy	annoying	짜증나게 하는	annoyed	짜증난
bore	boring	지루하게 하는	bored	지루하게 느끼는
surprise	surprising	깜짝 놀라게 하는	surprised	깜짝 놀란
amaze	amazing	놀라게 하는	amazed	놀란
depress	depressing	우울하게 하는	depressed	우울한

Check up!

Answer Keys p. 63

A 보기와 같이 주어진 단어를 분사 형태로 바꾸어 빈칸에 쓰시오.

보기
① I am interested in studying English.
② This movie is interesting.

1 move ① This TV program was __________.
② I was __________ by his letter.

2 satisfy ① Mom was __________ with my present.
② The food of the restaurant is __________.

3 disappoint ① His answer was __________.
② Daniel is __________ because he can't go hiking.

4	bore	① I was __________ because the play was not funny. ② Studying math is too __________.
5	excite	① Sally is __________ to go to the concert. ② Camping is __________! I love it.
6	annoy	① Noah was __________ because of Ann's joke. ② Today's weather is __________ me.
7	surprise	① I was __________ because Richard left without saying goodbye. ② That's a very __________ news to me.
8	fright	① I was __________ by the loud noise. ② It was a __________ message for him.
9	shock	① He is __________ by that rumor. ② That is a __________ rumor.
10	please	① They will be very __________ with the picnic. ② The taste of this food is very __________.

B 괄호 안에 주어진 단어 중 알맞은 것을 고르시오.

1 Sammy always looks (tired / tiring).

2 He did (amazed / amazing) things.

3 This story is (surprising / surprised).

4 The game is somewhat (excited / exciting).

5 They were very (satisfied / satisfying) with the result.

6 I was (depressing / depressed) because I didn't pass the exam.

7 Tyler is (surprised / surprising) by his girlfriend's present.

8 She was deeply (moved / moving) by the movie.

Lesson 12-7 분사구문

• **분사구문**: 현재분사를 이용하여 부사절을 부사구로 간단히 나타낸 표현으로, '이유, 양보, 때, 조건, 동시 동작' 등의 여러 의미를 나타낼 수 있다.

1. 분사구문 만들기

(1) 접속사를 생략한다.

(2) 주어를 생략한다.

(3) 동사를 '동사원형 + ing'의 형태로 바꾼다.

When he arrived at the station, he felt the train schedule was wrong.

= **Arriving** at the station, he felt the train schedule was wrong.

Grammar Plus +

• 분사구문의 맨 앞에 'Being'이 오는 경우 생략할 수 있다.
(Being) **Tired** today, I couldn't keep my promise.

2. 분사구문의 종류

• **이유**: because, as, since (~해서)
Feeling very tired, I will go to bed early.
(= As I feel very tired, I will go to bed early.)

• **양보**: though, although (~에도 불구하고)
Being good at that, you still had to try harder.
(= Although you are good at that, you still had to try harder.)

• **때**: when, as (~할 때), after (~후에), before (~전에), while (~하는 동안)
Being sick, you should go to the doctor.
(= When you are sick, you should go to the doctor.)

• **조건**: if (~하면)
Going straight, you'll find the building.
(= If you go straight, you'll find the building.)

• **동시 동작**: while, as, and (~하면서, ~하다가)
Watching TV, I fell asleep.
(= While I watched TV, I fell asleep.)

3. 분사의 부정: [not/never + 분사]

• **Not understanding** that theory, John did not answer at all.

Grammar Plus +

- 부사절의 시제가 주절의 시제보다 앞선 경우 완료 분사구문을 쓴다.
  - 완료 분사구문: [having + 과거분사]

  After she had turned on the music, she started cleaning the house.
  (부사절: After she had turned on the music / 주절: she started cleaning the house)

  ➡ **Having turned** on the music, she started cleaning the house.

Check up!

Answer Keys p. 63

A 다음 문장을 분사구문으로 바꾸어 빈칸을 채우시오.

1 Because I felt tired, I went to bed early.
➡ ___Feeling___ tired, I went to bed early.

2 After I graduated from university, I could get a job.
➡ __________ from university, I could get a job.

3 Because she dosen't live with her family, she usually feels lonely.
➡ __________ with her family, she usually feels lonely.

4 Although I know it's Neil's mistake, I won't blame him.
➡ __________ it's Neil's mistake, I won't blame him.

5 When I waited for a bus, I ran into my old friends.
➡ __________ for a bus, I ran into my old friends.

6 When Nick got the prize, he felt so happy.
➡ __________ the prize, Nick felt so happy.

7 If you turn left, you will find the hospital on your right.
➡ __________ left, you will find the hospital on your right.

8 After father saw my report card, he went into his room.
➡ __________ my report card, father went into his room.

9 If you had taken my advice, you wouldn't have regrets now.
➡ __________ my advice, you wouldn't have regrets now.

10 Because I had lost my wallet, I couldn't go anywhere.
➡ __________ my wallet, I couldn't go anywhere.

Practice More Ⅱ

Answer Keys p. 63~64

A 다음 밑줄 친 부분이 현재분사인지 동명사인지 구분하시오.

1 In the morning, you can see the rising sun. 현재분사

2 Her dream is traveling all over the world. ________

3 Thanksgiving Day is coming soon. ________

4 His job is making a romantic movie. ________

5 The leaves are falling from the branch. ________

6 John is waiting for me at the cafe. ________

7 The dining room is so dirty. ________

8 The girl swimming in the pool is my girlfriend. ________

9 Robert's hobby is watching TV. ________

10 Her wish is buying a new house. ________

B 다음 문장의 괄호 안에서 알맞은 것을 고르시오.

1 Don't be (surprised / surprising) at the results.

2 I was so (disappointed / disappointing) because Alex didn't come to my party.

3 The performance was (amazing / amazed).

4 She was (annoyed / annoying) because of her son.

5 We should respect all (lived / living) things.

6 I had my sunglasses (fixed / fixing) by the mechanic.

7 They are (confusing / confused) by the situation.

8 The (sleeping / slept) baby is my little sister.

9 The soccer game was really (interesting / interested).

10 I gave a (walking / walked) stick to my grandmother.

Practice More Ⅱ

C 다음 주어진 문장들을 밑줄 친 부분의 쓰임에 유의하여 각각 해석하시오.

1 I was very <u>surprised</u> at the valuable gift.
= 나는 그 귀중한 선물에 매우 놀랐다.

2 William lost his <u>swimming</u> suit.
= ____________________

3 There are many people <u>walking</u> in the park.
= ____________________

4 Kate was <u>moved</u> by her daughter's letter.
= ____________________

5 I need more <u>shopping</u> bags.
= ____________________

6 <u>Keeping</u> a diary is important.
= ____________________

7 They are <u>talking</u> about K-pop.
= ____________________

8 Who will take away that <u>broken</u> chair?
= ____________________

9 People call her a <u>living</u> doll.
= ____________________

10 My son likes <u>cooking</u>.
= ____________________

D 다음 우리말 해석에 유의하여 주어진 단어를 알맞게 배열하시오.

1 그들은 지금 Zoe를 기다리는 중이다. (waiting, now, are, Zoe, for)
= They *are waiting for Zoe now*.

2 이것은 정말 신나는 영화야! (what, this, movie, an, is, exciting)
= ____________________!

3 나는 지루하기 때문에 체스를 좋아하지 않는다.
(because, playing, it, chess, boring, is)
= I don't like ____________________.

Answer Keys p. 63~64

4 Lucas는 시험 결과에 만족하니?
(with, the test result, satisfied, Lucas)
= Is ________________________?

5 나는 엄마가 만들어준 드레스를 입는 것을 좋아해.
(made, my mother, a dress, by)
= I like to wear ________________________.

6 그녀는 Mark의 사고 소식에 놀랐어.
(was, at, she, Mark's accident, surprised)
= ________________________.

7 벤치 위에서 자고 있는 강아지는 나의 것이다.
(on the bench, sleeping, mine, is)
= The puppy ________________________.

8 저 산은 눈으로 덮여있다.
(with, is, that mountain, covered, snow)
= ________________________.

9 나는 이제 막 세차를 끝냈다.
(finished, my car, I, washing, just)
= ________________________.

10 그 남자는 계속 나를 보고 있었다.
(the man, at, kept, me, looking)
= ________________________.

11 나에게 할아버지께서 그려주신 그림이 있다.
(my grandfather, a picture, by, I, drawn, have)
= ________________________.

12 Linda가 쓴 책은 전 세계적으로 유명해졌다.
(famous, written, the book, became, by Linda)
= ________________________ all over the world.

Note

- **result** 결과
- **satisfied** 만족하는
- **surprised** 깜짝 놀란
- **mine** 나의 것
- **famous** 유명한
- **all over the world** 전 세계적으로

중간 기말고사 예상문제

내신 최다 출제 유형

01 다음 밑줄 친 부분의 용법이 나머지 넷과 다른 것을 고르시오. [출제 예상 90%]

① She was playing the cello when I came back home.
② Listening carefully in class is very important.
③ I don't like watching horror movies.
④ His favorite thing is traveling with his friends.
⑤ Would you mind closing the door?

02 다음 밑줄 친 부분이 어법상 옳은 것을 고르시오. [출제 예상 90%]

① Helen is exciting to watch the magic show.
② He was disappointing at his grades.
③ The children were frighten of the wolves.
④ The musical was amazing.
⑤ I was shock to hear about the news.

03 다음 문장 중 어법상 어색한 것을 고르시오. [출제 예상 80%]

① Luna was bored of doing homework.
② I was exciting at the tomato festival.
③ Lily's family went to the art gallery.
④ They are interested in tap dance.
⑤ The rainy days make me depressed.

04 다음 문장의 밑줄친 부분과 바꿔 쓸 수 있는 것을 고르시오. [출제 예상 80%]

Having a lot of work to do, I couldn't cook dinner.

① Because I have a lot of work to do
② Because I'm having a lot of work to do
③ Because I had a lot of work to do
④ I have a lot of work to do
⑤ I had a lot of work to do

[05~06] 다음 그림을 보고 괄호 안의 단어를 사용하여 문장을 완성하시오. [출제 예상 85%]

05

➡ The old lady ________ ________ ________ is my grandmother. (water, the, garden)

06

➡ The house ________ ________ is Kelly's house. (paint, blue)

[01~04] 다음 빈칸에 들어갈 알맞은 말을 고르시오.

★★★
01

We saw our car __________ in the car wash.

① washed ② wash ③ is wash
④ washes ⑤ being washed

★★★
02

Eric doesn't like music class because it is __________.

① bored ② boring ③ to bore
④ is boring ⑤ bores

★★★
03

The house __________ with the red bricks is ours.

① build ② is building ③ built
④ to build ⑤ builds

★★★
04

__________ an audition, Miranda bought some clothes.

① Having ② Had ③ To have
④ Has ⑤ Had

[05~06] 다음 빈칸에 공통으로 들어갈 알맞은 말을 고르시오.

05

• Someone's phone is __________.
• We heard the door bell __________.

① ringing ② ringed ③ rings
④ rang ⑤ rung

06

• His parents want to buy a __________ truck.
• They have __________ their truck for five years.

① using ② use ③ used
④ be using ⑤ be used

[07~08] 다음 빈칸에 들어갈 단어가 바르게 짝지어 진 것을 고르시오.

07

• The musical was so __________.
• We were so __________ by the musical.

① exciting – exciting ② excited – excited
③ exciting – excite ④ excite – excited
⑤ exciting – excited

08

• I saw you __________ red boots.
• She heard the __________ news.

① wear – surprised
② wearing – surprising
③ wearing – surprised
④ wears – surprising
⑤ worn – surprised

[09~10] 다음 대화의 빈칸에 들어갈 수 없는 말을 고르시오.

09

A Jaeho likes kungfu, doesn't he?
B Yes, he thinks it is __________.

① fun ② interesting ③ boring
④ exciting ⑤ enjoyable

10

A Oh, god! Look at that ________ building.
B What is going on?

① burned ② destroyed ③ fallen
④ burning ⑤ leaned

[11~12] 다음 대화에서 밑줄 친 부분의 알맞은 형태를 고르시오.

11

A What is your favorite food?
B We like hash brown potatoes.

① hashed ② hash ③ hashing
④ hashes ⑤ to hash

12

A How was your first class?
B I didn't like it. It was bore.

① bore ② boring ③ bored
④ to bore ⑤ born

[13~16] 다음 밑줄 친 부분의 쓰임이 나머지 넷과 다른 것을 고르시오.

13 ① My mom wants to buy a new washing machine.
② Look at the dancing boy in the subway.
③ Some birds are flying away.
④ I have been waiting for him for a long time.
⑤ Mina is taking care of her younger sister.

14 ① Sean's family likes going camping on weekends.
② We remembered her singing alone on the stage.
③ This movie is so boring.
④ Tommy has a good fixing skill.
⑤ He is looking for a sleeping bag.

15 ① My younger brother's hobby is listening to music.
② She enjoys climbing mountains on the weekends.
③ His dream is building a hospital for wild animals.
④ They are talking about the history of America.
⑤ His plan was going to Spain to see a tomato festival.

16 ① You wanted to meet that dancing girl.
② Jack drives a watering cart.
③ John and Wendy are having dinner at a Chinese restaurant.
④ The birds are singing in the woods.
⑤ My parents are jogging every morning.

Note watering cart 살수차

17 다음 중 밑줄 친 부분이 어색한 것을 모두 고르시오.

① The news is interested.
② Jack was very surprised.
③ She felt tiring.
④ I was so bored.
⑤ His humor isn't exciting.

18 다음 중 밑줄 친 부분이 올바른 것을 모두 고르시오.

① The roller coaster was not scared.
② We are so excited.
③ The show was a quite satisfied job.
④ Her new fashion style was so shocking.
⑤ Jamie doesn't feel interesting at all.

[19~21] 다음 보기 문장의 밑줄 친 부분과 쓰임이 같은 것을 고르시오.

19

보기
Helping others makes us happy.

① Jeremy was studying wild animals.
② My cat is crawling.
③ Jasmine heard you singing in the room.
④ What were you doing at that time?
⑤ Swimming in the river is so fun.

20

보기
The sun is shining in the sky.

① Jenny finished doing her work.
② We are rolling on the grass.
③ Maria takes a sleeping pill.
④ We keep writing in our diaries.
⑤ Thomas enjoys doing the dishes.

21

보기
You had better make real friends instead of meeting people online.

① We are waiting for the pajama party to start.
② They are looking at a burning house.
③ The old man uses a walking stick.
④ I watched a boring movie.
⑤ Jack is buying a glass of lemonade.

[22~23] 다음 우리말을 바르게 영작한 것을 고르시오.

22

나는 너무 피곤해서 집에 일찍 갈 것이다.

① Feel too tired, I will go back home early.
② To feel too tired, I will go back home early.
③ I feeling too tired, I will go back home early.
④ Feeling too tired, I will go back home early.
⑤ As feeling too tired, I will go back home early.

23

그들은 숙제를 하지 못했기에 벌을 받았다.

① Doing not their homework, they got the punishment.
② Not doing their homework, they got the punishment.
③ Their not doing homework, they got the punishment.
④ Cannot doing their homework, they got the punishment.
⑤ Not do their homework, they got the punishment.

[24~25] 다음 두 개의 문장들이 같은 뜻이 되도록 할 때 빈칸에 들어갈 알맞은 것을 고르시오.

24

While Mr. Black read a book, he fell asleep.
= ____________, Mr. Black fell asleep.

① Reads a book ② To read a book
③ Reading a book ④ Read a book
⑤ Be reading a book

25

When you leave here, you should tell us the reason.
= ________________, you should tell us the reason.

① Leave here ② Leaving here
③ Left here ④ To leave here
⑤ Leaves here

◇◇◇◇◇◇◇◇◇◇◇ 서술형 평가 ◇◇◇◇◇◇◇◇◇◇◇

[26~28] 다음 두 문장의 의미가 같도록 빈칸에 알맞은 말을 쓰시오.

26

I saw a man. He was playing the violin on the street.

= I saw a man __________ the violin on the street.

27

There is a little boy. He is crying.

= There is a __________ little boy.

28

We watched a house. The house was destroyed with dynamite.

= We watched the house that was __________ house with dynamite.

[29~31] 다음 괄호 안의 단어를 문맥에 맞게 알맞은 형태로 쓰시오.

29

The opera Carmen was __________. (amaze)

➡ ________________

30

The police officer found my __________ (steal) wallet.

➡ ________________

31

Jenny's boss is __________ (satisfy) with her reports.

➡ ________________

[32~34] 다음 글을 읽고 물음에 답하시오.

Emily ⓐ was tired today. So she went to bed early. Emily is in her dream. She ⓑ meets a boy who is never ⓒ grown up. His name is Peter Pan. He is a (A) 사랑 받는 boy. Everyone likes him.Over there, Emily saw him ⓓ fought with Captain Hook. That makes Emily ⓔ excited. (B) Because she has read a book 'Peter Pan,' she was very excited.

32 윗글 ⓐ～ⓔ의 밑줄 친 부분 중 어법상 어색한 것을 골라 고쳐 쓰시오.

➡ ________________

Answer Keys p. 64~65

33 윗글 (A)의 우리말을 문맥에 맞게 영어 단어로 고쳐 쓰시오.

➡ ____________________

★★★

34 윗글의 (B)를 분사구문으로 만들 때 빈칸에 알맞은 말을 쓰시오.

➡ __________ __________ ______ __________
__________, she was very excited.

[35~38] 다음 우리말에 맞춰서 괄호 안의 단어를 알맞게 배열하여 문장을 만드시오.

35

많은 사람들이 그 영화에 감동을 받았다. (people / a lot of / by / the film / were / moved)

➡ ____

36

Rachel은 그의 청혼에 기뻤다. (Rachel / proposal / his / pleased / was / with)

➡ ____

37

그녀는 그의 사고 때문에 우울했다. (depressed / she / accident / his / was / by)

➡ ____

38

저기 웃고 있는 소녀가 내 딸이다. (laughing / is / girl / my / daughter / that)

➡ ____

[39~40] 다음 문장을 우리말로 바르게 해석하여 쓰시오.

39

Being sick too much, she didn't go to the party.

➡ ____

40

Tommy was disappointed because he didn't get the first prize.

➡ ____

Note

13

Chapter
접속사

Point Check I

◆ **접속사 :** 두 개 이상의 단어와 단어, 구와 구, 문장과 문장을 연결하는 말을 가리킨다.
접속사에는 대등한 것들을 연결하는 접속사, 짝을 이루는 접속사, 여러 절을 이끄는 접속사 등이 있다.

◈ 접속사의 종류

접속사의 종류		예문
등위 접속사	**and** ~와, 그리고, ~하고 나서	My family likes strawberries and tomatoes very much.
	but 하지만, 그러나	She likes watching sports but doesn't like playing.
	or 또는, 아니면	Do you want red roses or pink roses?
	so 그래서, 그러므로	Sam had a headache, so he took some medicine.
	*** 명령문 and / or** • and (그러면, 그렇게 하면) Exercise harder, and you'll be healthy. • or (그렇지 않으면) Be more diligent, or you'll get left behind.	
상관 접속사	**both A and B** A와 B 둘 다 ~	Her favorite subjects are both English and Korean.
	either A or B A와 B 둘 중 하나는	Either Angela or Thomas will come to the party.
	neither A nor B A와 B 둘 다 아닌	Neither Mary nor John will leave here.
	not A but B A가 아니라 B	He is not a police officer but a firefighter.
	not only A but (also) B A뿐만 아니라 B도	She must not only do the dishes but (also) clean her room.

Lesson

13-1 and / but / or / so

'and, but, or, so'는 서로 비슷한 단어나 문장을 연결하는 데 사용된다.

- **and**: '~와', '그리고'라는 뜻으로 비슷하거나 대등한 내용을 나란히 연결할 때 쓴다.
- **but**: '그러나', '하지만'의 뜻으로 서로 반대되거나 대조되는 내용을 연결할 때 쓴다.
- **or**: '또는', '~이나'라는 뜻으로 둘 또는 여러 개 중 선택하는 내용을 연결할 때 쓴다.
- **so**: '그래서', '그러므로'라는 뜻으로 앞의 내용은 원인을, 뒤의 내용은 결과를 나타낸다.

1. **and**: ~와, 그리고, ~하고 나서
   - She gave me a pen **and** a notebook.
   - I got up **and** took a shower.

2. **but**: 하지만, 그러나
   - My little brother is short **but** he is strong.
   - Kate is smart **but** she is unkind.

3. **or**: 또는, 아니면
   - Do you like playing tennis **or** basketball?
   - Is he an astronaut **or** a pilot?

4. **so**: 그래서, 그러므로
   - Ethan felt dizzy, **so** he went to the doctor.
   - They practiced hard, **so** they won the game.

Grammar Plus +

- **'and, but, or, so, for'**를 **등위접속사**라고 한다.
- **등위접속사**: 문법적 역할이 서로 비슷하거나 대등한 요소들을 연결하는 접속사를 말한다.

Check up!

Answer Keys p. 66

A 다음 두 문장을 하나로 합칠 때 알맞은 접속사를 쓰시오.

1 I bought some cookies. I gave them to my friends.
➡ I bought some cookies ___and___ gave them to my friends.

2 She is tall. Her sister is small.
➡ She is tall _______ her sister is small.

3 He went to the store. He bought a blue bag.
➡ He went to the store _______ bought a blue bag.

4 Mr. Kim is smart. He is impatient.
➡ Mr. Kim is smart _______ impatient.

5 I like him. He doesn't like me.
➡ I like him _______ he doesn't like me.

6 She was tired. She didn't go hiking.
➡ She was tired, _______ she didn't go hiking.

7 He has a daughter. He doesn't have a son.
➡ He has a daughter _______ doesn't have a son.

8 Do you like oranges? Do you like apples?
➡ Do you like oranges _______ apples?

9 I went to the park. I jogged.
➡ I went to the park _______ jogged.

10 He has no time to meet her. She is so angry.
➡ He has no time to meet her, _______ she is so angry.

11 Does she go to the theater? Does she go to the park?
➡ Does she go to the theater _______ the park?

12 He is busy. He has a lot of work to do.
➡ He is busy _______ he has a lot of work to do.

13 Joseph is short. Joseph is strong.
➡ Joseph is short _______ strong.

14 Today is my birthday. I have a party tonight.
➡ Today is my birthday, _______ I have a party tonight.

15 Ally needs a help. She can't move those heavy boxes alone.
➡ Ally needs a help, _______ she can't move those heavy boxes alone.

Note

- **impatient** 참을성 없는
- **go hiking** 도보여행을 가다
- **help** 명 도움, 동 돕다
- **alone** 혼자서

Lesson

13-2 명령문과 and / or

• **and**: '~와', '그리고'라는 뜻으로 비슷하거나 대등한 내용을 나란히 연결할 때 쓴다.

• **or**: '또는', '~이나'라는 뜻으로 둘 또는 여러 개 중 선택할 내용을 연결할 때 쓴다.

1. **명령문+and**: ~해라, 그러면

Work hard, **and** you'll be successful.
(= If you work hard, you'll be successful.)

2. **명령문+or**: ~하지마라(~해라), 그렇지 않으면

Hurry up, **or** you can't get to the train on time.
(= If you don't hurry up, you can't get to the train on time.)
(= Unless you hurry up, you can't get to the train on time.)
➡ if not은 unless와 바꿔 쓸 수 있다.

Check up!

Answer Keys p. 66

A 괄호 안에 주어진 접속사 중 알맞은 것을 고르시오.

1 Study hard, (and / or) you will fail the exam.
2 Do exercise regularly, (and / or) you will get in shape.
3 Make haste, (and / or) you will miss the bus.
4 Bring your umbrella, (and / or) you will be wet.
5 Read this article, (and / or) you will know exactly about the disease.
6 Think positively, (and / or) you will achieve your goal.
7 Turn off the TV, (and / or) your mom will be very angry.
8 Work hard, (or / and) you will live a wealthy life.
9 Eat healthy food, (and / or) your health will be better.
10 Take note, (and / or) you can remember what you should do first.

Note
• **get in shape** 좋은 몸상태를 유지하다
• **haste** 서두름
• **disease** 병, 질병
• **achieve** 달성하다, 성취하다
• **goal** 목표
• **wealthy** 부유한

Lesson

13-3 both A and B / either A or B

• **상관접속사**: 두 단어 이상이 짝을 이루어 사용되는 접속사를 말한다.
상관접속사는 서로 떨어져 있는 두 개의 단어나 표현, 문장을 이어주면서 강조나 첨가의 의미를 나타낸다.

1. **both A and B**: A와 B 둘 다

   I like to play **both** soccer **and** baseball.

2. **either A or B**: A와 B 둘 중 하나는

   Either you can draw pictures **or** you can take pictures.

3. **neither A nor B**: A와 B 둘 다 ~아닌

   They can write **neither** Japanese **nor** Korean.

4. **not A but B**: A가 아니라 B

   We will **not** go swimming **but** go shopping.

5. **not only A but (also) B**: A뿐만 아니라 B도

   You should **not only** do your English homework **but** (also) study math.

Check up!

Answer Keys p. 66

A 다음 문장의 괄호 안에서 알맞은 것을 고르시오.

1 Jiho likes both listening to music (and / or) playing computer games.

2 He is not in Korea (but / or) in France.

3 Either I (or / nor) you should go to the grocery store.

4 Liam is not only handsome (but also / but) gentle.

5 I can go (neither / either) fishing nor hiking.

6 Mom can cook (both / not only) Chinese food and Japanese food.

Check up!

Answer Keys p. 66

7 Jacob can play (not only / both) the piano but also the violin.

8 This flower is (not / neither) a lily but a rose.

9 They can study either biology (or / nor) science.

10 I can buy neither that bag (nor / or) this machine.

B 다음 각 문장의 빈칸에 알맞은 접속사를 쓰시오.

1 We like ___both___ horror movie and the romantic comedies.

2 _______ you or Semi will go to America.

3 Susan has _______ a red hat but a black one.

4 Jack will bring not only some apples _______ cookies.

5 Neither Tom _______ his brother can play baseball.

6 Both Emma _______ her daughter are lovely.

7 She passed not the English test _______ the math test.

8 We brought _______ the umbrella nor the raincoat.

9 It's _______ Helen's phone but mine.

10 I want to take pictures of _______ birds but also flowers.

Practice More Ⅰ

A 다음 문장의 괄호 안에서 알맞은 것을 고르시오.

1 He went to the hospital (and / but) had a checkup.

2 The musical was really exciting, (so / for) I want to see it one more time.

3 Which one do you prefer, fried chicken (or / for) beef?

4 Jennifer bought a shirt for me, (but / for) I don't like its color.

5 Tim bought chocolate chips and flour, (and / but) he started making cookies.

6 We can choose butter (or / and) chocolate.

7 Turn right, (or / but) you won't see the post office.

8 I arrived late, (so / but) I missed the bus.

9 Take a shower (and / for) have some milk.

10 We prepared lunch by ourselves (for / so) mom was sick.

11 Study hard, (and / for) you will achieve your goal.

12 Jack is a slow learner (but / and) Jim is a fast learner.

13 She has no time for lunch, (so / or) she is very hungry.

14 Leave me alone, (and / or) I'll be alright.

15 Which jacket do you like, blue one (or / nor) red one?

B 다음 문장의 빈칸에 알맞은 접속사를 쓰시오.

1 He likes both pasta __and__ pizza.

2 Peter is not in Daejeon _______ in Daegu.

3 Jean likes _______ skirts but also high heels.

4 He can't remember _______ Jane nor Camila.

5 _______ Lina or Justin is a criminal.

Answer Keys p. 66

6 My aim is _______ to be a millionaire but to be a saint.

7 I would like to meet _______ Samuel and his wife.

8 This seminar is _______ interesting but also useful.

9 Jina was _______ a singer but an actress.

10 I think you can speak _______ Chinese nor Japanese.

C 다음 문장에서 어법상 어색한 것을 찾아 바르게 고치시오.

1 Either James nor Linda is a university student.

nor ➡ or

2 Both soccer and baseball is interesting sports.

_______ ➡ _______

3 Not his mother but his father like to go fishing.

_______ ➡ _______

4 Not only babies but also mothers wears white shirts.

_______ ➡ _______

5 My plan is to neither study English or finish homework today.

_______ ➡ _______

6 I don't want to run but also want to take a walk.

_______ ➡ _______

7 Not only Denny but also his friends goes to the concert.

_______ ➡ _______

8 Neither a pen nor an eraser are on the table.

_______ ➡ _______

9 Both Kevin or Christina went to the park for exercise.

_______ ➡ _______

10 Not only her hat but also her skirt are black.

_______ ➡ _______

Practice More I

Answer Keys p. 66

D 다음 우리말 해석에 맞게 주어진 단어를 배열하여 문장을 완성하시오.

1 그녀는 현명하지만 힘이 약하다. (but, smart, weak)
➡ She is ___smart but weak___.

2 여름 방학에 콘서트나 미술관에 가자.
(go to the, concert, the museum, or, either)
➡ During summer vacation let's ______________________.

3 Stella는 피아노를 칠 줄 알지만 춤은 못 춘다.
(can't, play, dance, can, the piano, but)
➡ Stella ______________________.

4 그의 목표는 축구선수가 되거나 가수가 되는 것이다.
(or, a singer, a soccer player, either)
➡ His goal is to be ______________________.

5 나는 국어와 영어 둘 다 공부하는 것을 좋아한다.
(study, Korean, both, English, and)
➡ I like to ______________________.

6 Valentina와 그녀의 남편 모두 아들의 졸업식에 가지 않을 것이다.
(is, neither, attend, going to, Valentina, her husband, nor)
➡ ______________________ their son's graduation ceremony.

7 그것은 내 방에 없고 테이블 위에 있다.
(not, but, in my room, on the table)
➡ It's ______________________.

8 그 과학자들은 로봇을 발명했을 뿐만 아니라 인공 위성도 발명했다.
(the satellite, not only, the robot, but also)
➡ The scientist invented ______________________.

9 우리는 영화 보러 가는 것과 테니스 치는 것을 다 좋아한다.
(both, play, to the theater, and, go, tennis)
➡ We like to ______________________.

10 Lucas나 Helen이 영어 시험에서 A를 받았다.
(either, an A, Lucas, got, Helen, or)
➡ ______________________ on English test.

Point Check Ⅱ

◆ **종속접속사:** 독립적이지 않고 한 문장의 일부로만 쓰이는 절을 이끈다. 종속접속사는 문장 안에서 명사절, 부사절, 형용사절을 이끌 수 있다.

◈ 접속사의 종류_종속접속사

접속사의 종류		예문
명사절을 이끄는 접속사	**that** ~라는 것	That Jane read that book is right. [주어] I know (that) she tells lies. [목적어] The news is that the pumpkins were sold out because of Halloween. [보어]
	whether (or not) ~인지 아닌지	Whether he is a genius (or not) doesn't matter. [주어]
	if ~인지 아닌지	I'm not sure if it is good or bad. [목적어]
시간의 부사절을 이끄는 접속사	**when** ~할 때	When the typhoon comes, you should be at home.
	while ~하는 동안, ~하면서	I always listen to music while I'm studying.
	before ~하기 전에	Before you go, please turn off the light.
	after ~한 후에	Wash your hands first after you come home.
	until ~할 때까지	Until he got back, I have waited for him here.
조건의 부사절을 이끄는 접속사	**if** 만약 ~이라면	If you get a good grade, we can eat out.
	unless 만약 ~이 아니라면	We can't go back home unless you finish it.
이유의 부사절을 이끄는 접속사	**because** ~때문에, 왜냐하면	Sophia was sad because she didn't pass the exam.

Lesson

13-4 that의 쓰임

• **that**: '~라는 것'으로 해석되며, 문장 맨 앞에 'that'이 붙으면 이 절은 명사절이 된다.

1. 주어의 역할: ~라는 것은

That she was a science teacher is true.
(= It is true **that** she was a science teacher.)

➡ 주어의 의미를 가지는 'that'은 'It ~ that' 구문으로 바꾸어 쓸 수 있다. 이때 it은 가주어, that절은 진주어가 된다.

That he told the truth is certain.

It is certain **that** he told the truth.

Grammar Plus +

동사 바로 앞까지의 문장을 that절이라고 하며, 이 문장이 진짜 주어이다. 'It~ that' 구문으로 바뀔 때, It은 that절을 대신하므로 뜻이 없고, 주어의 역할을 하는 가주어이다.

2. 목적어의 역할: ~라는 것을

We believe (**that**) Mrs. Brown will come back again.

➡ that절이 동사의 목적어로 쓰일 경우 that은 생략이 가능하다.

Grammar Plus +

'that' 은 **'think, know, believe, say'** 등의 목적어 역할을 하며, 이때 that은 생략이 가능하다.

3. 보어의 역할: ~라는 것이다

The problem is that we can't understand the question at all.

Check up!

Answer Keys p. 67

A 각 문장에서 밑줄 친 that이 이끄는 명사절이 어떤 역할을 하는지 쓰시오.

1 It is surprising that Michael became an actor. 주어
2 I think that they will get married soon. ________
3 The news is that he killed someone last night. ________
4 Tom didn't say that he could go to the conference. ________
5 That this novel is educational is false. ________
6 She knows that he will come back soon. ________
7 It is certain that we should go back to school. ________
8 The problem is that he can't remember what he did. ________
9 He believes that she doesn't leave him alone. ________
10 The fact is that the streets are covered with garbage. ________

Check up!

Answer Keys p. 67

B **우리말 해석과 일치하도록 괄호 안에 주어진 단어를 알맞게 배열하시오.**

1 나는 그 그림이 멋있다고 생각한다.
(think, I, great, the picture, is, that)
➡ *I think that the picture is great.*

2 그는 그 소녀가 창문을 깼다고 믿는다.
(that, the window, he, the girl, believes, broke)
➡ ______________________

3 거짓말 하는 것은 나쁘다. (it, a lie, you, that, is, tell, bad)
➡ ______________________

4 문제는 우리가 실수를 했다는 것이다.
(we, that, a mistake, made, the problem, is)
➡ ______________________

5 나는 내가 시험을 합격하기를 바랐다.
(wished, that, could, I, the exam, pass, I)
➡ ______________________

6 그가 그 학교에 입학했다는 것은 그릇된 정보이다.
(that, misinformation, is, he, the school, entered)
➡ ______________________

7 나는 그녀를 사랑했다는 것을 깨달았다.
(loved, I, her, realized, that, I)
➡ ______________________

8 교수님은 시험이 쉽다고 생각했다.
(easy, the test, thought, the professor, was, that)
➡ ______________________

9 좋은 소식은 내일 날씨가 맑을 것이라는 점이다.
(tomorrow, it, be, sunny, will, is, the good news, that)
➡ ______________________

10 Kelly가 하이킹을 못 가는 것은 사실이다.
(Kelly, go, that, can't, it, true, is, hiking)
➡ ______________________

11 나는 Jack이 늦을 것이라는 것을 안다.
(late, I, Jack, will, that, know, be)
➡ ______________________

Note
- **tell a lie** 거짓말하다
- **believe** 믿다
- **mistake** 실수
- **misinformation** 그릇된(잘못된) 정보
- **realize** 깨닫다
- **professor** 교수

Lesson

13-5 whether (or not)

• **whether (or not)** : '~인지 아닌지'의 뜻으로, 'whether'가 앞에 붙으면 이 절은 의문의 뜻을 가진 명사절이 된다.

1. 주어의 역할

Whether they get back (**or not**) is not important.

= It isn't important **whether** they get back (**or not**).

2. 목적어의 역할

I wonder **whether** it will snow tomorrow morning (**or not**).

= I wonder **whether or not** it will snow tomorrow morning.

= I wonder **if** it will snow tomorrow morning.

➡ 'whether'가 목적어의 역할을 할 때는 'if'로 바꿔 쓸 수 있다.

그렇지만 'whether or not'이 부사절로 쓰일 때는 'if'와 바꿔 쓸 수 없다.

Whether you like it **or not**, you must go there. (➡ if와 바꿔 쓸 수 없음)

3. 보어의 역할

Her question is **whether** she can teach math (**or not**).

Grammar Plus +

• **'whether와 that'** 은 명사절을 이끄는 **종속접속사**이다.

➡ **if**가 '~인지 아닌지' 라는 뜻으로 쓰일 경우 종속접속사에 해당된다.

• **간접의문문**에서 동사의 목적어로 **'whether'** 나 **'if' 의 명사절**이 쓰일 수 있지만, 'that' 절은 올 수 없다.

➡ I don't know **whether (if)** he is honest or not. (that절은 쓸 수 없음)

Check up!

Answer Keys p. 67

A 다음 괄호 안에서 알맞은 것을 고르시오. (답이 두 개면 모두 체크하시오)

1 It is important to her (if / whether) her teacher is angry or not.

2 The problem is (if / whether) she doesn't bring her key.

3 He wonders (whether / if) they will come back soon.

4 My question is (whether / if) he will arrive or not.

5 He's not sure (whether / that) it is dangerous or not.

6 Thomas doesn't care (whether / if) he passed the exam.

7 Mrs. Lee asked (if / that) I knew her.

8 I wonder (if / whether) it will snow next week.

Lesson 13-6

if / unless / because

• **if/unless**: '만약 ~라면'이라는 뜻으로, 조건을 나타내는 부사절을 이끈다.
'if'는 긍정의 의미로, 'unless'는 부정의 의미로 사용된다.

• **because**: '왜냐하면'이라는 뜻으로, 원인, 이유를 나타내는 부사절을 이끈다.

1. **if**: ~라면, ~한다면

If it gets dark, you can use this flashlight.

2. **unless**: ~하지 않는다면 (= if ~not)

• **Unless** you wake up early, you'll be late for school.
= **If** you do**n't** wake up early, you'll be late for school.

• Turn off the light **unless** you stay up late.
= Turn off the light **if** you do**n't** stay up late.

3. **because**: 왜냐하면

I didn't pass the exam **because** I didn't study at all.

Grammar Plus +

'**if / unless**'는 **조건**의 **부사절**을, **because**는 **원인**, **이유**의 **부사절**을 이끄는 **종속접속사**이다.

Check up!

Answer Keys p. 67

A **다음 우리말에 맞게 빈칸에 알맞은 것을 쓰시오.**

1 다음 주 날씨가 좋으면 야외에서 수업하자.
➡ ___*If*___ it is sunny next week, let's have an outdoor class.

2 서두르지 않으면 그곳에 제시간에 가지 못 할거야.
➡ ________ you hurry up, you won't be there on time.

3 어젯밤 악몽을 꿔서 너무 피곤해.
➡ I'm so tired ________ I had a nightmare last night.

4 질문이 있다면 내게 전화해도 돼.
➡ ________ you have a question, you can call me.

5 네가 나를 도와줘서 숙제를 빠르게 끝낼 수 있었다.
➡ I could finish my homework quickly ________ you helped me.

6 입장권이 없으면 이 영화를 볼 수 없다.
➡ ________ you have an entrance ticket, you can't watch this movie.

7 Olivia가 그 소설책을 읽고 싶어한다면 내가 그녀에게 보낼게.
➡ ________ Olivia wants to read the novel, I'll send it to her.

Lesson

13-7 when / while

- when/while : '~할 때'의 뜻으로 시간을 의미하며, 절 앞에 붙어 부사절이 된다.
- 시간을 나타내는 부사에는 '**when, while, before, after, until**' 등이 있다.

1. **when** : ~할 때

   When you are tired, you had better go to bed early.

2. **while** : ~하는 동안, ~하면서

   While I'm cooking, you set the table.

3. **before** : ~하기 전에

   Check the weather **before** you go outside today.

4. **after** : ~한 후에

   Brush your teeth **after** you eat a meal.

5. **until** : ~할 때까지

   I will stay here **until** he arrives.

Check up!

Answer Keys p. 67

A **다음 우리말 해석에 맞게 알맞은 접속사를 빈칸에 쓰시오.**

1 수영 하기 전에 준비 운동을 해야 한다.
➡ You should do warm-up exercises __before__ you swim.

2 그가 방에 들어 왔을 때 나는 빵을 잘랐다.
➡ _______ he entered the room, I cut the bread.

3 나는 버스가 떠난 뒤에 그곳에 도착했다.
➡ I arrived there _______ the bus left.

4 나는 해가 뜰 때까지 잠이 들지 못했다.
➡ I couldn't sleep _______ the sun came up.

5 남동생이 방에서 자는 동안 우리는 깜짝 파티를 준비했다.
➡ _______ my brother slept in his room, we prepared his surprising party.

Answer Keys p. 67

B 다음 보기에서 의미상 자연스러운 것끼리 연결하여 문장을 완성하시오.

1 Finish your homework •		• ① don't listen to music.
2 While you are studying, •		• ② before you sleep.
3 You need to set your priorities •		• ③ after you read this book.
4 Write a book report •		• ④ when you start new works.
5 I bought some snacks •		• ⑤ before the game started.

C 다음 보기 와 같이 괄호 안의 우리말과 뜻이 같도록 문장을 다시 쓰시오.

보기

I got up. + The alarm clock rang.
(나는 알람시계가 울리기 전에 일어났다.)
➡ I got up before the alarm clock rang.

1 Johnny came back. + We were very glad.
(Johnny가 돌아왔을 때 우리는 매우 기뻤다.)
➡ ______________________________

2 Read a book several times. + You understand it.
(이해할 때까지 한 권의 책을 여러 번 읽어라.)
➡ ______________________________

3 My mom is cooking. + I and my sister set the table.
(엄마가 요리를 하시는 동안 나와 언니는 식탁을 정리한다.)
➡ ______________________________

Practice More Ⅱ

A 다음 빈칸에 알맞은 접속사를 쓰시오.

1 The fact is ___that___ we should find a solution.

2 She doesn't know ________ he wants to meet her or not.

3 ________ it is cheap or not, I don't buy it.

4 People generally think ________ students should study hard.

5 He should prepare for the exam ________ you want it or not.

6 I heard ________ there will be a festival this month.

7 They wonder ________ he will come back soon.

8 The truth is ________ there was no one in the room at that time.

9 ________ you go to the concert or not is up to you.

10 I believe ________ heaven helps those who help themselves.

B 다음 보기 에서 문맥상 알맞은 접속사를 찾아 빈칸에 쓰시오.

보기

because / when / because of / after / before / until / if / unless / while

1 He usually sings a song ___while___ he is taking a shower.

2 ________ he was 13, his dream was to be a pilot.

3 Drive carefully ________ you are good at driving.

4 We can't go hiking ________ rain.

5 ________ you are sick, you can go home now.

6 You will fail the exam ________ you keep playing computer games.

7 ________ I was preparing for the party, people already came in.

8 ________ you finish the work, we will go out with Tina's family.

9 I can't go out with you ________ I don't have much time to study this week.

10 ________ you turn right, there will be a hospital.

11 ________ they arrived at the bus station, the bus hadn't arrived yet.

12 I couldn't sleep last night ________ my dog.

13 ________ you don't hurry up, you will be late.

14 ________ it is sunny outside, let's go on a picnic together.

15 ________ I entered the room, I heard the baby crying.

Answer Keys p. 67~68

C 다음 문장에서 어법상 어색한 것을 찾아 바르게 고치시오.

1 It's not important that she will come back or not.

that ➡ *whether*

2 What I arrived here, he came to pick me up.

________ ➡ ________

3 She will lose weight until she exercises regularly.

________ ➡ ________

4 Because construction, people can't enter this building.

________ ➡ ________

5 You don't have to worry if or not you pass the exam.

________ ➡ ________

6 Unless I was sleeping, mom made a cake for me.

________ ➡ ________

7 Noah can't participate in the dance contest because his condition.

________ ➡ ________

8 You will win the game unless you practice hard.

________ ➡ ________

9 Turn off the TV unless you aren't watching it.

________ ➡ ________

10 Robert couldn't go to school because of he was sick.

________ ➡ ________

Practice More Ⅱ

Answer Keys p. 67~68

D **다음 주어진 단어를 이용하여 우리말 해석에 맞게 문장을 완성하시오.**

1 Sally가 머리 색을 바꾸든 안 바꾸든 중요하지 않다.
(whether, or not, changes, her hair color, Sally)
➡ It isn't important *whether Sally changes her hair color or not*.

2 그녀의 게으름 때문에 그녀는 미국에 여행 갈 기회를 놓쳤다.
(her, because of, laziness)
➡ ______________________, she missed the chance to travel to America.

3 문제는 Lily가 그를 기억 못한다는 것이다.
(that, him, can't, Lily, remember)
➡ The problem is ______________________.

4 만약 네가 글짓기를 마치지 못한다면 너는 축구를 할 수 없다.
(if, the essay, can't, you, finish)
➡ ______________________, you will not be able to play soccer.

5 Nick이 그녀를 다시 보았을 때 그녀는 William과 함께 걷고 있었다.
(Nick, when, again, her, saw)
➡ ______________________, she was walking with William.

6 네가 시험에서 A를 받으면 부모님이 행복하실 것이다.
(If, on the test, get, an A, you)
➡ ______________________, your parents will be happy.

7 빨리 걷지 않으면 너는 기차를 놓칠 것이다.
(unless, fast, walk, you)
➡ ______________________, you will miss the train.

Note
- **laziness** 게으름
- **because of** ~때문에
- **remember** 기억하다
- **be able to** ~할 수 있다
- **miss** 놓치다

중간 기말고사 예상문제

Answer Keys p. 68

내신 최다 출제 유형

01 다음 중 밑줄 친 부분이 어법상 어색한 것을 고르시오. [출제 예상 90%]

① Jack loves his dog because it is so cute.
② Barbara didn't have breakfast because she is hungry.
③ My father made a cake because it was my birthday today.
④ We went to the car wash because our car was so dirty.
⑤ I went to bed early because I was so tired.

02 다음 밑줄 친 부분 중 생략할 수 있는 것을 고르시오. [출제 예상 90%]

① The problem is that we don't have any ideas.
② That she was a thief is true.
③ I think that my dog is not fat.
④ The truth is that Jack plays the flute well.
⑤ I don't know that singing girl.

03 다음 밑줄 친 부분 중 쓰임이 나머지 넷과 다른 것을 고르시오. [출제 예상 85%]

① When Emily goes out, it is raining.
② I like to take a bath when I'm tired.
③ When Linda came to the party, everyone shouted.
④ I feel excited when I finish a puzzle.
⑤ When is the next train leaving?

04 다음 중 어법상 어색한 것을 고르시오. [출제 예상 90%]

① You can eat all this food if you are hungry.
② When it rains, I feel good.
③ If you will knit a sweater, he'll be so happy.
④ When she was young, she was a little fat.
⑤ If it is snowy, I'll have a snowball fight with my friends.

05 다음 문장 중 어법상 바른 것을 고르시오. [출제 예상 85%]

① James likes to play both basketball and table tennis.
② She can speak neither Korean or English.
③ I should not take care of my pet but also feed it.
④ Either you can draw trees nor flowers.
⑤ My mom and I won't go shopping and go hiking.

06 Which conjunction is the most natural for this sentence? [출제 예상 85%]

I can't read Japanese __________ speak Chinese.

① with ② but ③ if
④ to ⑤ therefore

중간 기말고사 예상문제

[01~05] 다음 빈칸에 들어갈 말로 올바른 것을 고르시오.

01

__________ Jacky is on her way, I will prepare to welcome him warmly.

① While ② When ③ What
④ If ⑤ Whether

02

Mia wanted to be the prettiest woman __________ she participated in the beauty contest.

① while ② what time ③ until
④ when ⑤ where

03

Some people had to go back home __________ they didn't bring any stationery to write on.

① when ② because ③ unless
④ if ⑤ until

04

I really don't like math, social studies, __________ physics.

① but ② or ③ when
④ if ⑤ and

05

Some students became lawyers, __________ some students became homeless 10 years later.

① but ② or ③ and
④ with ⑤ unless

[06~07] 다음 문장에 밑줄 친 부분 대신 쓸 수 있는 것을 고르시오.

06

Jackson wonders <u>if</u> he will perform well at the rap concert.

① that ② because ③ whether
④ so ⑤ or

07

<u>If</u> you do <u>not</u> save money, you'll be poor.

① Whether not ② Unless
③ When not ④ That not
⑤ For not

[08~10] 다음 빈칸에 공통으로 들어갈 알맞은 단어를 고르시오.

08

- Cathy wanted to learn the piano __________ she's playing the guitar now.
- Cleaning the house and washing blankets hard, __________ we felt proud of ourselves.

① but ② and ③ so
④ or ⑤ if

09

> • Korean people respect Lee Sun-shin ________ he was the bravest general and protected from Japan's attack.
> • I was hungry ________ I didn't eat all day.

① and ② but ③ or
④ because ⑤ unless

10

> • Mulan was very brave, ________ she went to war instead of her father.
> • He was feeling bad, ________ he went to bed early last night.

① and ② but ③ so
④ because ⑤ or

[11~13] 다음 중 밑줄 친 부분의 쓰임이 어색한 것을 고르시오.

11 ① My sister is tall, but I am not.
② Harry can jump high, but his younger sister can't.
③ It's cloudy now, and it'll be rainy soon.
④ You are kind, and your older brother isn't.
⑤ This pie tastes good, but I don't like it.

12 ① Take the subwa, and you can get there in time.
② Hurry up, or you'll be late.
③ Just try it, and you will feel more confident.
④ Do your best, and you will do better.
⑤ Get up early, or you won't miss the first subway.

13 ① Jack was sad, but he lost his umbrella.
② I was hungry, so I ate all the cookies on the plate.
③ Paul likes summer because he likes swimming a lot.
④ The room was dirty, so we started cleaning.
⑤ Madison wrote a letter to him, but she didn't send it.

[14~15] 다음 중 어법상 올바른 것을 모두 고르시오.

★★★
14 ① Unless you feel good, you should rest.
② If you want to have it, you should buying it.
③ Jackson is knowing that the rumor was not true.
④ I need to exercise, but I don't want to do it.
⑤ She doesn't like going shopping, and she has to go today.

★★★
15 ① My problem is whether I cannot do it.
② Angela looks like an angel, but she is so mean.
③ It isn't important whether we can go on a picnic or not.
④ That is not true that he is a model.
⑤ Unless she overslept, she was late for her work.

[16~17] 다음 주어진 문장의 밑줄 친 부분과 용법이 같은 것을 고르시오. (답이 여러 개일 경우 모두 고르시오.)

16

When Mr. White goes into the classroom, the students are making a noise.

① When does she stop by Joe's office?
② I didn't know when Helen's birthday was.
③ When Hera dialed home, nobody took the phone.
④ When we arrived the concert hall, the concert started already.
⑤ Laura remembered when they visited her.

17

Please don't do that as teacher said.

① When you go somewhere, do as they say.
② As I arrived there, nobody was there.
③ As he grew up, she became a famous rapper.
④ They were shocked as they heard Jenny's accident.
⑤ As I went to a new place, I lost the way.

[18~20] 다음 두 문장을 한 문장으로 연결할 때 빈칸에 들어갈 알맞은 말을 고르시오.

18

Make your mind gentle. You will be prettier than before.
= Make your mind gentle, __________ you'll be prettier than before.

① so ② but ③ as
④ when ⑤ and

19

A man made a useful smartphone app. He earned a lot of money.
= A man made a useful smartphone app, __________ he earned a lot of money.

① as ② so ③ but
④ or ⑤ because

20

I came back home from outside. My mom was cooking dinner.
= My mom was cooking dinner __________ I came back home from outside.

① when ② what ③ who
④ because ⑤ and

21 다음 중 어법상 올바른 것을 고르시오.

① We went to the department store or didn't buy anything.
② I'm studying hard because I have a test tomorrow.
③ When do you leave, this weekend and next weekend?
④ We played soccer or tennis all day.
⑤ Go to bed early, and you'll get up late.

22 다음 중 빈칸에 and를 썼을 때 문장이 어색한 것을 고르시오.

① She can speak both Spanish ________ Chinese.
② When I was sick, Patricia visited me ________ cooked for me.
③ Sebastian ________ I are good classmates.
④ The actress is young ________ she looks old.
⑤ Mickey was singing ________ dancing on the stage.

23 다음 문장에서 that이 들어갈 알맞은 위치를 고르시오.

> I ① think ② she'll ③ be ④ better ⑤ soon.

[24~25] 다음 주어진 문장의 뜻과 알맞은 것을 고르시오.

★★★
24

> Leave now, or you'll miss the first scene of the movie.

① If you don't leave now, you won't miss the first scene of the movie.
② If you leave now, you'll miss the first scene of the movie.
③ If you leave now, you won't miss the first scene of the movie.
④ If you don't leave now, you'll miss the first scene of the movie.
⑤ Unless leave now, you won't miss the first scene of the movie.

★★★
25

> Check your email, and you'll know everything.

① If you don't check your email, you'll know everything.
② If you check your email, you won't know everything.
③ If you check your email, you'll know everything.
④ If you don't check your email, you won't know everything.
⑤ If you check your email, you know everything.

[26~27] 다음 두 문장을 한 문장으로 바르게 만들어진 것을 고르시오.

26

> Jean did her best.
> She became a famous designer.

① Jean did her best and became a famous designer.
② Jean did her best and becomes a famous designer.
③ Jean did her best but she became a famous designer.
④ Jean did her best or became a famous designer.
⑤ Jean did her best but became a famous designer.

27

You are tired.
You should take a rest.

① If you are not tired, you should take a rest.
② You are tired, or you should take a rest.
③ If you are tired, you should take a rest.
④ You are tired, and you should take a rest.
⑤ Unless you are tired, you should take a rest.

[28~32] 다음 빈칸에 알맞은 말을 고르시오.

28

Suzie likes to play ________ tag and hide-and-seek.

① but ② or ③ if
④ and ⑤ both

Note play tag 술래잡기하다
play hide-and-seek 숨바꼭질하다

29

Tory wants to draw ________ a landscape nor a still life picture.

① neither ② either ③ not
④ but ⑤ both

Note landscape 풍경화
still life picture 정물화

30

Jerry has to not only finish his project ________ arrange data of his team.

① but then ② and ③ but also
④ not only ⑤ either

Note arrange data 자료를 정리하다

31

________ we write a short story or make a paper craft.

① Either ② Neither ③ Not
④ Both ⑤ Not only

Note paper craft 종이공예

32

________ I finish reading this book, I won't write a report of it.

① If ② Unless ③ Whether
④ Or ⑤ Because

33 다음 중 나머지 네 문장과 뜻이 다른 것을 고르시오.

① I wonder whether it will be sunny tomorrow.
② I wonder whether or not it will be sunny tomorrow.
③ I wonder if it will be sunny tomorrow.
④ I'm not sure whether it will be sunny tomorrow.
⑤ I hope that it will be sunny tomorrow.

★★★
34 다음 문장 중 어법상 올바른 것을 고르시오.

① I don't know that he is sad or not.
② She asked me if I can go camping with her.
③ If or not they will come doesn't matter.
④ He asked them if or not they wanted to go on a picnic.
⑤ The question is if she moved to India or not.

Answer Keys p. 68~69

35 다음 중 주어진 문장과 뜻이 같은 것을 고르시오.

Turn off the radio unless you are listening to music.

① Turn off the radio if you are listening to music.
② Turn off the radio after you are listening to music.
③ Turn off the radio when you are listening to music.
④ Turn off the radio if you aren't listening to music.
⑤ Turn off the radio if you listen to music.

◇◇◇◇◇◇◇◇◇◇◇ 서술형 평가 ◇◇◇◇◇◇◇◇◇◇◇

[36~38] 다음 주어진 문장에서 틀린 곳을 찾아 고쳐 쓰시오.

36

Because of it is raining, I and my younger brother have to wear raincoats and rain boots.

__________ ➡ __________

37

He is very smart. He can speak only not English but also Spanish.

__________ ➡ __________

38

Both Jasmine or her sister are good at singing.

__________ ➡ __________

[39~40] 다음 주어진 문장을 that을 사용하여 하나의 문장으로 만들어 다시 쓰시오.

39

• It is true.
• Oscar bought a new sports car.

➡ ____________________

40

• We knew it.
• Kevin wanted to marry with her.

➡ ____________________

[41~42] 다음 주어진 문장을 'and' 또는 'or'를 사용하여 같은 뜻의 문장으로 다시 고쳐 쓰시오.

★★★
41

If you read a book many times, you'll understand it better.

➡ ____________________

Answer Keys p. 68~69

★★★
42

Unless you take the test, you'll not pass this semester.

➡ ____________________

[43~45] 다음 괄호 안의 단어를 우리말에 맞게 배열하여 문장을 완성하시오.

43

그녀와 여동생은 둘 다 유명한 오페라 가수들이다.
(opera / and / her / sister / are / she / both / famous / divas)

➡ ____________________

Note diva 주연 여가수, 프리마돈나

44

나는 그가 더 많은 유용한 물건들을 발명할 수 있을 것이라고 생각한다.
(useful / things / I / that / think / more / invent / can / he)

➡ ____________________

45

나는 오늘 밤 그들이 그 뮤지컬을 즐길지 아닐지 궁금하다.
(I / wonder / the / will / they / musical / tonight / enjoy / whether)

➡ ____________________

[46~47] 다음 주어진 문장을 우리말로 바르게 해석하고, 밑줄 친 that의 역할을 쓰시오.

46

It is possible that you can make them happy.

➡ ____________________
(__________)

47

I know that many people have a dream, and they do their best for it.

➡ ____________________
(__________)

48 다음 글의 (A)와 (B)에 들어갈 알맞은 단어를 쓰시오.

My father is a cook. He makes delicious food for us every weekend. He likes basketball, ____(A)____ we often play basketball together. My mother is an English teacher. She speaks English very well. She likes camping, ____(B)____ she doesn't like bugs.

➡ (A) __________
(B) __________

14 Chapter 전치사

Point Check I

◆ **전치사 :** 전치사는 명사나 대명사 앞에 위치하며 '시간, 장소, 위치, 방향' 등을 나타낸다.

◈ 전치사의 종류

시간, 때를 나타내는 전치사	at during	on before	in after	for until	 from	 since
장소를 나타내는 전치사	at	on	in			
방향을 나타내는 전치사	to across	from along	into through	out of around	up	down
위치를 나타내는 전치사	under next to	over beside	behind by	in front of between	 among	
도구, 수단을 나타내는 전치사	with	by				
기타 주요 전치사	without	like	about			

Lesson

14-1 여러 가지 전치사

• **전치사:** 전치사는 명사나 대명사 앞에 위치하며 '시간, 장소, 위치, 방향' 등을 나타낸다.

◈ 전치사의 종류

시간, 때를 나타내는 전치사	at	on	in	for		
	during	before	after	until	from	since
장소를 나타내는 전치사	at	on	in			
방향을 나타내는 전치사	to	from	into	out of	up	down
	across	along	through	around		
위치를 나타내는 전치사	under	over	behind	in front of		
	next to	beside	by	between	among	
도구, 수단을 나타내는 전치사	with	by				

Check up!

Answer Keys p. 70

A 각 문장에서 전치사에 동그라미하고 전치사 뒤에 오는 명사(구)에 밑줄을 그으시오.

1 There is a restaurant at the corner.

2 Jiho comes in January.

3 I slept at two o'clock.

4 A man is standing in front of the public library.

5 There are dolls under my bed.

6 We will go to Japan during winter vacation.

7 I always have breakfast in the morning.

8 Sam will enter the university in 2015.

9 She met her mom at the bus stop.

10 We have to finish the project by next month.

11 Jerry will go back to Korea on December 12th.

12 I traveled in Italy for a month.

13 The teacher divided up cookies among the students.

14 She waited for her daughter by 7 p.m.

15 I have lived in Russia since 1997.

Lesson 14-2 시간, 때를 나타내는 전치사 (1)

• 시간을 나타내는 전치사는 시간, 요일, 계절의 정확한 때를 말해 준다.

• **at**: 시각, 시점 • **on**: 요일, 날짜 • **in**: 월, 연도, 계절

◈ at, on, in의 주요 쓰임

전치사	예시		쓰임
at	• at 5 o'clock	• at 7:30	구체적인 시각
	• at noon • at the end of this year	• at midnight	특정한 시점
on	• on July 4th	• on Saturday	날짜/요일
	• on my birthday	• on Easter	특정한 날
	• on Monday morning • on Friday night		특정한 날의 아침, 점심, 저녁
in	• in the morning • in the afternoon	• in the evening	아침, 점심, 저녁
	• in November	• in 2015	월/연도
	• in the 21st century		세기
	• in (the) spring		계절
	• in the past • in the present	• in the future	과거, 현재, 미래

Check up!

Answer Keys p. 70

A 다음 빈 칸에 at, on, in 중에 알맞은 전치사를 골라 쓰시오.

1 My father always does light exercise __*in*__ the morning.
2 I met my old friends ________ Sunday.
3 There are 31 days ________ a month.
4 I came home ________ midnight.
5 They will go hiking ________ Sunday afternoon.
6 Her dream is to be a doctor ________ the future.
7 His new movie will be released ________ the end of this year.
8 He will be back ________ my birthday.
9 Cherry blossoms bloom ________ March.
10 I went fishing with my dad ________ noon.

Grammar Plus +

시간의 전치사는 **at** ➡ **on** ➡ **in** 순으로 나타내는 시간의 범위가 넓어진다.

Lesson

14-3 시간, 때를 나타내는 전치사 (2)

• **before, after, during, for**와 같은 시간의 전치사들은 시간의 전후 관계나 특정한 기간 등을 나타낼 때 사용한다.

◈ 시간, 때를 나타내는 전치사

전치사		예시	쓰임
before ~전에		• before noon • before eight o'clock	구체적인 시간이나 특정 시점
after ~후에		• after dinner • after 2 o'clock	
during	~하는 동안	• during winter vacation	특정 기간
for		• for an hour • for two months	시간의 길이를 나타내는 숫자 표현
by	~까지	• by 9:00	특정 시간까지 일이 완료
until		• until midnight	특정 시간까지 상태가 계속
from ~로부터		• from last month	시작된 시점만 나타내며, 완료형이 아닌 시제와 함께 쓰임
since ~이래로		• since 1998	과거에 시작된 일이 지금까지 계속되는 것을 나타내며, 완료형 시제와 함께 쓰임

- You should finish this project by 9 o'clock.
- We did our homework until midnight.
- I started writing in a diary since last week.
- Anna has lived in Seoul since 2010.

Check up!

Answer Keys p. 70

A 다음 괄호 안에서 알맞은 전치사를 고르시오.

1 We played soccer (for / during) three hours.

2 I went to my grandmother's house (during / for) summer vacation.

3 She has worked for this company (for / since) 2001.

4 I have been studying English (from / since) last week.

5 John has to turn in his homework (until / by) tomorrow morning.

6 They waited for Sally (until / by) five.

7 Julia has to finish her homework (before / from) eating.

8 We studied English (since / for) five years.

9 The conference will start (after / until) 3 o'clock.

10 The rent is due (by / since) the end of the month.

Lesson

14-4 장소를 나타내는 전치사

• 명사나 대명사 앞에서 사람이나 물건이 있는 장소를 정확하게 말해주는 역할을 한다.

◈ 장소를 나타내는 전치사

전치사	예시		쓰임
at	• at home • at the bus station	• at the door	하나의 지점을 나타낼 때
	• at school	• at work	건물의 용도에 맞는 일을 하고 있을 때
	• at a party	• at a meeting	행사나 모임을 말할 때
on	• on the wall	• on the ground	표면에 맞닿은 것을 말할 때
	• on the road	• on Main Street	길을 말할 때
	• on a bus	• on a train	교통수단을 말할 때
	• on TV	• on the Internet	통신수단을 말할 때
in	• in town • in Seoul	• in America	마을, 도시, 국가와 같이 넓은 장소일 때
	• in a car	• in a building	탈것, 건물, 용기 등의 내부를 말할 때
	• in space	• in the sky	우주, 하늘을 말할 때

Check up!

Answer Keys p. 70

A 다음 문장의 빈칸에 at, on, in 중 알맞은 전치사를 쓰시오.

1 Let's meet ___at___ the left corner.

2 There is a beautiful picture ________ the wall.

3 He grew up ________ America.

4 Minji teaches English ________ school.

5 We met Hanna ________ the road.

6 I will see my old friend ________ my birthday party.

7 There are many stars ________ the sky.

8 Let's meet ________ Samsung Station.

9 There will be a big festival ________ our town.

10 Bill usually listens to music ________ the radio.

Lesson 14-5

방향을 나타내는 전치사

• 명사나 대명사 앞에 쓰여서 방향을 정확하게 말해주는 역할을 한다.

◈ 장소를 나타내는 전치사

전치사		예시
to	~로, ~에	• We go to school.
from	~로부터	• She is from China.
into	~안으로	• The dog walks into its house.
out of	~밖으로	• He came out of the house.
up	~위로	• We are going up the stairs.
down	~아래로	• We are climbing down the mountain.
across	~을 가로질러	• The stream is flowing across the street.
along	~을 따라서	• Sam and I are walking along the river.
through	~을 통하여	• The ball flew through the window.
around	~주위에	• There are many stores around the famous statue.

Check up!

Answer Keys p. 70

A 다음 그림을 보고 보기 에서 알맞은 전치사를 골라 빈칸에 쓰시오.

보기

down along into through across up

1 Let's go ___up___ the hill.

2 Tim walked ________ the street.

3 The car is passing ________ a tunnel.

4 The dog ran ________ the river.

5 They go ________ the stairs.

6 She went ________ the store.

Lesson 14-6 위치를 나타내는 전치사

• 명사나 대명사 앞에서 사람이나 물건이 있는 위치를 정확하게 말해주는 역할을 한다.

◈ 위치를 나타내는 전치사

전치사		예시
under	~아래에	• There are two cats under the table.
over	~위에	• A bird is flying over the building.
in front of	~앞에	• She danced in front of a building.
behind	~뒤에	• The cat is behind the tree.
next to		• The post office is next to the hospital.
beside	~옆에	• Jane stands beside her puppy.
by		• I'll wait for you by the front door.
between	~사이에 (둘 사이)	• There is a big cake between the two girls.
among	~사이에 (셋 이상)	• There is a cute kitten among the pets up for adoption.

Check up!

Answer Keys p. 70

A 다음 그림을 보고 괄호 안에서 알맞은 것을 골라 쓰시오.

1 There are people ___under___ the tree. (under, over)

2 Tim should choose one person __________ the students. (between, among)

3 John is standing __________ my house. (by, near)

4 The birds are flying __________ the bridge. (over, below)

5 The baby is sleeping __________ the dog. (beside, behind)

6 She is sitting __________ him. (next to, in front of)

7 There is a house __________ two trees. (between, among)

Lesson

14-7 도구/수단을 나타내는 전치사

• **with** : '~을 가지고'라는 뜻으로 도구를 사용할 때 함께 쓰인다.

• **by** : '~을 타고'라는 뜻으로 교통수단과 함께 쓰인다. 이때 'by + 교통수단' 사이에는 'the'가 들어가지 않는다.

1. **with** : ~을 가지고

My father and I drew a big picture **with** crayons.

2. **by** : ~을 타고(교통수단), ~을 통해(수단)

• We usually go to work **by** subway. [교통수단]

• They got the report card **by** email. [수단]

Check up!

Answer Keys p. 70

A 다음 빈칸에 전치사 with, by 중 알맞은 것을 쓰시오.

1 I cut the bread ___with___ a knife.

2 Sam usually goes to school __________ bus.

3 She drew that picture __________ a pencil and a pastel.

4 He will go to America __________ airplane.

5 We will send information __________ email.

6 My sister likes to play __________ dolls.

7 We will go to Busan __________ express train.

8 People can go to space __________ spaceship.

9 Cindy likes to write letters __________ a fountain pen.

10 I will send today's timetable __________ a text message.

B 다음 괄호 안에서 알맞은 것을 고르시오.

1 You can contact him (by / with) phone.

2 She did her homework (by / with) a laptop.

3 My dog likes to play (with / by) a ball.

4 We can go to the concert (by / in) bus.

5 I got the report card (by / to) letter.

Lesson

14-8 기타 전치사

• **without/like/about**: 시간, 장소, 위치 등을 표현하는 전치사 외에 문장에서 자주 사용되는 주요 전치사들이다.

1. without: ~없이

• People can't live **without** water.

2. like: ~처럼, ~같이

• I want to be pretty **like** my sister.

Grammar Plus +

'**like**'가 동사로 사용될 때와 전치사로 사용될 때를 잘 구분해야 한다.

• **동사**로 사용될 경우: 주어 뒤에 위치 - She **likes** singing songs.
• **전치사**로 사용될 경우: be동사나 감각동사 뒤에 위치 - I look **like** my father.

3. about: ~에 관하여

• We study **about** the history of computers.

Check up!

Answer Keys p. 71

A 다음 빈칸에 without, like, about 중 알맞은 전치사를 쓰시오.

1 She didn't know ___about___ today's homework.

2 Matthew runs ________ a cheetah.

3 Don't go to school ________ an umbrella. It'll be rainy today.

4 I don't want to talk ________ the party. It was so terrible.

5 Sam wants to be a pilot ________ his brother.

6 She took the class ________ peace and war.

7 I can't read anything ________ glasses.

8 Let's think ________ air pollution. It's a serious issue.

9 Mrs. White sings ________ a bird.

10 We can't go ________ her.

Practice More I

Answer Keys p. 71

A 다음 괄호 안에 알맞은 것을 고르시오.

1 Kate and I went to the restaurant (at / in) lunchtime.

2 My family will come to my house (to / at) 7:00.

3 Let's talk (about / with) the test result.

4 It will rain (on / in) Christmas evening.

5 The rabbit jumped (into / on) the hole.

6 Mom cut the cake (with / by) a knife.

7 Ann has lived in L.A. (since / in) 1993.

8 They usually go hiking (in / for) the summer.

9 My son looks (alike / like) a prince.

10 I like to write a letter (by / with) hand.

11 Lisa finally had a baby (at / in) the end of August.

12 We must finish our homework (by / to) tomorrow.

13 I heard about the accident (by / with) email.

14 I usually get up early (in / on) the morning.

15 John is climbing (up / to) the mountain.

B 다음 보기 에서 빈칸에 알맞은 전치사를 골라 쓰시오.

보기

to through in on down across along
since by around out of after

1 There is a stream _through_ the forest.

2 My office is ________ the third floor of this building.

3 There is a Thai restaurant ________ here.

4 We played computer games ________ school.

5 I have graduated ________ 2016.

6 Our parents usually walk ________ the river.

7 Mr. Hwang and I went ________ the office to have lunch.

8 Going to our grandmother's home ________ bus will take longer.

9 There was a subway station ________ the school.

Practice More I

10 The hospital is on the way _______ my home.

11 Ann has traveled all over the world _______ 2013.

12 Don't jump _______ the bridge.

C 다음 주어진 우리말 해석에 맞게 빈칸을 채우시오.

1 나의 할아버지는 지팡이 없이는 걸을 수 없다.
➡ My grandfather can't walk __without__ a walking stick.

2 나는 여동생과 아빠 사이에 서 있었다.
➡ I stood _________ my father and my sister.

3 그들은 토요일 아침에 낚시를 갈 것이다.
➡ They will go fishing _________ Saturday morning.

4 그때 나는 달리기에 지쳐 있었다.
➡ _________, I was tired of running.

5 Jessica는 과제를 5시까지 제출해야 한다.
➡ Jessica has to turn in her homework _________ 5.

6 남산에 있는 봉우리는 고깔모자처럼 보인다.
➡ The peak of Namsan Mountain looks _________ a cone.

7 Mr. Han은 집 주변에 나무들을 심었다.
➡ Mr. Han planted trees _________ his house.

8 그는 그 끈을 가위로 잘랐다.
➡ He cut the rope _________ the scissors.

9 나의 취미는 산을 오르는 것이다.
➡ My hobby is _________ the mountain.

10 새들이 강 위로 날아가고 있다.
➡ The birds are flying _________ the river.

11 이번 시간에는 그 작가의 작품에 대해 배워보자.
➡ Let's learn _________ the painter's work.

12 우리는 공항까지 Tim의 차를 타고 갈 것이다.
➡ We will go to the airport _________ Tim's car.

13 너는 그녀의 친구들 사이에서 그녀를 쉽게 찾을 수 있다.
➡ You can spot her easily _________ her friends.

14 소파 뒤에서 동전 몇 개가 발견됐다.
➡ Several coins were found _________ the sofa.

중간 기말고사 예상문제

Answer Keys p. 71

내신 최다 출제 유형

01 다음 문장 중 어법상 <u>어색한</u> 것을 고르시오. [출제 예상 90%]

① Flowers are everywhere on May.
② Jina was singing in the rain.
③ I go to church on Sundays.
④ She gets up early in the morning.
⑤ All my family plants flowers or trees on April 5th.

02 다음 문장 중 어법상 올바른 것을 고르시오. [출제 예상 90%]

① I'm so hungry. Can you bring a hamburger of me?
② I want to buy a present for my dad.
③ This letter is for Greg. Can you send it for him?
④ I'm going to make Korean dishes to him.
⑤ You had better buy a scarf to her.

03 다음 중 밑줄 친 부분이 어법상 <u>어색한</u> 것을 고르시오. [출제 예상 90%]

① We have two classes <u>between</u> science and math.
② They will go <u>to</u> the zoo this Saturday.
③ I sometimes walk <u>from</u> my office to my home.
④ <u>During</u> three days, we enjoyed the water festival.
⑤ Is this bus <u>for</u> Gwangju?

04 다음 짝지어진 문장의 의미가 서로 <u>다른</u> 것을 고르시오. [출제 예상 85%]

① There is a flower shop next to the park.
→ There is a flower shop beside the park.
② The McDonald's is near here.
→The McDonald's is not far from here.
③ Emily is across from the post office.
→ Emily is in the middle of the post office.
④ There is a stream under the bridge.
→ There is a bridge over the stream.
⑤ He stands in front of me.
→ I stand behind him.

05 다음 대화의 빈칸에 들어갈 단어들로 바르게 짝지어진 것을 고르시오. [출제 예상 90%]

A Lily, can you guess? Who is the most famous woman ⓐ __________ the world?
B Mother Teresa?
A No. She is ⓑ __________ Italy. But she lives in France now.
B I don't know. I give ⓒ __________. Who is she?
A Mona Lisa.

① in – from – up ② in – in – up
③ in – from – at ④ on – in – of
⑤ at – in – up

중간 기말고사 예상문제

[01~05] 다음 빈칸에 들어갈 알맞은 전치사를 고르시오.

01

My parents allowed me to play computer games ________ Sundays.

① in ② at ③ from
④ on ⑤ of

02

Our winter vacation begins ________ December.

① in ② on ③ at
④ by ⑤ to

03

Joan is from England. She helps us ________ English.

① on ② with ③ by
④ for ⑤ in

04

Hi, everyone. Nice to see you. I am Yuna. I am ________ Ulsan.

① in ② on ③ from
④ for ⑤ with

05

It's summer. We have to be ready ________ the rainy days.

① of ② at ③ in
④ from ⑤ for

[06~08] 다음 우리말과 같은 뜻이 되도록 빈칸에 알맞은 것을 고르시오.

06

아버지께서는 저녁식사 후에 설거지를 하신다.
➡ My father washes the dishes ________ dinner.

① before ② in ③ after
④ during ⑤ at

07

그는 잠시 동안 우리들과 이야기하기를 원했다.
➡ He wanted to talk with us ________.

① on a minute ② by a minute
③ with a minute ④ for a minute
⑤ in a minute

08

그 교회는 우체국과 병원 사이에 있어요.
➡ The church is ________ the post office and the hospital.

① between ② during ③ for
④ next to ⑤ beside

[09~13] 다음 빈칸에 공통으로 들어갈 알맞은 것을 고르시오.

09

- Speaking and writing Chinese is too difficult ________ me.
- Let's go to a bazaar ________ poor old people this afternoon.

① on ② in ③ to
④ for ⑤ by

Answer Keys p. 71~72

10

- The weather changes often ________ spring.
- There are a few people ________ the building.

① at ② in ③ to
④ for ⑤ by

11

- What's ________ channel 7 at 6:30 on Sunday nights?
- My favorite TV show is now ________ TV.

① on ② by ③ in
④ to ⑤ for

12

- Laura always leaves ________ work at 7:30 in the morning.
- Thank you ________ your nice advice.

① at ② of ③ to
④ by ⑤ for

13

- A big pine tree is ________ the lake.
- My brother delivers milk ________ bicycle.

① with ② beside ③ by
④ next to ⑤ in

★★★
14 다음 밑줄 친 단어의 뜻이 나머지 넷과 다른 것을 고르시오.

① We've never seen a wonderful thing like that.
② You want to be a singer like her, don't you?
③ What do you like to eat?
④ Does she swim like a fish?
⑤ A Turtle Ship looks like a turtle.

★★★
15 다음 주어진 문장의 밑줄 친 부분과 뜻이 같은 것을 고르시오.

Which one do you want for dessert?

① I was at camp for the last two days.
② We are looking for Jenny's ring.
③ She is never late for school.
④ I just want to eat steak for dinner.
⑤ Thank you for your help.

[16~17] 다음 질문에 알맞은 대답을 고르시오.

16

A When do you go to the library?
B ________________________.

① In Sundays ② At Tuesdays
③ On Thursdays ④ Of Thursdays
⑤ By Tuesdays

17

A What time do you take a subway?
B ______________________.

① In 8:20. ② At 8:20. ③ On 8:20.
④ For 8:20. ⑤ By 8:20.

[18~20] 다음 빈칸에 들어갈 전치사들이 알맞게 짝지어 진 것을 고르시오.

18

- The Whites go to the mall ________ the evening.
- I really hate getting up ________ the sun rises.

① in – on ② in – at
③ in – after ④ in – before
⑤ at – after

★★★
19

- We swim everyday ________ the summer.
- They were doing their homework ________ two hours.

① for – during ② for – for
③ during – for ④ during – during
⑤ before – during

20

- ________ Halloween, children go around the town to get some candies and chocolate.
- Joan always jogs ________ the morning.

① On – in ② In – in ③ In – on
④ On – on ⑤ At – in

[21~23] 다음 주어진 우리말을 바르게 영작한 것을 고르시오.

21

커다란 은행나무 아래에 한 소녀가 있다.

① There is a girl by the big ginkgo tree.
② There is a girl over the big ginkgo tree.
③ There is a girl under the big ginkgo tree.
④ There is a girl in the big ginkgo tree.
⑤ There is a girl at the big ginkgo tree.

22

그것이 갑자기 내 앞에 나타났다.

① It appeared suddenly in front of me.
② It appeared in front of me sudden.
③ It suddenly appeared to me.
④ It suddenly appeared at me.
⑤ It suddenly appeared in front of me.

23

풍선이 다리 위를 날아가고 있는 중이다.

① The balloon fly over the bridge.
② The balloon is flying over the bridge.
③ The balloon flies on the bridge.
④ The balloon is fly over the bridge.
⑤ The balloon flies over the bridge.

[24~25] 다음 중 밑줄 친 부분이 어색한 것을 모두 고르시오.

24
① We go to the beach in Saturday.
② She is reading a book in the bench.
③ There are some clouds in the sky.
④ I have three birds in the cage.
⑤ There are many trees in the park.

25 ① I and Jenna played badminton at night.
② Oliver had lunch at noon.
③ Jack usually gets up early at the morning.
④ I like to listening to music while I'm reading a book at the evening.
⑤ We were at school at that time.

[26~27] 다음 중 어법상 올바른 것을 모두 고르시오.

26 ① His grandfather grows tomatoes in his farm.
② Overeating is very bad of your health.
③ Look in that picture.
④ Mom pours the milk into the glass.
⑤ Her younger brother is afraid of dogs.

27 ① The first train leaves in 5:00 a.m.
② They went around the forest.
③ Fred works for a publishing company.
④ What do you do in special holidays?
⑤ There are a lot of buildings on the town.

[28~29] 다음 중 밑줄 친 부분의 쓰임이 잘못된 것을 고르시오.

★★★
28 ① Where will you go during the summer vacation?
② Kelly works from 9 a.m. to 6 p.m.
③ I sent him a card in his birthday.
④ There are no classes on Saturday and Sunday.
⑤ Our family usually eats dinner at 7:30.

★★★
29 ① I can make many friends through the Internet all over the world.
② It snows a lot in winter.
③ On the way home, I saw a man falling.
④ Most of people go ice fishing in January.
⑤ I sometimes go to the shopping mall in subway.

30 다음 중 빈칸에 on이 들어갈 수 없는 문장을 고르시오.

① They enjoyed themselves ________ the beach.
② I bought a beautiful scarf ________ Jenny.
③ Johnny is ________ a diet now.
④ People usually wear their traditional clothes ________ special holidays.
⑤ What do you do ________ Sundays?

31 다음 글의 빈칸에 들어갈 전치사들로 바르게 짝지어진 것을 고르시오.

> Dear Julie,
> Hi, Julie. I am ⓐ ________ Los Angeles with my family. We went to an Indian restaurant tonight. Here, I learned some new facts. To order food, I saw a menu. But there's no beef ⓑ ________ the menu. I was surprised at it. But dad said, "Indian people don't eat beef, and some people eat food ⓒ ________ their hands."

① on – in – with ② in – in – with
③ in – on – with ④ at – in – with
⑤ in – at – with

[32~33] 다음 글을 읽고 물음에 답하시오.

This picture is called *Mona Lisa*. Leonardo da Vinci started to paint this picture in 1503. And he finished it in 1505. *Mona Lisa* is ⓐ __________ the Louvre Museum ⓑ __________ Paris, France. *Mona Lisa* is a famous picture because there are many mysteries about the painting. And Leonardo's another famous painting is *The Last Supper*.

32 윗글의 ⓐ와 ⓑ에 들어갈 알맞은 전치사로 짝지어 진 것을 고르시오.

① at – in ② in – at ③ in – in
④ at – at ⑤ of – in

33 윗글을 읽고, 다음 질문들 중 답할 수 없는 것을 고르시오.

① When did Leonardo da Vinci start painting the *Mona Lisa*?
② What can you see in the painting, *The Last Supper*?
③ What is the title of this picture?
④ Where is the *Mona Lisa* now?
⑤ Why is the *Mona Lisa* very famous?

[34~37] 다음 물음에 답하시오. (객관식 2문항, 서술형 2문항)

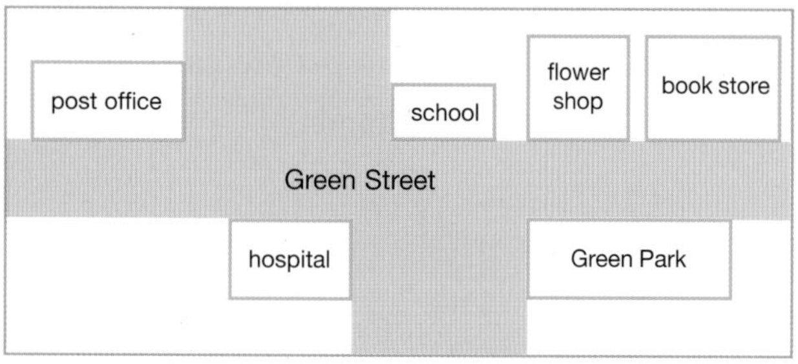

[34~35] 위 그림을 참고하여 다음 문장의 빈칸에 알맞은 말을 고르시오.

34

The Green Park is __________ from the hospital.

① next to ② across ③ on
④ between ⑤ beside

35

The flower shop is __________ the school and the bookstore.

① between ② next to
③ beside ④ across from
⑤ over

[36~37] 위의 그림을 보고 다음 우리말을 바르게 영작하시오.

36

병원은 Green Street에 있습니다.

➡ ______________________________

37

서점은 꽃집 옆에 있습니다.

➡ ______________________________

Answer Keys p. 71~72

◇◇◇◇◇◇◇◇◇◇◇ 서술형 평가 ◇◇◇◇◇◇◇◇◇◇◇

[38~40] 다음 우리말에 맞게 각 빈칸에 알맞은 전치사를 쓰시오.

38

- 그는 아버지를 닮았다.
  ➡ He looks ________ his father.
- 그것은 진짜 같다.
  ➡ It is ________ a real.

➡ ____________

39

그녀는 아이들을 위해 일하는 것에 흥미를 갖고 있다.
➡ She is interested ________ working ________ children.

➡ ____________

★★★
40

그는 겨울 방학 동안 Ann 숙모 집에 머물렀다. 그리고 이틀 동안 영어캠프에 다녀왔다.
➡ He stayed at Aunt Ann's ________ winter vacation. And he went to English Camp ________ two days.

➡ ____________

[41~43] 다음 주어진 문장에서 어법상 틀린 곳을 찾아 고쳐 다시 쓰시오.

41

Nobody lives within air.

➡ ____________________________

42

It was so long time to see Henry in the meeting.

➡ ____________________________

43

Eddie's hobby is climbing in the mountain.

➡ ____________________________

[44~47] 다음 우리말에 맞게 괄호 안의 단어를 배열하여 문장을 완성하시오.

44

나는 지난주부터 영어로 일기를 쓰기 시작했다.
(I / started / my / diary / in / writing / English / in)

➡ ____________________________ last week.

45

Mr. Wang은 한국에 3년 동안 머물면서 한국어를 공부했다.
(Mr. Wang / Korean / for / studied / years / three)

➡ ____________________________ in Korea.

Answer Keys p. 71~72

46

르네상스에 관하여 우리는 지난 한 달 동안 공부하였다.
(we / Renaissance / the / about / studied)

➡ ______________________ last month.

47

그 배우 주위에는 많은 팬들이 있다.
(there / are / around / fans / many)

➡ ______________________ the actor.

[48~50] 다음 주어진 단어를 이용해 우리말에 맞게 빈칸을 채우시오.

48 상자 앞에 곰 인형이 세 개 있다.
(in front of teddy bear)
➡ There are ____________________

49 가방 한 개가 상자들 사이에 있다. (between)
➡ There is ____________________

50 장난감들 사이에 꽃 한송이가 있었다. (among)
➡ There was ____________________

51 다음 문장의 빈칸에 공통으로 들어갈 알맞은 말을 쓰시오.

- Jake listens to music ________ weekends.
- I don't have free time ________ Wednesday.

➡ ____________

52 다음 밑줄 친 ⓐ~ⓔ중 어법상 알맞지 <u>않는</u> 것의 기호를 쓰고, 그 옆에 바른 단어를 쓰시오.

Dear my friends,
I wanted to make some dresses ⓐ <u>for</u> you. So I designed one hundred pictures ⓑ <u>of</u> dresses ⓒ <u>of</u> all ⓓ <u>of</u> you. The green dresses were for Gina, and the blue ones were for Miran. You were so special ⓔ <u>on</u> me.

➡ ____________, ____________

Note

Grammar Master Level 1

펴낸이	임 병 업
펴낸곳	(주)월드컴 에듀
디자인	임예슬 · 김지현
저자	신은진
편집	김채원
감수	Amy Smith
등록	2015년 10월 15일
주소	서울특별시 강남구 언주로 120 912호 (도곡동, 인스토피아)
전화	02)3273-4300 (대표)
팩스	02)3273-4303
홈페이지	www.wcbooks.co.kr
이메일	wc4300@wcbooks.co.kr

GRAMMAR MASTER 1

정답 및 해설

WorldCom Edu

Chapter 01 문장의 기초

Lesson 1-1 인칭대명사와 be동사

Check up! p. 011~012

A	1	it	2	we
	3	he	4	they
	5	you	6	they
	7	he	8	we
	9	it	10	they
B	1	is	2	are
	3	is	4	are
	5	is	6	are
	7	are	8	are
	9	is	10	is
C	1	They're	2	X
	3	He's	4	X
	5	We're	6	She's
	7	X	8	I'm
	9	You're	10	X

Lesson 1-2 be동사의 부정문

Check up! p. 013

A
1 I'm not
2 Your daddy isn't
3 Her brothers aren't
4 You aren't(You're not)
5 It isn't(It's not)
6 They aren't(They're not)

B	1	am not	2	is not
	3	aren't	4	is not
	5	aren't		

Lesson 1-3 일반 동사

Check up! p. 014~015

A	1	reads	2	watches
	3	tries	4	loves
	5	works	6	goes
	7	studies	8	looks
	9	plays	10	brushes
B	1	makes	2	watch
	3	go	4	runs
	5	agrees	6	loves
	7	takes	8	do
	9	washes	10	tries
C	1	goes → go	2	have → has
	3	likes → like	4	watches → watch
	5	cry → cries	6	plays → play
	7	listens → listen	8	read → reads
	9	wash → washes	10	likes → like

Lesson 1-4 일반 동사 부정문

Check up! p. 016~017

A	1	play	2	don't
	3	go	4	do not
	5	does	6	do/have
B	1	doesn't play	2	doesn't do
	3	doesn't visit	4	doesn't have
	5	don't swim	6	doesn't use
	7	don't like	8	don't teach
	9	don't buy	10	doesn't eat

C
1 My daddy doesn't cook well.
2 Anna and her sister don't go fishing.
3 Emma doesn't speak English well.
4 Sammy doesn't like to sing songs.
5 She doesn't play the drum well.
6 Everyone doesn't love that TV show.

Lesson 1-5 Yes / No 의문문

Check up! p. 019

A
1 Do 2 Is
3 Am 4 Are
5 Do

B
1 she does 2 they don't
3 I am 4 she is
5 they don't

C
1 Is my family going to the zoo?
2 Does Sam want to go to the party?
3 Do John and his father go to the same health center?
4 Do I write in my diary every day?
5 Are you kind to people?

Lesson 1-6 There is / There are

Check up! p. 020

A
1 is 2 There is
3 any 4 Are
5 Is there 6 There isn't/any

Practice More I p. 021~023

A
1 is 2 are
3 are 4 is
5 am 6 are not
7 is not 8 are not
9 is not 10 are not

B
1 teaches 2 go
3 read 4 wash
5 buys 6 doesn't use
7 doesn't like 8 don't need
9 don't cook 10 doesn't catch

C
1 doesn't 2 water
3 do not 4 isn't
5 don't sing 6 works
7 has 8 are
9 don't

D
1 I am
2 she isn't (she is not)
3 I don't (I do not)
4 they do
5 she doesn't (she does not)
6 there isn't (there is not)

E
1 go → goes / Wendy는 상점에 갑니다.
2 is → are / 민수와 Suzie는 좋은 친구들입니다.
3 does → is / Mary는 요리에 관심이 많습니다.
4 watch → watches / Tony는 해리포터 라는 영화를 봅니다.
5 sings → sing / 내 이웃들은 아주 큰 소리로 노래를 부릅니다.

F
1 Do Sally and her family travel to London? / they do
2 Does he want to meet Tina today? / he doesn't (he does not)
3 Are there any carrots and tomatoes in the basket? / there are
4 Is it raining outside? / it isn't (it's not, it is not).
5 Am I mean to you? / you aren't (you're not, you are not)

서술형 연습

G
1 My new jacket is nice.
2 Your brother is tall and fat.
3 Does he speak English well?
4 You don't understand the meaning.
5 My father is in the living room.

Lesson 1-7 Wh- 의문문

Check up! p. 026

A 1 when 2 what
3 where 4 which

B 1 Why 2 When
3 What 4 When

C 1 ④ I want to go Gangwondo
2 ① Because she was very sick.
3 ③ I don't know.
4 ② She usually gets up at 7.

Lesson 1-8 선택 의문문

Check up! p. 027

A 1 Which / or / water
2 Which / or / science
3 Who / or / Mrs. Kim
4 Does / or / a hamburger
5 Are / or / magicians

Lesson 1-9 부가의문문

Check up! p. 029

A 1 isn't it 2 doesn't she
3 can you 4 isn't it
5 does he

B 1 does he 2 did you
3 aren't they 4 isn't it
5 aren't we 6 are they
7 wasn't it 8 doesn't he
9 do they 10 aren't I

Practice More Ⅱ

p. 030~032

A 1 who 2 when
3 where 4 what
5 why 6 how
7 which

B 1 Who 2 What
3 doesn't she 4 When
5 Which 6 doesn't he
7 What 8 do we
9 doesn't it 10 does he

C 1 What 2 Who
3 Why 4 When (what time)
5 How 6 Where
7 Which / or 8 Do / or
9 Is / or 10 Who

D 1 is he? 2 aren't they
3 don't they 4 do you
5 is he? 6 Does she
7 do they 8 aren't we?
9 is it? 10 don't you?

E 1 What / ⓑ 2 Who / ⓒ
3 How / ⓓ 4 Where / ⓐ

F 1 are(go) → X (going)
2 watches → watch
3 Who → What
4 Which → Who
5 does → doesn't
6 When → Where
7 Anna and Tony → they
8 is not → isn't
9 When → How
10 and → or

서술형연습

G 1 When / cook turkey
2 Why does he exercise
3 take the subway / don't you?
4 on the farm / is she
5 a farmer or a fisherman?

Lesson 1-10 명령문

Check up! p. 034~035

A 1 Be 2 wash
3 Let's not 4 be
5 Don't tell

B 1 Don't run in the hall
2 Let's not make a noise.
3 Don't be unkind to the others
4 Don't eat only meat.
5 Let's not throw the garbage.

C 1 Prepare the umbrella.
2 Let's meet at five
3 Clean your room
4 Let's not make a mess
5 Let's go to the movies

D 1 and 2 or
3 work / and 4 Don't be / or

Lesson 1-11 명령문의 부가 의문문

Check up! p. 036

A 1 will you 2 will you
3 will you 4 shall we
5 will you 6 shall we
7 will you 8 will you
9 shall we 10 will you

Lesson 1-12 감탄문

Check up! p. 037

A 1 How / she 2 What / has
3 How / he(Martin) 4 What / are
5 What / he

Practice More Ⅲ p. 038~040

A 1 Be 2 brush
3 Let's 4 Let's not
5 Throw 6 will you
7 shall we 8 will you
9 shall we 10 will you

B 1 Turn on
2 Be kind to
3 Help people
4 Let's drink
5 Let's watch
6 Don't make noise.
7 Don't throw
8 Don't waste water
9 Don't touch dry ice
10 Don't hit

C 1 will you 2 will you
3 shall we 4 will you
5 shall we 6 will you
7 shall we 8 will you
9 shall we 10 will you

D 1 Don't / or 2 Sleep / and
3 Brush / or 4 Don't / or
5 Do / and

E 1 How slow 2 What a beautiful
3 How cold 4 What an awesome

F 1 What a wonderful camera she has!
2 How horrible they are!
3 How smart Jenny is!
4 What a mysterious scene it is!

서술형 연습

G 1 Be a positive person.
2 You won't cry if you fall down, will you?
3 Let's do homework in the library.
4 How clean your room is!

Lesson 1-13 문장의 기본 구성 요소

Check up! p. 042~043

A	1	My family	2	We
	3	They	4	Mary and Jane
B	1	fly	2	has
	3	looks	4	arrived
C	1	him	2	the truth
	3	a serenade	4	a mistake
D	1	Mr. Black	2	honest
	3	a cook	4	cold
E	1	주어	2	주격보어
	3	목적격보어	4	목적어
	5	동사	6	주어

Lesson 1-14 문장의 1, 2형식

Check up! p. 045

A	1	ⓒ	2	ⓓ
	3	ⓑ	4	ⓐ
	5	ⓔ		
B	1	2형식, is	2	1형식, live
	3	1형식, runs	4	2형식, felt
	5	2형식, smells		

C
1 looks handsome.
2 are husband and wife.
3 A lot of stars are
4 a kind nurse
5 Tim and Jerry work

Lesson 1-15 문장의 3, 4형식

Check up! p. 046~047

A	1	coffee	2	some flowers
	3	her cat	4	a question
	5	me		

B
1 us(간목) a fairy tale(직목)
2 me(간목) a present(직목)
3 our son(간목) a big kite(직목)
4 her(간목) a glass of water (직목)
5 her (간목) an email (직목)
6 us (간목) good news (직목)

C	1	us a big cake	2	buys
	3	us a picture	4	likes
	5	me	6	explains
	7	her		

Lesson 1-16 4형식 문장의 3형식 전환

Check up! p. 048~049

A	1	to us	2	of him
	3	me	4	us
	5	her		
B	1	for	2	to
	3	to	4	for
	5	of	6	for

C
1 Maria asked a difficult question of me.
2 He cooked spaghetti for her.
3 We bought some apples for you.
4 Mrs. Green gives some chocolate to me.
5 Sam showed a pearl necklace to me.
6 Ann requires some advice of me.

Lesson 1-17 문장의 5형식

Check up! p. 050

A	1	her son / a great architect		
	2	us / go out	3	you / dry
	4	his car / washed	5	them / happy

Practice More IV

p. 051~053

A
1 My grandparents / live
2 Jenny and I / are
3 That monster / is
4 Michael / came
5 The pretty girl / is

B
1 fish / X
2 dogs are "loyal animals" / X
3 me / happy
4 a household account book / X
5 X / an artist

C
1 1형식
2 2형식
3 3형식
4 1형식
5 4형식
6 3형식
7 4형식
8 5형식

D
1 me
2 her
3 for
4 me"puppy"
5 me
6 participate
7 impressive
8 me
9 man
10 kind

E
1 sends/to
2 the magic tricks to him.
3 brought/to
4 a scary tale to
5 teaches/to us
6 cooks me pizza
7 Jack his favorite pen.
8 her some information.
9 him a new oven
10 her friends Christmas cards

F
1 him happy
2 she advised
3 go to the party
4 him an honest man
5 them finish

서술형 연습

G
1 Lucy sings very well
2 Jenny and Sammy read books every day.
3 A stone feels hard.
4 He gave me a bunch of roses.
5 I call them heroes

중간 기말고사 예상문제

내신 최다 출제 유형

p. 054

01 ⑤ 02 ② 03 ① 04 ③ 05 ④
06 ③ 07 ①

해설

01 Ms. Lee와 Mr. Brown 두 사람이 주어로 나왔기 때문에 복수 동사가 와야 한다. 복수형의 be동사는 are이다.

02 ①,③,④,⑤의 'is'는 '~이다'의 뜻으로 쓰였고, ②의 'is'는 '~에 있다'의 뜻으로 쓰였다.

03 ② 'a(n)+형용사+명사+주어+동사'의 감탄문은 what을 사용한다. ③ 'let's'의 부정은 바로 뒤에 not을 붙여 'let's not'이라고 표현한다. ④ 명령문은 항상 동사원형으로 시작한다. cleaning → clean. ⑤ '형용사+주어+동사'의 감탄문은 'how'를 사용한다.

04 ① Does → Do, ② go → goes, ④ don't → doesn't, ⑤ Do → Does

05 ①,②,③,⑤는 '~이다'의 뜻으로 쓰였고, ④는 '~에 있다'라는 뜻으로 쓰였다.

06 ①,②,④,⑤는 2형식의 문장이고, ③은 3형식의 문장이다.

07 Today we have a new student today → 두 개의 'today' 중 하나를 삭제한다.

p. 055~062

01 ②	02 ②	03 ②	04 ④	05 ⑤
06 ①	07 ⑤	08 ①	09 ⑤	10 ①
11 ③	12 ④	13 ④	14 ③	15 ③
16 ③	17 Let's	18 don't make		19 ④
20 ③	21 ③	22 ⑤		

23 (1) when, (2) where, (3) who, (4) what, (5) how

24 which, or		25 Is, or	26 ④	27 ③
28 ②	29 ③	30 ③	31 ①	32 ②
33 ①	34 ③	35 ①	36 ④	37 ③
38 ④	39 ④	40 ②	41 ④	
42 She is a good player.			43 ④	44 ②
45 ③	46 ②			

〈서술형 평가〉

47 aren't they/is she? 48 and 49 or

50 The patient doesn't suffer form a toothache.

51 Is Tom Sawyer a brave boy?

52 Let's not go into the haunted house

53 What a great singer Michael Jackson was!

54 smells → smell 55 like/are/have/live

56 The man tells us the truth.

57 Jenny brings some cake to them

58 Mr. Brown makes us laugh 59 shall we

60 will you

해설

01 The puppy와 My mother은 각각 단수를 나타내고 있으므로 단수동사인 'is'가 정답이다.

02 Mary and John과 Those cute girls는 복수형이므로 복수동사 'are'이 정답이다. 'Those'는 'that(저것, 저 사람)'의 복수 형태로서 이 단어를 모른다 해도 'girl' 뒤에 복수를 나타내는's'와, 문장 끝 'classmate'뒤의 's'를 통해 복수 문장임을 알 수 있다.

03 ① you're – you are, ③ aren't – are not, ④ she's – she is, ⑤ isn't – is not의 줄임말 형태이다. 하지만 ②번은 amn't는 'am not'이라고 써야 올바르다. 'am not'는 줄임말이 없다.

04 ① isn't – is not, ② They're – They are, ③ isn't – is not, ⑤ She's – She is의 줄임말 형태이다. ④ 일반명사와 be동사 사이에는 줄임말 형태를 사용할 수 없다.'Many birds are'이라고 써야 한다.

05 주어진 문장의 동사는 'is'로서 단순동사를 뜻한다. ①,②,③,④번은 모두 단수이나 ⑤번은 복수로서 빈칸에 들어갈 수 없다.

06 ② wash → washes, ③ buy → buys, ④ do → does, ⑤ brush → brushes

07 work → works

08 3인칭 단수 주어가 쓰였기 때문에 그 다음에 오는 동사도 단수 형태로 알맞게 바꿔줘야 한다. 'don't → doesn't'

09 'visit'은 일반동사이므로 이를 부정문으로 바꿀 때는 'do/dose'를 쓰고 'not'을 붙인다. 주어가 3인칭 단수형태이므로 'does not'을 사용하고, 그 뒤의 동사는 원형으로 써야한다.

10 be동사 부정문은 be동사 바로 뒤에 'not'을 붙여 사용한다.

11 일반동사 의문문은 'Do / Does+주어+동사원형' 순서로 만든다. 주어가 3인칭 단수 일 경우 does를 사용하며, 동사는 원형을 사용한다.

12 be동사의 의문문은 'be동사+주어~?' 순서대로 쓴다. 주어의 인칭에 따라 be동사는 'am, are, is' 중에 하나를 선택하여 쓴다.

13 Yes/No의문문에 대한 대답은 질문의 주어는 대명사로, 동사는 일치시킨다. 'Mr. and Mrs. Smith'는 두 사람이며, be동사 의문문을 사용한것에 주의하여 답을 찾는다.

14 Yes/No의문문에 대한 대답은 질문의 주어는 대명사로, 동사는 일치시킨다. 'Jack'은 남자아이 이름이며, 3인칭 단수이다. 일반동사 의문문이라는 것에 주의하여 답을 찾는다.

15 평서문을 명령문으로 바꿀 때 주어는 생략하고, 동사는 원형의 형태로 문장 제일 앞에 놓는다. 동사가 'am, are, is' 중의 하나일 경우는 이의 원형인 'be'를 써 준다.

16 be동사의 부정은 be동사(am, are, is)뒤에 바로 'not'을 붙인다.

17 Shall we~? 로 시작하는 문장은 제안을 하는 의미가 강하며, 명령문에서도 제안의 의미를 가지고 있는 'Let's'를 써 준다.

18 명령문의 부정문은 주어가 빠진 동사 원형 앞에 'Don't'를 붙여 만든다. 이때의 'don't'는 동사가 be동사나 일반동사나 상관없이 모두 사용한다.

19 ① doesn't → don't, ② is → are, ③ are → X, ⑤ has → have

20 'I'는 단수이나 1인칭 이므로 동사 변화가 없다. doesn't → don't

21 무엇을 좋아하냐는 질문에, 그것을 사지 않겠다고 대답하였다.

22 ① A: 무엇을 사고 싶니? B: 난 그렇게 생각 안해.
② A: 너는 언제 집으로 돌아가니? B: 버스정류장에 있어.
③ A: 넌 이번 주에 어디 가니? B: 나는 병원에 있어.
④ A: 오늘 기분이 어때? B: 오늘은 너무 더워.

23 ① 'go to bed (잠자리에 들다)' 의 뜻을 정확히 인지하고, 시간을 나타내는 when을 사용한다.
② '살다'라는 뜻의 장소를 나타내는 동사가 왔으므로 where을 사용한다.
③ 사람을 의미하는 하는 단어를 보며 '누구'를 뜻하는 who를 사용한다.

④ 표정이 슬퍼 보인다는 문장이 바로 뒤에 옴으로 무슨 일이 있었는지에 묻는 것으로 유추 할 수 있다.

24 둘 중 어느 것을 선택 하냐는 질문은 의문사 'which'를 사용한다. 뒤에 나오는 선택 사항 중간에는 'or'를 꼭 써 주어야 한다.

25 바로 '이것 또는 저것'을 뜻하는 질문에는 굳이 의문사가 아니라 be동사 또는 일반동사가 올 수 있다. 대답에서 be동사가 나왔으므로 주어에 맞는 be동사를 사용한다.

26 부가의문문은 주절의 동사와 시제를 일치시키며, 주절의 주어는 대명사로 바꿔 주어야한다. 주절이 부정이면 부가의문문은 긍정을, 주절이 긍정이면 부가의문문은 부정을 사용한다. 또한 부가의문문의 동사가 부정일 경우에는 반드시 줄임말을 사용한다.

27 부가의문문은 주절의 동사와 시제를 일치시키며, 주절의 주어는 대명사로 바꿔 주어야한다. 주절이 부정이면 부가의문문은 긍정을, 주절이 긍정이면 부가의문문은 부정을 사용한다. 또한 부가의문문의 동사가 부정일 경우에는 반드시 줄임말을 사용한다.

28 4형식의 문장으로 '주어+동사+간접목적어+직접목적어'순으로 배열한다. 동사가 일반동사인데, 목적어만 2개가 나왔을 경우 하나가 사람, 다른 하나가 사물이면 4형식의 목적어라고 생각한다.

29 4형의 문장이며, 일반동사 뒤에는 목적어가 온다. 'I'는 주격대명사이다.

30 전치사를 사용한 3형식의 문장이다. 4형식에서 3형식으로 문장을 전환할 때 각 동사에 맞는 전치사를 사용한다. 'require'의 전치사는 'of'이다.

31 주어와 동사, 형용사로 이루어진 문장은 'how' 감탄문으로 만든다. 'How+형용사+주어+동사' 순으로 만든다.

32 주어 외에 명사가 하나 더 나올 경우 'what'감탄문으로 만든다. 'What+a(n)+형용사+명사+주어+동사' 순으로 만든다.

33 'teach'의 전치사는 'to', 'cook'의 전치사는 'for'이다.

34 'ask'의 전치사는 'of', 'tell'의 전치사는 'to'이다.

35 'how'가 '어떻게'라는 뜻의 방법을 물어보는 표현으로 쓰였으므로, 방법을 제시하는 ①번이 정답이다

36 'what time'이라는 시간을 물어봤기 때문에 ④번이 정답이다.

37 ①,②,④,⑤는 모두 동사 '좋아하다'의 뜻으로 쓰였고, ③번은 전치사로 '~같은'이라는 뜻으로 쓰였다.

38 ①,②,③,⑤는 모두 주어가 복수 형태로 'are'을 사용하고, ④번은 단수로 'is'를 사용한다.

39 첫 번째 문장의 주절이 긍정이므로 부가의문문은 부정이, 두번째 문장의 주절이 부정이므로 부가의문문은 긍정이 나와야 한다.

40 ①,③,④,⑤는 모두 2형식의 문장이고, ②번은 1형식의 문장이다. 각 문장 제일 앞, 또는 뒤에 부사구가 붙어도 문장의 요소에 표함되지 않으므로 하나의 형식으로 하지 않는다.
즉, 생략한 표현이라 생각하고 문장의 요소를 나누는 것이 좋다.

41 ⓐ ten-minutes → the ten-minute, ⓓ classes → class

42 She is a good player.

43 모두 4형식의 문장을 3형식으로 전환한 것이다. ④번 'sent'는 전치사 'to'와 함께 사용한다.

44 모두 4형식의 문장을 3형식으로 전환한 것이다.
① make – for, ③ bought (buy) – for,
④ showed (show) – to, ⑤ gave (give) – to

45 5형식의 문장으로 '주어+동사+목적어+목적보어'의 형태이다.
① 3형식, ② 4형식, ④ 3형식, ⑤ 3형식

46 2형식의 문장으로 '주어+동사(be동사, 감각동사)+보어'의 형태이다. ① 3형식, ③ 1형식, ④3형식, ⑤ 4형식

〈서술형 평가〉

47 주절이 긍정이면 부가의문문은 부정, 주절이 부정이면 부가의문문은 긍정이다. 주절의 동사와 형태 및 시제를 일치 시켜 사용한다.

48 만일 네가 어려운 사람을 돕는다면, 그들은 너에게 고마워 할 것이다. → 어려운 사람을 도와라, 그러면 그들은 너에게 고마워 할 것이다. 'if'문장을 명령문으로 바꿀 때 긍정의 의미를 가지면 'and'를 사용 한다

49 만일 너가 정크푸드만을 먹는다면, 너는 뚱뚱하고 약해질 것이다. → 정크푸드만 먹지 말아라, 그렇지 않으면 너는 뚱뚱하고 약해질 것이다. 'if'문장을 명령문으로 바꿀 때 부정의 의미를 가지면 'or'를 사용한다.

50 일반동사의 부정문은 'do/does+not+동사원형'의 형태이다.

51 be동사의 의문문은 be동사를 문장의 제일 앞에 놓는다.

52 'Let's'의 부정형은 바로 뒤에 'not'을 붙여준다.

53 'What'의 감탄문이다. 'What+a(n)+형용사+명사+주어+동사'

54 주어인 'The roses'가 복수형이므로, 동사에 변화가 필요없다. smells → smell

55 나는 치타를 아주 많이 좋아한다. 그들은 제일 빠른 동물이다. 그들은 강한 다리를 가지고 있다. 치타의 대부분은 아프리카에 산다.

56 3형식의 문장을 4형식으로 전환할 때, 문장 끝의 전치사구에서 전치사는 생략하고 목적어가 동사 뒤로 간다.

57 4형식의 문장을 3형식으로 전환할 때, 간접목적어는 전치사와 함께 문장의 제일 끝으로 간다. 'bring'의 전치사는 'to'이다.

58 5형식의 문장으로 '주어+동사+목적어+목적격보어'의 형태이다. 주어인 Mr. Brown이 먼저 나오고, 그 뒤를 이어 동사 makes, 목적어 us, 그리고 목적격보어의 역할을 하는 laugh 순으로 배열한다.

59 'Let's'명령문의 부가의문문은 긍정/부정에 상관없이 'shall we?'를 사용한다.

60 일반 명령문의 부가의문문은 긍정/부정에 상관없이 'will you?'를 사용한다.

Chapter 02 동사의 시제

Lesson 2-1 일반동사 3인칭 단수 (1)

Check up! p. 065~066

A	1	am	2	is
	3	are	4	are
	5	is		
B	1	asks	2	stands
	3	cleans	4	reads
	5	agrees	6	meets
	7	finds	8	wears
	9	sits	10	knows
	11	reaches	12	wishes
	13	teaches	14	arrives
	15	misses	16	dresses
	17	passes	18	goes
	19	brushes	20	has
C	1	wants	2	wears
	3	mix	4	draws
	5	help	6	touches
	7	does	8	takes
	9	passes	10	catches

Lesson 2-2 일반동사 3인칭 단수 (2)

Check up! p. 067

A	1	envies	2	lays
	3	hurries	4	flies
	5	says	6	copies
	7	cries	8	marries
	9	stays	10	obeys
	11	pays	12	dries
	13	worries	14	supplies
B	1	brings	2	worry
	3	makes	4	fly
	5	carries	6	wakes
	7	studies	8	tries

Lesson 2-3 일반동사 현재형

Check up! p. 068~069

A	1	watches	2	get
	3	misses	4	reads
	5	look	6	makes
	7	goes	8	deserves
	9	has	10	calls
B	1	taste	2	walks
	3	cry	4	goes
	5	writes	6	rises/sets
	7	is	8	changes
	9	makes	10	fall
	11	say	12	tries
	13	make	14	has
	15	sends		

Lesson 2-4 현재진행형

Check up! p. 071

A	1	calling	2	drawing
	3	waiting	4	flying
	5	entering	6	writing
	7	bringing	8	saving
	9	cutting	10	beginning
B	1	is reading	2	is pouring
	3	is standing	4	am sending
	5	is making		

C
1 Are birds flying
2 She isn't (is not) making
3 Is he using
4 We aren't (are not) drawing
5 They aren't (are not) building
6 The flowers aren't (are not) blooming

Lesson 2-5 현재형과 현재진행형

Check up! p. 072

A	1	drinks	2	goes
	3	are singing	4	am writing
	5	like	6	are dancing
	7	reads	8	practice

Practice More I p. 073~075

A	1	③	2	⑤
	3	③	4	①
	5	②	6	①
B	1	looks	2	keep
	3	knows	4	rains
	5	is coming	6	has
	7	are not drawing	8	likes
	9	goes	10	are not practicing
C	1	goes	2	plays
	3	rides	4	gets up
	5	tries	6	am leaving (leave)
	7	is buying	8	visit
	9	is planning (plans)	10	is teaching

D
1 going → are going
2 take → are taking
3 is going → goes
4 looks → is looking
5 is writing → are writing
6 is belonging → belongs
7 is walking → walks
8 am remembering → remember
9 are speaking → speak
10 is having → are having

E	1	is / helping	2	is / taking
	3	drink	4	are having
	5	sets		

서술형연습

F
1 Isabella is laughing at me.
2 Kim is sitting next to Robert.
3 I am looking for my glasses now.
4 He goes to school at 8:30 in the morning.
5 She is not talking on the phone now.

Lesson 2-6 be동사 과거형

Check up! p. 078

A	1	was	2	were
	3	Were/were	4	were not
	5	Was/was not		
B	1	wasn't(was not)	2	Were/were
	3	Were/weren't(were not)	4	was
	5	Was/wasn't(was not)	6	Were
	7	were	8	Were/were

Lesson 2-7 일반동사의 과거형_규칙동사 변화

Check up! p. 079~080

A	1	stopped	2	raised
	3	discussed	4	happened
	5	talked	6	lived
	7	shopped	8	answered
	9	worried	10	cleaned
	11	hugged	12	planned
	13	hopped	14	worked
	15	played	16	escaped
	17	cooked	18	studied
	19	invented	20	served
B	1	Did/work	2	did not(didn't) live
	3	did not(didn't) play	4	Did/buy
	5	Did/study		
	6	did not (didn't) think		
	7	Did/have	8	did not (didn't) fall
	9	did not (didn't) draw	10	Did/show

Lesson 2-8 일반동사의 과거형_불규칙동사 변화

Check up! p. 084

A
1 spread→spread 2 cost→cost
3 read→read 4 caught→caught
5 burnt(burned)→burnt(burned)
6 found→found 7 held→held
8 fed→fed 9 kept→kept
10 made→made 11 meant→meant
12 slid→slid 13 stood→stood
14 thought→thought 15 put→put
16 dreamed(dreamt)→dreamed(dreamt)
17 sat→sat 18 told→told
19 won→won 20 was/were→been
21 wore→worn 22 slept→slept
23 laid→laid 24 bore→born
25 began→begun 26 bit→bitten
27 woke→woken 28 rode→ridden
29 ran→run 30 grew→grown

Lesson 2-9 과거진행형

Check up! p. 085~086

A
1 were flying 2 were enjoying
3 was making 4 was digging
5 was laying 6 were singing
7 was writing

B
1 Was/running
2 Was/caring
3 Was/looking
4 wasn't (was not) having
5 wasn't (was not) listening
6 wasn't (was not) speaking
7 Was/asking
8 weren't (were not) crossing
9 was/watering
10 wasn't(was not) lying

C
1 We weren't (were not) watching TV.
2 They were studying for the test at that time.
3 Was she swimming in the pool?

Practice More Ⅱ

p. 087~089

A
1 did 2 spread
3 sang 4 studied
5 ate 6 meant
7 kept 8 burnt(burned)
9 spoke 10 wore

B
1 was 2 were
3 was 4 was
5 were 6 went
7 left 8 cooked
9 thought 10 brought

C
1 She did not (didn't)
2 Did Helen like
3 Jack did not (didn't) finish
4 I was not (wasn't)
5 Did Jane run
6 Did she leave China
7 The concert was not (wasn't)
8 Did he come
9 Did they sleep
10 Joe and Helen were not (weren't)

D
1 Did/they/didn't 2 Was/she was
3 Did/didn't 4 Was/he was
5 Did/she didn't 6 Were/we weren't

E
1 was playing computer games
2 were reading the newspaper
3 was washing his car
4 watched a movie
5 did my homework
6 brought a loaf of bread

F
1 Was
2 moved
3 was having
4 was not
5 were going (went)
6 stayed
7 practiced
8 enjoyed

서술형연습

G 1 Was / taking a nap
2 Was / playing tennis
3 did not(didn't) study
4 Was not(wasn't) sleeping
5 did not(didn't) play

Lesson 2-10 will / be going to

Check up!

p. 091~092

A 1	be	2	will play
3	will not	4	is not
5	going to	6	aren't going to
7	going to		

B 1 am going to run
2 will go
3 is going to meet
4 will take part
5 are going to wake
6 is not going to have (will not have)
7 will take a shower
8 aren't(are not) going to be
9 Will

C 1	going to/we are	2	Will/will
3	Is/going to/she is	4	is not going to
5	will not		

Lesson 2-11 현재형의 미래표현

Check up!

p. 093

A 1	is	2	play
3	arrives	4	leave
5	is doing	6	are visiting
7	are going to	8	are
9	read	10	will

Practice More Ⅲ

p. 094~096

A 1 am going to go
2 is going to visit
3 is going to snow / will make
4 are going to
5 are going to tell
6 is going to have a date
7 will
8 are going to be back
9 is going to be
10 are going to play

B 1	help	2	be
3	carry	4	go
5	will arrive		

C 1	is → will	2	drinks → drink
3	makes → make		
4	go → going (is → will)		
5	doing → do	6	starts → start
7	stayed → stay	8	painting → paint
9	going → go (will → is)	10	starts → start

D 1	leaves	2	coming
3	love	4	arrives
5	help	6	tell

서술형 연습

E 1 Sam will lead the soccer team this year.
2 Minsu and Jihye are going to quit the band
3 The news won't(will not) make him happy.
4 The bad rumor isn't going to spread all over the world.

F 1 will go/is
2 is going to leave
3 will/watch
4 am going to read
5 arrives/will not miss
6 will cancel/rains
7 is going to start
8 will call/find
9 will help(is going to help)
10 are you going to meet

중간 기말고사 **예상문제**

내신 최다 출제 유형

p. 097

01 ③	02 ③	03 ①,④	04 ④	05 ③, ⑤
06 ②				

해설

01 형용사인 'nice'가 그 앞의 'history teacher'를 보충 설명하는 문장으로 동사는 be동사가 와야 한다. Does → Is

02 Jacky는 3인칭 단수이므로 does 가 와야 한다. Do → Does

03 ① 'Everything'은 해석은 '모든'이지만 단수 취급을 하기 때문에 be동사 'is'가 와야한다.
④ 'your teacher'은 단수 이므로 동사 역시 단수동사를 사용해야 한다. Are → Is

04 ① have, ② went, ③ studied, ⑤ read(read는 현재형과 과거형의 형태가 같다.)

05 ① played, ② enjoyed, ④ bought

06 ①,③,④,⑤는 모두 일반 동사이다. be동사와 일반동사는 함께 쓰일 수 없다. ② 'be동사+동사-ing'의 형태로 현재진행형이다

p. 098~104

01 ④	02 ②	03 ④	04 ④	05 ③
06 ⑤	07 ③	08 ①	09 ④	10 ③
11 ③	12 ④	13 ⑤	14 ③	15 ⑤
16 ④	17 ③	18 ②	19 ③,④	20 ②,⑤
21 ③	22 ⑤	23 ⑤	24 ⑤	25 ①
26 ④	27 ③	28 ②,④	29 ②,④	30 ③
31 ④	32 ③	33 ④	34 ②	35 ①
36 ①,③	37 ③	38 ③	39 ②	40 ④

〈서술형 평가〉

41 are going to
42 will not
43 ① are going to, ② are climbing
44 ① see → saw, ② takes → took
45 she was walking along the river
46 (1) No, she doesn't, (2) It's a bird.
47 Dan is going on a picnic next Tuesday.
48 She didn't bring any money at all.
49 We were studying English for the final exam.
50 She will leave for Singapore tomorrow.
51 Tom and I go to school on foot every day.

해설

01 watch → watches

02 play → plays

03 wash → washes

04 lay의 과거형은 'laid'이다. 'lain'은 lie의 과거분사형이다.

05 feed의 과거형은 'fed'이다. feed는 과거형과 과거분사형이 같은 불규칙 동사형이다. 'feed - fed - fed'의 형태로 변화한다

06 ride의 과거형은 'rode'이다. ride는 원형과 과거, 과거분사형이 모두 다른 불규칙 동사형으로 'ride - rode - ridden'의 형태로 변한다.

07 'played'와 'went'가 과거 동사이므로 과거를 나타내는 부사 'last week'가 정답이다.

08 첫 번째 문장: 'next week'가 오는 것으로 보아 시제가 미래임을 알 수 있다. 두 번째 문장: 부사절에 현재형 동사를 쓰는 것으로 보아 시제가 미래임을 알 수 있다. 그러므로 will이 정답이다.

09 ⓐ 일반동사의 과거형 의문문에서 'did+주어' 다음에는 동사원형이 온다. ⓑ last week로 보아 과거 시제이므로 동사의 과거형이 온다. ⓒ 일반동사 과거형의 부정문에서 didn't 뒤에는 동사원형이 온다.

10 '단모음+단자음'으로 끝나는 동사는 마지막 자음을 한 번 더 써서 진행형을 만든다. 'winning'이 옳은 형태이다.

11 과거 부사 'last week'를 통해 과거 시제임을 알 수 있다. 과거 동사인 ③ went to가 정답이다

12 현재시제는 습관, 반복되는 사건 등을 나타낼 때 쓸 수 있다. 'every day'를 통해 매일의 습관임을 알 수 있으므로 빈칸에는 현재시제인 ④sleep이 와야 한다.

13 일반 동사 과거형 의문문으로 긍정의 대답일 경우 'Yes, 주어+did'로 답한다.

14 ③ 'be going to' 질문형은 대답을 'be going to'로 답해야 한다. 질문의 주어가 'you' 이므로 대답의 주어는 'I'가 와야 한다. 그러므로 'I'm going to go picnic with father'가 답이 된다. ①,④ 의문사로 시작하는 의문문은 Yes나 No로 대답할 수 없다.

15 과거 부사 last year가 왔으므로 시제가 과거임을 알 수 있다. 그러므로 1인칭 be동사 'am'의 . 과거형인 was가 와한다.

16 ①,②,③,⑤ 본동사를 보조하는 조동사로 쓰였으며 아무런 뜻이 없다. ④ 일반 동사 '~하다'의 뜻을 가진다.

17 ③ have: 첫번째 문장 : 먹다, 두번째 문장: 'the time'은 '시계'의 의미로 쓰였다. 직역을 하면 '시계를 가지고 있습니까?'가 되고 즉, 몇 시냐는 의미의 표현이 된다.

18 'play+the 악기이름', 'play+운동'

19 ③ uses → use (주어가 복수형태), ④ going → go (부사 on Sundays는 일요일마다의 뜻으로 반복적인 일상생활에 대한 표현)

20 ② is → are, ⑤ is comes → comes(또는 is coming)

21 일반동사 과거형 부정문: did not+동사원형

22 일반동사 과거형 의문문: Did+주어+동사원형~?

23 현재진행형: be동사(am, are, is)+동사-ing

24 (A) 조동사+동사원형, (B) 'Will'에 대한 대답은 'will'로 한다.

25 (A) be동사 과거+동사-ing (과거진행형)
(B) 'Were'에 대한 대답은 'were'로 한다.

26 ①,②,③,⑤ 미래형 'be going to' ~할 것이다, ④ 현재 진행형 'is going to' ~로 가고 있는 중이다

27 ①,②,④,⑤ 미래의 뜻을 가진 부사와 함께 쓰여 가까운 미래를 표현, ③ 일상생활의 반복을 표현

28 ②,④ 동사가 과거형이므로 부사 역시 과거형태를 사용한다.

29 ②,④ 동사가 현재진행형인데, 미래를 뜻하는 부사와 쓰여 가까운 미래를 표현한 문장 이다.

30 ③ 'were'로 대답을 하였으며, 주어가 복수이다. 주어 'we'로 대답할 수 있는 질문에는 'you'가 들어가야 한다.

31 ④ 'did'로 대답을 하였으며, 주어가 복수이다. 주어 'they'로 대답할 수 있는 질문에는 'I, you'가 들어갈 수 없다.

32 ③ 미래형 'be going to+동사원형', ①,②,④,⑤는 현재진행형 문장이다.

33 ④ 단순 과거형, ①,②,③,⑤는 과거진행형 문장이다.

34 '고치다-fix'는 일반동사이다. 일반동사 부정문은 '주어+did not+동사원형'

35 주절은 과거진행형, 부사절은 과거형이다. (when 이하 문장을 부사절이라 한다.)

36 ① was meeting → met,
③ drink some coke → drank some coke

37 ③ 미래형에 쓰이는 동사: will, be going to

38 ③ 미래형에 쓰이는 동사: will, be going to
→ '현재진행형 + 미래형 부사어'로도 미래를 표현할 수 있다.

39 ① tomorrow → 미래를 뜻하는 단어, 삭제
③ to playing → to play, ④ yesterday → 과거형 단어, 삭제
⑤ Does → Do

40 ④ were bringing → are bringing

〈서술형 평가〉

41 'will'과 'be going to'는 미래시제를 나타내는 조동사로 사용할 수 있다.

42 현재진행형 문장 뒤에 미래를 뜻하는 부사어가 오면 가까운 미래를 뜻한다. 미래를 나타내는 표현의 부정형으로 'will+not'을 사용할 수 있다.

43 ① 'be going to' 미래형 조동사,
② 현재진행형 + 미래형 부사: 미래를 뜻함

44 ① 함께 속해있는 부사절의 동사가 과거형이므로, 주절의 동사도 과거형으로 한다.
② 함께 속하는 'and'이하 접속절 문장이 과거형이므로 시제를 일치시켜준다.

45 과거진행형: be동사 과거(was, were)+동사-ing

46 (1) 'Yes/No' question의 대답은 질문의 주어와 동사를 일치시켜 답한다.
(2) 'Wh-' question은 'yes/no'로 대답할 수 없다.

47 현재진행형: be동사(am, are, is)+동사-ing

48 과거형 부정문: 주어+did not+동사원형

49 과거진행형: be동사 과거(was, were)+동사-ing

50 '~로 떠나다' leave for(+장소)

51 'every day'매일

Chapter

03 조동사

Lesson 3-1 조동사의 종류와 역할

Check up! p. 108

A
1 swim
2 go
3 eat
4 do
5 stop
6 come
7 pay
8 accept
9 get
10 suggest

B
1 snow
2 will be able to
3 make
4 Alex study
5 may not
6 not
7 go
8 are going to
9 draw
10 had

Lesson 3-2 미래형 will

Check up! p. 109

A
1 will go
2 will make
3 will send
4 will do
5 will have
6 will finish
7 will have
8 will participate

Lesson 3-3 will의 부정문과 의문문

Check up! p. 110

A
1 Mr. Han will not (won't) go to school.
2 Will she bring some delicious cookies for Jane?
3 My teacher will not (won't) be upset because of Tom.
4 Will this robot clean the floors?
5 Helen will not (won't) buy a cup of coffee.
6 Jenny will take a test next week
7 Will Steven practice soccer harder?
8 They will go to Africa to help sick people.

Lesson 3-4 미래형 be going to

Check up! p. 111~112

A
1 will not
2 will
3 will
4 are going to
5 is not going to

B
1 am going to draw / next week.
2 is not going to write / tomorrow
3 are going to take / today
4 is not going to bring / tonight
5 are going to join / next semester

C
1 she isn't (is not)
2 Are / going to / are
3 are going to
4 going to / am not('m not)
5 is going to

Practice More I

p. 113~115

A
1 watch
2 go
3 swim
4 wash
5 have
6 bark
7 come
8 writes
9 study
10 remember

B
1 I will make pizza for my family.
2 Sam will go hiking with his brother.
3 He will finish his project.
4 Jinju will travel all around the world this year.
5 My grandmother will go there.
6 Daniel and you are going to visit Japan on a tour.
7 The library is going to be closed during the summer vacation.
8 I am going to go to John's birthday party
9 Mom is going to buy a new coffee machine.
10 Phillip is going to sing a song from The Phantom of the Opera.

C
1 Will Mary tell her brother an interesting story?
2 I am not going to practice tennis every weekend.

3 He will not watch the baseball game tonight.
4 Are they going to leave Busan tomorrow?
5 She will not stay here for a few days.

D 1 not is going to → is not going to
2 wants → want
3 moving → move
4 wills → will
5 be rain → rain
6 goes → go
7 to give → give
8 writing → to write
9 Does → Is
10 is held → be held

서술형 연습

E 1 I will make a chocolate cake tomorrow.
2 They will play soccer this Sunday.
3 Linda isn't going to make lunch for us.
4 Will you be there tonight?
5 Sam will become a great scientist in the future.

F 1 Denny는 다음 학기에 우리 독서 동아리에 가입할 것이다.
2 나는 다음 주에 해리 포터 역에 오디션을 볼 것이다
3 Mr. Moon은 오늘 오지 않을 예정이다.
4 너희 가족은 다음 달에 서울로 이사를 갈거니?

Lesson 3-5 can

Check up!

p. 117

A 1 making → make
2 cans → can
3 to play → play
4 discussed → discuss
5 plays → play

B 1 나를 도와 주시겠습니까?
2 Jack은 친구를 아주 잘 사귄다.
3 그들은 이제 답안지를 제출해도 된다.
4 우리는 그곳에 걸어서 갈 수 있습니까?
5 오늘 밤에 TV를 봐도 되나요?

Lesson 3-6 can의 부정문

Check up!

p. 118

A 1 can't 2 can
3 can't 4 can
5 can't 6 can't

B 1 Monkeys cannot (can't) swing the branches.
2 They cannot (can't) go up the mountain.
3 Children cannot (can't) run here and there all day.
4 An ant cannot (can't) hold up heavy things.

Lesson 3-7 can의 의문문

Check up!

p. 119

A 1 speak 2 can
3 can 4 can't
5 Can/can't

B 1 Can / park / you can't
2 Can / borrow / you can
3 Can / go / I can't
4 Can / play / he can / can
5 Can / turn / I can

Lesson 3-8 be able to

Check up!

p. 120~121

A 1 am not able to
2 is able to
3 are able to
4 is not(isn't) able to
5 are not(aren't) able to
6 is able to
7 Are / able to
8 is not(isn't) able to
9 Are / able to
10 are not(aren't) able to

B 1 playing → play 2 are → is
3 able not → not able 4 using → use
5 ables → is able 6 is → are
7 runs → run 8 not are → are not
9 helped → help 10 does → is

Lesson 3-9 be able to의 과거와 미래

Check up! p. 122

A
1 was able to
2 was not(wasn't) able to
3 will be able to
4 will not(won't) be able to
5 was able to
6 Were / able to

Lesson 3-10 could

Check up! p. 123~124

A
1 ride a bike / could not(couldn't)
2 could / play badminton

B
1 could
2 play
3 Could
4 not eat
5 can
6 could not
7 have
8 could not
9 fix
10 go

Lesson 3-11 may

Check up! p. 125~126

A
1 추측 2 허가
3 허가 4 추측
5 추측 6 허가
7 추측 8 추측
9 허가 10 추측

B
1 may be 2 may rain
3 may go/play 4 may use
5 may be 6 may come
7 may leave 8 may be
9 may play 10 may eat
11 may be 12 may take
13 may get 14 may go
15 may jog

Lesson 3-12 may의 부정문과 의문문

Check up! p. 128

A
1 May I 2 go
3 may not 4 tell
5 use 6 May
7 may not 8 throw

B
1 May / take 2 may go
3 may not solve 4 may not watch
5 May / ask 6 may not come
7 May / introduce 8 May / buy
9 may not sit 10 May / speak

Practice More Ⅱ p. 129~131

A
1 am able to 2 can't
3 were able to 4 was not able to
5 is able to 6 are able to
7 was able to 8 Are/able to
9 was able to 10 isn't able to

B
1 cans → can
2 has → have
3 to go → go
4 will can → will be able to (will/can)
5 ate → eat
6 plays → play
7 speaking → speak
8 may can → may (can)
9 is able to → are able to
10 reading→ read

C
1 Can I borrow some books?
2 He may not go there because of his sister.
3 Seon is not able to go hiking with his father.
4 Is Mary able to drive a car?
5 My sister could not make kimchi.
6 Can you bring some cookies?
7 He may not go to the airport tonight.
8 Could they borrow some pens?
9 She is not able to go home early.
10 I can't cook well.

D 1 ④ 2 ①
3 ③ 4 ④

서술형연습

E 1 I was not able to buy the car.
2 They could go to the concert yesterday.
3 May I close the door?
4 She was not able to move the furniture alone.

C 1 She must not hit animals.
2 Must men wear a black hat tonight?
3 You must not eat too much.
4 You must be kind to your friends.
5 He must not laugh at us.
6 We must save energy.
7 They must be comedians.

Lesson 3-13 must

Check up! p. 133~134

A 1 must be 2 must move
3 must find 4 must keep
5 must be 6 must come back
7 must be

B 1 obeys → obey 2 turning → turn
3 studying → study 4 have → has
5 being → be 6 is → be
7 hide → hiding

C 1 They must be honest.
2 You must not play now.
3 She must be a nurse.
4 We must not cross the street
5 I must finish my homework

Lesson 3-14 must의 부정문과 의문문

Check up! p. 135~136

A 1 O 2 X
3 O 4 X
5 X

B 1 must not 2 Must
3 must not 4 Must
5 must not

Lesson 3-15 have to

Check up! p. 137~138

A 1 have to 2 have to
3 has to 4 have to
5 has to 6 have to
7 has to 8 has to
9 have to 10 has to

B 1 has → have
2 practicing → practice
3 has → have
4 helped → help
5 studied → study
6 has → have
7 have → has
8 stopped → to stop
9 has → have
10 have → has

Lesson 3-16 have to의 부정문과 의문문

Check up! p. 139

A 1 don't 2 Do
3 don't 4 have to take
5 doesn't have 6 have
7 doesn't 8 go

Lesson 3-17 should

Check up! p. 140

A 1 must 2 should
3 should 4 should
5 have to 6 should
7 should 8 should

Lesson 3-18 should의 부정문과 의문문

Check up! p. 141~142

A 1 should 2 should not
3 should 4 be
5 go 6 not join
7 should 8 cut
9 throw 10 should not

B 1 ⓒ 2 ⓐ
3 ⓓ 4 ⓑ

C 1 Should I take off my hat here?
2 You should not make excuses for your mistake.
3 Should I move the mouse here?
4 Tyler should not spend too much money.

Practice More Ⅲ p. 143~145

A 1 의무 2 추측
3 조언 4 의무
5 불필요 6 금지
7 추측 8 금지
9 불필요 10 의무

B 1 has to → have to
2 don't → doesn't
3 Do I should → Should I
4 doesn't → don't
5 Do you must → Must you (Do you have to)
6 must be → must
7 not should → should not
8 tell not → not tell
9 following → follow
10 has to → have to

C 1 don't have to finish
2 Do/have to get up
3 don't have to find
4 should go
5 must not throw
6 should not play soccer
7 must be

D 1 그들은 내일 아침 일찍 일어나야 한다.
2 나는 일기를 써야만 하는데, 그것이 숙제이기 때문이다.
3 그녀는 그 일을 금요일까지 끝낼 필요가 없다.
4 우리는 영어 말하기 대회에 참가해야만 한다.
5 나는 학생들이 그들의 미래를 위해 열심히 공부해야 한다고 생각한다.

서술형 연습

E 1 must, have to
2 doesn't have to, doesn't need to, need not
3 should

F 1 Does she have to buy the doll for her daughter?
2 Jane and Kate don't have to go to the hospital.
3 Should I take care of them?
4 They should not buy the green chair
5 John mustn't (must not) exercise regulary.

Lesson 3-19 must not과 don't have to의 차이

Check up! p. 147~148

A 1 don't have to 2 must not
3 doesn't have to 4 must not
5 don't have to 6 doesn't have to
7 must not 8 don't have to
9 must not 10 must not

B 1 don't → doesn't
2 getting → to get
3 doesn't → don't
4 studying → study
5 going → go
6 cleaned → clean
7 has → have

8 doesn't must → must not
9 don't must → don't have
10 have not → doesn't have

Lesson 3-20 should / have to / must

Check up!

p. 149

A
1 must
2 should
3 must
4 don't have to
5 should
6 must
7 should not
8 have to
9 must not
10 have to

Lesson 3-21 had better

Check up!

p. 150

A
1 have → had
2 wearing → wear
3 to take → take
4 has → had
5 not better → better not
6 listened → listen
7 are → X

Lesson 3-22 would like (to)

Check up!

p. 151

A
1 Would / like
2 would like to
3 wants
4 would like
5 wants to
6 would like to
7 Does / want to

Practice More IV

p. 152~154

A
1 don't have to
2 would like to
3 must
4 would like
5 don't have to
6 had better
7 had better not
8 should
9 should

B
1 don't have to eat
2 must not enter
3 should visit
4 doesn't have to go
5 must not hit
6 must be
7 don't have to prepare
8 should exchange
9 must not listen
10 doesn't have to read

C
1 Would you like to go
2 had better not plant
3 don't have to repair
4 have to follow
5 had better go
6 need not (don't need to)

D
1 going → go
2 has → had
3 chages → change
4 to buy → buy
5 are → X
6 could → would
7 change → to change

서술형연습

E
1 should exchange it for
2 had better take a rest
3 don't have to buy
4 have to finish
5 had better hurry up
6 has to go shopping
7 don't have to eat
8 would like to start

중간 기말고사 **예상문제**

내신 최다 출제 유형 p. 155

01 ② 02 ② 03 ⑤ 04 ①,⑤ 05 ③
06 ②

해설

01 조동사 will 다음에는 동사원형이 온다. (주어의 인칭 변화 없음) ① has → have, ③ does → do, ④ goes à go, ⑤ swimming → swim

02 will 다음에는 동사원형이 온다. (주어의 인칭 변화 없음) ① 조동사는 2개가 나란히 올 수 없다.③ 조동사 뒤에는 동사원형이 온다. ④ 2명일 경우 동사는 복수 동사로 바꿔주어야 한다. ⑤ when절이 과거형인데 반해, 주절은 현재진행형이다.

03 ①,④ 요청 – ~해 줄까요, ②,③ 허락 – ~해도 될까요, ⑤ 가능/능력을 의미 – ~할 수 있다

04 ①, ⑤ – 조동사 뒤에는 동사원형이 와야 한다.
② didn't가 바뀐 형태이므로 뒤의 동사는 원형이 와야 한다.
③ It means 'a cute person.'
④ 조동사 can의 뒤에는 동사원형 'be'가 와야 한다.

05 첫 번째 빈칸에는 허락을 뜻하는 'may' 또는 'can'이 와야 한다. 두 번째는 건물 앞에 주차 하는 것을 금지 하고 있기 때문에 'must not'이 알맞다.

06 ② will 뒤에는 동사원형이 온다.

p. 156~163

01 ⑤	02 ①	03 ⑤	04 ②	05 ⑤
06 ③	07 may	08 will	09 can	10 ①
11 ②	12 ⑤	13 ④	14 ②	15 ①
16 ②	17 ③,④	18 ①,④	19 ③	20 ④
21 ③	22 ③	23 ④	24 ③,⑤	25 ⑤
26 ④	27 ②	28 ④	29 ②	30 ④
31 ③	32 ②,④	33 ①,③	34 ①,④	35 ④,⑤
36 ①	37 ③	38 ②	39 ②,⑤	40 ②
41 ③				

〈서술형 평가〉

42 are able to 43 ⓐ can ⓑ can't ⓒ can
44 They can't jump high
45 Kelly would like to drink some orange juice.
46 Mr. Brown speaks so fast and I can't understand at all.
47 Paul will give her a hand.
48 She must be a famous actress.
49 He may not remember me.
50 Sumi didn't want to go there.
51 We stayed up late last night/We weren't tired
52 He got first prize.
53 Jessy was able to jump high when she was young. / We are able to sing a song at the band
54 He may be a gentle man. / You may not leave here before you finish your work.
55 Students must follow the rules of the school. / They must not laugh at other children.

해설

01 'I'm sorry'는 미안한 감정을 나타내는 표현으로 그 뒤의 문장에 대한 부정적인 의견에 대한 유감을 표시하므로, 알맞은 답은 cannot이다.

02 밖이 점점 어둑해 진다는 앞의 문장처럼 구름이 잔뜩 끼었으니 곧 비가 올 예정이란 것을 알 수 있다.

03 능력을 나타내는 표현은 조동사 can 이다.

04 도움을 줘도 괜찮겠냐는 것은 허락을 구하는 표현으로 'May I~' 또는 'Can I~'가 될 수 있다. (B) 의 대답은 원하는 색상의 사이즈를 찾을 수 없다는 표현이 되므로 'can't'을 써준다. 알맞은 답은 '② May – can't' 이다.

05 허락을 구하거나, 요청을 할 때 'May' 또는 'Can'을 사용할 있다. 질문과 대답의 동사가 일치해야 하므로 '⑤ can – can'이 알맞다.

06 ③ 무언가를 권유할 때는 주로 'would'를 사용한다. 'Would you~?'라고 물었을 때의 대답으로는 긍정일 경우 'Yes, I would.'로 할 수 있지만, 보다 정중한 표현으로 'Yes, please' 라고도 표현 할 수 있다.

07 '아마'라는 추측을 의미하는 단어는 may 이다.

08 '~할 것이다'의 미래 표현은 조동사 'will'을 사용한다.

09 '~할 수 있다'의 능력을 표현하는 것은 조동사 'can'을 사용한다.

10 ② 동사 'be'와 'play'는 원형으로 함께 올 수 없다.
③ 조동사 뒤에는 동사원형이 온다.
④ 'can' 대신 'is'가 와야 한다. 또는 'able to'를 뺀다.
⑤ 조동사 뒤에는 동사원형이 온다.

11 ① 조동사 뒤에는 동사원형이 온다. ③ 'could'가 이미 과거형으로 바뀌어 졌으니 뒤의 동사는 원형이 와야한다. ④ 'can't'와 'be able to' 모두 조동사 이므로 함께 쓰일 수 없다. She can't (또는 is able to) buy a new bag. ⑤ 'weren't'는 과거형이므로 미래를 나타내는 부사어 'tomorrow'가 오면 안 된다.

12 ①,②,③,④는 능력을 의미하는 '~할 수 있다'의 뜻이다. ⑤ '~해도 된다'는 뜻으로 허락을 의미한다.

13 ①,②,③,⑤는 '~해도 된다'는 허락을 의미하고, ④는 '~일 것이다'라는 추측을 의미한다.

14 ①,③,④,⑤는 '~해야 한다'의 강한 의무를 의미하고, ②는 '~임

이 틀림없다'라는 강한 추측을 의미한다.

15 '~할 예정이다'의 미래를 나타내는 표현은 'be going to'이다.

16 '~할 예정이다'의 미래를 나타내는 또 다른 표현은 'will'이다.

17 '~해도 될까요'라는 요청의 의미를 담고 있는 또 다른 표현으로 'Can / Could'를 사용할 수 있다. 'could'는 'can, may' 보다 조금 더 정중한 표현이다.

18 '~해야 한다'는 의무의 의미를 표현한다.

19 '~좀 하실래요 (해 주실래요)'의 권유를 표현할 때는 'would like+명사' 또는 'would like to+동사원형'을 사용한다.

20 '~하는 것이 낫겠다'의 충고 및 조언을 의미하는 표현은 'had better'를 사용한다. 'had better'뒤에는 동사원형이 온다.

21 무엇을 사고 싶냐는 질문에 약간의 치즈를 산다고 답하였다.

22 'Yes, I can.' 또는 'No, I can't.'로 답할 수 있다.

23 'Yes, I will.' 또는 'No, I won't.'로 답할 수 있다

24 ①,②,④, '~할 수 없다'의 불가능의 뜻이고, ③,⑤ '~하면 안된다'의 금지의 뜻으로 쓰였다.

25 ①,②,③,④ 는 허락이나 추측을 나타내는 'may'. ⑤나에게 꽃을 사주겠냐고 물어보는 문장으로 'will'이 들어가는 것이 알맞다.

26 숙제 하는 것을 도와달라 요청했는데, '너는 그것을 하면 안된다' 라는 답변은 어색하다.

27 'May I~?'의 질문에 대한 답으로 'No, I can't.'는 잘못된 응답이다.

28 '~을 할 수 없다'는 'can't'를 사용한다.

29 '~을 해야 한다'라는 의무를 표현하는 긍정문이기 때문에 'should'만 사용해야한다.

30 (a) 'must not' ~해서는 안된다' 금지의 뜻, (b) 'be careful' 조심하다, (c) 'Are – be able to' ~ 할 수 있다.

31 (a) 'have to' ~해야 한다 의무의 뜻 – 그들은 매번 손을 씻어야 한다. (b) 'will' ~할 것이다 – 우리는 약간의 사진을 찍을 것이다. → 조동사 뒤에는 동사원형 (c) 'would like to' ~하고 싶어하다– 당신은 오렌지 좀 드시겠어요? →'eat'이라는 동사원형이 왔으니 그 앞에는 'like to' 가 오는 것이 맞다.

32 ① be able to+동사원형, ③ could not+동사원형, ⑤ to add → add

33 ② could not+동사원형, ④ may not is → may not be, ⑤ will+동사원형

34 ① will+동사원형, ④ is not able speak → is not able to speak

35 ④ 주어가 'they'로 복수형이고, 'models'는 주어를 가리키는 주격보어로 복수형이다. 'a'를 뺀다. ⑤ 'could'는 과거형이고, when 절 역시 동사의 시제를 일치시켜야 하므로, is → was 가 알맞다.

36 'can't be' ~일리가 없다

37 'should' (~해야 한다)+동사원형 (be kind 친절하다)

38 'must be' ~임에 틀림없다

39 ⓑ were → are: 문장 끝에 'now'는 현재를 뜻하므로 be동사 현재형이 와야 한다. ⓔ likes → likes to: 한 문장에 동사가 두 개 나란히 올 수 없다.

40 윗 글에서 Jenny는 컴퓨터, 라디오, TV등을 수리할 수 있고, 또한 약간의 전기 제품도 만들 수 있다는 표현으로 봐서 그녀의 직업은 'engineer (기술자)' 가 알맞다.

41 had better ~하는 것이 낫겠다.

〈서술형 평가〉

42 'can' 과 바꾸어 쓸 수 있는 '~할 수 있다'의 다른 표현으로는 'be able to'를 사용할 수 있다.

43 ⓐ 앞 문장에서 캥거루는 세상에서 가장 점프를 잘 한다고 했기 때문에 'can'이 알맞으며, 'but'은 앞 뒤 문장이 서로 상반되는 뜻을 가지고 있는 접속사로서, 윗 글의 ⓒ는 원숭이의 특징을 잘 나타내주는 긍정의 의미가 되므로 그 와 반대인 ⓑ는 'can't' 가 알맞다.

44 우리말과 영어의 주어의 위치는 항상 문장의 제일 앞에 위치하게 된다. '주어+can't+동사원형…'의 순서로 영작한다.

45 'Kelly는 약간의 오렌지 주스를 마시고 싶어 한다.' '주어+would like to+동사원형+명사' 순으로 배열한다

46 Mr. Brown은 굉장히 빨리 말을 하고 나는 전혀 이해할 수 없다.

47 'will' ~할 것이다

48 'must be' ~임이 틀림없다

49 'may not' ~않을지도 몰라

50 일반동사 과거형의 부정문 이다. '주어+didn't+동사원형'의 순서대로 문장을 완성한다.

51 일반동사 과거형 문장과 be동사 과거형 부정문이다. be동사 부정형인 'weren't' 뒤에 형용사가 오도록 한다.

52 'get+서수+prize' ~번째 상을 타다

53
- I am able to 동사원형
- you, we, they, 사람 또는 사물 둘이상 are able to 동사원형
- he, she, it, 사람 또는 사물 하나 is able to 동사원형

위의 법칙을 잘 지켰는지, 동사원형이 알맞게 사용되었는지에 중점을 둔다.

54
- I, you, we, they, he, she, it, 사람(사물) 하나 또는 여러 개 may (not)+동사원형

동사원형이 알맞게 사용되었는지에 중점을 둔다.

55 I, you, we, they, he, she, it, 사람(사물) 하나 또는 여러 개 must (not)+동사원형
동사원형이 알맞게 사용되었는지에 중점을 둔다.

Chapter

04 명사와 관사

Lesson 4-1 명사의 종류

Check up! p. 167

A 셀 수 있는 명사

(1) cow, box, pencil, nurse, cup, computer, movie, actor, window

(2) family, cattle

셀 수 없는 명사

(1) love, hate

(2) Mary, Russia, Tim, John

(3) coffee, salt, bread

Lesson 4-2 명사의 복수형

Check up! p. 169~170

A 1	kites	2	eggs
3	hats	4	pens
5	nails	6	dishes
7	beaches	8	knives
9	oxen	10	heroes
11	oranges	12	umbrellas
13	subjects	14	apples
15	daughters	16	ladies
17	roofs	18	windows
19	parties	20	friends
21	teeth	22	sandwiches
23	rings	24	mice
25	men	26	baths
27	children	28	diaries
29	cookies	30	questions
31	flowers	32	shirts
33	ideas	34	bottles
35	beliefs	36	monkeys
37	toys	38	erasers
39	boats	40	mistakes

B 1	sheep	2	geese
3	numbers	4	legs
5	women	6	feet
7	factories	8	leaves
9	sports	10	hours
11	cliffes	12	fish
13	deer	14	problems
15	churches	16	days
17	pants	18	ducks
19	inches	20	branches
21	cakes	22	scarves
23	seasons	24	girls
25	radios	26	dictionaries
27	cars	28	babies
29	wives	30	blouses
31	keys	32	lives
33	cameras	34	Japanese
35	stories	36	butterflies
37	elephants	38	actresses
39	seeds	40	reports

Practice More I p. 171~173

A 1	X	2	a
3	a	4	X
5	X	6	an
7	a	8	a
9	an	10	X
11	X	12	an
13	X	14	X

B 1	companies	2	heroes
3	candies	4	dishes
5	echoes	6	keys
7	classes	8	mistakes
9	stories	10	bushes
11	moths	12	letters
13	boxes	14	phones
15	lives	16	safes
17	ideas	18	toys
19	baths	20	songs
21	churches	22	tomatoes
23	cups	24	zoos
25	brushes		

C 1 ② sheep – sheep
2 ③ child – children
3 ① ox – oxen
4 ⑤ clay – clays

D 1 money
2 coffee
3 Love
4 a cup
5 wisdom
6 monkeys
7 brushes
8 salt
9 daughters
10 axes

서술형 연습

E 1 three sons
2 water
3 three sheep and two cakes
4 five candies and three sandwiches
5 thirteen-year-old
6 five marbles / ten marbles
7 ten hotdogs
8 friendship
9 coffee
10 two lollipops

Lesson 4-3 주의해야 할 명사의 수량

Check up! p. 175~176

A 1 much
2 much
3 a few
4 a little
5 little
6 a little
7 little

B 1 much
2 some
3 a lot of / some
4 many
5 some
6 a lot of
7 any

C 1 much friends → many friends
2 any candy → some candies
3 a lot of fan → a lot of fans
4 Any thieves → Some thieves
5 many information → much information

Lesson 4-4 셀 수 없는 명사의 수량 표현

Check up! p. 177

A 1 two spoonfuls of
2 two pieces of / a cup of
3 a slice of
4 two bottles of / a bar of
5 three pieces of

Lesson 4-5 명사의 소유격

Check up! p. 178~179

A 1 Jim's dream
2 a dog's life span
3 woman's bathroom
4 king's crown
5 Plato's theory
6 Edison's invention
7 men's average height
8 teacher's ring
9 Socrates' words
10 Venus' love

B 1 today's
2 The legs of chair
3 The title of the novel
4 Lucas's wife
5 tomorrow's weather
6 wheels of the cart
7 a bird's wings
8 today's news
9 ten million dollars'
10 quality of the furtniture

Lesson 4-6 명사의 동격

Check up! p. 180

A
1 my niece
2 John
3 the tallest woman in our office
4 my best friend
5 a recently married couple
6 Harry Potter
7 Jessica
8 the most famous actor in Britain
9 Amy's letter
10 a rose

B
1 나의 가장 친한 친구인 Mary는 다음 달에 서울로 이사를 간다.
2 네가 어제 만났던 그 소녀가 바로 내 여동생 Emily였다
3 나의 역사 선생님이신 Mrs. Green은 항상 나를 격려해 주신다.
4 너는 그들 Isabella와 Jackson이 너의 좋은 친구들이라고 생각해?
5 너는 너의 여동생 Jessy와 함께 내 파티에 올것이니?

Practice More Ⅱ p. 181~183

A
1 many　2 a little
3 much　4 little
5 much　6 few
7 a few　8 few
9 much　10 a few

B
1 three cups of　2 a spoonful of
3 two pieces of　4 few
5 three pieces of / two pounds of
6 four bottles of　7 four slices of
8 My sister　9 little
10 one of the most famous actors in Korea

C
1 sheeps → sheep
2 waters → water
3 girl's → girls'
4 loafs → loaves
5 The desk's legs → The legs of the desk
6 your's → yours
7 glove → gloves
8 piece → pieces
9 Shes' → She's
10 name of the boy → the boy's name

서술형 연습

D
1 Linda ordered two glasses of juice.
2 She brought Mason's book.
3 I couldn't see today's news.
4 Dorothy brought her daughter's bags and glasses.
5 There are few books to read in the room.
6 The legs of the table are made from metal.

E
1 오늘의 날씨는 아주 덥다.
2 John은 자기 양말을 찾고 있다.
3 우리는 아이들의 건강을 돌봐야 한다.
4 나는 그 셔츠의 색깔이 싫다.

Lesson 4-7 부정관사 a / an

Check up! p. 185

A
1 a　2 an
3 an　4 a
5 a　6 a
7 a　8 an

Lesson 4-8 정관사 the

Check up! p. 186

A
1 the　2 the
3 an　4 the
5 the　6 a
7 a　8 the
9 The　10 the
11 a / a

Lesson 4-9 'the'가 쓰이지 않는 경우

Check up! p. 187

A 1 X 2 the
3 the 4 X
5 the 6 X
7 the 8 X
9 the 10 X
11 X 12 the
13 the 14 X
15 X

Practice More Ⅲ p. 188~190

A 1 the 2 An
3 the 4 a
5 the 6 an
7 a / the 8 the
9 the 10 the

B 1 France
2 school
3 the first
4 an old man
5 an apple
6 The girl
7 The chair
8 the piano
9 the smartest
10 The boys

C 1 an 2 X
3 X 4 the
5 the 6 a
7 the 8 the / X
9 A 10 X
11 a / The 12 the
13 X 14 the
15 The (A)

서술형 연습

D 1 Seoul is the capital of Korea.
2 Sally is an elementary school student.
3 Andrew is the best soccer player in our class.
4 My brother is good at playing the flute.
5 The rooms in the house are big.

E 1 나는 외동이다.
2 우리 사무실은 이 건물 4층에 있다.
3 Tom은 항상 아침을 먹는다.
4 나는 내 여자친구 에게 꽃을 주기 위해 교회에 갔다.
5 모든 사람들이 지구가 둥글다는 것을 알고 있다.

중간 기말고사 예상문제

내신 최다 출제 유형 p. 191

01 ④ 02 ②,④ 03 ④,⑤ 04 ① 05 ③,④
06 ③ 07 ④

해설

01 ① dresses → dress, ② brothers → sisters: 자매는 영어로 'sisters'라고 표현한다. ③ a MP3 → an MP3 : 알파벳 'm'은 자음이지만, 첫소리발음이 모음으로 시작하기 때문에 'an'을 붙여주는 것이 알맞다. ⑤ a pencils → a pencil

02 ①'water'은 셀 수 없는 명사이다. many → much
③ 'amimals and plants'는 셀 수 있는 명사 복수형이다. much → many (또는 a lot of) ⑤ 'paper'는 셀 수 없는 명사이다. many → much

03 ④ restaurants가 복수형이므로, 복수 동사 'Are there~?' 이라고 하는 것이 알맞다. ⑤ 'There isn't' 뒤에 또 'not'이 반복되는 부정형을 뺀다.

04 'sheep'의 복수형은 'sheep'이다.

05 'There are'는 셀 수 있는 명사의 복수형을 표현할 때 사용한다. 복수형 단어로는 'young men, children' 뿐이다.

06 ①,②,④,⑤의 'a'는 '하나의' 뜻으로 쓰였고, ③의 'a'만 종족을 대표하는 뜻으로 쓰였다.

07 운동경기 앞에는 관사를 사용하지 않는다.

p. 192~197

01 ②	02 ④	03 ③	04 ①	05 ⑤
06 ④	07 ⑤	08 ④	09 ④	10 ③
11 ③	12 ⑤	13 ⑤	14 ④	15 ③
16 ②	17 ①	18 ③	19 ④	20 ②,③
21 ①	22 ④	23 ①,⑤	24 ③,④	25 ①,④,⑤
26 ①	27 ③	28 ①	29 ①	30 ③
31 ⑤	32 ⑤	33 ③	34 ②	

〈서술형 평가〉

35 an old woman **36** a glass of water

37 once a week

38 She eats a bowl of mushroom soup every morning.

39 They eat two pieces of pizza and drink two cups of black tea.

40 They emphasized the importance of it

41 Jane and I went home by taxi

42 ⓐ a Australian → an Australian / ⓒ any chopped cucumber → some chopped cucumbers

43 a bottle of water

44 She comes from Australia.

45 three sheep, ten pounds of, milk

46 Jennifer washes her hands, teeth, and feet before dinner

47 I bought two packs of milk, three bottles of orange juice, and two bunches of grapes.

해설

01 photo – photos

02 belief – beliefs

03 goose – geese

04 monkey – monkeys

05 deer – deer

06 'milk'는 셀 수 없는 명사이므로 'many'와 함께 쓸 수 없다.

07 ⑤ 'skirt'는 단수 일 때 한 개, 복수일 때 두개, 세 개… 셀 수 있는 명사이다. ①,②,③,④ 는 단어 자체가 복수 형태이므로 한 개, 두개 셀 때는 앞에 반드시 수량을 표현하는 단위가 나와야 한다.

08 ④ loves of bread → (a) loaf of bread

09 ① benchs → benches, ② foots → feet, ③ heros → heroes, ⑤ gooses → geese

10 ① moneys → money, ② puppys → puppies, ④ waters → water, ⑤ boxs → boxes

11 'university'는 모음으로 시작하지만, 첫소리 발음이 '반자음'으로 시작하므로 'a'를 붙여준다.

12 운동경기 앞에는 'the'를 붙이지 않는다.

13 'uniform'은 모음으로 시작하지만, 첫 소리 발음이 '반자음'으로 시작하므로 'a'를 붙여준다.

14 악기 앞에는 정관사 'the'를 붙여준다.

15 'foot – feet'의 형태이다. → 길이의 단위로도 사용한다.

16 a bunches of roses → a bunch of roses

17 a piece of: bread, cheese, pizza등을 세는 단위이다.

18 a pound of: sugar, meat, pork, beef등을 세는 단위 이다.

19 집, 사무실, 상점 등을 나타내는 명사가 소유격 뒤에 오면 생략이 가능하다.

20 집, 사무실, 상점 등을 나타내는 명사가 소유격 뒤에 오면 생략이 가능하다.

21 ①'stars'는 셀 수 있는 명사의 복수형이므로 'much'가 아닌 'many'가 와야 한다.

22 'energy'는 셀 수 없는 명사이기 때문에 'many'가 아닌 'much'가 와야 한다.

23 ② 'some'과 'a pound of' 모두 명사의 수량을 나타내 주는 표현으로 함께 나란히 쓸 수 없다. ③ 'tea'는 셀 수 없는 명사이다. ④ 'This food'는 단수 형태이므로 단수 동사 'is'가 와야 한다.

24 ① 부정문에서는 'some'이 아닌 'any'를 사용한다. ② 'homework'는 셀 수 없는 명사이므로 'much'를 사용한다. ⑤ friend' → friend's : 어포스트로피를 찍을 때는 위치를 주의, 단수 명사일 경우 ['s]를 붙여야 한다.

25 ② 'books'는 셀 수 있는 명사의 복수형이므로, 동사로서 'are'가 나와야 한다. ③ 긍정문은 'some' 사용한다. ⑤ 'email'은 셀 수 없는 명사로서 's'를 붙이지 않는다.

26 friends's → friends' : –s로 끝나는 단어는 [']만 붙인다.

27 halfs → halves

28 a monkeys → monkeys: 부정관사 'a'와 복수명사 'monkeys'는 함께 쓸 수 없다.

29 ② a little → a few, ③ any → some, ④ much → many, ⑤ much → many

30 ① doctors's → doctor's, ② his's → his, ④ teachers → a teacher, ⑤ wents → went

31 ① sing → sings, ② play the hockey → play hockey ③ a Chinese → Chinese, ④ a him → him

32 ⑤ 'by+교통수단'에는 'the'를 붙이지 않는다.

33 'a lot of, lots of'는 셀 수 있는 명사와 셀 수 없는 명사 둘 모두 사용할 수 있다. 'money'는 셀 수 없는 명사로 'much'를, 'dishes'는 셀 수 있는 명사 복수형으로 'many'와 바꿔 쓸 수 있다.

34 Some students like reading books a little hard. 몇몇 학생은 조금 어려운 책을 읽는 것을 좋아한다. → 'a little' 수량이 아닌 정도의 의미에서 '조금'이라는 뜻으로 사용된다.

〈서술형 평가〉

35 old는 모음으로 시작하므로 an이 붙는다.

36 a glass of: water, milk, juice, 등의 수량표현이다.

37 'a'는 per (~마다)의 의미로도 사용 된다.

38 a bowl of: soup, rice의 수량표현이다.

39 a piece of: pizza, bread, paper등의 수량표현
a cup of: coffee, tea등의 수량표현

40 emphasize: 주장하다

41 교통수단(taxi) 이므로 관사를 붙이지 않는다.

42 '~나라 사람'을 이야기 할 때 개인일 경우 관사 'a / an'를 붙여준다.

43 a bottle of: water, ink, juice등의 수량표현이다.

44 come from ~출신이다

45 a pound of: cheese, sugar, meat등의 수량표현이다.
a bottle of: milk, beer, juice등의 수량표현이다.

46 tooth - teeth, foot - feet

47 two packs of milk (우유 두 팩), three bottles of orange juice (오렌지 주스 세 병), two bunches of grapes (포도 두 송이)

Chapter

05 대명사

Lesson 5-1 대명사의 종류

Check up! p. 202~203

A
1 mine
2 They
3 He
4 He
5 It
6 his
7 Our
8 us
9 hers
10 Its
11 his
12 He
13 She
14 hers
15 them

B
1 my
2 her
3 his
4 us
5 yours
6 its
7 ours
8 her
9 our
10 yours
11 Her
12 mine / them
13 their
14 Their
15 me

Lesson 5-2 재귀대명사

Check up! p. 204~205

A
1 himself
2 myself
3 herself
4 myself
5 himself
6 herself
7 yourself
8 himself
9 myself
10 themselves

B
1 O
2 O
3 X
4. X
5 X
6 O
7 O
8 X
9 X
10 O

C
1 himself / 재귀용법, 생략 불가능
2 herself / 강조용법, 생략 가능
3 yourself / 강조용법, 생략 가능
4 itself / 재귀용법, 생략 불가능
5 himself / 강조용법, 생략 가능

Lesson 5-3 비인칭 주어 'it'

Check up! p. 206

A
1 비인칭주어
2 대명사
3 비인칭주어
4 대명사
5 비인칭주어
6 비인칭주어
7 대명사

Lesson 5-4 지시대명사

Check up! p. 207

A
1 Those
2 This
3 This
4 That
5 these
6 This
7 Those
8 This
9 That
10 This

Practice More I

p. 208~210

A
1 your
2 Its
3 them
4 you
5 It's
6 These
7 Her
8 This
9 My
10 It
11 mine
12 They
13 This
14 yourself
15 himself

B
1 me
2 yours
3 my
4 His
5 himself
6 its
7 their
8 her
9 yours
10 him
11 myself
12 us
13 our
14 mine
15 themselves

C
1 This
2 those
3 These
4 That
5 This

서술형연습

D
1 It will be sunny tomorrow.
2 Look at that lady!
3 Cindy met him and his daughters
4 It's not your fault.
5 Linda worried about her test results
6 Steven likes that picture on the wall.
7 Did you make this pasta by yourself?
8 Let me introduce myself
9 That book isn't mine
10 I bought this car for Helen's family.

Lesson 5-5 부정대명사_one/another

Check up!

p. 212

A
1 one
2 one another
3 another
4 ones
5 another
6 ones
7 One/another
8 another
9 it

Lesson 5-6 부정대명사_others/the other(s)

Check up!

p. 213

A
1 others
2 the others
3 the other
4 the others
5 others
6 Some/others
7 the others

Lesson 5-7 부정대명사_some/any

Check up!

p. 214

A
1 Some
2 any
3 any
4 some
5 some
6 any
7 some
8 any
9 some
10 any
11 any
12 some

Lesson 5-8 부정대명사_each/every

Check up!

p. 215

A
1 men → man
2 classes → class
3 are → is
4 presents → present
5 go → goes
6 need → needs
7 nights → night
8 moments are → moment is
9 others → other
10 are → is

Lesson 5-9 부정대명사_-thing/-one/-body

Check up! p. 216~217

A
1 is
2 loves
3 is
4 are
5 something special
6 celebrates
7 calls
8 wants
9 Nothing
10 reads

B
1 anybody → somebody
2 something → anything
3 beautiful something → something beautiful
4 Non → None
5 Anybody → Somebody
6 No thing → Nothing
7 Anyone → Someone
8 anyone → someone
9 nothing → anything
10 Anyone → Everyone

Practice More Ⅱ p. 218~219

A
1 one
2 it
3 ones
4 It
5 One, the other (another)
6 another
7 One
8 Some/others
9 others
10 another

B
1 the others
2 others
3 the other
4 another
5 the others
6 Some/others
7 the others
8 One

C
1 anyone → someone
2 children → child
3 any → some
4 anything → something
5 have → has
6 No → None
7 Other → Others
8 ones → one

D
1 Some/others
2 Some/the others
3 One/the other
4 ones
5 one

Lesson 5-10 부정대명사_so/same/such

Check up! p. 221

A
1 so
2 so
3 such as
4 the same as
5 the same

Lesson 5-11 의문대명사

Check up! p. 222~223

A
1 Who
2 Who(m)
3 Whose
4 Who
5 Who(m)
6 Who
7 Whose
8 Who
9 Who(m)
10 Who

B
1 Which
2 What
3 What
4 Which
5 or
6 What
7 which
8 What
9 Which
10 What

C
1 의문형용사
2 주격
3 의문형용사
4 목적격
5 소유대명사

Lesson 5-12 타동사+대명사+부사 (이어동사)

Check up!

p. 225

A
1 up it → it up
2 to up → up
3 his baby for → for his baby
4 off him → him off
5 him for → for him
6 away it → it away
7 it at → at it
8 on it → it on
9 this position for → for this position
10 it about → about it
11 music to → to music
12 up him → him up
13 her idea to → to her idea
14 up them → them up
15 up it → it up
16 on it → it on
17 Suzie with → with Suzie
18 out it → it out
19 away them → them away
20 in it → it in

Practice More Ⅲ

p. 226~228

A
1 What
2 so
3 Whom
4 Which
5 turn it off
6 the
7 Whose
8 carry it out
9 the same as
10 such as

B
1 ⓓ
2 ⓐ
3 ⓒ
4 ⓔ
5 ⓑ
6 ⓙ
7 ⓘ
8 ⓗ
9 ⓖ
10 ⓕ

C
1 to → so
2 a → the
3 same → such
4 What → Which
5 Whose → Whom
6 same → such
7 What → Whose
8 her at → at her
9 such as→ same
10 turn in it → turn it in

서술형연습

D
1 Whom did you meet yesterday?
2 Whom does Jack talk to?
3 Do you like the same music genre as Kate?
4 Such was the teacher's explanation
5 He and I have the same car.
6 You don't throw it out the window.
7 Whose computer is this?
8 Sara put the appointment off.
(=Sara put off the appointment.)
9 Each of them bought some apples there.
10 Which food does Jenny eat for lunch?

E
1 Helen은 그를 배웅해야 하는 것을 잊었다.
2 너는 그 소문을 믿니?
3 너는 그 제안을 받아들여야 한다.
4 나는 그것들을 다 써버렸다
5 미래에 어떤 일을 하고 싶니?

중간 기말고사 예상문제

내신 최다 출제 유형

p. 229

01 ② 02 ⑤ 03 ⑤ 04 ① 05 ④
06 ①

해설

01 첫 번째 문장에서는 '하나'의 의미로 쓰였고, 두 번째 문장에서는 부정대명사로서 불특정한 사물을 가리키고 있다

02 주어의 목적어 역할을 하는 재귀대명사가 나와야 한다.

03 ①,②,③,④는 비인칭 주어 'it', ⑤는 대명사 'it'

04 ② 악기 앞에는 정관사 'the'가 붙어야 한다. ③ 부정문에서는 'some'이 아닌 'any'를 쓴다. ④ 부정문에서 부정의 의미가 있는 'nobody'대신 'anybody'를 써야 한다. ⑤ 긍정문에서는 'any'가 아닌 'some'을 사용한다.

05 소유대명사 뒤에는 명사가 올 수 없다. 문맥상 'my friend'라고 해야 알맞다.

06 'hers' 나는 지우개가 없었다. 그래서 수미가 '그녀의 것'을 주었다.

p. 230~235

01 ⑤	02 ②	03 ④	04 ②	05 ④
06 ④	07 ③	08 ①,⑤	09 ③,⑤	10 ②,④
11 ④,⑤	12 ②	13 ①	14 ③	15 ①
16 ②	17 ⑤	18 ③	19 ③	20 ④
21 ④	22 ①	23 ④	24 ①	25 ④
26 ①	27 ④	28 ④	29 ③	30 ②
31 ⑤				

〈서술형 평가〉

32 This is

33 This is my brother's new bag.

34 What time does Jenny go to school

35 One / the other

36 Some / the others

37 One / another / the other

38 Some marbles / the others (the other marbles)

39 They

40 ⓐ some ⓑ others

41 A: Whose is this dictionary?
B: It's hers.

42 Sam makes the birthday cake by himself.

43 There are many flowers. Some choose roses, and the others choose lilies.

해설

01 ① His → He, ② Her → She
③ He's → His, ④ name's → name

02 ① he → his, ③ he's → his, ④ It's → Its, ⑤ Hers → Her

03 you're → your

04 ①,③,④,⑤는 소유격 her (그녀의), ② 목적격 her (그녀를)

05 앞 문장에서 'she'라는 주어가 나옴으로 그녀의 이름을 물어보는 것을 알 수 있다.

06 〈보기, ④〉 his, ① its, ② Its, ③ her, ⑤ her

07 〈보기, ③〉 Its, ① Her, ② her, ④ their, ⑤ her

08 ① you're → your, ⑤ 'a' 또는 'her' 둘 중 하나를 지운다.

09 ③ he's → his, ⑤ he → him

10 ① their → her, ③ Her → She, ⑤ ours → our

11 ① her → his, ② her → my, ③ Yours → Your

12 This is Woody. → 전화상에서 '저는 ~입니다'라고 표현 할 때는 'This is~'를 사용한다.

13 Of course. (물론이지)

14 They are so kind to me. 주격인칭대명사
I want you to introduce them. 목적격인칭대명사
Here are their pictures. 소유격인칭대명사

15 ① 강조용법으로 쓰인 재귀대명사는 생략이 가능하다.
②,③,④,⑤ 재귀용법은 생략이 불가능하다.

16 ①,③,④,⑤ 대명사, ② 가주어 it

17 ①,②,③,④ 비인칭 주어 'it'

18 women은 복수명사이기 때문에 복수동사 'are'이 와야 한다.

19 'Nobody'자체가 부정의 뜻을 가지고 있으므로 'doesn't'가 올 필요가 없다. 'Nobody'는 단수 취급하므로 'knows'로 동사의 형태를 바꿔준다.

20 그녀가 영어 선생님이라는 정보를 토대로 누구인지를 물어보는 질문인지 알 수 있다.

21 앞에서 언급한 명사와 같은 종류의 물건일 경우 'one'을 사용한다. 앞에서 언급한 명사를 다시 한 번 중복해서 언급할 경우 'it'을 사용한다.

22 앞에서 언급한 명사를 다시 한 번 중복해서 언급할 경우 복수형의 명사는 'them'을 사용한다. 눈앞의 있는 것 외에 다른 하나를 말 할 경우 'another'를 사용한다.

23 yours → mine

24 감탄문은 'how' 또는 'what'을 사용하는데, 문장에 관사 'a(n)'이 나올 수 있는 문장은 'what'으로 시작하는 문장이다.

25 방법이나 날씨를 물어보는 표현은 주로 'how'를 사용한다.
→ 'what'을 사용하여 날씨를 물을 경우: what's the weather like?

26 날씨, 날짜, 시간 등을 표현할 때는 비인칭 주어 'it'을 사용한다.

27 문맥 상 한 늙은 여성에 대해 이야기 하고 있으니 'an old woman'이 알맞다.

28 every는 단수를 나타내므로 Every student likes him이 알맞다

29 '몇몇은 ~이고, 나머지 몇몇은~'의 표현은 'some~ others(또는 other+복수명사)'를 사용한다.

30 한정되어 있는 명사 두 개 중 '하나는 ~이고, 나머지 하나는 ~이다'의 표현으로는 'one~ the other~'을 사용한다.

31 'his - his' 인칭대명사 'he'의 소유격과 소유대명사는 형태가 같다.

〈서술형 평가〉

32 전화상에서 '저는 ~입니다'라는 표현을 할 때는 'This is~'를 사용한다.

33 단수명사(bag)를 가리키므로 'This is~'를 쓴다.

34 What time +do(es)+주어+동사원형~?

35 one~ the other… (하나는~, 다른 하나는…)

36 some~ the others… (몇몇은~, 다른 것들은…)

37 one~ another… and the other (하나는~, 다른 하나는…, 그리고 나머지 하나는)

38 some~ the others… (몇몇은~, 다른 것들은…)

39 '질문에서 'old people'이라고 정체를 언급 하였으므로, 대답에서는 명사의 반복을 피하기 위하여 이의 복수형 대명사인

'They'를 사용한다.

40 '어떤 사람들은~이고, 다른 어떤 사람들은~'은 'some~, others~'라고 표현한다.

41 소유대명사: mine, yours, hers, his, ours, theirs
의문사: whose 위의 단어들을 이용하여 적절한 문장을 만들었는지 확인한다.
예시〉 • Please, never forget to bring yours.
• I don't know where mine is?

42 재귀대명사의 강조용법은 주어, 보어, 목적어를 강조하여 설명한 것으로 생략이 가능하다. 재귀대명사: myself, yourself, itself, herself, himself, ourselves, yourselves, themselves
예시〉 • Jenny herself believes it's true.
• We make ourselves at home.

43 'some~, the others' 몇몇은~하고, 다른 나머지들은~한 이라는 뜻을 잘 살려서 썼는지 확인 한다.
예시〉 • I saw many people in the swimming pool. Some were swimming themselves, but the others were using tubes.

Chapter 06 형용사

Lesson 6-1 형용사의 쓰임

Check up! p. 239

A
1 your dress/beautiful
2 good/time
3 red/shirt
4 serious/problem
5 good/actress
6 She/lovely
7 wonderful/place
8 Your sister/cute, old/she
9 This lecture/boring
10 something/exciting

Lesson 6-2 형용사의 위치

Check up! p. 240

A
1 a great time
2 she is beautiful
3 our new English teacher
4 his lovely baby Ann
5 The big concert hall
6 makes people happy
7 a cute cat

Lesson 6-3 수량형용사_many/much

Check up! p. 241

A
1 Many
2 many
3 much
4 many
5 much
6 How many
7 How much
8 How much

Lesson 6-4 수량형용사_(a) few / (a) little

Check up! p. 242

A
1 a few
2 a little
3 few
4 a little
5 a little
6 a few
7 a few
8 a little
9 a few
10 a little
11 a little
12 few
13 a few
14 little
15 a little

Lesson 6-5 수량형용사_some/any

Check up! p. 243

A
1 some
2 any
3 any
4 some
5 any
6 some
7 any
8 some
9 any
10 some
11 any
12 some
13 any
14 some
15 any

Lesson 6-6 기타 형용사

Check up! p. 244~245

A
1 something sweet
2 four
3 anything else
4 two
5 something important
6 anything cold
7 something to drink
8 nobody else
9 something wrong
10 something good

B
1 anything
2 no one
3 nothing
4 nothing
5 doesn't have any
6 nothing
7 anything
8 no water
9 anything
10 any

Practice More I

p. 246~248

A
1 great
2 delicious
3 a few
4 nice
5 famous
6 sweet
7 beautiful/kind
8 wonderful

B
1 baby, deer, dog, friend
2 money, coffee, water
3 baby, deer, dog, friend
4 money, baby, deer, coffee, dog, friend, water
5 money, coffee, water
6 money, baby, deer, coffee, dog, friend, water
7 baby, deer, dog, friend

C
1 Sally is a diligent student.
2 I have an interesting book .
3 There is a tall boy.
4 I have nothing special to say for her.
5 Tim has artistic talent.
6 Father gave me a difficult puzzle.
7 He has a nice sense of humor.
8 I love your beautiful smile.
9 I don't have much time.

D
1 a few → a little
2 beautifully → beautiful
3 few → little
4 any → some
5 terribly → terrible
6 much → many
7 interesting something → somsething interesting
8 well → good
9 day (two) → days (second)

서술형연습

E
1 His face turned pale.
2 She will be a good mother.
3 Would you like something cold to drink?
4 Kelly needed a few cookies and a little water.
5 The organization helps the sick dogs
6 The new house is so big.
7 I want something fast.
8 The song makes me gloomy.
9 There are a few fish in the fishbowl.
10 How much money did you spend on going on a picnic?

Lesson 6-7 기수와 서수

Check up!

p. 251

A
1 ninth
2 first
3 second
4 fifteenth
5 one thousandth
6 third
7 fortieth
8 seventh
9 tenth
10 twenty-second
11 thirtieth
12 eighteenth
13 ninty-ninth
14 twentieth
15 seventeenth
16 eighth
17 eleventh
18 fourth
19 sixty-seventh
20 fifth
21 one hundredth
22 twenty-third
23 seventy-fourth
24 sixty-sixth
25 fifty-first
26 thirty-third

B
1 second
2 twentieth
3 third
4 fifth
5 thirteenth
6 first
7 fourth

Lesson 6-8 기수와 서수를 이용한 숫자 읽기 (1)

Check up!

p. 252~253

A
1 four hundred twenty-eight
2 thirty-two thousand, eight hundred fifty
3 seven thousand, seven hundred (and) eighty-nine
4 six hundred sixty
5 nine point eight seven
6 nine thousand eight hundred seven
7 six hundred fifty-eight
8 two thousand five hundred eighty
9 five sixths
10 seven hundred forty-eight
11 five hundred thirty
12 zero point nine eight
13 two and a third (two and one third)
14 sixty-six
15 nineteen thousand four hundred eighty-seven
16 six point five eight nine
17 a half (one half)
18 twenty-one thousand two hundred three
19 one thousand four

20 zero point zero seven eight

B 1 seven three two, one seven one seven
2 two nine four eight, eight nine zero three
3 four five eight eight, nine seven four eight
4 one one(double one) two
5 zero one eight, six nine one four, eight one five four
6 one, eight four seven, nine eight five, two zero three five
7 two zero one five, four eight seven five

Lesson 6-9 기수와 서수를 이용한 숫자 읽기 (2)

Check up! p. 255

A 1 two thousand eighteen
2 March twenty-first (the twenty-first of March)
3 nineteen ninety-seven
4 January twenty-fifth (the tewenty-fifth of January)
5 October twelfth (the twelfth of October)
6 nineteen eighty-nine
7 November twenty-second (the twenty-second of November)
8 March seventeenth, nineteen ninety-nine (the seventeenth of March, nineteen ninety-nine)
9 December thirteenth (the thirteenth of December)
10 July tenth, two thousand fifteen (the tenth of July, two thousand fifteen)

B 1 thirty dollars (and) eighty-five cents
2 fifteen dollars (and) seventy-four cents
3 eight thousand, six hundred (and) forty-eight won
4 ninety-five dollars (and) seventy-four cents
5 seventy-four dollars (and) eighteen cents
6 eighty-four thousand, five hundred (and) ten won

C 1 sixty nine degrees Celsius
2 seventeen degrees Fahrenheit
3 six hundred forty-eight degrees Celsius
4 one hundred seventy-four degrees Fahrenheit
5 two hundred eleven point eight five degrees Celsius
6 one hundred forty seven point six five five degrees Fahrenheit
7 zero point one four five degrees Fahrenheit

Lesson 6-10 시각 표현

Check up! p. 256~257

A 1 five thirty-five
2 nine twenty-three
3 one twenty-nine
4 twelve thirty-seven
5 four twenty-six
6 twelve (oh) six
7 eleven (oh) two
8 four twenty-eight
9 three (oh) four
10 five fifty-seven

B 1 twenty-five after ten
2 fifteen to eight
3 twenty to ten
4 half past eleven
5 a quarter past five
6 twenty-five after eleven
7 ten to nine
8 a quarter past three
9 five to two
10 ten after two
11 twenty to five
12 fifteen to seven
13 twenty after one
14 twenty-five to six
15 a quarter past twelve
16 twenty-five to two
17 ten after one
18 twenty after two
19 twenty-five to four
20 fifteen to five
21 a quarter after eleven
22 five to seven
23 five after seven
24 twenty-five past eight
25 ten to ten

Lesson 6-11 형용사의 관용표현

Check up!
p. 258

A
1 dozens of
2 Thousands of
3 hundreds of
4 dozens(scores) of
5 Tens of thousands of
6 hundreds of
7 hundreds of
8 Millions of

Practice More Ⅱ
p. 259~260

A
1 four
2 third/two
3 fifteen
4 two
5 sixth
6 first
7 nine
8 thirteenth
9 seventy
10 twenty-four
11 fourteenth
12 sixty
13 ten thousand
14 fifth
15 five

B
1 two thousand five hundred (and) eighty-one
2 March twenty-seventh
3 zero point two nine three
4 nineteen eighty-nine
5 a million
6 three point five nine one
7 January twenty-sixth, two thousand five
8 eighty-eight dollars nineteen cents
9 four sevenths
10 June twelfth, two thousand fifteen
11 the thirteenth century
12 six and four fifths
13 one hundred thirty-eight point one seven
14 the seventeen thirties
15 Seven thousand four hundred (and) fifty-nine won.

C
1 It's half past eight.
2 It's a quarter past three.
3 It's a quarter past ten.
4 It's a quarter to six.
5 It's ten past two.
6 It's half past eleven.

서술형 연습

D
1 the third
2 zero one zero, seven three two, one seven one seven.
3 the sixteenth floor
4 a quarter to nine
5 thirty-three degrees Celsius
6 Hundreds of people
7 six hundred (and) sixty-five stamps
8 Two millions of people
9 June nineteenth (the nineteenth of June)
10 tens(dozens, scores) of

중간 기말고사 예상문제

내신 최다 출제 유형
p. 261

01 ① 02 ③ 03 ④ 04 many → much
05 ⓑ → How much time
06 they use them too much 07 is no one

해설

01 ⓑ some → any, ⓒ many → much, ⓔ Much → Many
02 a little → a few (또는 some)
03 부정대명사 ('-thing, -body, -one'으로 끝나는) 뒤에는 형용사가 온다. ④번은 동사
04 'water'은 셀 수 없는 명사이기 때문에 'much'로 바꿔준다.
05 ⓑ 'time'이 시간을 의미하며, 시간은 셀 수 없는 명사에 속하므로 'much'가 맞다.
06 teenagers → 복수, 주격 they / smartphones → 복수, 목적격 them
07 'not~anyone'은 'no one'으로 바꿀 수 있다.

p. 262~267

01 ④	02 ③	03 ①	04 ③	05 ③
06 ⑤	07 ③	08 ②	09 ⑤	10 ①
11 ④	12 ③	13 ⑤	14 ①	15 ④
16 ①	17 ③	18 ④	19 ②	20 ④
21 ④	22 ②	23 ②,③	24 ④,⑤	25 ③,⑤
26 ①,②	27 ④	28 ①	29 ④	30 ③
31 ②	32 ③	33 ①	34 ⑤	35 ②
36 ④				

〈서술형 평가〉

37 a very pretty lady **38** a really fantastic picture

39 That clown looks very sad.

40 This is a very exciting ride.

41 ① There is little rain in Africa.

42 ② Would you like some cold water?

43 ⓐ much → many

44 (A) 약간의: some
(B) 3,000원: three thousand won

45 the twenty-third of March, nineteen seventy-six
(= March (the) twenty-third, nineteen seventy-six)

46 Gijoon's birthday is (Gijoon was born on) the twenty-fourth of May, nineteen ninety-eight.
(= May the twenty-four, nineteen ninety-eight)

47 It is thirty-six degrees Celsius

48 He doesn't have any time to exercise.

해설

01 ①,②,③,⑤ 형용사+명사, ④ 명사+명사

02 ①,②,④,⑤ 감각동사+형용사, ③ 감각동사 뒤에 부사는 올 수 없다.

03 ② feels softly → feels soft, ③ warm anything → anything warm, ④ makes me happily → makes me happy, ⑤ are looks dirty → look dirty

04 ① smells → smell, ② a moive funny → a funny movie, ④ There is → There are, ⑤ hot something → something hot

05 ①,②,④,⑤ 형용사, ③ 부사

06 ①,②,③,④ 형용사, ⑤ 명사

07 three-third

08 twenty-one → twenty-first

09 'much'는 셀 수 없는 명사 앞에 온다.

10 'a little'은 셀 수 없는 명사 앞에 온다.

11 감각동사+형용사

12 감각동사+형용사+명사

13 1979년 → nineteen seventy-nine

14 57 → fifty-seven

15 two and three fourths

16 '10시 15분 전=9시 45분'시간을 표현할 때 'to'는 '~전에' 라는 뜻이고, 'a quarter'은 4분의 1 즉, 한 시간의 4분의 1은 15분을 뜻한다. 'a quarter to'는 '15분 전' 이고, 그 뒤에 'ten'이 나왔으니 10시 15분 전이라는 뜻이다.

17 날짜, 시간 등을 나타낼 때는 비인칭 주어 'it'을 사용한다.

18 월/일, 연도 순으로 읽는다.

19 셀 수 없는 명사 coffee에 어울리는 형용사는 'much'이다.

20 많은: a lot of, lots of, a plenty of, many

21 December twenty-eighth (= the twenty-eighth of December)

22 the thirty-first of August (= August thirty-first)

23 ① many → much, ④ some → any, ⑤ a few → some

24 ① There is → There are, ② much → many, ③ any → some

25 ③ some → any: 부정문에서는 'any'를 사용한다.
⑤ any → some: 권유문에서는 의문문이라 할지라도 'some'을 사용한다.

26 ① confusing → confused, ② exciting → excited
→ 사람이 감정을 느끼는 주체가 되어 주어로 나오면 과거분사 형용사를 사용한다.

27 ① 'Hundreds of' 수백의, ② 'Lots of' 많은, ③ 'Most of' 대부분의, ⑤ 'Dozens of' 수십의

28 며칠 : 'a few days'

29 6:45 → fifteen to seven

30 감정을 느끼는 주어가 사람일 경우 과거분사형태의 형용사를 사용한다.

31 감정을 느끼는 주어가 사물일 경우 현재분사형태의 형용사를 사용한다.

32 be동사+형용사, 감각동사+형용사, be동사+동사-ing

33 person → people

34 'how many'는 셀 수 있는 명사의 수를 물어보는 표현이다. 'water'은 셀 수 없는 명사이다.

35 부정의 문장에는 'anything'을 사용한다.

36 ①,②,③,⑤의 'nice'는 뒤의 명사를 설명한다. (한정적용법)
④번은 주어의 성질을 설명한다. (서술적용법)

〈서술형 평가〉

37 부사+형용사+명사

38 부사+형용사+명사

39 감각동사+형용사

40 be동사+사물이 느끼는 감정 형용사 (현재분사)

41 셀 수 없는 명사: 'little' 사용한다.

42 권유하는 의문문은 'some'을 사용한다.

43 셀 수 있는 명사: 'many' 사용 (ride-기구)

44 (A) 셀 수 있는 명사의 복수형이므로 'some'을 사용한다.
(B) 삼(3) three+천(1,000) thousand=three thousand

45 영어로 연도를 포함한 날짜를 읽을 때는 '일-월 년' 또는 '월-일-년' 순으로 읽는다.

46 영어로 연도를 포함한 날짜를 읽을 때는 '일-월-년' 또는 '월-일-년' 순으로 읽는다.

47 온도-섭씨를 나타낼 때는 'Celsius'를 사용한다.

48 부정문에서는 'any'를 사용한다.

Chapter

07 부사

Lesson 7-1 부사의 역할

Check up!

p. 271

A
1 carefully
2 happily
3 very much
4 fast
5 really
6 fluently
7 very
8 certainly
9 quite
10 suddenly

B
1 John solves the problem easily.
2 I usually wake up early.
3 She studies hard to pass the exam.
4 Tim looks so tired.

Lesson 7-2 부사의 종류

Check up!

p. 272

A
1 upstaris
2 today
3 yesterday
4 sometimes
5 abroad
6 heavily

Lesson 7-3 형용사를 부사로 바꾸는 방법 (1)

Check up!

p. 273

A
1 nicely
2 newly
3 easily
4 closely
5 loudly
6 usually
7 really
8 greatly
9 quickly
10 angrily
11 happily
12 beautifully
13 gladly
14 suddenly
15 quietly
16 clearly
17 wonderfully
18 bravely
19 sadly
20 poorly
21 safely
22 similary
23 variously
24 mainly
25 possibly
26 busily
27 badly
28 surely
29 strongly
30 strangely

Lesson 7-4 형용사를 부사로 바꾸는 방법 (2)

Check up!

p. 274

A
1 부사
2 형용사
3 형용사
4 부사
5 부사
6 형용사
7 부사
8 형용사
9 형용사
10 부사

Practice More I

p. 275~276

A
1 weakly
2 softly
3 calmly
4 terribly
5 seriously
6 politely
7 heavily
8 sensibly
9 specially
10 hugely
11 importantly
12 richly
13 surprisingly
14 differently
15 equally
16 wisely
17 coldly
18 dangerously

B
1 late
2 well
3 really
4 happily
5 high
6 long
7 hard
8 fast
9 fluently
10 Fortunately

C
1 Luckily
2 fast
3 carefully
4 heavily
5 hard
6 early
7 quite (pretty)
8 late
9 happily
10 soon

D
1 Julia dance well.
2 Eric starts quickly.
3 Sam works slowly.
4 My father smokes heavily.
5 He runs fast.
6 Tim acts strangely.
7 They talk loudly.
8 He plays soccer amazingly.
9 She plays the piano well.
10 It changes suddenly.

Lesson 7-5 빈도부사의 종류와 의미

Check up! p. 278

A
1 always 2 often
3 rarely 4 never
5 sometimes 6 often
7 never

Lesson 7-6 빈도부사의 위치

Check up! p. 279

A
1 often sing 2 seldom rains
3 is always 4 rarely watches
5 should never

B
1 The baby usually sleeps 17 hours a day.
2 The English class always starts 8:30 a.m.
3 John and I often go to school by bus.
4 I will never leave without saying good bye.

Lesson 7-7 의문부사

Check up! p. 280~281

A
1 Where 2 When
3 How long 4 Where
5 How 6 Why
7 Where 8 How often
9 Why 10 When
11 How old 12 How much
13 Why 14 How many
15 When 16 Where
17 How long 18 Why
19 How often 20 How far

Lesson 7-8 시간을 나타내는 부사표현

Check up! p. 283

A
1 this morning 2 last night
3 this year 4 in May
5 on Thanksgiving Day 6 last night
7 in 2003 8 next week
9 every weekend 10 this afternoon
11 at midnight 12 next year
13 in fall
14 on Sundays (every Sunday)
15 in May 16 on New Year's Day

Practice More Ⅱ p. 284~285

A
1 often 2 always
3 never 4 sometimes
5 sometimes 6 always

B
1 He usually plays tennis
2 I am sometimes
3 He is never late
4 often stay
5 John always eats breakfast
6 usually take
7 will never forget
8 always eat

C
1 Where 2 How
3 Why 4 How
5 When 6 when
7 How

D
1 Why did you call me last night?
2 Susan has parties on Fridays.
3 How far is the school?
4 Alice usually eats dinner at 8 o'clock.
5 We will go to a farm to see sheep the day after tomorrow.
6 How long have you been to France?

중간 기말고사 예상문제

내신 최다 출제 유형

p. 286

01 ③	02 ④	03 ③	04 ③	05 ①
06 ③	07 ①			

해설

01 ① always am → am always, ② What → Who
④ play → plays ⑤ has → have

02 빈도부사는 be동사 뒤에 위치한다.

03 부사의 위치: '일반동사+부사'

04 빈도부사 위치: 일반동사 앞, be동사 뒤

05 ① 형용사: 훌륭한, ②,③,④,⑤ 부사: 잘

06 ①,②,④,⑤ 부사, ③ 형용사가 와야 한다.
beautifully → beautiful

07 빈도부사 'usually'는 일반동사 앞에 위치한다.

p. 287~292

01 ③	02 ⑤	03 ②	04 ②	05 ④
06 ②	07 ③	08 ⑤	09 ①	10 ②
11 ②	12 ②	13 ③	14 ⑤	15 ②
16 ③,④	17 ①,⑤	18 ②	19 ④	20 ⑤
21 ①	22 ②	23 ④	24 ①,③	25 ②,④
26 ①	27 ⑤	28 ③	29 ④	30 ②,④
31 ①	32 ⑤	33 ②	34 ④	35 ⑤

〈서술형 평가〉

36 well 37 fast 38 ⓐ many(a lot of, lots of)
ⓑ Every morning ⓒ usually

39 always takes care of

40 always/often/sometimes

41 When was Thomas born?

42 How long did you live in Beijing?

43 How often does he play football?

44 Jenny swims very fast.

45 I speak slowly.

46 Billy Elliot dances well.

47 Sam rarely practices the piano .

48 They climb mountains every week.

해설

01 ①,②,④,⑤ 형용사+ly = 부사, ③ 명사+ly = 형용사

02 ①,②,③,④ 형용사+ly = 부사, ⑤ 동사+ly = 형용사

03 ①,③,④,⑤ 형용사+ly = 부사, ② 'late-late'-형용사와 부사의 형태가 같다. 'lately'는 '최근에'라는 뜻을 가진 원래 형태가 부사이다.

04 'hard-hard'-형용사와 부사의 형태가 같다. 'hardly'는 '거의 ~않다'라는 뜻을 가진 원래 형태가 부사이다.

05 'bad-badly', 'worse'는 '더 나쁜'이라는 뜻을 가진 형용사이다

06 'How cute!' 정말 귀엽다! (감탄문), 'How is it going?' 잘 지냈어? (안부인사 = How are you?)

07 'how high~' 얼마나 높은~, 'fly high' 높이 날다

08 'What is the weather like?' 날씨가 어때?
'What does she do?' 그녀의 직업은 무엇이니?

09 빈도부사는 일반 동사 앞에 위치한다.

10 빈도부사는 be동사 뒤에 위치한다.

11 언제, 몇 시에 'when = what time'

12 빈도부사는 be동사 뒤에 위치한다. 'is never'

13 빈도부사는 일반동사 앞에 위치한다. 'sometimes laugh'

14 ①,②,③,④ 부사: 꽤, 매우, ⑤ 형용사: 예쁜

15 ①,③,④ 부사: 열심히, ⑤ 부사: 꽤, 상당히, ② 형용사: 어려운

16 ③ studies always → always studies, ④ lately → late

17 ① good → well, ⑤ stay usually up → usually stay up

18 ② 'How often~? (얼마나 자주~?)'라는 뜻으로 횟수나 빈도를 물어보는 질문이다.
① one time → once, ⑤ two time → twice

19 'How can~? (어떻게 ~할 수 있니?)'의 뜻으로 방법을 물어보는 질문이다.

20 'How far~? (얼마나 먼~?)'이라는 뜻으로 거리를 물어보는 질문이다.

21 'How far is the church from here?' → '거리'에 대한 질문
'How can I go there?' → '방법'에 대한 질문

22 'Why was she absent?' → '이유'에 대한 질문
'How did you know that?' → '방법'에 대한 질문

23 ~전에 'ago', 이번 'this'

24 ② at the morning → in the morning
④ in Wednesday → on Wednesday
⑤ in Jim's birthday → on Jim's birthday

25 ① read usually → usually read
③ at the marathon → in the marathon
⑤ invited → inviting

26 ① 'a lot of = much': 'milk'가 셀 수 없는 명사이다.
②,③,④,⑤ 'a lot of = many': 셀 수 있는 명사들이다.

27 hardly → hard

28 surf usually → usually surf

29 ①,②,③,⑤ 동사를 수식하는 부사: 빠르게
④ 명사를 수식하는 형용사: 빠른

30 ①,③,⑤ 셀 수 없는 명사와 쓰인다.

31 'pick + 대명사(목적어) + up'의 형태가 되어야 한다.

32 'never' 절대 ~않는 – 빈도부사가 있어도 뒤의 일반동사의 시제에는 변화가 없다.

33 가끔씩 한다는 대답에 대한 질문은 빈도수를 물어보는 것이 된다. 'How often ~?' – 얼마나 자주~?

34 ① usually finishes, ② is always, ③ does the dishes, ⑤ safely

35 sometimes drinks

〈서술형 평가〉

36 Jenny의 삼촌은 요리를 잘 한다. 잘 – 'well'

37 미란은 빨리 달린다. 빨리 – 'fast'

38 ⓐ 셀 수 있는 명사 – 'many, ⓑ ~마다 – 'Every', 아침 – 'morning' ⓒ 보통 – 'usually'

39 빈도부사는 일반동사 앞에 사용한다.

40 항상 – 'always', 보통 – 'often', 가끔 – 'sometimes'

41 날짜가 나온 답의 질문에는 의문사 'when'을 사용한다.

42 시간이 나온 답의 질문에는 의문사 'how long'을 사용한다.

43 빈도수를 묻는 질문으로는 'how often~?'을 사용한다.

39 빈도부사는 일반동사 앞에 사용한다.

40 항상 – 'always', 보통 – 'often', 가끔 – 'sometimes'

41 날짜가 나온 답의 질문에는 의문사 'when'을 사용한다.

42 시간이 나온 답의 질문에는 의문사 'how long'을 사용한다.

43 빈도수를 묻는 질문으로는 'how often~?'을 사용한다.

44 fast → fast

45 slow → slowly

46 good → well

47 빈도부사는 일반동사 앞에 위치한다. 'rarely' 거의 ~않은

48 시간을 나타내는 부사는 주로 문장 맨 끝에 위치한다.

Chapter

08 비교구문

Lesson 8-1 비교급과 최상급의 규칙변화 (1)

Check up! p. 295~296

A
1 larger - largest
2 weaker - weakest
3 harder - hardest
4 wiser - wisest
5 milder - mildest
6 dirtier - dirtiest
7 cleaner - cleanest
8 louder - loudest
9 stronger - strongest
10 prettier - prettiest
11 smaller - smallest
12 poorer - poorest
13 fatter–fattest
14 happier - happiest
15 safer - safest
16 cheaper - cheapest
17 lower - lowest
18 noisier - noisiest
19 politer (more polite) - politest (most polite)
20 easier - easiest
21 more friendly - most friendly
22 busier - busiest
23 closer - closest
24 taller - tallest
25 sooner - soonest
26 braver - bravest
27 luckier - luckiest
28 faster - fastest
29 thinner - thinnest
30 longer - longest
31 higher - highest
32 colder - coldest
33 lighter - lightest
34 heavier - heaviest
35 greater - greatest
36 warmer - warmest
37 hungrier - hungriest
38 wetter - wettest
39 stricter - strictest
40 angrier - angriest
41 nearer - nearest
42 funnier - funniest
43 stranger - strangest
44 earlier - earliest
45 thicker - thickest
46 tastier - tastiest
47 shorter - shortest
48 lovelier - loveliest
49 uglier - ugliest
50 softer - softest

Lesson 8-2 비교급과 최상급의 규칙변화 (2)

Check up! p. 297~298

A
1 more hopeful - most hopeful
2 more ridiculous - most ridiculous
3 more critical - most critical
4 rarer - rarest
5 more interesting - most interesting
6 more quickly - most quickly
7 more pleasing - most pleasing
8 more exciting - most exciting
9 quieter - quietest
10 more expensive - most expensive
11 more careful - most careful
12 more important - most important
13 more complicated - most complicated
14 more creative - most creative
15 more alone - most alone
16 more awesome - most awesome
17 more familiar - most familiar
18 more convenient - most convenient
19 more positive - most positive
20 more afraid - most afraid
21 more colorful - most colorful
22 more famous - most famous
23 more beautiful - most beautiful
24 more tired - most tired
25 cleverer (more cleverer) - cleverest (most clever)
26 more boring - most boring
27 more special - most special
28 more useful - most useful
29 more difficult - most difficult
30 more delicious - most delicious
31 more different - most different
32 more hopeless - most hopeless
33 more foolish - most foolish
34 brighter - brightest
35 more popular - most popular
36 more curious - most curious
37 more slowly - most slowly
38 more ashamed - most ashamed
39 more excellent - most excellent
40 more nutritious - most nutritious

Lesson 8-3 비교급과 최상급의 불규칙변화

Check up!

p. 300

A
1 later – latest
2 worse – worst
3 better – best
4 elder – eldest
5 fewer – fewest
6 worse – worst
7 more similar – most similar
8 more – most
9 further – furthest
10 more – most
11 better – best
12 older – oldest
13 costlier–costliest
14 slimmer – slimmest
15 farther – farthest
16 less – least
17 more useless – most useless
18 more patient – most patient
19 latter – last
20 deeper – deepest

Practice More I

p. 301~303

A
1 slimmer – slimmest
2 slower – slowest
3 faster – fastest
4 longer – longest
5 lower – lowest
6 better – best
7 more ridiculous – most ridiculous
8 worse – worst
9 larger – largest
10 older – oldest
11 milder – mildest
12 hotter – hottest
13 tastier – tastiest
14 more hopeless – most hopeless
15 more important – most important
16 fewer – fewest
17 easier – easiest
18 more tired – most tired
19 tougher – toughest
20 lovelier – loveliest

B
1 taller
2 more beautiful
3 hotter
4 more important
5 newer
6 harder
7 deeper
8 higher
9 more delicious
10 brighter
11 older
12 more interesting
13 earlier
14 more expensive
15 more
16 smaller
17 more difficult
18 slower
19 more quickly
20 older

C
1 shorter
2 longer
3 smarter
4 less
5 bigger
6 stronger
7 more handsome
8 older
9 more interesting
10 more famous

Lesson 8-4 원급의 비교

Check up!

p. 305

A
1 smart
2 small
3 not so
4 many
5 fast
6 not as
7 interesting
8 not as
9 twice
10 cold
11 new
12 many
13 not as
14 three times

Lesson 8-5 비교급의 비교

Check up! p. 306~307

A
1 more expensive
2 taller
3 older
4 more interesting
5 colder and colder
6 earlier
7 more quickly
8 better
9 younger
10 newer
11 bigger
12 more careful
13 longer
14 more colorful
15 richer/richer
16 smaller
17 more popular
18 better
19 more
20 deeper/deeper

B
1 as → than
2 more cheap → cheaper
3 strong → stronger
4 to → than
5 bad → worse
6 kind → kinder
7 rich → richer
8 thin → thinner
9 yours → you
10 fast → faster
11 then → than
12 many and many → more and more
13 a lot→ a lot more
14 strong → stronger
15 more strict → stricter

Lesson 8-6 최상급의 비교

Check up! p. 308~309

A
1 the thinnest
2 the most powerful
3 the best
4 the highest
5 the oldest
6 the shortest
7 the most famous
8 the most valuable
9 the most diligent
10 the coldest

B
1 Tim is one of the happiest people I've ever met.
2 The ring is one of the most expensive things in my room.
3 Sujin is one of the most talented students in our class.
4 John is one of the bravest men in the group.
5 He is one of the heaviest boys in our village.

C
1 Jack is the tallest in class.
2 Laura is the most famous in her country.
3 My brother is the mildest man in the world.
4 Hong Kong is one of the busiest cities.
5 T-Rex is one of the fiercest dinosaurs.

Practice More Ⅱ p. 310~312

A
1 thin
2 tall
3 the most famous
4 faster
5 much
6 the most
7 prettier
8 faster
9 actors
10 fat

B
1 then → than
2 cheaper → cheapest
3 the → X
4 player → players
5 old → older
6 coldest → colder
7 expensivier → more expensive
8 than → as
9 most late → latest
10 most lovely → loveliest

C
1 not as tall as
2 not as young as
3 as long as
4 not as big as
5 not as big as

D
1 twice as much as
2 not as old as
3 not as high as
4 one of the most beautiful flowers in the garden
5 not as dark as black

E
1 Jina is as smart as Linda.
2 Baseball is one of the most popular sports in Korea.
3 My chair is as new as yours.
4 Samantha is the best student in our class.
5 Lily has three times as many clothes as her husband.

6 Seoul is one of the most beautiful cities in the world.
7 Jane's bag is as small as Jim's.

F
1 Mary는 엄마만큼 요리를 잘한다.
2 그는 Tom만큼 용감하지 않았다.
3 그들은 전국을 통틀어 최고의 춤꾼들이다.
4 햄버거는 가장 건강에 좋지 않은 음식이다.
5 나는 Tina보다 정직하다.

중간 기말고사 **예상문제**

내신 최다 출제 유형

p. 313

01 ①　02 ③　03 ④　04 ③　05 ②
06 is the biggest lizard

해설

01 감각동사+형용사 -er+than. ① happy → happier
02 ③ ⓐ the+최상급, ⓑ the+최상급, ⓒ 비교급+than
03 ① not as so → not as (또는 not so),
② they → them (또는 they are), ③ fat than → fatter than
⑤ the faster → faster
04 ①,②,④,⑤ 'most + 형용사 = 최상급',
③ 'most + 명사' → 'many'의 최상급
05 명사를 수식하는 형용사가 와야 한다. gooder → better
06 'the + 최상급' – 'big'은 '단모음+단자음'으로 이뤄진 단어이므로 자음을 한 번 더 써주고 '-est'를 붙인다.

p. 314~319

01 ④	02 ②	03 ⑤	04 ③	05 ⑤
06 ②	07 ③	08 ⑤	09 ②	10 ③
11 ③,⑤	12 ③,④	13 ④,⑤	14 ②	15 ⑤
16 ①	17 ④	18 ③	19 ③	20 ②
21 ②	22 ③	23 ②,③	24 ③	25 ⑤
26 ②	27 ①	28 ③	29 ⑤	30 ③,⑤
31 ③,④				

〈서술형 평가〉
32 Ted is as good at speaking English as Tina.
(=Tina is as good at speaking English as Ted.)
33 shorter and shorter
34 the most expensive
35 ① youngest, ② strongest, ③ most diligent,
④ tallest
36 China is much larger than Korea.
37 You are not as ugly as her.
38 겨울은 사계절 중에서 가장 추운 계절이다.
39 셰익스피어는 세계에서 가장 위대한 작가 중 하나이다.
40 스마트폰은 컴퓨터보다 더 편리하다.
41 Phillip is as honest as Larry.
42 Jessica is more popular than Cindy.
43 Jerry is the most handsome in his class.

해설

01 little – less – least: 불규칙 변화를 가진다.
02 big – bigger – biggest '단모음 + 단자음'으로 끝나는 형용사는 뒤의 자음을 한 번 더 써주고 '-er', '-est'를 붙여준다.
03 foolish – more foolish – most foolish 2음절 이상의 형용사의 경우 비교급에는 'more', 최상급에는 'most'를 붙여준다.
04 Jack의 키는 167이고 Sue의 키는 170으로 Sue가 더 크다.
'A 비교급 + than B' B보다 A가 더 ~한
05 Jessica와 Saewon 모두 95점을 받았고 '둘 다 똑똑한 학생들'이라는 의미이다. 'as+형용사 원형+as' …만큼 ~하는
06 주어가 'Harry'로 시작하였고, Jack보다는 덜 뚱뚱하니 원급의 부정문을 사용하는 것이 맞다. 'not as 형용사원급 as'
07 키가 작은 이들 중 세번째라는 의미, 셋 이상을 비교할 때는 최상급을 사용한다. 'the+최상급+in 장소' ~에서 가장 ~한
08 'one of the 최상급' 가장 ~한 것(사람) 중 하나
09 '최상급 + of~' ~에서 가장~한/ '비교급 + than' ~보다~한
10 재준은 기은보다 나이가 더 많다.
→ Jaejoon is older than Gieun
11 ① An airplane is faster that a taxi.
② A snake is longer than an earthworm.

④ This building is the tallest.

12 ① taller → tall, ② slow → slow as, ⑤ powerfuler → more powerful

13 ① 'It's getting colder and colder.' – '비교급+and+비교급' 점점 더 ~한, ② This book is heavier than that one.
③ You are prettier than Anne. ④ 'even, much, still' 등이 비교급 앞에 쓰여서 '훨씬, 더욱 더'라는 뜻을 가짐
⑤ '원급' 문장에 배수사가 들어가면 '…배로 ~한'이라는 뜻.

14 He is the kindest man.

15 Tommy's grades became better and better.

16 Ellen is the busiest girl in class.

17 '점점 더 ~한' 이라는 뜻은 '비교급 + and + 비교급' 구문을 사용한다.

18 third: '세 번째'라는 뜻으로 서수이다. '~배'는 배수를 사용하며, 영어에서는 '3 이상'부터는 '숫자 + times'라고 표현한다.

19 '~보다 …한' : 비교급 + than

20 부사 'become, still, far, much' 등은 비교급 앞에 쓰여서 '훨씬, 더욱'의 뜻으로 사용 한다.

21 ①,③,④,⑤ 형용사 원급 – 비교급, ② 동사 – 명사

22 ①,②,④,⑤ 형용사 비교급의 규칙변화, ③ 형용사 비교급의 불규칙변화

23 ① very → much, ④ as lazy as so → as lazy as, ⑤ as thinner as → as thin as.

24 '배수사 + as + 원급 + as A' – A보다 …배 ~한

25 비교급 앞에 쓰여 '훨씬, 더욱'이라는 뜻으로 사용되는 단어들: 'even, much, still, far' 등

26 'the+최상급+of~' (한 집단에서) 가장 ~한

27 'one of the 최상급+복수명사' 가장 ~한 것들 중 하나

28 '원급: not as ~ as…'는 '비교급: –er(more) than'구문과 바꿔 쓸 수 있다. 비교급 구문을 원급 구문의 부정형으로 바꿀 때 주어와 목적어의 자리 역시 바뀐다.

29 ①,②,③,④ 'Susan이 학교에서 가장 최고의 무용수'라는 의미
⑤ 'Susan은 학교에서 가장 최고의 무용수 중 한 명'이라는 의미

30 ③ '비교급 + than'
Tina의 키가 162cm이고, Ted의 키가 157cm인 것을 봐서 Tina가 더 크다고 표현한다.

31 ③ 'not as (=so) ~ as…' 구문을 사용
Tina is not so fast as Ted. Tina는 Ted 만큼 빨리 달리지 못한다. → Ted가 더 빨리 달린다는 의미.
② '비교급 + than'

〈서술형 평가〉

32 둘 모두 영어 말하기를 잘한다고 했으므로 문장 처음과 끝의 이름이 바뀌어도 괜찮다. 'as ~ as' 사이에는 형용사 원형이 오며 'good at speaking English'는 하나의 '형용사구' 로 묶은 상태로 'as ~ as' 사이에 넣어준다.

33 '점점 더 ~한'은 '비교급 + and + 비교급'으로 표현한다.

34 '가장 ~한'은 'the + 최상급'으로 표현한다.

35 'the + 최상급'

36 비교급에서 '훨씬, 더욱'이라는 의미로 쓰이는 단어: 'still, much, even'

37 '…만큼 ~한'의 원급비교 부정형: 'not as ~ as...'

38 'the+최상급'

39 'one of the + 최상급 + 복수명사'

40 '비교급 + than'

41 'as ~ as' 사이에는 형용사 또는 부사의 원형이 들어가는 것에 주의한다. 'not as ~ as'에서 첫 번째 'as' 대신에 'so'를 넣어도 괜찮다.
예시〉 • Maria is not as pretty as Gina.

42 비교급 단어 형태를 만들 때, '형용사 + –er' 또는 'more + 형용사'를 쓴다.
예시〉 • You are cleverer than him.
→ 'clever : cleverer, more clever' 모두 사용 가능하다.

43 최상급 단어 형태를 만들 때, '형용사 + –est' 또는 'most + 형용사'를 쓴다.
최상급 문장 뒤의 전치사구: 'in + 장소', 'of + 집단'에 주의한다.
예시〉 • Max is the tallest of his friends.

Chapter

09 부정사

Lesson 9-1 부정사의 형태

Check up! p. 323~324

A 1 명사적 용법 2 형용사적 용법
3 부사적 용법 4 부사적 용법
5 명사적 용법 6 형용사적 용법

B 1 playing → play 2 being → be
3 eating → eat 4 doing → do
5 collected → collect 6 to clean → clean
7 winning → win 8 being → be
9 taking → take 10 saving → save

C 1 is to eat 2 is to go
3 to come 4 to drink
5 to wear

Lesson 9-2 to부정사의 명사적 용법

Check up! p. 325~326

A 1 주어 2 보어
3 주어 4 목적어
5 보어 6 목적어

B 1 what 2 how
3 where 4 when
5 what 6 how
7 when

C 1 to buy 2 to go
3 to eat 4 to visit
5 to ride

Lesson 9-3 to부정사의 형용사적 용법

Check up! p. 327~328

A 1 to drink 2 to study English
3 to do 4 to write with
5 to live in 6 to tell
7 to eat 8 to take care of
9 to fall in love with 10 to study in

B 1 candies to eat
2 to remember
3 air to breathe
4 to say
5 to talk about
6 to sit on
7 to exercise
8 to study for
9 to live in
10 to talk with

C 1 to eat 2 to do
3 to go 4 to read
5 to get

Lesson 9-4 to부정사의 부사적 용법

Check up! p. 330

A 1 원인 2 목적
3 근거 4 결과
5 근거 6 목적
7 결과 8 근거
9 원인 10 목적

B 1 I went to the park to run.
2 Joe studies hard to pass the exam.
3 Camilla must be a fool to love him.
4 They are disappointed to lose the soccer game.
5 Samuel must be kind to do such a thing.

Practice More I

p. 331~333

A
1	주어	2	보어
3	목적어	4	주어
5	목적어	6	보어
7	주어	8	목적어
9	목적어	10	보어

B
1	부사	2	명사
3	형용사	4	부사
5	명사	6	부사
7	형용사	8	부사
9	명사	10	형용사

C
1 Be → To be
2 going → to go
3 to something → something to
4 riding → ride
5 wants to not eat → doesn't want to eat
6 being → be
7 playing → play
8 telling → tell
9 gone → go
10 buying → buy
11 to not → not to
12 wearing → to wear
13 going → to go
14 went → go
15 writing → write

D
1	to	2	in
3	with	4	with
5	on		

E
1 to hear the news
2 began to rise
3 try to walk for 30 minutes
4 happy to meet her again
5 decided to make a new movie
6 to win the soccer game
7 to be 99 years old
8 something sweet to eat
9 try to think positive
10 went to the store to buy the groceries.

Lesson 9-5 사역동사+목적어+원형부정사

Check up!

p. 335~336

A
1	had/paint	2	Let/show
3	made/clean	4	Let/introduce
5	let/sleep	6	helps/(to) do
7	made/keep	8	makes/smile
9	helps/(to) listen	10	had/clean

B
1	do	2	try
3	to clean	4	hold
5	read	6	to do
7	finish	8	fly
9	stop	10	cut

Lesson 9-6 지각동사+목적어+원형부정사

Check up!

p. 337

A
1	dance	2	sing
3	jogging	4	do
5	shaking	6	running
7	steal	8	touch
9	talking	10	playing
11	going	12	crying
13	shout	14	blow
15	calling		

Lesson 9-7 too… to ~ / enough to ~

Check up!

p. 338~339

A
1 too
2 to
3 enough
4 so
5 to reach
6 couldn't
7 to travel
8 to cut
9 so
10 smart enough

B
1 too/to
2 so/that
3 so/that
4 clever enough
5 so/that

C
1 can → couldn't
2 enough strong → strong enough
3 going → go
4 can → can't
5 to impatient too → too impatient to

Practice More Ⅱ

p. 340~342

A
1 cross
2 introduce
3 smile
4 to
5 gather
6 too
7 tell
8 enough time
9 clean
10 turn in
11 go / going (둘 모두 맞음)
12 eat
13 barking
14 solve
15 to play

B
1 too young to watch
2 so smart that
3 kind enough to show
4 so sad that he couldn't do anything
5 too much luggage to carry
6 tall enough to reach
7 too early to go

C
1 throw → to throw
2 solving → to solve
3 to weak → too weak
4 enough brave → brave enough
5 laughed → laugh(laughing)
6 can → can't
7 going → go
8 enough rich → rich enough
9 stolen → steal(stealing)
10 to show → show

D
1 so heavy that I can't move it
2 let me read his old books
3 felt someone put his hand on her head
4 had me not wear a short skirt
5 made me bring back old memories.
6 see the girls playing football
7 had his son not clean the front yard
8 too young to understand the lecture
9 too sleepy to do her homework
10 heard him sing in the bathroom

중간 기말고사 예상문제

내신 최다 출제 유형

p. 343

01 ④ 02 ① 03 ④ 04 ④ 05 ④
06 ⑤

해설

01 ①,②,③,⑤ 명사적 용법의 목적어 역할, ④ 부사적 용법의 '목적'

02 ② have → to have, ③ to getting → to get, ④ make → to make, ⑤ learning → learn

03 ① starting → starts, ② learning → learn, ③ going → to go, ⑤ read → to read

04 〈보기〉,④ 명사적 용법으로 동사의 목적어 역할을 한다. ①,⑤ 주어 역할, ②,③ 보어 역할

05 to부정사가 형용사처럼 쓰이는 경우 '~하는, ~할'이라고 해석하며, 대명사 뒤에 위치 한다.

06 ①,④ 'in order to'는 '~하기 위하여'라는 뜻으로 to부정사 부사적용법 '목적'을 의미하며 대신 바꿔 쓸 수 있다. ②,③ 동사를 목적어로 취하는 to부정사로 바꿀 수 있다. ⑤ 'enjoy'는 항상 동명사만을 목적어로 취한다.

p. 344~350

01 ①	02 ④	03 ②	04 ④	05 ③
06 ①	07 ④	08 ①	09 ②	10 ①, ③
11 ②	12 ④	13 ①	14 ②	15 ③
16 ③	17 ③	18 ③	19 ①	20 ③
21 ④	22 ②	23 ⑤	24 ③	25 ①
26 ①,④	27 ③,⑤	28 ⑤	29 ①	30 ③
31 ②	32 ③	33 ⑤	34 ①	35 ④
36 ②	37 ①	38 ①	39 ③	40 ⑤

〈서술형 평가〉

41 to buy a car
42 To eat breakfast every morning
43 She should decide where to move.
44 John doesn't know what to buy.
45 They teach how to read a book.
46 so/that I can't
47 so/that she can be
48 have enough/to read/hours
49 let (made, had)/play badminton/homework
50 grew/to be/nurse/she wished

해설

01 'like to' ~하는 것을 좋아하다, 'be going to' ~할 예정이다
02 'how to부정사' ~하는 방법
03 go → to go (명사처럼 쓰이는 to부정사)
04 'like to + 동사원형': opens → open
05 〈보기〉 ①,②,④,⑤ 명사적 용법의 목적어 역할, ③ 명사적 용법의 보어 역할
06 〈보기〉 ②,③,④,⑤ 형용사적 용법, ① 원인을 나타내는 부사적 용법
07 〈보기〉 ①,③ 명사적 용법의 주어 역할, ②,⑤ 명사적 용법의 가주어(it), 진주어(to have), ④ 부사적 용법
08 'need'는 to부정사를 목적격 보어로 쓴다.
09 감정을 나타내는 형용사 뒤에 오는 to부정사는 부사 역할을 하며 감정의 이유를 나타낸다.
10 ①, ③ 지각동사는 목적어를 원형부정사로 하지만, 동작의 강조를 위해 현재분사를 사용 하기도 한다.
11 'love' 뒤에는 to부정사를 사용한다.
go → to go (또는 동명사 going)
12 'wan to+동사원형' want to watching → want to watch
13 'want'는 to부정사를 목적어로 쓰기 때문에 'want to make'의 순서가 되고, 'Wh-의문문'의 동사가 일반동사일 경우 조동사 'do'가 의문사 바로 뒤에 온다.
14 ① I wish to be a famous singer. ③ Sometimes, to eat out is good. ④ It is not easy to speak English well. ⑤ He won't go there to help people.
15 ① She wants something to eat. ② It is not good to waste your time. ④ I don't have much time to do homework. ⑤ It is hard to make him happy.
16 ⓐ I like to ride in-line skates. ⓒ He will go to America next month. ⓓ They were happy to see me.
17 ①,②,④,⑤는 to부정사로 쓰였고, ③은 방향을 나타내는 전치사이다.
18 ①,②,④,⑤ to부정사 형용사적 용법, ③ to부정사 부사적 용법의 '목적' 의미
19 '~하기 위해' 목적을 나타내는 to부정사 부사적 용법이다.
20 '~하는 것은' to부정사의 명사적용법으로 쓰였다.
21 사역동사의 목적격보어로 원형부정사를 사용한다.
22 ①,③,⑤의 감각동사와, ④의 사역동사의 목적격보어는 원형부정사를 사용한다. ②의 'help'는 to부정사와 원형부정사 모두 사용할 수 있다.
23 〈주어진 문장, ⑤〉 '~해서' to부정사의 부사적 용법으로 '이유'를 뜻한다. ①,④ 명사적용법_주어, ②,③ 형용사적 용법
24 〈주어진 문장, ③〉 to부정사 부사적 용법의 '결과'를 의미한다. ①,④,⑤ to부정사 명사적용법 ② to부정사 부사적용법의 '원인'
25 〈주어진 문장,①〉 to부정사 부사적 용법의 '목적'을 나타낸다. ②,③,④ to부정사의 명사적 용법, ⑤ to부정사의 형용사적 용법
26 ①,④ 지각동사 + 원형부정사, 지각동사 + 현재분사(동사ing) → 지각동사의 목적격보어로는 원형부정사가 오며, 동작의 진행을 강조하고 싶을 경우에는 현재분사를 사용하기도 한다.
27 ③,⑤ 지각동사+원형부정사, 지각동사 + 현재분사(동사ing) → 지각동사의 목적격보어로는 원형부정사가 오며, 동작의 진행을 강조하고 싶을 경우엔 현재분사를 사용하기도 한다.
28 'write on some paper'에서 'on'을 써야 한다.
29 'live in a big house'에서 'in'을 써야 한다
30 'talk with some friends'에서 'with'를 써야 한다.
31 결과를 나타내는 to부정사의 부사적 용법이다.
32 첫 번째 문장: to부정사의 형용사적 용법이다. 두 번째 문장: 5형식문장의 목적격보어의 역할을 한다.
33 to부정사를 목적어로 취하는 동사 - 'want, hope'
34 ⓑ being → be, ⓒ go → to go
35 'notice'는 지각동사이기 때문에 목적격보어로 원형부정사 (또는 현재분사)가 와야 한다. to get → get (or getting)
36 사역동사의 목적격보어는 원형부정사를 사용한다.
37 ① 'love + to부정사(또는 동명사)'
38 ② want to → wants to, ③ wearing → wear, ④ walking → walk, ⑤ drink → to drink
39 ① listening → listen, ② studies → study, ④ eating → eat, ⑤ to dance → dance(dancing)
40 ① entering → enter, ② bigger → big ③ not to play → not play, ④ to help → help

〈서술형 평가〉

41 'enough + 명사 + to부정사' 구문이다.

42 to부정사의 명사적 용법 중 '주어 역할'을 하는 to부정사

43 'where + to부정사' 어디로(~해야) 할지

44 'what + to부정사' 무엇을(~해야) 할지

45 'how + to부정사' 어떻게(~해야) 할지

46 'too + 형용사 + to + 동사원형'은
'so ~ that + 주어 + can't + 동사원형'과 바꿔 쓸 수 있다.

47 '형용사 + enough to + 동사원형'은
'so + 형용사 + that + 주어 + can + 동사원형'과 바꿔
쓸 수 있다.

48 'enough to + 동사원형' ~하기에 충분한

49 사역동사의 목적격보어로는 원형부정사가 온다.

50 to부정사 부사적 용법의 결과를 의미 한다.

Chapter

10 동명사

Lesson 10-1 동명사의 규칙

Check up! p. 353

A
1 is
2 swimming
3 Exercising
4 her
5 is
6 him
7 is
8 not calling
9 walking
10 is

Lesson 10-2 동명사의 역할

Check up! p. 354~355

A
1 reading
2 talking
3 drawing
4 Driving
5 repairing
6 cooking
7 talking
8 Listening
9 winning
10 Meeting
11 joining
12 working
13 writing
14 learning
15 telling
16 doing
17 eating
18 playing
19 leaving
20 becoming

B
1 gave up buying
2 started laughing
3 practiced playing
4 loves cooking
5 enjoyed dancing

Lesson 10-3 동명사와 to부정사의 동사

Check up! p. 357

A
1 to live
2 doing
3 taking
4 to go
5 playing
6 to go out
7 to participate in
8 speaking
9 to travel
10 to buy
11 playing
12 to visit
13 to eat
14 to stay
15 talking

B
1 exercising
2 eating
3 to go
4 singing
5 to use
6 to study

Lesson 10-4 동명사의 관용 표현

Check up! p. 359

A
1 go camping
2 are used to doing
3 looked forward to traveling
4 cannot help loving
5 busy doing
6 spent / watching
7 feels like going
8 spend / playing
9 keeps talking to
10 kept me from sleeping
11 feel like
12 spent / finishing
13 waiting for
14 didn't feel like answering
15 How about eating

Practice More Ⅰ

p. 360~362

A

1	inviting	2	doing
3	studying	4	playing
5	listening	6	Learning
7	saying	8	riding
9	watching	10	laughing

B

1	주어	2	보어
3	목적어	4	목적어
5	보어	6	주어
7	목적어	8	주어
9	목적어	10	보어

C

1 living → live
2 to participate → participating
3 learn → learning
4 to write → writing
5 played → playing
6 eating → to eat
7 to help → helping
8 play → playing
9 make → making(to make)
10 are → is

D

1 waiting for
2 go skiing
3 busy preparing for Jack's birthday party
4 cannot help loving
5 feel like going fishing
6 keep me from going out alone
7 How about playing tennis
8 went hunting
9 spent a lot of money taking pictures
10 is looking forward to going

중간 기말고사 예상문제

내신 최다 출제 유형

p. 363

01 ①　02 ④,⑤　03 ②　04 ②　05 ④
06 ⓐ exercise, ⓑ playing, ⓒ watching, ⓓ do
07 Jennifer loves playing

해설

01 ① 동명사를 목적어로 취하는 동사가 와야 한다. ②,③,④,⑤는 to부정사만을 목적어로 취하는 동사들이다.
02 ④,⑤ 문장의 주어로 to부정사나 동명사의 형태가 와야 한다.
03 ① ride → riding, ③ take → taking, ④ play → playing, ⑤ do → doing
04 ① touching → touch (지각동사 + 원형부정사) ③ want be → want to be (want + to부정사), ④ she → her, ⑤ drawing → draw
05 ① teach → teaching, ② staying → stay, ③ sing → singing, ⑤ traveling → travel
06 ⓐ 'do exercise' 운동을 하다, ⓑ,ⓒ 'enjoy + 동명사', ⓓ 'want + to부정사'
07 'love'는 to부정사, 동명사를 모두 목적어로 취할 수 있다.

p. 364~368

01 ③	02 ④	03 ⑤	04 ②	05 ①
06 ③	07 ④	08 ①	09 ④	10 ②
11 ①	12 ④	13 ①	14 ①	15 ③
16 ⑤	17 ③	18 ②	19 ⑤	20 ④
21 ①,③	22 ④,⑤	23 ③	24 ④	25 ①
26 ②	27 ⑤	28 ④	29 ③	30 ①

〈서술형 평가〉

31 skating
32 meeting
33 running
34 He enjoys telling his childhood stories.
35 Walking every day is good for your health.
36 He spent a lot of money buying his house.
37 Philip goes skiing every winter.
38 I'm not used to getting up early in the morning.

해설

01 'go+동명사' ~하러 가다의 과거형
02 'be busy 동명사' ~하느라 바쁘다
03 'mind'는 동명사만을 목적어로 취한다.
04 'look forward to 동명사' ~하기를 학수고대하다.
05 주어로 동명사가 쓰였다.
06 첫 번째 문장은 to부정사, 두 번째 문장은 동명사를 목적어로 취한다.
07 첫 번째 문장 – 'stop + 동명사' (~하는 것을 멈추다), 두 번째 문장 – 'stop + to부정사' (~하기 위해 멈추다)
08 ② to run → running, ③ Use → Using, ④ join → joining, ⑤ read → reading
09 ① exercise → exercising, ② tell → telling, ③ to jump → jumping, ⑤ sing → singing
10 'stop + 동명사' ~하는 것을 멈추다
11 'What(How) about 동명사' ~하는 것은 어때?
12 'hope'는 to부정사만을 목적어로 취한다.
13 'want'는 to부정사만을 목적어로 취한다
14 ① 동명사의 주어 역할, ②,③,④,⑤ 동명사의 목적어 역할
15 ③ 현재분사 (동작)를 나타냄, ①,②,④,⑤ 동명사 보어 역할
16 ①,②,③,④ 동명사 목적어 역할, ⑤ 현재분사
17 ① want to do this weekend, ② will (또는 is going to) ④ are you going to do, ⑤ go fishing
18 'hope, want, feel like' 동명사 → 'enjoy'는 동명사만을 목적어로 취한다.
19 'look forward to + 동명사' ~하는 것을 학수고대하다
20 'love + to부정사' ~하는 것을 좋아하다
21 ① 'hope to부정사' – visit → to visit ③ 'what about + 동명사' – catch → catching
22 ④ become → becoming, ⑤ sing → singing
23 문장의 주어와 동명사의 주어가 다를 경우 동명사의 의미상의 주어로 소유격 또는 목적격을 사용한다.
24 ① playing not → not playing, ② are → is, ③ open → opening, ⑤ in-line skate → in-line skating
25 ① 'go + 동명사' ~하러 가다: 'go traveling' 여행을 가다
26 〈보기, ②〉동명사의 보어 역할 ①,③ 전치사의 목적어 역할, ④,⑤ 동사의 목적어 역할
27 〈보기,①,②,③,④〉 동명사의 주어 역할, ⑤ 명사
28 'avoid+동명사' ~하는 것을 피하다 (→ to부정사는 사용할 수 없다.)
29 'dream about + 동명사' ~하는 것을 꿈꾸다.
30 'decide to + 동사원형' ~하기로 결정하다

〈서술형 평가〉

31 'go + 동명사' ~하러 가다
32 'How(What) about + 동명사' ~하는 것이 어때?
33 'run': 달리다, (가게)를 운영하다 의 뜻을 가지고 있다. 마지막 문장의 'running'은 '달리는'이라는 뜻으로 현재분사로 쓰였다.
34 'enjoy'는 동명사만을 목적어로 취한다.
35 'Walking every day'는 주어역할을 하는 동명사 이다.
36 'spend 시간 / 돈 동명사' ~하는 데 시간 / 돈을 쓰다
37 'go + 동명사' ~하러 가다
38 'be used to 동명사' ~하는 데 익숙하다

Chapter 11 수동태

Lesson 11-1 수동태의 사용

Check up! p. 371

A
1 능동 2 능동
3 수동 4 능동
5 수동 6 능동
7 수동 8 수동
9 능동 10 수동
11 능동 12 수동
13 능동 14 수동
15 수동

Lesson 11-2 수동태에 많이 쓰이는 불규칙 동사

Check up! p. 373

A
1 ate - eaten 2 gave - given
3 told - told 4 thought - thought
5 was/were - been 6 blew - blown
7 cooked - cooked 8 hit-hit
9 did - done 10 wrote - written
11 used - used 12 spoke - spoken
13 got - got(ten) 14 flew - flown
15 held - held 16 threw - thrown
17 found - found 18 laid - laid
19 came - come 20 lost - lost
21 made - made 22 read - read
23 broke - broken 24 drew - drawn
25 agreed - agreed 26 carried - carried
27 cried - cried 28 chose - chosen
29 fixed - fixed 30 rode - ridden
31 took - taken 32 killed - killed
33 built - built 34 knew - known
35 bore - born 36 sent - sent
37 taught - taught 38 sang-sung
39 meant - meant 40 stole - stolen
41 worried - worried 42 fed - fed
43 destroyed - destroyed 44 saw - seen
45 visited - visited 46 kept - kept
47 spent - spent 48 woke - woken
49 cleaned - cleaned 50 put - put
51 bit - bitten 52 began - begun
53 invited - invited 54 dried - dried
55 drove - driven
56 understood - understood
57 planned - planned 58 hid - hidden

Lesson 11-3 능동태를 수동태로 바꾸기

Check up! p. 374

A
1 are invited 2 is sent
3 are collected 4 is visited
5 was opened 6 were made
7 is fixed

Lesson 11-4 'by+목적격' 생략하기

Check up! p. 375

A
1 Many books were published (by them).
2 Photos are taken here (by people).
3 The cup was broken (by someone).
4 These letters were written by him.
5 Fresh vegetables are sold in the store (by them).
6 Sujin was elected class president by the students.
7 The park is visited (by people) every day.
8 A jar of apple jam is made by Lilly.
9 The dove is considered a symbol of peace (by people).

Lesson 11-5 'by' 이외의 전치사를 사용하는 수동태

Check up! p. 376

A
1 is scared of
2 am bored with
3 was surprised at
4 is filled with
5 is interested in
6 is covered with
7 is known for
8 is made from

Lesson 11-6 수동태의 현재와 과거

Check up! p. 377

A
1 is sent
2 was washed
3 is recommended
4 was made
5 is built
6 were invited
7 is delivered
8 were broken
9 was used

Practice More I p. 378~380

A
1 in
2 at
3 by
4 with
5 of
6 by
7 by
8 by
9 of
10 at
11 with
12 by

B
1 was invented
2 was washed
3 was scolded
4 was drawn
5 was eaten
6 was surprised at
7 was caught
8 was fixed
9 were written
10 were seen

C
1 is eaten
2 is seen
3 was chosen
4 are withered
5 was painted
6 were finished

D
1 was played by
2 were adopted by
3 is interested in
4 were written by
5 is opened

E
1 Many songs were composed by him.
2 My brother was bitten by the dog.
3 Strawberries are grown by my grandfather.
4 The expensive diamonds were stolen by the thief.
5 The baby was taken care of by her.

중간 기말고사 예상문제

내신 최다 출제 유형 p. 381

01 ① 02 ④ 03 ③ 04 ③ 05 ①
06 ⓐ → was bought
07 Other students are always laughed at by her.

해설

01 ② I → me, ③ park → parked, ④ they → them, ⑤ hold → held
→ 수동태: 'be동사 + 과거분사 ~ by + 목적격'
02 is make → is made
03 행위자가 막연한 사람이거나 분명하지 않을 때 생략할 수 있다.
04 ① is become → became, ② made → is made (was made), ④ setted → set (set-set-set), ⑤ 'be filled with' ~로 가득차다
05 능동태의 동사가 과거형이기 때문에 수동태에서는 be동사의 과거형을 써야 한다. 행위자가 'Elsa'인 것이 확실하기 때문에 'by+목적격'은 생략할 수 없다.
06 새 시계가 잃어버린 행위를 당한 수동태 문장이다. 수동태의 동사 형태: 'be동사 + 과거분사'
07 주어: 능동태의 목적어, 동사: be동사 + 과거분사, by + 목적격: by + 능동태 주어

p. 382~387

01 ⑤ 02 ④ 03 ② 04 ③ 05 ①
06 ② 07 ③ 08 ⑤ 09 ① 10 ③
11 ③ 12 ④ 13 ② 14 ④ 15 ①
16 ② 17 ⑤ 18 ④ 19 ① 20 ③
21 ② 22 ⑤ 23 ② 24 ③ 25 ③
26 ② 27 ③ 28 ③ 29 ④ 30 ⑤
31 ①,③ 32 ④,⑤ 33 ②,③ 34 ①,② 35 ③,④
36 ②,④

〈서술형 평가〉

37 is held 38 by Eddie
39 from 40 with
41 causes 42 were planted
43 The computer program was developed by a programmer.
44 The outline of the picture was drawn by Leonardo.
45 The beautiful tower was built by an Italian artist.
46 The juice was spilled by my brother.

해설

01 ① keep – kept, ② ride – ridden, ③ break – broken ④ bear – born

02 ① am – been → 'am'은 be동사 중 하나이고, 현재와 과거의 형태는 각각 다르지만 과거분사형은 주어의 인칭에 관계없이 'been'을 사용한다. ② do – done, ③ wake – woken, ⑤ bite – bitten

03 ① give – given, ③ sing – sung, ④ swim – swum, ⑤ wear – worn

04 'be made of' ~로 만들어지다 (재료의 성질에 변화가 없다.)

05 'be covered with' ~로 뒤덮여있다

06 'be filled with' ~로 가득 차다

07 능동태 문장의 동사가 과거형이므로, 수동태의 be동사도 과거형으로 써준다.

08 문장의 동사가 현재형이므로, 수동태의 be동사도 현재형으로 써준다.

09 'Hamlet'이 셰익스피어에 의해 쓰여졌다는 수동태 문장이며, 이미 끝난 과거의 일이므로 수동태 과거형을 써준다.

10 새끼 캥거루를 'Joey'라고도 부르는 것은 과거의 끝나버린 일이 아니다. 'be동사의 현재형+과거분사' 형태가 알맞다.

11 is draw → draws

12 'was broken': 수동태의 동사는 'be동사 + 과거분사' 형태이다.

13 능동태의 목적어→ 주어, 능동태의 동사→ be동사+과거분사, 능동태의 주어→ by+목적격
The light bulb / was invented / by Thomas Edison
→ 행위자가 구체적인 사람으로 언급될 경우 반드시 'be+목적격'의 형태를 만들어준다.

14 능동태의 목적어 → 주어, 능동태의 동사 → be동사+과거분사, 능동태 주어 → by+목적격
a garage sale / is held / by Mr. and Mrs. Green (on their garden)

15 능동태의 목적어 → 주어, 능동태의 동사 → be동사+과거분사, 능동태 주어 → by+목적격
The flowers / were watered / by me

16 '공을 던지다'에서 'throw'의 수동태는 'is thrown'이 알맞다

17 '메일을 보내다'에서 'send'의 수동태는 'was sent'가 알맞다.

18 '~을 굽다'의 'bake'의 수동태는 'was baked'가 알맞다.

19 수동태의 동사는 'be동사 + 과거분사'이다.
is written, is broken

20 수동태의 동사는 'be동사 + 과거분사'이다.
is watched, were caught

21 능동태의 동사가 과거형이므로 수동태의 동사도 'be동사 과거형 + 과거분사'로 사용된다.

22 능동태의 동사가 과거형일 경우 수동태에서는 'was(were)+과거분사'의 형태가 된다.

23 능동태의 동사가 과거형이므로 수동태의 동사도 'be동사 과거형 + 과거분사'로 사용된다.

24 수동태 동사가 'be동사의 과거형 + 과거분사'이기 때문에 능동태 동사는 과거형이 된다.

25 'be covered with' ~로 덮이다.
'be tired of' ~에 지치다, 피곤하다

26 'be pleased with' ~에 즐거워하다
'be surprised at' ~에 놀라다

27 'be bored with' ~에 지루해하다,
'be worried about':~에 대해 걱정하다

28 3형식의 문장 (능동태)으로 '주어 + 동사 + 목적어 + 부사'로 이루어졌다.

29 'be interested in' ~에 흥미를 가지다

30 이미 끝나버린 과거의 일을 수동태 문장으로 표현할 때 be동사는 과거형이 사용된다.

31 ② is rode → is ridden, ④ is poped → is popped,
⑤ is blocking → is blocked

32 ① was stole → was stolen
② were broken → was broken, ③ is → are(were)

33 ① is sell → is sold, ④ was send → were sent
⑤ comic book → comic books

34 ① was hearing → was heard,
② were catch → were caught

35 ③ was knit → was knitted, ④ is spinned → is spun

36 ② were played → was played
④ was drown → was drawn

〈서술형 평가〉

37 'hold'의 과거분사는 'held'이다.

38 수동태의 목적격은 'by + 목적격'으로 표현된다.

39 'be made from' ~로 만들어지다 – 재료의 성질이 화학적으로 변화된 경우에 사용된다.

40 'be covered with' ~로 덮이다

41 수동태의 be동사가 현재형이므로, 능동태의 동사도 현재형으로 써주며, 주어의 인칭에 따라 '–es'를 붙여준다.

42 수동태의 동사는 능동태 동사의 시제와 일치시킨다.
능동태 동사가 과거형일 경우, 수동태에서는
'be동사과거 + 과거분사'로 표현된다.

43 주어: 능동태의 목적어,
동사: be동사의 과거+'develop' 과거분사,
목적어: by+능동태 주어

44 주어: 능동태의 목적어, 동사: be동사의 과거 + 'draw' 과거분사,
목적어: by + 능동태 주어

45 수동태 어순: 주어 + be동사 + 과거분사 + by + 목적격

46 수동태 어순: 주어 + be동사 + 과거분사 + by + 목적격

Chapter

12 분사

Lesson 12-1 분사의 종류와 형태

Check up! p. 391

A 1 boring 2 smiling
3 falling 4 broken
5 forgotten 6 rising
7 sleeping 8 crying
9 interesting 10 closed

Lesson 12-2 현재분사

Check up! p. 392~393

A 1 running 2 interesting
3 standing 4 flying
5 surprising 6 crossing
7 eating 8 sleeping
9 taking 10 singing

B 1 cleaned → cleaning
2 sat → sitting
3 crossed → crossing
4 washing → washed
5 played → playing
6 cried → crying
7 shone → shining
8 had → having
9 cooked → cooking
10 floated → floating

Lesson 12-3 과거분사

Check up! p. 394

A 1 I want to read the novel written in English.
2 I want to exchange my broken chair.
3 She found a lost dog.
4 Is this the picture drawn by your mom?
5 The money spent on Children's Day is too much.

B 1 repaired 2 beloved
3 broken 4 named
5 washed

Lesson 12-4 분사의 쓰임

Check up! p. 395

A 1 looking 2 broken
3 having 4 practicing
5 been 6 running
7 preparing 8 listening
9 canceled 10 waiting
11 planted 12 lived
13 watching 14 born
15 done

Practice More I

p. 396~398

A 1 boring 2 holding
3 surprising 4 exiting
5 climbing 6 interesting
7 crossing 8 written
9 spent 10 rolling

B
1 running 2 listening
3 pleased 4 born
5 missing 6 written
7 following 8 stolen
9 been 10 repaired

C 1 excited → exciting
2 chewed → chewing

3 flew → flying
4 sat → sitting
5 cleaned → cleaning
6 playing → played
7 lived → living
8 walked → walking
9 shocking → shocked
10 amazed → amazing

D
1 Look at that crying baby.
2 The girl jumping rope is my sister.
3 I heard an exciting story in the morning.
4 We were shocked to hear of his accident.
5 Joe wears a coat given to him by his girlfriend.
6 I saw Nick standing on the hill.
7 She sits surrounded by the flowers.
8 Mr. Lee always looks tired.
9 She lies around reading books all day.
10 I was disappointed because I couldn't pass the exam.

Lesson 12-5 현재분사와 동명사

Check up! p. 400

A
1 현재분사 2 동명사
3 현재분사 4 동명사
5 현재분사 6 현재분사
7 동명사 8 동명사
9 현재분사 10 동명사

Lesson 12-6 감정을 나타내는 분사

Check up! p. 401~402

A
1 moving / moved
2 satisfied / satisfying
3 disappointing / disappointed
4 bored / boring
5 excited / exciting
6 annoyed / annoying
7 surprised / surprising
8 frightened / frightening
9 shocked / shocking
10 pleased / pleasing

B
1 tired 2 amazing
3 surprising 4 exciting
5 satisfied 6 depressed
7 surprised 8 moved

Lesson 12-7 분사구문

Check up! p. 404

A
1 Feeling 2 Graduating
3 Not living 4 Knowing
5 Waiting 6 Getting
7 Turning 8 Seeing
9 Having taken 10 Having lost

Practice More Ⅱ p. 405~407

A
1 현재분사 2 동명사
3 현재분사 4 동명사
5 현재분사 6 현재분사
7 동명사 8 현재분사
9 동명사 10 동명사

B
1 surprised 2 disappointed
3 amazing 4 annoyed
5 living 6 fixed
7 confused 8 sleeping
9 interesting 10 walking

C
1 나는 그 귀중한 선물에 매우 놀랐다.
2 William은 자기의 수영복을 잃어버렸다.
3 공원에는 산책 중인 사람들이 많다.
4 Kate는 자기 딸의 편지에 감동 받았다.
5 나는 쇼핑백이 몇 개 더 필요해.
6 일기를 쓰는 것은 중요하다.
7 그들은 K-pop에 대해 얘기를 하는 중이다.
8 누가 저 부서진 의자를 치울 거야?
9 사람들은 그녀를 살아있는 인형이라고 부른다.
10 내 아들은 요리하는 것을 좋아한다.

D
1 are waiting for Zoe now
2 What an exciting movie this is!
3 playing chess because it is boring
4 Lucas satisfied with the test result

5 a dress made by my mother
6 She was surprised at Mark's accident.
7 sleeping on the bench is mine
8 That mountain is covered with snow
9 I just finished washing my car
10 The man kept looking at me
11 I have a picture drawn by my grandfather.
12 The book written by Linda became famous

중간 기말고사 **예상문제**

내신 최다 출제 유형

p. 408

01 ① 02 ④ 03 ② 04 ③
05 watering the garden 06 painted blue

해설
01 ① 현재분사, ②,③,④,⑤ 동명사
02 ① exciting → excited
② disappointing → disappointed
③ frighten → frightened, ⑤ shock → shocked
03 감정의 주체가 사람일 경우 과거분사를 사용 한다.
04 '이유'의 분사구문이다. 접속사와 주어를 생략하고 '동사+ing'의 형태가 부사절의 주어가 된다.
05 물을 뿌리고 있는 할머니가 주체이므로 현재분사가 사용된다.
06 이미 페인트가 칠해져 있는 집이 대상이 되므로 과거분사가 사용 된다.

p. 409~413

01 ⑤	02 ②	03 ③	04 ①	05 ①
06 ③	07 ⑤	08 ②	09 ③	10 ④
11 ①	12 ②	13 ①	14 ③	15 ④
16 ②	17 ①,③	18 ②,④	19 ⑤	20 ②
21 ③	22 ④	23 ②	24 ③	25 ②

〈서술형 평가〉
26 playing (play) 27 crying
28 destroyed 29 amazing
30 stolen 31 satisfied
32 ⓓ, fighting (fight) 33 loved
34 Having read the book 'Peter Pan'
35 A lot of people were moved by the film.
36 Rachel was pleased with his proposal.
37 She was depressed by his accident.
38 That laughing girl is my daughter
39 너무 아팠기 때문에 그녀는 파티에 가지 않았다.
40 Tommy는 자기가 일등을 하지 못해서 실망했다.

해설
01 '세차 중인'을 의미하므로 현재분사 'being washed'가 알맞다.
02 감정을 나타내는 분사는 사물이 주어가 되는 경우 현재분사형이 사용된다.
03 '지어진 집'을 의미하므로 과거분사 'built'가 알맞다.
04 분사구문의 '이유 (~때문에)'를 의미한다.
05 첫 번째 문장: 'be동사+현재분사'의 형태로 진행형을 뜻한다. 두 번째 문장: 지각동사는 목적어로 원형부정사 또는 현재분사를 취한다.
06 첫 번째 문장: 뒤의 'truck'을 수식하는 과거분사이다. 두 번째 문장: 'have / has+과거분사'의 완료 형태이다.
07 첫 번째 문장: 'The musical'이 감정을 일으키는 대상이므로 현재분사가 사용된다. 두 번째 문장: 'We'가 감정을 느끼는 대상이므로 과거분사가 사용된다.
08 지각동사는 목적어로 원형부정사 또는 현재분사를 취한다.
09 쿵푸를 좋아한다고 하였기 때문에 'boring (지루한)'은 답이 될 수 없다.
10 이미 '~해버린 집'이라는 의미의 과거분사가 사용되어야 한다. 'burning'은 현재분사로 능동, 진행의 의미를 가지고 있다.
11 명사를 꾸며주는 과거분사: hashed brown potatoes
12 감정을 느끼게 하는 주어가 사물일 경우 현재분사를 사용한다.
13 ① 동명사, ②,③,④,⑤ 분사
14 ③ 분사, ①,②,④,⑤ 동명사
15 ④ 분사, ①,②,③,⑤ 동명사
16 ② 동명사, ①,③,④,⑤ 분사
17 ① 감정을 느끼게 하는 주어가 사물일 경우 현재분사가 사용된다. ③ 감정을 느끼는 주어가 사람일 경우 과거분사가 사용된다.
18 ① scared → scaring, ③ satisfied → satisfying, ⑤ interesting → interested
19 〈보기, ⑤〉 동명사, ①,②,③,④ 분사
20 〈보기, ②〉 분사, ①,③,④,⑤ 동명사
21 〈보기, ③〉 동명사, ①,②,④,⑤ 분사
22 분사구문의 '이유'를 나타낸 표현이다. 부사절이 문장 맨 앞에 나올 때 접속사와 주어는 생략하고, 동사를 '현재분사' 형태로 바꾼다
23 분사구문의 부정형은 분사형태 앞에 'not'을 붙인다.
24 '동시 동작'을 나타내는 분사구문이다. 접속사와 주어를 생략하고, '동사원형+ing'를 주어로 쓴다.
25 '때(시간)'를 나타내는 분사구문이다.

〈서술형 평가〉

26 지각동사 'saw' 뒤에는 원형부정사 또는 현재분사가 와야 한다.

27 'boy'를 꾸며주는 현재분사이다.

28 'house'를 꾸며주는 과거분사이다.

29 감정을 느끼는 주체가 사물인 경우 현재분사가 사용된다.

30 'wallet'을 꾸며주는 과거분사이다

31 감정을 느끼는 주체가 사람인 경우 과거분사가 사용된다.

32 지각동사 뒤에는 원형부정사 또는 현재분사가온다.

33 '~된'이라는 수동의 의미이므로 과거분사가 사용된다.

34 'have / has + 과거분사'의 완료 형태의 분사구문은 'having + 과거분사'의 형태를 가진다.

35 '주어 + be동사 + 과거분사 + by + 목적격'의 수동태 형식이다. 감동을 받은 주체가 사람이기 때문에 과거분사 'moved'를 사용한다.

36 '주어 + be동사 + 과거분사 + by + 목적격'의 수동태 형식이다. 감동을 받은 주체가 사람이기 때문에 과거분사 'moved'를 사용한다.

37 'be depressed' ~에 우울하다

38 '웃고 있는 소녀'에서 진행을 의미하는 현재분사 'laughing'이 명사 'girl'을 꾸며준다.

39 파티에 가지 않았다는 이유가 앞의 부사절이기에 '~때문에'로 해석된다. → Because she was sick too much, she didn't go to the party.

40 because절에는 Tommy가 실망했다는 내용이 쓰였다.

Chapter
13 접속사

Lesson 13-1 and / but / or / so

Check up! p. 418

A	1	and	2	but
	3	and	4	but
	5	but	6	so
	7	but	8	or
	9	and	10	so
	11	or	12	because
	13	but	14	so
	15	for		

Lesson 13-2 명령문과 and / or

Check up! p. 419

A	1	or	2	and
	3	or	4	or
	5	and	6	and
	7	or	8	and
	9	and	10	and

Lesson 13-3 both A and B / either A or B

Check up! p. 420~421

A	1	and	2	but
	3	or	4	but also, but
	5	neither	6	both
	7	not only	8	not
	9	or	10	nor
B	1	both	2	Either
	3	not	4	but (also)
	5	nor	6	and
	7	but	8	neither
	9	not	10	not only

Practice More I

p. 422~424

A	1	and	2	so
	3	or	4	but
	5	and	6	or
	7	or	8	so
	9	and	10	for
	11	and	12	but
	13	so	14	and
	15	or		
B	1	and	2	but
	3	not only	4	neither
	5	Either	6	not
	7	both	8	not only
	9	not	10	neither
C	1	nor → or	2	is → are
	3	like → likes	4	wears → wear
	5	or → nor	6	but also → but
	7	goes → go	8	are → is
	9	or → and	10	are → is

D
1 smart but weak
2 go to either the concert or the museum
3 can play the piano but can't dance
4 either a soccer player or a singer
5 study both Korean and English
6 Neither Valentina nor her husband is going to attend
7 not in my room but on the table
8 not only the robot but also the satellite
9 both go to the theater and play tennis
10 Either Lucas or Helen got an A

Lesson 13-4 that의 쓰임

Check up! p. 426~427

A
1 주어
2 목적어
3 보어
4 목적어
5 주어
6 목적어
7 주어
8 보어
9 목적어
10 보어

B
1 I think that the picture is great.
2 He believes that the girl broke the window.
3 It is bad that you tell a lie.
4 The problem is that we made a mistake.
5 I wished that I could pass the exam.
6 That he entered the school is misinformation.
7 I realized that I loved her.
8 The professor thought that the test was easy.
9 The good news is that it will be sunny tomorrow.
10 It is true that Kelly can't go hiking.
11 I know that Jack will be late.

Lesson 13-5 whether (or not)

Check up! p. 428

A
1 whether
2 whether
3 whether / if
4 whether
5 whether
6 whether / if
7 if
8 if / whether

Lesson 13-6 if / unless / because

Check up! p. 429

A
1 If
2 Unless
3 because
4 If
5 because
6 Unless
7 If

Lesson 13-7 when / while

Check up! p. 430~431

A
1 before
2 When
3 after
4 until
5 While

B
1 ②
2 ①
3 ④
4 ③
5 ⑤

C
1 When Johnny came back, we were very glad. (We were very glad when Johnny came back.)
2 Read a book several times until you understand it.
3 While my mom is cooking, my sister and I set the table. (My sister and I set the table while my mom is cooking.)

Practice More Ⅱ

p. 432~434

A
1 that
2 whether / if
3 whether
4 that
5 whether
6 that
7 if/whether
8 that
9 whether
10 that

B
1 While
2 When
3 until
4 because of
5 If
6 if
7 While
8 After
9 because
10 If
11 when
12 because of
13 If
14 If
15 Before

C
1 that → whether
2 What → When
3 until → if
4 Because → Because of
5 if → whether
6 Unless → While
7 because → because of
8 unless → if
9 unless → if
10 because of → because

D 1 whether Sally changes her hair color or not
2 Because of her laziness
3 that Lily can't remember him
4 If you can't finish the essay
5 When Nick saw her again
6 If you get an A on the test
7 Unless you walk fast

중간 기말고사 **예상문제**

내신 최다 출제 유형

p. 435

01 ② 02 ③ 03 ⑤ 04 ③
05 ① 06 ②

해설

01 아침식사를 하지 않아서 배가 고프다는 원인과 결과를 말해주고 있다. 'so (그래서)'가 알맞다.

02 ①,④ 보어 역할, ② 주어 역할, ⑤ 지시형용사, ③ 동사의 목적어로 쓰일 경우 생략이 가능하다.

03 ①,②,③,④ '~할 때'의 뜻을 가진 접속사이다. ⑤ '언제'라는 뜻의 의문사이다.

04 ③ 시간이나 조건을 나타내는 부사절에서는 미래를 표현할 때 현재 시제를 사용한다. will knit → knit

05 ② 'neither A nor B' : A와 B 둘 다 아니다, ③ 'not only A but also B': A뿐만 아니라 B도 아니다, ④ 'either A or B' : A와 B 둘 중 하나, ⑤ 'not A but B' : A가 아니라 B이다

06 접속사를 경계로 앞뒤의 내용이 서로 반대일 때 접속사 'but'를 쓴다.

p. 436~442

01 ① 02 ④ 03 ② 04 ⑤ 05 ①
06 ③ 07 ② 08 ① 09 ④ 10 ③
11 ④ 12 ⑤ 13 ① 14 ①,④ 15 ②,③
16 ③,④ 17 ① 18 ⑤ 19 ② 20 ①
21 ② 22 ④ 23 ② 24 ④ 25 ③
26 ① 27 ③ 28 ⑤ 29 ① 30 ③
31 ① 32 ② 33 ⑤ 34 ② 35 ④

〈서술형 평가〉

36 Because of → Because
37 only not → not only
38 or → and
39 It is true that Oscar bought a new sports car.
40 We knew that Kevin wanted to marry with her.
41 Read a book many times, and you'll understand it better.
42 Take the test, or you'll not pass this semester.
43 Both she and her sister are famous opera divas.
44 I think that he can invent more useful things.
45 I wonder whether they will enjoy the musical tonight.
46 네가 그들을 행복하게 만들 수 있는 것은 가능한 일이다. (주어)
47 나는 많은 사람들에게 꿈이 있고, 그들이 그 꿈을 위해 최선을 다한다는 것을 안다. (목적어)
48 (A) so, (B) but

해설

01 '~하는 동안'의 의미인 'while'이 알맞다.
→ Jacky가 올 동안 나는 따뜻하게 맞이할 준비를 한다.

02 '~할 때'의 의미인 'when'이 알맞다.
→ 미인 대회에 참석했을 때 Mia는 최고로 예쁜 여인이 되고 싶었다.

03 '~때문에'의 의미인 'because'가 알맞다.
→ 그림을 그리는 어떠한 물품도 가져오지 않았기 때문에 몇몇 사람들은 집으로 돌아가야 했다.

04 'and'는 '~와, 그리고'의 뜻으로 대등한 단어와 단어, 문장과 문장 등을 서로 연결할 때 쓰인다.
서로 대등한 것들을 연결할 때 'A, B, and C'의 형식이다.

05 'but'은 '하지만'의 뜻으로, 앞뒤의 항목이 대조되거나 반대일 때 사용한다.

06 'if = whether' (~인지 아닌지)

07 'if not = unless' (만약 ~않는다면)

08 앞뒤 항목의 내용이 대조되거나 반대일 경우 'but'을 사용한다.

09 'because' ~때문에

10 'so'는 앞의 문장은 원인을, 뒤의 문장은 결과를 나타낼 때 사용된다.

11 앞뒤 문장이 대조적일 경우 'but'을 사용한다.

12 or → and
→ Get up early, and you won't miss the first subway.

13 but → because

14 ② buying → buy, ③ is knowing → knows
⑤ and → but

15 ① I cannot do it → I can do it or not
④ 'It ~ that 용법', That is not true → It is not true
⑤ Unless → Because

16 〈보기, ③,④〉 '~할 때', ①,②,⑤ '언제'

17 〈보기, ①〉 '~처럼' ②,③,④,⑤ '~할 때'

18 '~해라, 그러면'의 의미로, 명령문을 연결하는 긍정문이다.

19 원인과 결과를 보여주는 문장을 연결할 때는 접속사 'so'를 쓴다.

20 때를 나타내는 접속사 'when'을 쓴다.

21 ①' or → but, ③ and → or, ④ or → and, ⑤ and → or

22 앞뒤 문장이 서로 반대된다. 'but'을 사용하는 것이 알맞다.

23 타동사 뒤에 쓰여서 목적어 역할을 한다.
→ 'that'을 목적어로 받는 타동사
: 'think, know, believe, say' 등이 있다.

24 '명령문 or = If you don't~, you'll~ '

25 '명령문 and = If you~, you'll~ '

26 앞뒤의 문장을 연결해 주는 접속사 'and'를 쓴다.

27 '만약 네가 피곤하다면, 조금 쉬는 게 낫겠다.'의 표현으로 쓸 수 있다. '만약 ~하다면'의 뜻을 가진 접속사는 'if'이다.

28 'both A and B' : A와 B 둘 다 ~이다

29 'neither A nor B' : A와 B 둘 다 아니다

30 'not only A but also B' : A뿐 아니라 B도 역시

31 'either A or B' : A와 B 둘 중 하나는

32 'unless = if not' 만약~하지 않는다면

33 ①,②,③,④ 내일 날이 맑을지 아닐지 궁금해 한다.
⑤ 내일 날이 맑기를 바라고 있다.

34 ① 의문사가 없는 간접의문문은 'if'나 'whether'을 써 준다.
that → whether, ③ If or not → Whether or not
④ if → whether, ⑤ 주절 이하의 문장이 보어로 쓰였으므로 whether가 쓰여야 한다. If → whether
→ 'if'의 명사절은 목적어로만 사용된다.

35 'unless = if~not' 만약 ~하지 않는다면

〈서술형 평가〉

36 'because of + 명사', 'because + 문장'

37 'not only A but also B' : A뿐 아니라 B도 역시

38 'both A and B' : A와 B 둘 다 ~이다

39 'It is true that~' :~한 것은 사실이다

40 'We knew that~' : ~이라는 것을 알고 있었다

41 'If'절을 명령문으로 바꾸고, 긍정의 뜻을 가질 경우 'and'를 붙인 후 나머지 문장은 그대로 써준다.

42 'If'절을 명령문으로 바꾸고, 부정의 뜻을 가질 경우 'or'를 붙인 후 나머지 문장은 그대로 써준다.

43 'both A and B' : A와 B 둘 모두~

44 '동사 (think)' 뒤의 'that'절은 목적어로 쓰인다.

45 'wonder (궁금하다) + whether (~인지 아닌지)'

46 'It'은 가주어이고, 'that'이하가 진주어이다.

47 'that' 이하의 문장은 동사 'know'의 목적어로 쓰였다.

48 (A) 'so' 그래서 (B) 'but' 하지만

Chapter

14 전치사

Lesson 14-1 여러 가지 전치사

Check up! p. 445

A
1 at the corner
2 in January
3 at two o'clock
4 in front of the public library
5 under my bed
6 during winter vacation
7 in the morning
8 in 2015
9 at the bus stop
10 by next month
11 on December 12th
12 for a month
13 among the students
14 by 7 p.m.
15 since 1997

Lesson 14-2 시간, 때를 나타내는 전치사 (1)

Check up! p. 446

A
1 in | 2 on
3 in | 4 at
5 on | 6 in
7 at | 8 on
9 in | 10 at

Lesson 14-3 시간, 때를 나타내는 전치사 (2)

Check up! p. 447

A
1 for | 2 during
3 since | 4 since
5 by | 6 until
7 before | 8 for
9 after | 10 by

Lesson 14-4 장소를 나타내는 전치사

Check up! p. 448

A
1 at | 2 on
3 in | 4 at
5 on | 6 at
7 in | 8 at
9 in | 10 on

Lesson 14-5 방향을 나타내는 전치사

Check up! p. 449

A
1 up | 2 across
3 through | 4 along
5 down | 6 into

Lesson 14-6 위치를 나타내는 전치사

Check up! p. 450

A
1 under | 2 among
3 by | 4 over
5 beside | 6 in front of
7 between

Lesson 14-7 도구/수단을 나타내는 전치사

Check up! p. 451

A
1 with | 2 by
3 with | 4 by
5 by | 6 with
7 by | 8 by
9 with | 10 by

B
1 by | 2 with
3 with | 4 by
5 by

Lesson 14-8 기타 전치사

Check up!

p. 452

A
1 about　2 like
3 without　4 about
5 like　6 about
7 without　8 about
9 like　10 without

Practice More I

p. 453~454

A
1 at　2 at
3 about　4 on
5 into　6 with
7 since　8 in
9 like　10 by
11 at　12 by
13 by　14 in
15 up

B
1 through　2 on
3 around　4 after
5 in　6 along
7 out of　8 by
9 across　10 to
11 since　12 down

C
1 without　2 between
3 on　4 At that time
5 by　6 like
7 around　8 with
9 climbing up　10 over
11 about　12 in
13 among　14 behind

중간 기말고사 예상문제

내신 최다 출제 유형

p. 455

01 ①　02 ②　03 ④　04 ③　05 ①

해설

01 '달(month)' 앞에는 전치사 'in'을 붙인다.

02 ① of → to, ③ for → to, ④ to → for, ⑤ to → for

03 ④ 구체적인 시간의 길이가 나올 때는 'for'를 사용한다

04 'across from' ~의 건너편에,
'in the middle of' ~의 한가운데에

05 장소의 전치사 'in', 출신지를 나타내는 'from',
숙어 'give up' (포기하다)

p. 456~462

01 ④	02 ①	03 ②	04 ③	05 ⑤
06 ③	07 ④	08 ①	09 ④	10 ②
11 ①	12 ⑤	13 ③	14 ③	15 ④
16 ③	17 ②	18 ④	19 ③	20 ①
21 ③	22 ⑤	23 ②	24 ①,②	25 ③,④
26 ④,⑤	27 ②,③	28 ③	29 ⑤	30 ②
31 ③	32 ①	33 ②	34 ②	35 ①

〈서술형 평가〉

36 The hospital is on Green Street.
37 The bookstore is next to(=beside) the flower shop.
38 like
39 in, for
40 during, for
41 Nobody lives without air.
42 It was so long time to see Henry at the meeting.
43 Eddie's hobby is climbing mountains.
44 I started writing in my diary in English
45 Mr. Wang studied Korean for three years
46 We studied about the Renaissance
47 There are many fans around
48 three teddy bears in front of the box
49 a bag between the boxes
50 a flower among the toys
51 on
52 ⓒ for, ⓔ to

해설

01 요일 앞에는 'on'을 쓴다.

02 달 앞에는 'in'을 쓴다.

03 'with' (~을 가지고) 도구와 함께 쓰인다.
→ 그녀는 영어를 사용해 우리를 도와준다.

04 'be from (=come from)' ~출신이다, ~로부터 오다

05 'be ready for' ~을 준비하다

06 'after' ~후에

07 ④ 'for a minute' 잠시 동안, ⑤ 'in a minute' 곧, 즉시

08 'between A and B': A와 B 사이에

09 'for' : 첫 번째 문장 – ~에게
두 번째 문장 – ~을 위한

10 'in + 계절/장소'

11 통신수단을 말할 때는 'on'을 쓴다.

12 'leave for' ~을 향해 떠나다/출발하다

13 'by' : 첫 번째 문장 – ~옆에,
두 번째 문장 – ~을 타고 (by+교통수단)

14 ③ 좋아하다, ①,②,④,⑤ ~처럼, ~같이

15 〈보기, ④〉 ~을 위하여, ① 'for' ~동안, ② 'look for' ~을 찾다, ③ 'be late for' ~에 늦다, ⑤ 'thank ~ for'··· ···에 대해 ~에게 고맙게 여기다

16 요일 앞에는 전치사 'on'을 쓴다. 요일 뒤에 '-s'가 붙으면 '그 요일마다'의 의미가 된다.
'on Thursday' 목요일에, 'on Thursdays'목요일마다

17 시간 앞에는 전치사 'at'을 붙여준다.
→ 'in 10 minutes' 경우 10분 후에'라는 의미로 'in'이 여기에서는 '~후에'의

18 'in the evening' 저녁에,
'before the sun rises' 해가 뜨기 전에

19 'during+특정 기간의 명사', 'for + 정확한 기간의 숫자 표현'

20 'on + 특별한 날', 'in the morning'

21 'under' ~아래

22 'in front of' ~의 앞에, 'suddenly' 갑자기 (→ 부사, 일반동사 앞에 위치한다.)

23 ② 'be동사 + 동사-ing' ~하고 있는 중이다, 'over' ~위로

24 ① in → on, ② in → on

25 ③ at → in, ④ at → in

26 ① in → on ② of → for ③ in → at

27 ① in → at ④ in → on ⑤ on → in

28 in → on

29 in → by

30 for

31 ③ ⓐ 'in 장소', ⓑ 'on the menu', ⓒ 'with 도구'(→ 손으로 음식을 먹는다고 하였으므로 손이 도구이다.)

32 장소와 장소가 나란히 올 경우, 작은 것 순으로 'at'과 'in'을 사용한다.

33 위의 이야기는 모나리자에 초점을 맞추어 이야기하고 있다.
'최후의 만찬'이라는 그림도 그렸다라는 사실만 나열했다.

34 'across from' ~의 건너편에

35 'between A and B' A와 B 사이에

〈서술형 평가〉

36 길 위에서 어떤 건물이 있다는 것을 표시할 때는 전치사 'on'을 사용한다.

37 'next to (=beside)' ~옆에

38 'like': ~와 같은, ~처럼

39 'be interested in' ~에 흥미를 갖다,
'work for' ~을 위해 일하다

40 'during': 특정한 기간 (명사로 표현),
'for': 정확한 기간 (숫자로 표현)

41 'without' ~없이 within → without

42 모임이나 행사를 말할 때는 전치사 'at'을 쓴다.

43 'climb up' ~위를 오르다

44 'start + 동사-ing': ~하는 것을 시작하다

45 'for + 숫자표현 (시간의 길이)'

46 'about' ~에 관하여

47 'around' ~주위에

48 'in front of' ~앞에

49 'between' ~사이에(두 개)

50 'among' ~사이에(셋 이상)

51 요일 앞에는 전치사 'on'을 사용한다.

52 ⓒ 'for' ~을 위해, ⓔ 'to' ~에게